Victorian women poets lived in a time when religion was a vital aspect of their identities. Cynthia Scheinberg examines Anglo-Jewish (Grace Aguilar and Amy Levy) and Christian (Elizabeth Barrett Browning and Christina Rossetti) women poets, and argues that there are important connections between the discourses of ninteenth-century poetry, gender, and religious identity. Further, Scheinberg argues that Jewish and Christian women poets had a special interest in Jewish discourse; calling on images from Judaism and the Hebrew Scriptures, their poetry created complex arguments about the relationships between Jewish and female artistic identity. She suggests that Jewish and Christian women used poetry as a site for creative and original theological interpretation, and that they entered into dialogue through their poetry about their own and each other's religious and artistic identities. This book's interdisciplinary methodology calls on poetics, religious studies, feminist literary criticism, and little read Anglo-Jewish primary sources.

Cynthia Scheinberg is Associate Professor of English at Mills College in Oakland, California. She has published articles in *Victorian Studies, Victorian Literature and Culture, Victorian Poetry,* and has contributed chapters to *The Cambridge Companion to Victorian Poetry* (Cambridge, 2000), *Women's Poetry, Late Romantic to Late Victorian: Gender and Genre, 1830–1900,* and *Critical Essays on Elizabeth Barrett Browning.*

CAMBRIDGE STUDIES IN NINETEENTH-CENTURY
LITERATURE AND CULTURE

General editor
Gillian Beer, *University of Cambridge*

Nineteenth-century British literature and culture have been rich fields for interdisciplinary studies. Since the turn of the twentieth century, scholars and critics have tracked the intersections and tensions between Victorian literature and the visual arts, politics, social organization, economic life, technical innovations, scientific thought – in short, culture in its broadest sense. In recent years, theoretical challenges and historiographical shifts have unsettled the assumptions of previous scholarly syntheses and called into questions the terms of the older debates. Whereas the tendency in much past literary critical interpretation was to use the metaphor of culture as "background," feminist, Foucauldian, and other analyses have employed more dynamic models that raise questions of power and of circulation. Such developments have reanimated the field.

The series aims to accommodate and promote the most interesting work being undertaken on the frontiers of the field of nineteenth-century literary studies: work which intersects fruitfully with other fields of study such as history, or literary theory or the history of science. Comparative as well as interdisciplinary approaches are welcomed.

A complete list of titles published will be found at the end of the book.

WOMEN'S POETRY AND RELIGION IN VICTORIAN ENGLAND

Jewish Identity and Christian Culture

CYNTHIA SCHEINBERG

CAMBRIDGE
UNIVERSITY PRESS

PUBLISHED BY THE PRESS SYNDICATE OF THE UNIVERSITY OF CAMBRIDGE
The Pitt Building, Trumpington Street, Cambridge, United Kingdom

CAMBRIDGE UNIVERSITY PRESS
The Edinburgh Building, Cambridge CB2 2RU, UK
40 West 20th Street, New York, NY 10011-4211, USA
477 Williamstown Road, Port Melbourne, VIC 3207, Australia
Ruiz de Alarcón 13, 28014 Madrid, Spain
Dock House, The Waterfront, Cape Town 8001, South Africa

http://www.cambridge.org

© Cynthia Scheinberg 2002

First published 2002

Printed in the United Kingdom at the University Press, Cambridge

Typeface Baskerville Monotype 11 / 12.5 pt.   *System* LATEX 2$_\varepsilon$ [TB]

A catalogue record for this book is available from the British Library

Library of Congress Cataloguing in Publication data
Scheinberg, Cynthia.
Women's poetry and religion in Victorian England : Jewish identity and Christian culture/
Cynthia Scheinberg.
p.   cm. – (Cambridge studies in nineteenth-century literature and culture; 35)
Includes bibliographical references and index.
ISBN 0 521 81112 0
1. Religious poetry, English – History and criticism.
2. Christianity and literature – England – History – 19th century.   3. Judaism and
literature – England – History – 19th century.   4. Women and
literature – England – History – 19th century.   5. English poetry – Jewish authors – History
and criticism.   6. English poetry – Women authors – History and criticism.
7. English poetry – 19th century – History and criticism.   8. Rossetti, Christina Georgina,
1830–1894 – Religion.   9. Browning, Elizabeth Barrett, 1806–1861 – Religion.
10. Christian poetry, English – History and criticism.   11. Aguilar, Grace,
1816–1847 – Religion.   12. Jewish poetry – History and criticism.   13. Levy, Amy,
1861–1889 – Religion.   I. Title.   II. Series.

PR508.R4 S34   2002
821′.809382 – dc21   2001052972

ISBN 0 521 81112 0 hardback

This book is dedicated to:
Daniel A. Harris, teacher and friend
Denise and Herbert Scheinberg, parents and friends
Eliahu J. Klein, husband and friend.

*****

The David L. Kalstone Memorial Fund,
administered by the Department of English at Rutgers University,
offered generous support towards the publication of this book.

Contents

Acknowledgments

> Exposing a work, which has long been the darling object of an author's cares, the treasured subject of his secret thoughts, the companion of private hours, to the eye of a censorious world, must ever be attended with many varied and conflicting feelings, more particularly if that treasured subject be theology . . .
>
> (Grace Aguilar, *The Spirit of Judaism*, 9)

This book has been ten years in the making; there are a number of individuals and institutions to thank, for both tangible and intangible gifts that have helped me persevere despite "varied and conflicting feelings."

I am grateful for the support this project received while in the dissertation stage, specifically from the Rutgers University Graduate Department of English and its graduate fellowship and assistantship program. Dr. Robert Goheen and The Woodrow Wilson National Fellowship Foundation supported my graduate work in the form of a generous Mellon Fellowship, without which this project would not have been born. A grant from The Memorial Foundation for Jewish Culture gave me an early boost of confidence that my work had relevance for Jewish studies. The women in my dissertation group, Deborah Gussman, Loretta Stec and Rebecca Brittenham, were committed, kind and tough first critics. Hugh English deserves mention for much emotional support, as does Myron Gessner. My mentors and teachers at Rutgers, Barry V. Qualls, Caroline Williams, and Cora Kaplan, gave valuable assistance. Catharine Stimpson offered valuable professional advice throughout. The project would have been unthinkable and impossible to execute without the unflagging efforts of my dissertation chair, Daniel A. Harris. His mentoring and extraordinary teaching are evident on every page of this book.

I am grateful to the staff and collections at the Rutgers University Library, Jewish Theological Seminary Library, New York Public Library, Memorial Library and Divinity School Library at Harvard University,

University College Library, London, The Bodleian Library, Oxford and the F. W. Olin Library at Mills College. Access to the Amy Levy papers was provided by Camellia Plc., London. Special thanks go to Clarence Maybee and Carol Jarvis at the Mills College Library. For last-minute computer help, I thank Rachel Newman and Jean Weishan at Mills College Academic Computing Services.

Thanks are also due to the following institutions whose support helped in the transition from dissertation to book: the National Endowment for the Humanities, the Mills College English and Women's Studies Departments, Mills College Faculty Development Fund, the Harvard Divinity School's Program in Women's Studies and Religion, and the Oxford Centre for Hebrew and Jewish Studies. My colleagues at the Harvard Divinity School Program in 1996–7 – especially Constance Buchanan, Bonna Devora Haberman, and Joycelyn Moody – helped transform the theoretical frame of this project significantly.

Special thanks go to Linda Hunt Beckman and Michael Galchinsky for their published scholarship on Amy Levy and Grace Aguilar, respectively, and the unpublished advice and texts they both generously offered throughout this project. I have learned much from my discussions with Joseph Bristow, Nadia Valman, Meri-Jane Rochelson, and Michael Ragussis. I am grateful to my colleagues, students, and friends in the Division of Letters at Mills College and especially: Madeleine Kahn, Brinda Mehta, Libby Potter, Ruth Saxton, Linda Moody, Erin Merk, Carol Pal, Rebekah Edwards, Carrie Pickett, and Erin Carlson.

Some ideas and passages in this book have appeared in earlier forms in the following publications: *Victorian Studies*, *Victorian Poetry* and *Victorian Literature and Culture*; each has kindly given permission to reprint. I am especially grateful to the editors of the latter journal, John Maynard and Adrienne Munich, for their early support of my scholarship. Some material was also revised from an earlier publication in *Women's Poetry, Late Romantic to Late Victorian: Gender and Genre 1830–1900*, edited by Isobel Armstrong and Virginia Blain.

The staff and editors at Cambridge University Press have been of inestimable help. Linda Bree offered guidance and advice from the very beginning of the publication process. Rachel de Wachter was always available for logistical support; Neil de Cort guided the book through the production stage. Special mention goes to my copy editor Audrey Cotterell, whose patient and wise counsel improved the typescript greatly.

Family and friends who have also supported this work include Leora Lawton, Amy Pratt, Alice Steinman, and Joe Roman. David Scheinberg and Anne Scheinberg have always shown interest in and respect for my work that I have not taken for granted. My parents, Denise Mangravite Scheinberg and I. Herbert Scheinberg, taught me through their example my first lessons in social conscience, creativity, intellectual rigor, and wise humor. My daughter, Rachel Gavriella Klein, was born near the end of the project; her joyful presence has taught me afresh the importance of a balanced life. Finally, Eliahu J. Klein has been a devoted partner in this process, helping in all facets of the project; along with being my foremost Judaica expert, he has also made me laugh at the most stressful moments. His own example as a scholar and writer has helped me see this project through to the bitter (and sweet) end.

CHAPTER I

Introduction

"BEHOLD HOW WE PREACH": WOMEN'S RELIGIOUS POETRY
AND CONTRADICTIONS OF LITERARY HISTORY

Christianity provided [nineteenth century women writers] with subject matter, justification and authority for many kinds of writing, but almost always at the price of accepting their inferiority to men and restricting their imaginative and intellectual scope. (Dorothy Mermin, *Godiva's Ride*, xvii)

> Of man's first disobedience, and the fruit
> Of that forbidden tree, whose mortal taste
> Brought death into the world, and all our woe,
> With loss of Eden, till one greater Man
> Restore us, and regain the blissful seat,
> Sing Heav'nly Muse . . . (John Milton, *Paradise Lost*, I: 1–6).

> > The lilies say: Behold how we
> > Preach without words of purity.
> > The violets whisper from the shade
> > Which their own leaves have made:
> > Men scent our fragrance on the air,
> > Yet take no heed
> > Of humble lessons we would read.
> > (Christina Rossetti, "Consider the
> > Lilies of the Field," lines 11–17)

The history of English literary criticism is not without its contradictions. One of the most glaring of these contradictions is the very different critical attention that has been offered to religious poetry written by men and religious poetry written by women. Although the triumphs of the past twenty years of active feminist literary criticism have suggested that women writers deserve as much recognition as the male writers who have been at the center of literary canons for centuries, women's poetry that deals with explicitly religious topics and texts still faces a kind of discriminatory

I

treatment by both male-centered and feminist critical orientations. One generalized assumption that supports this very different treatment of religious poetry by men and women is the idea that women whose poetry asserts significant commitments to religious traditions are "restrict[ed]" in "imaginative or intellectual scope," and that any woman who engaged with religious traditions must have been "accepting [her] inferiority to men." In short, women poets who write on explicitly religious themes have most often been seen as passively regurgitating "male" religious traditions which have often been categorized as repressive to women. This set of assumptions in turn creates the idea that women who write poetry on religious topics are not creative agents of either literary art or religious philosophy, while those male poets in the English literary tradition who write on religious themes deserve to be our most revered and canonized of authors.

Milton's opening lines from *Paradise Lost* typify the deep engagement with religion and Biblical texts that marks so much writing by men in the English literary tradition; for the most part, this engagement with religion has been seen as a central organizing principle for constructing a canon of male English Christian writers in which Milton takes his place with George Herbert, John Donne, Alfred Lord Tennyson, Matthew Arnold, Gerard Manley Hopkins, T. S. Eliot, etc. In this tradition, Milton's rewriting of Biblical narrative has been lauded as one of the most influential literary creations of British literary history, in part for its imaginative reworking of a Biblical text. However, while Christina Rossetti's poem "Consider the Lilies of the Field" also offers an imaginative reworking of Biblical text (Matthew 6: 27–30 and Luke 12: 27), it has rarely been read as offering creative reworking of the Bible. Instead, Rossetti's poem might fall – for some – into a category I once heard described as "that dreadful tradition of poems by women that paraphrase the Bible." When I first heard that phrase, I immediately began to wonder why Milton was not also classified as a "paraphraser of the Bible"; suddenly, the reality of the absolutely different treatment offered to women's and men's religious poems was crystallized for me.

It would be difficult to prove that Rossetti's poem merely "paraphrases" Jesus' parable about the "lilies of the field" which "toil not, neither do they spin" but are nevertheless "clothed" in beauty by God; in short, Jesus' message is that one must not worry about material conditions and anxious work, but rather have faith in God. Rossetti's poem, calling on that text, says something quite different; it certainly does not contradict the idea that one should have faith, but it puts a very different context around that message. Highlighting the connection between flowers and women that is so common to English poetic and Biblical traditions, Rossetti's poem suggests that women-cum-flowers actually do have lessons to teach men – a teaching that may take a different form than men's "preaching" but is nevertheless full of "humble lessons." In short, Rossetti's poem suggests that along with being objects of beauty, women have a unique set of religious experiences, ideas, and lessons to teach, lessons that she perceives are rarely "heed[ed]" by men.

While feminist critics have long understood the double standards that women writers have faced in literary history, both feminists and non-feminists tend to reject women's religious verse as marginal to larger issues in Victorian studies, as well as less important in the history of women's creativity and literary agency. The goal of this book, at its broadest level, is to suggest that women's religious poetry is a site in which we find evidence of women's creative and original engagements with religious text and theology. Further, a focus on women poets and their religious affiliations is one way to get a clearer historical understanding of how the discourses of poetry, gender, and religion collided in Victorian England. Examining these historical intersections, I argue that women used poetry as a site to do the theological work from which they were excluded in most Victorian religious institutions.

A more specific goal of this book is to insist on the importance that the discourse about Jewish identity had in the poetry of both Jewish and Christian women poets, and so my readings focus on the ways Jewish and Christian women turn to the discourse of the Judaic, Hebraic, and Jewishness in their poetry.[1] Because the Hebrew Scriptures serve as a shared text for both Jewish and Anglican traditions, the comparison of Jewish and Anglican women's uses of Judaic texts and Biblical figures in their poetry illuminates these women's complex relationships to their own religious traditions, as well as to their respective religious "others." I argue that poetry is an especially important generic site for this inquiry, because hegemonic Victorian Christian culture claimed the genre of poetry as an essentially Christian theological enterprise, as suggested by my readings of John Keble, John Henry Newman, and Matthew Arnold in chapter 2.[2] That alliance between Christian ideology and poetry affected not only the Christian women writers who have been most canonized in literary history, but also impacted the lesser-known Jewish women writers' own bids for literary authority in their own day and by later critical history. Recognizing the importance Victorian poetics invest in the Judaic and Jewishness, we are in a better critical position to understand how and why women poets in particular turned to this discourse of Jewishness in order to claim alternative kinds of literary identity.

In this study, I realign the discourses of gender, poetry, and religion to account for their historical specificity in the nineteenth century. In so doing, I acknowledge a number of important historical/events and phenomena that are coincident with the construction of poetic and national identity in Victorian England: the emergence of women poets as enfranchised figures in mainstream literary culture, the growing presence of a Jewish community as an increasingly legitimated political entity, and the renewed attention to the Hebrew Scriptures in the wake of the German higher criticism and the theories of Hebrew poetry generated, in part, by Johann Gottfried Herder and Bishop Lowth. These historical trends intersect with other larger ideological concerns in Victorian English culture: the increasing anxiety about the meaning of English Christian identity within an active imperialist regime, and the increasing anxiety about the status of women.

Within these larger historical contexts for understanding Victorian poetic identity and its theological implications, it becomes possible to rethink the position of women's religious poetry in feminist and literary contexts. Women of both Christian and Jewish affiliations did assert a theological voice through the act of writing poetry, and so I argue that these women should be read as creative agents of theological inquiry rather than merely passive recipients of a patriarchal tradition. Poetry was one of the most important generic sites in Victorian culture to accommodate this radical and public theological work of women – radical not in the sense that this theological poetry always positioned itself against traditional notions of gender or religion – but radical at the moment poetry provided a sanctioned public forum through which women could voice their theological ideas and participate in debates about religious, political, and gendered identity. Of course, the novel was an equally important force in this emergence of women's voices into a public sphere, yet the very different generic history of the novel and its very different cultural position in Victorian England meant that the novel has never claimed the deep relationship to religion that poetry has in the English literary tradition. It is precisely the power of the connection between religion and poetry, often understood to be rooted in the familiar figure of the poet/prophet, that has profound effects for Victorian women's poetry.

My comparative methodology reads Jewish and Christian women poets in juxtaposition; nevertheless, I put a special emphasis on the historical fate of Anglo-Jewish women poets and their double marginalization in both Victorian and contemporary critical discourse. Suggesting that poetry was a rich site for women's theology, therefore, does not imply that I find either poetry or theology politically neutral sites. On the contrary, the vexed history of Jewish and Christian relations in the Diaspora is reflective of the fact that theology has been a site of profound ethnic and political conflict, while the hegemony of Christian theology in most Western societies has created persistent persecution of Jewish individuals and communities in a variety of historical periods. In this context it is worth nothing that most feminist criticism of Victorian women poets has tended to uncritically (and inaccurately) assume that Christian values were universal for all Victorian women writers; the Jewish poets I include in this study suggest otherwise, and indicate through a variety of poetic strategies how they challenged this assumed association between "woman" and "Christian" in their own poetry.

Thus, on one level, this is a specifically textual and historical study of Elizabeth Barrett Browning, Christina Rossetti, Grace Aguilar, and Amy Levy. My literary analysis pays close attention to the ways each of these women conceptualize the relationships between Jewish and Christian, gendered, sexual, and literary identity. But on another level, this book also engages in comparative cultural studies; by comparing the work of the two most famous Christian women poets in the Victorian canon with two of the most important Jewish women poets of the era, this book asks readers to first consider how the canonized women poets turn to discourses of Hebrew Scriptures to construct quite particular Christian literary identities, and then to consider how Jewish women poets created their own literary identities with and against this more familiar Christian female poetic enterprise. I hope readers will be, by the end of the book, in a position to think about the larger theo-literary politics that operated between Victorian Christian and Jewish women, and to observe the implicit and often explicit dialogue about Jewishness that pervades Victorian women's poetry. Including Anglo-Jewish writers in this study is thus more than an act of canon revision; reading from both Christian and Jewish perspectives, I expose the anti-Judaic and anti-Semitic assumptions that structure so much of Christian Victorian poetic discourse.

In the rest of this Introduction, I explore the methods of some recent and not so recent critical studies that have perpetuated the historical inattention to Victorian women's theological poetics. Before turning to that analysis, however, it is important to clarify my own use of the terms "religious difference" and "religious affiliation" in this text. Readers will note that I rarely use terms of specific religious denomination in reference to the writers I examine, although I realize that there are very important differences between the Christian and Jewish denominations these writers might claim for themselves or others have claimed for them. Instead, I tend to use the more general terms "Jewish" and "Christian," though I do refer to "Anglicanism" as a marker for the Victorian period's most politically powerful form of Christian identity at different moments in the text. My use of the more general religious terms is strategic rather than an oversight. For, to explore the significance of the specific locations of these women in Christian and Jewish religious institutions – perhaps naming them "High Anglican" or "Anglo-Catholic" in the case of Rossetti, Broad Church, Dissenter, or Swedenborgian in the more slippery case of Barrett Browning, "traditional" in the case of Aguilar's Judaism, and "liberal or agnostic" in the case of Levy – might serve to limit the ways these women can be read as original religious thinkers. Further, these established labels often best refer to issues of practice and worship, but may not be useful when seeking to identify specific contours of the particular woman poet's religious thought.

However, my emphasis on the rather general terms "Jewish," "Christian," and the occasional more specific usage of "Anglican" are not intended to deny the complex histories of Victorian Christian and Jewish movements. The very real divisions in Christian identity that mark the Victorian period, such as: the struggle for Roman Catholic enfranchisement that rivaled the struggle of the Jewish community for similar rights; the attendant Catholic revival that marked the period; the power of evangelical Protestant movements in their own separation from the Established Church and their deep influence on that Church itself; and the myriad crises in the Established Church itself, as typified by the Oxford Movement – all of these are important examples of religious difference, though not the "difference" I am most interested in as I trace the discourse of Jewishness in the period. Similarly, a detailed study of Victorian Jewish history shows sweeping changes in the nature of worship, the growth of "liberal" synagogues, and the shifts in Jewish religiosity; yet the issue of where my writers did or did not worship, while important in other contexts, is less interesting to me than how they articulated their Jewish identity. Thus, while no religious historian would suggest that both Barrett Browning's quite anti-institutional Christianity and Rossetti's commitment to the Established Church are the "same" brand of Christianity, I position these women together and in contrast to demonstrate a range of Christian women's thinking about Jewish identity. Similarly, it is quite possible that Aguilar would not have approved of Levy's claims about Jewishness, yet in this study, they are read together to offer two divergent voices on Jewish self-understanding.

Though my hope is that later scholars will build on my analyses by perhaps linking this work to studies of denominational differences, my concerns in this project have been to explore how women who have some link to the "Established" dominant Christian culture of England situate themselves in relation to Jewish identity, and likewise how women who identify as Jewish situate themselves within a dominant Christian culture. Given the book's focus on the religious division between Christian and Jew, I am ultimately most interested in those basic tenets that connect Christian denominations rather than the differences that separate them: namely, that Jesus Christ was a Jew who became Messiah and Son of God, and that the Christian covenant and Scriptures supersede and replace the Jewish covenant of the Hebrew Scriptures. Conversely, within this context, "Jewish" can come to mean those who are born into a Jewish family, who reject the idea of Jesus as Messiah, and who base their faith on the understanding of the Torah as a divinely inspired text to which nothing can be deleted or added. The competing discourses which circulate around the Jewish texts which all Christianities and Judaisms claim to share – namely the "Old Testament" or Tanakh, is what initially motivated this study of women writers, and continues to motivate the readings I produce throughout.

FEMINIST LITERARY CRITICISM AND THE RELIGION "PROBLEM": CHRISTINA ROSSETTI AS TEST-CASE

Most scholars of American women . . . interpret religion as a variable *inside* the established framework of public and private spheres that reinforces women's assignment to the private and their exclusion from the public. Religion is often depicted, as if in a drama, in the role of the gatekeeper – even of prison guard – in the lives of historical women. Recognizing religion as shaping only the values or beliefs people hold, however, and not also the *structural* values their social institutions and arrangements embody and promote, misses the major aspect of its historical significance. (Constance H. Buchanan, *Choosing to Lead*, 43)

Our current critical moment is one in which the "lost" texts of so many women poets are again resurfacing, thanks to the pioneering research manifest in the new anthologies that have emerged in the last five years, including three new anthologies of Victorian poets by major publishers (Everyman, Blackwell, and Oxford University Press) and a number of recent books by important feminist scholars, including Angela Leighton's *Victorian Women Poets* (1992), Germaine Greer's *Slip-shod Sibyls* (1995), Dorothy Mermin's *Godiva's Ride* (1993), and Isobel Armstrong's *Victorian Poetry: Poetry, Poetics, Politics* (1993). In addition, an international conference in July 1995 titled "Rethinking Women's Poetry 1730–1930" (Birkbeck College, London), drew a number of scholars at the forefront of this resurgence of interest in Victorian women poets, as does the annual British Women Writers Conference. Given this new access to texts of women poets, then, the time is ripe to reconsider some of the critical assumptions that have attended the study of Victorian women writers.

This project of rethinking Victorian literary history from the starting points of women's poetry and religious identity has led me to examine certain critical narratives of Victorian literary history.[3] I begin with a generalized observation: feminist literary critics of the past thirty years have tended to dismiss the religious and theological as meaningful categories in an explicitly feminist literary history. Despite a handful of critics who have taken the lead in exploring women's religious identity in literature, discussed below, there has been a more general resistance to this approach in many critical studies of women's writing. This resistance has its roots in a much larger Western feminist myopia about the crucial role religion has played throughout history in women's lives, in both public and private dimensions.

Constance Buchanan has offered a cogent analysis of how scholars of women's history have repeatedly erased the powerful role religion has played in shaping women's public identity in American history. Buchanan points out that feminist scholarship has sought to construct a woman's history that focuses on what seem to be "strong and independent" women's voices; thus, feminist scholars who chart women's emergence in the public sphere tend, as Buchanan writes, to understand religion as a minor, and even negative force in women's history. Buchanan suggests that scholars who see religion as fully contained within the private sphere are unable to see the larger function of religion and theology in women's historical agency; thus, Buchanan suggests that for many feminist historians, "[t]heir assumptions about women and religion lead them to believe that only *non*religious and *non*domestic language signals the historical emergence of women's full public agency" (Buchanan, *Choosing to Lead*, 140).

Though Buchanan writes specifically about the political and historical work of American women reformists, her comments on the emergence of women's "full public agency" resonate with many feminist constructions of British women's literary identity. For, like constructions of feminist history which assume a certain understanding of "public" identity, so too have feminist literary critics tended to assume that the religious is a "private" category that did not contribute to women's emergence as public writers. This rejection of the religious or domestic as potential sites of women's power and resistance, Buchanan suggests, "tells us more about the values of modern scholars that about the lives [and I would add to this the texts] of historical women" (135).[4] It would seem that for many current feminist critics, women writers who actively supported religious institutions and affiliations were necessarily didactic, submissive, unenlightened, and uncreative reproducers of male religious hierarchy; they are, it would seem, somewhat of an embarrassment to our twenty-first-century secular feminism.[5]

We can chart this discomfort, and the subsequent critical contortions feminist critics have made, by a brief examination of some critical comments on Christina Rossetti, the most canonized – and yet perhaps the most religiously identified woman – in past and present Victorian studies. Rossetti's status in the feminist canon might challenge my thesis that women poets have been most dismissed when they engage with religious themes or identity in their poetry. Yet Rossetti has not been canonized in feminist circles for her religious poetry, but rather, I would suggest, despite it. As a self-identified, deeply devout Anglican, Rossetti has proven an interesting stumbling block for feminist criticism of Victorian poetry; in her work, religion can not be dismissed, and yet her stature in Victorian and contemporary canons insists that feminist critics find a way to position her within the hegemonic narrative of women's literary history, a narrative which often validates writers and texts which challenge the assumed oppression of patriarchal religious institutions, and has canonized those writers who take a stance for women's emergence in the public sphere.

Three milestone publications in feminist literary criticism on women's poetry will serve here to illustrate the complications Rossetti's work creates for feminists: the momentously important work by Sandra Gilbert and Susan Gubar, The *Madwoman in the Attic*, Angela Leighton's *Victorian Women Poets: Writing Against the Heart*, and Dorothy Mermin's *Godiva's Ride*.[6] As I offer a particular critique of some of the most influential books on women's poetry in the last thirty years, I want to assert my own intellectual debt to the critics I cite below. My intent in the following section is simply to suggest that certain assumptions about religious identity which are at play in these works deserve to be challenged; nevertheless, I recognize that the religious issues I am interested in exploring may not have been of central importance to these critics. Thus, the following criticisms are not intended to dismiss the immense importance and influence these writers have had on my own development as a critic, but rather to suggest why later criticism might take up new concerns in relation to women and religion as a way to build on this earlier, groundbreaking work.

In this history of twentieth-century feminist literary history there is perhaps no single text as important as Sandra Gilbert and Susan Gubar's 1979 *The Madwoman in the Attic: The Woman Writer and the Nineteenth-Century Literary Imagination*. As part of their theory of nineteenth-century women's "Poetics of Renunciation," Gilbert and Gubar read Rossetti's famous *Goblin Market*, writing "Obviously the conscious or semi-conscious allegorical intention of this narrative poem is sexual/religious ... Beyond such didacticism, however, 'Goblin Market' seems to have a tantalizing number of other levels of meaning – meanings about and for women in particular – so that it has recently begun to be something of a textual crux for feminist critics" (Gilbert and Gubar, *Madwoman*, 566). Gilbert and Gubar recognize that the "intention" of *Goblin Market* is "sexual/religious," though their conflation of these two terms is somewhat confusing. Within the passage from which I have quoted, the critics provide basic outlines of the poem's religious references to Christ's redemption narrative. The reading they go on to produce after this quotation is indeed quite complex, one that argues for the poem's concern with tropes of women's intellectual and sexual power. Situating *Goblin Market* in relation to work by Wollstonecraft, Keats, and Milton, they conclude that the poem contributes to Rossetti's theory that a woman must "bur[y] herself in a coffin of renunciation" in order to survive patriarchy's conflicted demands on women writers.

Gilbert and Gubar's reading is problematic, however, at the moment it sets up a binary opposition between the religious "allegorical intention" and those "tantalizing ... other levels of meaning ... for and about women in particular." Why is the religious necessarily linked to "didacticism" and then distinctly separated from "tantalizing ... levels of meaning ... for and about women in particular"? Of course, throughout their reading, Gilbert and Gubar make use of religious symbol and doctrine; it would be hard to read this particular poem without reference to Christian symbol. For these critics, however, what is important is Rossetti's depiction of the submission women artists must make to the patriarchal, Christian proscriptions against female pleasure and art.

Their theory of a "poetics of renunciation" hinges on the assumption that renunciation of women's creative energy/pleasure is required in an explicitly patriarchal/religious ideology, and that for women in such a culture, the terms "didactic" and "religious" are necessarily elided, and set against terms like "creative," "original," and "artistic." However, this opposition between the creative and the religious has structured much of men's literary production in Christian culture; renunciation is a figure that has been explored by male poets as fully as by women poets, and I would argue it takes its origins from deep structures within Christian theology, rather than as an explicit response to patriarchal oppression of women. In other words, Christian discourse provides a certain theological basis for the idea of renunciation, which is fully galvanized by Victorian discourses of gender, though not totally circumscribed by gender difference. Thus, the problem comes when feminist critics seek to isolate that renunciation as a specifically female response to patriarchy rather than seeing its deeper Christian theological roots.

Dorothy Mermin's *Godiva's Ride* is one of the most accessible summaries of Victorian women's literary life to emerge in recent years, and Mermin also includes an analysis of the ways Christian discourse asserts certain imperatives for humility in a chapter titled "Religion." What makes Mermin's analysis of women's interactions with religious discourses difficult to grasp is her elision between how Victorian women poets were perceived in their specific historical moment, and how "we" might perceive them today. Mermin writes:

For most women, however, religion was not just a way to enter literature, but a stopping place. Hymn writing was open to women, as it had been in the eighteenth century, and could enable them to reach large audiences, but devotional poetry of every sort had fallen into a minor if popular mode. Christina Rossetti wrote very powerful religious poems that had many admirers in the nineteenth century and are now being reclaimed by criticism, but they seemed to fall outside the mainstream of high culture and until very recently were considered minor if excellent work when considered at all. This is not just a problem of gender: as a convert to Catholicism and a Jesuit, Gerard Manley Hopkins, the other great devotional poet of the century and an admirer of Rossetti's work, was in a similarly marginal position, and his innovative verse was unappreciated and mostly unpublished in his lifetime. Still, gender expectations worked against women. Their poetic expressions of faith, by replicating the childlike submissiveness that was expected of them anyway, are apt to seem somewhat flat, since they lack the tension between the strength and independence men are presumed to possess and the devotional poet's humility before God. (Mermin, *Godiva's Ride*, 113–14)

This passage is, I think, more complex than it might appear at first, in part because of the slippage between Victorian and contemporary critical perspectives. It is hard to know how Rossetti's poetry can be seen to fall "outside the mainstream of high culture" as Rossetti was seen as an important poet in her contemporary moment, reviewed, as Tricia Lootens documents, in most major literary journals of the day.[7] Further, the comparison to Hopkins is telling; though Mermin suggests that his marginalization was a result of his non-establishment affiliation as a Catholic, linking Rossetti to Hopkins as in the "similarly marginal position" of the devotional poet neglects the fact that Rossetti was not part of a Catholic minority, but rather an Anglican elite. Indeed, whereas Hopkins specifically limited his own publishing activity to comply with his religious beliefs, Rossetti published and sold prolifically from her first book onward. Her success in fact helps prove that devotional poetry itself was not marginal in Victorian culture, but rather a dominant cultural form, as is evident when we remember that John Keble's *The Christian Year* – a volume of strictly devotional verse – outsold most if not all books of the day, going through over 159 editions in less than fifty years. Mermin's evaluation that all such "devotional" poetry was "popular" and "minor" reflects twentieth-century (and especially New Critical) disdain of the devotional mode of Victorian poetry, as well as disdain for that which was "popular," rather than any historical "truth" about the Victorian period's actual discourses on poetry itself.[8]

Ultimately, it is Mermin's last sentence that is most important to my argument here. When she writes that women's "poetic expressions of faith . . . are apt to seem somewhat flat, since they lack the tension between the strength and independence men are presumed to possess and the devotional poet's humility before God," we see the double bind in which much current feminist criticism places the Victorian women poet. For this woman poet is always judged against some "presumed" quality of "strength and independence" which must counter the "devotional poet's humility." Yet again, this critical model simplifies the ways gendered and religious characteristics are inseparable in this period, and likewise raises the question of to whom women's "poetic expressions of faith . . . are apt to seem flat." It would seem to me that the attribute of "flatness" here occurs only after a critical judgment about religious poetry has been made.

Angela Leighton calls on similar critical assumptions in her equally groundbreaking book, *Victorian Women Poets: Writing Against the Heart*. In her chapter on Rossetti, Leighton sets up the idea that Rossetti's religious devotion was a realm separate from her "imagination," writing in two different passages:

> The public facade of [Rossetti's] life provided, in some ways, a persuasive screen of domestic devotion and religious fervor, behind which her imagination had plenty of room to play. (129)
>
> Rossetti's religious patterns of thought are profoundly and disturbingly at odds with the imaginative vagaries of her verse. It is those vagaries, however, which create the essential tension of her writing . . . (160)

Again, my point here is not to disagree with the actual readings Leighton produces, which I often find quite compelling; my point is that the readings can only be persuasive when we accept the assumptions that Rossetti's religious devotion was a "screen," a barrier, and that her "imagination" could only operate behind that "facade." Leighton's language clearly posits that religious devotion must be "at odds" with the "imaginative vagaries . . . which create the essential tension of her writing"; thus again, the idea that religious devotion might produce its own creative power, rather than mask creative power, is the underlying assumption that propels Leighton's reading of Rossetti. Setting up religion as a "facade," Leighton can rescue Rossetti from the seemingly problematic role religion must play for a devout women writer when she is perceived from twenty-first-century, secular, Western feminist eyes.

   At this point, it is important to note that there have been many critics before me who have offered quite different critical trajectories than the dominant one I have outlined above; this set of critics offers important precursors to this book and its method. Christine Krueger's *The Reader's Repentance* (1992) links the traditions of eighteenth- and nineteenth-century evangelical women's preaching and novels. Krueger suggests that women novelists carried on a tradition of "evangelical hermeneutics [that] briefly vitiated male domination of public speech, allowing women to use the authoritative language of scriptures among men as they traditionally had with each other" (5). Thus, Krueger understands this "influential group of orators and writers" to "offer a model for empowerment of female authors and elucidate the uses Victorian women made of religious discourse" (5). Krueger thus isolates a crucial tradition of women's texts and public acts that counters the assumptions often reinscribed in feminist literary criticism; her book challenges more common critical assumptions "that all evangelists – given their medium, the phallocentric, logocentric texts of scripture and religious discourse – necessarily preach reconciliation with patriarchy" (4). Her work begins to ask new questions that link feminist analysis to the discourses of theology and women's prose.

Similarly, Ruth Jenkins' *Reclaiming Myths of Power: Women Writers and the Victorian Spiritual Crisis* and Janet Larson's "Lady Wrestling for the Victorian Soul: Discourse, Gender and Spirituality in Women's Texts" (in the special 1991 issue of *Religion and Literature* titled "Reconstructing the Word: Spirituality in Women's Writing") explore Victorian women writers' texts in relation to theology and Victorian culture. Jenkins argues that Brontë, Nightingale, Gaskell, and Evans (George Eliot) explored the narrative of "spiritual crisis" and used their writing to "resurrect the female aspects of God . . . tapping the historic privilege Christianity had given the oppressed to challenge the world . . . [b]y reclaiming the Judeo-Christian myth, then, women writers authorized their participation in literary production" (*Reclaiming Myths*, 26). Jenkins' work is important because it takes seriously the "theological foundations" of Victorian women's texts, and she suggests that women prose writers who sought to "reappropriate" the "Judeo-Christian myth" could "reconstruct the primary text used for women's subjugation" and thus "revise not just the literary canon but its theological foundation" (29).

Larson too argues the importance of the Victorian "connection of women with things spiritual" and suggests that such a link "appears to have entailed a major effort of reconceptualization in a period of numerous paradigm shifts" ("Lady Wrestling," 44–5). Thus Larson writes: "Victorian women's texts redefine, yoke, creatively confuse, and write these polarized terms ['public/private, flesh/spirit, body/soul, secular/religious'] into new discursive continuums . . . In these conversions of received discourse emerging through women's new words, disembodied Word again becomes Flesh. Angels become prophets, and 'women's spirituality,' escaping its domestication, takes up the burdens of history" (51). Larson, Jenkins, and Krueger all argue the crucial role theology takes in the ideology of gender in the period, and in the texts of Victorian women writers themselves. They call for a contextualization and historicization of literary and religious discourses, and thus explicitly and implicitly expose some of the differences between Victorian and twenty-first-century attitudes toward religion and literature. Though these writers concern themselves only with Christian writers, they help us complicate the idea that religion has only served as an "oppressive" force in women's literary history. With the exception of Larson's work, however, much of the most compelling work about women and religious identity has dealt with Victorian fiction and prose writing. I would argue that when we turn to women's poetry, the urgency of linking theological analysis and Victorian women's texts rises considerably.

In her 1991 article, "'A Word Made Flesh': The Bible and Revisionist Women's Poetry," Alicia Ostriker makes the bold statement that "women's poetry is one portion of a collective enterprise which on the one hand has as its ultimate goal the radical transformation of what used to be called 'the Judeo-Christian' tradition, and on the other hand stems directly from that tradition" (10). In her close examination of women's use of Biblical text and narrative, Ostriker offers this kind of quality of attention to women's religious texts, and goes further to situate those texts within the larger context of Biblical criticism. Further, Ostriker's self-conscious questioning of the term "Judeo-Christian" and her interest in American women poets of Jewish descent suggest her interest in de-naturalizing the assumed Christianity of English and American women writers. Larson likewise calls for "a much wider examination . . . of the testimonies of Jewish and Black women" though her own examples are taken primarily from white Christian women. By including the analysis of Jewish women poets in this book, I take up Ostriker's and Larson's challenges to diversify the texts we use to theorize women's literary identity, and question whether "the Judeo-Christian tradition" remains a productive term for any literary or theological inquiry in which Jewish perspectives are given central rather than marginal attention.

RELIGION AS A "MARK OF CULTURAL DIFFERENCE":
NEW QUESTIONS FOR WOMEN'S POETRY

There is much room for feminist work [in religion] . . . because western feminists have not so far been aware of religion as a cultural instrument rather than a mark of cultural difference . . . (Gayatri Spivak, "The Politics of Translation")

Another theory about the specifically feminist dismissal of the role religion has played in women's literary history comes out of an analysis of feminism's roots in Marxist theory. Amy Newman argues quite convincingly that attitudes toward women and religion in Western feminist studies are rooted in an unexamined acceptance of Marx's critique of religion, which is based, according to Newman, on profoundly imperialist and anti-Semitic assumptions. Noting that Marx "advocates the banishment of religion to the private sphere," Newman suggests that "although feminist theorists have criticized the privatization of gender relations in Marxist and neo-Marxist critical theories on the grounds that privatization has the effect of excluding women from public moral and political decision making . . . they have not questioned the privatization of religion in Western social and political theories" ("Feminist Social Criticism," 29). Newman goes on to write that "[f]ailure to criticize this aspect of Marx's theory of religion allows religion to be seen as irrelevant to moral and political considerations and to the formation of ethical subjects" (29). Concluding her argument, Newman invokes Gayatri Spivak's critique of Western feminism, and cites Spivak's call to revise certain assumptions about religion by "western feminists," cited above.

Spivak's and Newman's critique is directed primarily at feminist theory in religion and philosophy; to consider their critique within in the realm of recent work on Victorian women's poetry requires a few steps backward. For I would argue that in this genre, and for feminist literary critics in particular, religion has not yet been seen as a "mark of cultural difference," let alone a "cultural instrument." Feminist criticism of women's poetry in Victorian England repeatedly equates the term "religion" with Christianity, only occasionally (and usefully) making distinctions between Christian denominations of the period.[9] In most cases, since religious identity does not take a central place in the analysis, this elision between Christian theology and all religious discourses has not had a very important effect on particular readings. But the assumption that all women in Victorian England were Christians has lead to a skewed picture of English literary culture by constantly erasing the presence of those non-Christian subjects who, at the height of England's imperialism, had an increasing presence in the empire and on England's own shores. And of these multiple religious others existing within the British empire, the Jewish community was the most significant non-Christian community, subject to social discrimination and political disenfranchisement after both Catholic and Dissenting Protestant groups were given full citizenship in England.[10]

Feminist theologians, of course, have long since accepted the idea that women have been active participants in their unique religious traditions, and one of the main projects of feminist work in theology in the last twenty years has been to rewrite religious history to claim women's active roles in religious institutions, to produce theologies that offer to women full agency within traditional religious institutions, or to construct new institutions for women's religious action. This work has been pathbreaking, and I draw on its methods and theories throughout this literary study because I think feminist theologians have much to offer those of us in literary studies. However, feminist theology has not yet reaped the rewards of some feminist theory and literary research, which continues to uncover more and more texts by women which, while not explicitly written as theological tracts, nevertheless have important theological implications for reconstructing women's religious history through alternative genres. Indeed, because women were barred from theological education and clerical roles in most nineteenth-century religious institutions, they were likewise generally barred from the production of authorized theology – and this exclusion continued long after women became culturally authorized to produce literary texts.[11] It seems logical to suppose that as women became increasingly empowered in other textual arenas, those women for whom religion was a central aspect of their identity would use those venues to explore theological questions. Thus, women's exclusion from the canon of theological writing does not necessarily mean women did not produce theology. Yet, to get at this original theological work, feminist theologians will have to break down the constructed distinction between theology and literature in order to claim so-called "creative texts" as having theological import for women,[12] just as feminist literary critics will need to rethink simplistic attitudes toward religion and the possibilities for women's creativity within established religious traditions.

Ignoring the integral structural role religion and theology played in women's literary history obscures not just religious identity, but the complex mediations religious discourses performed in the construction of Victorian women's cultural, gendered, and literary identity. It is not that women writers merely had to position themselves with and against patriarchy *per se* in this historical moment; once we name the ways cultural power was organized in Victorian England not only along gendered axes, but also religious axes, we can see how literary identity is constructed with and against what feminist theologian Elisabeth Schussler Fiorenza has termed kyriarchy, a theoretical concept that helps counter a dualistic analytical approach to patriarchy as simply "domination of men over women." For Schussler Fiorenza, kyriarchy is defined as "a social-historical system of domination and subordination that is based on the rule of the lord/master/father" and which can "express the changing social relations of domination/subordination which are structured by the economic political discourses not only of gender but also race, class and colonialism" (*In Memory*, xviii–xix). If we apply this notion of kyriarchy to Victorian poetics, we need to acknowledge that religious difference was also implicated in the "changing social relations of domination/subordination" in Victorian England. Thus it was not just gender that determined authority and identity in Victorian England, but rather a kyriarchical pyramid that positioned Anglican, heterosexual, upper class, and male as the dominant and interlinked categories of identity for a "true poet" and likewise a "true Englishman."

With this recognition of the complex work a dominant religious ideology enacts on women of differing religious affiliations, it becomes possible to reconstruct the axes of power in Victorian England as not only dependent on gender, but also religious affiliation and ethnic/racial identity.[13] Such a reworking of analytical method can let us fruitfully revise questions from feminist history and offer some new answers. Gilbert and Gubar pose what should seem a highly relevant question to this study in *The Madwoman in the Attic*; analyzing the forces that impinged on woman's poetic authority, they write:

From the Renaissance to the nineteenth century the poet had a privileged, almost magical role in most European societies, and "he" had a quasi-priestly role after Romantic thinkers had appropriated the vocabulary of theology for the realm of aesthetics. But in Western culture women can not be priests ... How then – since poets are priests – can women be poets? (546)

In this passage, Gilbert and Gubar acknowledge the ways religious and gendered discourses converge in the figure of the poet as priest. The figure of the poet as priest is a somewhat broader, though clearly related formulation to the one I focus on in chapter 2, namely, the poet as prophet. Nevertheless, both figures, prophet and priest, share the same "privileged, almost magical role" of access to divine knowledge that Wordsworth, Carlyle, and Shelley (to name a few) all define as part of their figure of the Vates or prophet. But when Gilbert and Gubar name the Romantic thinkers as "appropriat[ing] the vocabulary of theology for the realm of aesthetics," they too quickly obscure the complexity of this theological and aesthetic relationship, and thus over-simplify the scope of their crucial question, which can be paraphrased as "how can women become poets in a culture that denies to them the religious authority associated with poetry?" In short, their question and its implicit answer (that women had to struggle to be poets in nineteenth-century England) privileges the analysis of women's identity in *patriarchal* culture over an analysis of women's identity in *Christian* culture, and thus elides the meaning of patriarchy and Christianity without delineating the distinct roles each might play in a kyriarchically conceived system of identity.

To follow Gilbert and Gubar's formulation of poetic identity would be to come to the inaccurate conclusion, implied in their own rhetorical question, that women could only become poets in Victorian England through an embattled and contestatory process, perhaps as impossible as becoming a female priest. Yet, as I argue in chapter 2 of this book, while certain theorists who remain linked to Romantic theories of the poet as prophet did maintain essentialist gender difference and positioned women as the "lacking" other in that system, other theorists of poetry constructed a powerful tradition of theological poetics which created very different relationships between gender and religion; in short, the feminization of both poetics and Christian identity may have enabled the rise of women poets rather than hindered it. Further, from the history of actual publishing records, we know that this model of theological poetics was extraordinarily influential in this period: it was John Keble's *The Christian Year*, a book of poetry constructed specifically along his own literary principles, that was the single most popular book of poetry in Victorian England, outselling all other volumes of the day.[14] Significantly, the next largest market in poetry belonged to women poets; as Dorothy Mermin has revealed, Elizabeth Barrett Browning – as well as more "overtly and strictly religious" poets, Christina Rossetti, Adelaide Proctor, and Jean Ingelow were "highly successful . . . in 1877, thirteen years after her death, Proctor outsold every living writer except Tennyson, and Ingelow's works sold over 200,000 copies in America alone" (*Godiva's Ride*, 76). Mermin suggests that these poets "exemplified the ideal of poetic womanhood" (76); however, when we link their market dominance with that of Keble's *Christian Year*, we see that it was not womanhood *per se* that was idealized; it was the connection between poetry, womanhood, and an explicit Christian identity that responded to certain idealized notions of Victorian poetry. These historical publishing facts challenge the once familiar idea that religious poetry and women's poetry (not to mention women's religious poetry!) were "minor" categories in Victorian England.

By taking into account a broader picture of Victorian poetics, which includes theological and religious analysis in chapter 2, I propose a revision to Gilbert and Gubar's question (or equation) for understanding women's poetic identity in nineteenth-century England: since poets were assumed to be Christians, and women were assumed to be the ideal of Christian identity, Christian women certainly could be poets. And finally, we can bring those two sets of questions together in understanding many Christian women poets' strategies for constructing their own poetic identity in and against figures of Jewishness; with this more comprehensive picture of the world of Victorian poetics, the original question takes on further complexity: since poets are understood to be Christian, and women are assumed to be Christian, then Christian women have particular stakes in interpreting Jewish identity in ways that might support their own specific Christian poetic authority. Likewise, Jewish women poets, in recognition of the links between poetic and Christian identity, construct quite different approaches to both Christian womanhood and Jewish identity.

In many of the readings that follow, I suggest that theological commitments not only inform the content of women's poems and lives, but also influence the "structural values" of poetry, that is, the very genres, forms, and rhetorics that constructed Victorian poetry. Women, no less than male poets, participated in cultural and theological assumptions about poetry, and thus absorbed and created the overarching theological values that structured their own poetry and sense of aesthetic value, just as they absorbed and created the hegemonic construction of gender identity.[15] Thus, whereas Mermin suggests that "[n]o women poets, moreover, not even Barrett Browning, used poetry as men did to work through the intellectual issues of Victorian faith and doubt . . . women could not afford to question the faith that gave them poetic authority" (*Godiva's Ride*, 114), I contend that Victorian women poets repeatedly engaged with questions of "faith and doubt" in their poetry, and while they did use their faith to claim poetic authority, women poets were often questioning and challenging the terms of that faith. I would go further, though, to suggest that beyond those quite basic categories of theological work ("faith and doubt"), women poets also engaged with more specific theological questions, including the authority of Biblical texts, traditional institutional authority, women's prophecy, and religious history. For example, I argue that Elizabeth Barrett Browning generates her own theory of Christian typology as she negotiates Christian theology and feminism in her epic, *Aurora Leigh*, and that Grace Aguilar paid very specific attention to theories of Jewish prophecy as she sought to construct poetic identity for herself as a devout Jewish woman. Thus, my readings of women's poetry offer to women poets the same quality of attention that has been paid to the "great" religious poetry of Christian men for centuries. In many ways, what I have termed "the quality of attention" distinguishes different critical methods, and ultimately different aesthetic criteria for judging poetry itself, as I suggest in the conclusion to chapter 2.

Comparing the work of uncanonized Jewish and canonized Christian women poets, then, exposes that the ways literary history has classified poetic value may not be based on logical or consistent premises and assumptions, but rather based on deeply held assumptions about the relationships between aesthetics, religious and sexual difference. Thus, "great men's poetry" can be explicitly religious while women's religious poetry is rarely seen as crucial to the narrative of English literary history. That such contradictions exist in methods and approaches to men's and women's poetry is no surprise, of course, to most feminist critics; yet here, I want to suggest that this particular contradiction in how we understand the deep relationships between Victorian gendered, religious, and poetic discourses is most fully evident at the moment we acknowledge that the category "Victorian women's poetry" contains heterogeneous dimensions, voices, and traditions within its bounds. Further, for most of its critical history, Victorian women's poetry has been subject to what might be termed a Christian critical bias.

Because poetic, religious, and gendered discourses were rarely separable in Victorian culture, it is imperative to shift the emphasis in feminist criticism from an exclusive focus on gender to a more complex analytical model that allows for the structural influence of *both* gender and theology on women's poetry. Of course, this drive to introduce other axes of difference – particularly race and class – in recent feminist work has been an imperative for most feminist thought in the last two decades. My point in this book is that there are unique historical reasons to consider the discourses of religion – and in particular of Jewishness – in Victorian poetry by Christian and Jewish women, and that so doing helps us recognize that Christian identity offered to some women poets certain literary and political privileges in Victorian England, while to others, the lack of Christian affiliation created barriers to full literary and national citizenship.

CONQUERORS AND EXILES: JEWISH DIFFERENCE
IN THE "CONTACT ZONE" OF VICTORIAN POETICS

No one sings,
Descending Sinai: on Parnassus-mount
You take a mule to climb and not a muse
Except in fable and in figure: forests chant
Their anthems to themselves, and leave you dumb.
But sit in London at the day's decline,
And view the city perish in the mist
Like Pharaoh's armaments in the deep Red Sea,
The chariots, horsemen, footmen, all the host,
Sucked down and choked to silence – then, surprised

> By a sudden sense of vision and of tune,
> You feel as conquerors though you did not fight,
> And you and Israel's other singing girls,
> Ay, Miriam with them, sing the song you choose.
>   (Elizabeth Barrett Browning, *Aurora Leigh*, III: 190–203)

> I stood ALONE 'mid thronging crowds who filled that stranger shrine
> For there was none who kept the faith I hold so dearly mine:
> An exile felt I, in that house, from Israel's native sod, –
> An exile yearning for my *home*, – yet loved still by my God.
>   (Grace Aguilar, "A Vision of Jerusalem: While Listening to a Beautiful
>   Organ in One of the Gentile Shrines," lines 21–4, in *The Spirit of Judaism*)

Once we destabilize the understanding of the Victorian poet as an identity not only tied to theories of sexual identity, but also deeply rooted in certain Christian theological principles, we can better understand why Jewish identity, Judaism, and Hebrew history are constantly referred to in Victorian women's poetry. For, in terming poetry a specifically Christian discourse, the figures of Christian otherness – Jewish and "Hebraic" figures from contemporary life and Biblical history – necessarily exist in tension with the figures of Christian self. Women poets, Jewish and Christian, operating in this moment when the very act of poetry was linked to Christian theology, thus engaged not only with issues of gendered authority (or lack thereof) but also with the role their respective religious affiliations played within this larger theological and literary nexus. In the passages above, we can glimpse the complex ways religious and literary identity collide for two of the most important women poets of the Victorian period, Elizabeth Barrett Browning and Grace Aguilar.

Elizabeth Barrett Browning takes up the figure of the Hebraic Miriam as a figure of the woman poet's victory, linking the moment in Exodus of Israel's victory over the Egyptians to the powerful agency of her own voice and "Israel's other singing girls" – a phrase which in the context of the poem must refer specifically to other Christian women poets. Barrett Browning's use of Christian typology allows her to claim this moment and figure from Hebrew history as her own even as she works throughout the poem to name a specifically Christian poetic identity. Her identification with the figure of a "conquering" woman poet is telling, reminding us of the cultural and ideological privileges granted to Anglican women in imperial England and the increasing recognition of women as literary figures in Victorian England – or at least Barrett Browning's own achievement of literary success. With her notion of "Israel's other singing girls," Barrett Browning effectively erases the possibility of those "other" women poets who might make a very different claim to the figure of "Israel's . . . singing girls" – namely, those Anglo-Jewish women poets who were writing and publishing in Barrett Browning's own day. Yet, as I explore in chapter 3, this claiming of the Israelite "singing girl" as a figure for Christian female literary authority eventually places Barrett Browning in a theological conundrum: how to extricate Christian transcendence from a figure of specifically Hebraic identity and history, and how to adapt models of Christian authority to a specifically feminist sensibility. Observing Barrett Browning's subsequent negotiations with this intersection between gendered and typological discourses demonstrates how *Aurora Leigh* can be read as a complex and original theological work whose religious philosophy does indeed have "tantalizing . . . levels of meaning . . . about and for women in particular."

Barrett Browning's rhetorical erasure of "real" Israelite women in Victorian England was, of course, prophetic in terms of later literary history. Though Grace Aguilar wrote prolifically and published widely in America and England before her early death, her name remains almost virtually unknown in Victorian studies of poetry.[16] And just as Barrett Browning confidently predicts the "conquering" effect of Christian women poets, so too does Aguilar find language to predict her own more marginal position within literary history, naming explicitly her status as "other" by situating her poem within the confines of a "Gentile Shrine." And, as I chart in my readings of Aguilar and Amy Levy, perhaps the two most important Jewish women poets in Victorian England, Anglo-Jewish women poets often identified themselves in terms of the exile rather than the conqueror, even as they turned to the same Biblical tradition that their Christian counterparts used to claim a certain poetic authority.

Aguilar's identification with the figure of the Jewish exile against Barrett Browning's identification with the "conqueror" suggests the heightened awareness Anglo-Jewish women had toward their own literary and religious identity in this period; reading their work in conjunction with the most famous Christian women poets of their day exposes the overt Christian assumptions that structure so much of the discourse on and about women poets. Aguilar's theological poetry works to claim Judaism as an ongoing and powerful religious tradition that offers special benefits to Jewish women, and she does so by turning to the hegemonic discourse of spirituality that marks so many Christian theories of womanhood. Claiming these hegemonic Christian principles of "spirituality" as essentially Jewish in origin, Aguilar recognizes the overt and covert Christianity that marks the construction of the women writer in Victorian England, and she successfully works against that tradition to emerge as a highly successful Jewish woman writer for both Jewish and Christian audiences.

Aguilar's prolific and successful career reminds us of the presence and subsequent erasure of an Anglo-Jewish literary tradition in Victorian England. Along with this fact of Jewish writers' presence in Victorian England and the critical need to recognize religious diversity in English literary history, there are also distinct historical and ideological connections between the rise of the Anglo-Jewish community in Victorian England and Victorian (Christian) England's obsession with Hebraic literary figures and history. In the last few years, much excellent research on the literature, history, and "problem" of Jewish identity in Victorian England has been published, most notably Michael Ragussis' *Figures of Conversion: "The Jewish Question" & English National Identity* (1995), David Feldman's *Englishmen and Jews: Social Relations and Political Culture 1840–1914* (1994), Bryan Cheyette's *Constructions of "the Jew" in English Literature and Society* (1993), and Andrea Freud Loewenstein's *Loathsome Jews and Engulfing Women* (1993); these texts all focus primarily on Anglo-Christian authors' perspectives on Jewish identity. Michael Galchinsky's monumentally important study, *The Origin of the Modern Jewish Woman Writer: Romance and Reform in Victorian England* (1996) is the first study devoted to specifically Anglo-Jewish women writers, with a focus on fiction.

Clearly, this outpouring of major books locates the discourse of Jewish identity as central in Victorian England. What we learn from these books is that the nineteenth century was the first in England's history to contend with a significant Jewish community, a minority population whose very presence in a nation with a state religion (Anglicanism) necessarily ruptured certain historical assumptions about national identity, racial politics, and religious authority. Questions of religious, racial, and national identity were already under heightened scrutiny throughout most of the nineteenth century due to a number of other historical phenomena: England was at the height of its imperialist mission, galvanizing new theories of racial difference (through which Jews were always seen as racial others); religious controversy reigned in High, Broad, and Low Church Anglicanism; and sexual difference became a site of increasing attention and concern. What is exciting about all the recent work on the discourse of Anglo-Jewish identity is how these new books insist that the "problem" Jewish identity posed in England intersected with almost all of England's major cultural upheavals, and so can be read not merely as "minority" history, but rather as a lens through which to reorganize basic assumptions about almost all aspects of Victorian culture.

However, little of the current work in Anglo-Jewish history and literature focuses on the work of women poets, nor do any really focus on specifically theological questions of Judaism; most of these studies have been primarily concerned with theories of Jewish cultural and/or racial identity. This book expands the current parameters of Jewish-Victorian studies by looking specifically at how women's poetry engages with the discourse of Jewish difference and Hebrew history. Similarly, this project goes beyond the current interest in non-fiction and fictional prose writing by exploring how the generic history of English poetry maintains connections with Christian traditions and generic formulas from the Renaissance onward. Thus, learning from the many fine works that have located Jewish differences as central to the discourse of the novel, I hope to show the important role Jewish difference has played in the Victorian discourse on poetry.

My hope is that reading chapters on both Jewish and Christian women poets in conjunction with each other and the larger Victorian discourse on theological poetry will create a new picture of Victorian poetry and poetics. As I account for a variety of women's religious and cultural positions in Victorian literary culture, I propose to reimagine the site of Victorian poetics itself, countering images of that world as a site where only one patriarchal theory of poetry reigned and silenced/oppressed women poets. Instead, I understand the world of Victorian poetics as what Mary Louise Pratt has termed "a contact zone," which she defines as a "social spac[e] where cultures meet, clash and grapple with each other, often in contexts of highly asymmetrical relations of power, such as colonialism, slavery or their aftermaths" ("Arts of the Contact Zone," 584). With such a theory, the dominant interests of hegemonic Christian culture, Christian male clerics, critics, and even politicians can be seen in "contact" with the often competing and "asymmetrically" empowered interests of Christian women, as well as Jewish communities, clerics, and politicians, and Jewish woman writers – all of whom sought to lay claim to the highest form of literary identity in Victorian England, the mantle of the poet.

Pratt suggests that the "literate arts of the contact zone" (590) are particularly complex for those who speak against hegemonic values and

ideologies. Once we read Jewish women poets into the contact zone
of Victorian poetics, a number of new possible interpretative strategies
emerge; indeed, Jewish women poets help us reinterpret that which
seemed "logical" or "normative" when we only looked at Christian
women poets. Likewise, because Jewish women poets were fully aware of
the ideological links between ideas of "woman," "poetry," and "religion/
Christianity" in the period, their responses to these dominant associations help us understand how minority writers negotiate majority culture.
It is this final comparison between Jewish and Christian women's texts
that generate the larger thesis with which I began this Introduction:
namely, that women's religious affiliation profoundly affects the ways
women conceive of themselves as poets in Victorian England.

This theory of the contact zone of Victorian poetics is particularly
useful for a feminist analysis of women's literary history, because it accounts for "asymmetrical relations of power" without over-simplifying
the patterns of those power asymmetries. That is, constructing Victorian
poetry as contact zone allows us to think about a number of different
ideological discourses simultaneously, and thus produce a kyriarchical
understanding of women's literary history that does not privilege gender
as the only category of power in Victorian England. Pratt suggest that
out of such a contact zone, a genre of text she calls "autoethnographic"
emerges, and she describes an autoethnographic text as ones in which
"people undertake to describe themselves in ways that engage with representations others have made of them. Thus if ethnographic texts are
those in which European metropolitan subjects represent to themselves
their others (usually their conquered others), autoethnographic texts are
representations that the so-defined others construct *in response* to or in
dialogue with those texts" (585). Translating Pratt's model based on colo-
nial encounters to the context of Victorian literary culture, I suggest we
read the dominant Anglican male critics as analogous to "European
metropolitan subjects" and Christian and Jewish women poets as
"so-defined others" – a multiple set of "others" who have often competing concerns. These multiple others are constructed in particular ways
in texts of dominant male Christian literary theory, and these constructions are then open for self-reinterpretation by those more marginally
positioned subjects. In the end, we can imagine how both Christian and
Jewish women use the hegemonic representations of their identity to
make counter claims to that vision of Christian poetic identity produced
by hegemonic male Anglican critics. And in understanding the more
dialogic activity of men's and women's, Jewish and Christian women's,

literary culture, we can rethink some of the more troublesome and indeed historically inaccurate constructions of women's literary history that a more simplistic analysis of "patriarchy" has produced.

The theory of the contact zone is particularly useful to the study of Victorian women's poetry, then, because it allows us to account for the very acute differences in cultural power that mark histories of men's and women's writing in the English tradition while also recognizing certain kinds of literary power that women could successfully construct within the paradigms of androcentric literary theory. In short, a contact zone model might ultimately let us complicate theories of women's literary history as a "separate" tradition of literary identity – a project I would enthusiastically endorse, as I think the tracing of separate male and female trajectories of literature has been an important phase in feminist criticism, but is not the end goal of a feminist critical project. Pratt's theory challenges binary divisions of the very concept of dominant and marginal writing traditions, however, by acknowledging the more dialogic context out of which writing emerges in a given historical moment. In understanding the texts of Christian and Jewish women poets as "autoethnographic," I want to suggest that these supposedly "marginal" texts are both expressive of particular aspects of Jewish and women's experience, while also fully engaged with the dominant discourses of male poetics.

Chapters 2–4 of the book argue collectively that Jewish identity was a central figure in Christian Victorian poetry and poetic theory. In chapter 2: "'Sweet singers of Israel': gendered and Jewish otherness in Victorian poetics," I sketch out the different ways mainstream theories of Victorian poetry and aesthetics are fully linked to religious and theological inquiry as well as a discourse on gender. Reading male Christian writers like John Keble, John Henry Newman, Eneas Dallas, and Matthew Arnold, I suggest that the mid-Victorian poetic theory significantly reworked the Romantic model of the poet as prophet, and reorganized the relationships between the discourses of gender, poetry, and religious identity in order to align poetry with a specifically Christian identity. In addition, I analyze why figures of Jewish identity emerged quite pervasively in the discourse on poetry, and demonstrate why there are distinct intersections between constructions of Jewish and gendered "lack"; in short, I suggest that hegemonic Anglican male critics call on both female and Jewish difference in order to confirm, albeit with much ideological slippage, the complete and superior identity of the Christian male poet. I go on to suggest what implications this construction of "theological poetry" might have had for the discourses of women's poetry and Jewish difference, and how women poets worked with and against this tradition of theological poetry to emerge as some of the most successful poets of their day.

Chapters 3 and 4, focusing on the most famous Christian women poets of the period, Elizabeth Barrett Browning and Christina Rossetti, offer readings that suggest these poets' full engagement with the discourse of theological poetry explored in chapter 2. I explore how these women call on and rewrite particular theories of religious identity in their project of constructing an authoritative female, Christian poetic self. What emerges here is that, though in radically different ways, both Barrett Browning and Rossetti rely on figures of Jewish difference to help construct their Christian female literary identity; the construction of a Christian poetic self for these women entailed a complex negotiation with their religious "other," the Jew and specifically the Jewish woman from the Hebrew Bible/Old Testament. In chapter 3, "Elizabeth Barrett Browning and the 'Hebraic monster,'" I first explore Barrett Browning's complex relationship to the Hebrew language, and demonstrate how Barrett Browning often configures the roots of true poetry as linked to Hebraic/Jewish discourse and identity, especially in the early works, "The Seraphim" and "Drama of Exile." I pay special attention to her little-studied dramatic monologue, "The Virgin Mary to the Child Jesus," suggesting that by figuring Mary with specifically Jewish roots, Barrett Browning links her to a tradition of poetic prophecy and claims her as an active agent of poetic speech rather than the traditional silent Pietà. Constructing a chronological narrative of Barrett Browning's theological concerns in these works, I position *Aurora Leigh* as the culmination of Barrett Browning's theological poetic project that identifies Jewishness as a crucial phase of poetic development, yet one that must be ultimately replaced by Christian conversion. Finally, examining *Aurora Leigh* in relation to theories of Christian typology, I suggest that Barrett Browning constructs female poetic identity as that which relies upon a complex linkage between Jewish conversion and heterosexual marriage.

Chapter 4, "Christina Rossetti and the Hebraic goblins of the Jewish Scriptures," turns to the work of Christina Rossetti and compares her figures of Jewish and Hebraic identity to Barrett Browning's, suggesting these two important women poets offered very different configurations for gendered and religious identity. I argue that Rossetti creates an essential connection between the construction of woman and the construction of the Jew/Hebrew in her poetry; both figures are understood to be incomplete, or "lacking" total subject status. Looking at poems rarely analyzed in Rossetti studies, including "Christian and Jew: A Dialogue" and "By the Waters of Babylon BC 570," I suggest that Rossetti's vision of women's ultimate agency within Christian theology hinges on rejecting Jewish difference. Concluding with readings of *Goblin Market* and "Monna Innominata," I argue that Rossetti constructs a complex typology of self and other that situates Christian women, Jewish women, Christian Scripture, and "Old Testament" in a dynamic relation to each other, though generally in relationships that are based on deeply anti-Judaic assumptions which have not yet been fully articulated in Rossetti studies.

In Chapters 5 and 6, the focus of the book shifts to explore the work of two lesser-known Jewish women poets of the Victorian era, Grace Aguilar and Amy Levy. Occupying different periods in the century, both Levy and Aguilar address the assumptions about women and Christian identity that pervade Christian England as they attempt to reclaim Jewishness from the representations of Jewish identity in Christian culture. At the moment the Jewish woman begins to produce and publish poetry – in English – she enters into a series of ideological conundrums; if the Christian woman poet is repeatedly marginalized by the fact of her gender, what we learn from reading Levy and Aguilar is that the Jewish woman is doubly or triply marginalized through her inability to participate in the discourse that claims poetry as an essentially Christian mode of expression; further, the Jewish woman becomes suspect in terms of her gender identity in a period which made hegemonic cultural links between the "true woman" and the "Christian." Although Levy and Aguilar share this problematic relationship to Christian discourse, they approach the problem of Jewish women's poetic identity from very different directions.

Chapter 5 "'Judaism rightly reverenced': Grace Aguilar's theological poetics," examines the work of Grace Aguilar, and argues that she galvanizes the power that poetry carried in the period as a strategy for creating a specifically Jewish and female spiritual identity. In her prose about Jewish women poets/prophets of the Bible, as well as in her own lyric poetry, Aguilar constructs a particular Jewish women's spiritual identity in and against models of Christian women's religious and literary identity. In order to deconstruct the assumed link between Christianity and "true womanhood" so pervasive in Victorian England, Aguilar turns to the male Romantic poets for a model of spiritual authority. If, as Michael Galchinsky has argued, Aguilar uses fiction to articulate a specifically political and historical understanding of the Jewish woman, I suggest that she uses poetry as the genre in which to develop a specific Jewish woman's theology and spiritual identity. Yet Aguilar is also profoundly concerned with the dynamics of Jewish history; in this chapter I also suggest that her unique understanding of Jewish history and its role in the development of traditional Judaism has a profound effect on her understanding of women's religious authority. I end the chapter by examining Aguilar's complex reading of Biblical women prophets, and the complex position being a "public" author posed for her own understanding of the ideal spiritual Jewish woman.

Chapter 6, "Amy Levy and the accents of minor(ity) poetry," is devoted to the work of an Anglo-Jewish poet who has been often read as an essentially non-religious poet. I suggest that regardless of the extent of Levy's own religious belief, her work repeatedly signals her awareness of the alliance between English literary history and Christian theology. Overtly concerned with the concept of "minority," Levy's poetry and poetic theory highlights the contingencies between religious, sexual, and literary identity as they have been constructed in English poetic tradition, and offers a series of challenges to those dominant constructions. I argue that Levy's significant work in the genre of dramatic monologue exposes the explicit Christian principles that structure poetic canonization and identity in the Victorian period; for example, her poem "Magdalen" seeks to show the convergence between figures of fallen women and Christian rhetorics of Jewish conversion. In other works, Levy seeks to destabilize the assumed heterosexuality of both Christian and Jewish religious verse, challenging an historical alliance between tropes of religious devotion and heterosexual desire. Moving finally to her lyric poetry, I suggest that there is an important Jewish subtext in many of her poems, and I suggest there are important moments where Levy, despite her own reservations about Jewish religion, aligns her own poetic identity with the classical tradition of Jewish devotional poetry.

Reading Jewishness, and especially Jewish women poets, into the contact zone of Victorian poetics insists that we see the complex ways Jewishness and femaleness are both deeply overdetermined sites of poetic identity. In this sense, Jewish women poets serve as crucially important teachers for feminist scholars who seek to take into account not only the commonalities but also the acute differences in women's experiences. Having essentially ignored the important role the Jewish "other" has played in the canonized tradition of English poetry, English critical tradition has likewise lost an opportunity to see the essential relatedness of gendered and religious identity, a relatedness that has helped obscure the work of many women poets until quite recently, and continues to obscure the specific challenges non-Christian women faced in the English literary tradition and critical history. Reading Anglican and Jewish women poets as part of a contact zone of Victorian theological poetics insists that we see these women of our literary past not only as victims of hegemonic patriarchal discourses of identity, but also as agents of those discourses. They did not simply accept the terms of the androcentric male criticism; they argue with those critical constructions as well as co-opt those that serve their purposes.

The following considerations of women's interventions in poetry, theology, and religion may take those of us committed to current feminist politics into uncomfortable places. It means considering Christian women's anti-Judaism and anti-feminism *as well as* their sisterhood with Jewish women and the more liberatory feminist practices we laud today. It means considering how some women sought to hold on to their commitments to traditional religion despite the limitations both Christianity and Judaism often placed on women's public religious agency; and it means acknowledging the sometimes anti-Judaic assertions of Christian women and indeed Jewish women themselves. Examining women's poetry in relation to theories of poetry and religion also means recognizing that women's poetry is not a genre of its own, but rather one that engages with the central ideas and concepts of androcentric literary theory of the day. Further, it reminds us that the idea of "a woman's tradition" obscures the crucially different historical experiences of non-Christian women writers. Recognizing the particular Christian theology that undergirds theories of English poetry reminds us that no religious identity exists outside of historical relationship with its religious "others." And finally, when we fully recognize the powerful links between religious and literary identity in this period, we can rethink certain assumptions of the role religion has played in women's lives, not only as a place of oppression, but also as a site of power and sustenance for Victorian women, both personally and publicly.

CHAPTER 2

"Sweet singers of Israel": gendered and Jewish otherness in Victorian poetics

"INSUFFICIENT AND PARTIAL": JEWISH PROPHETS, WOMEN POETS, AND THE TYPOLOGICAL PARADIGM

Certainly any one would be surprised to find how large a part Poetry plays in the Holy Scriptures. For, if I am not mistaken, nearly half the sacred volume was written in metre . . . Hence it is sufficiently clear that a kind of relationship exists between those subjects which God has ordained to prepare the way for his Gospel and the dispositions and tone of mind of those whom we honour pre-eminently as poets or at least as disciples of the poets . . . Therefore I cannot help believing that it was in more than one way that the Hebrew seers and poets prepared their nation to receive the later revelation of Truth. (John Keble, Lecture XL of *Lectures on Poetry (Praelectiones Academicae)* 474)

Her various writings show that she has drunk true inspiration from the fountain to which she has so often resorted with the graceful vase of her natural genius. Miss Barrett is singularly bold and adventurous. Her wing carries her, without faltering at their obscurity, into the cloud and the mist, where not seldom do we fail to follow her, but are tempted, while we admire the honesty of her enthusiasm, to believe she utters what she herself has but dimly perceived. (George Bethune, *The British Female Poets*, 452)

Christian hermeneutics has to "save" – in every sense – the Old Testament. Yet it also has to throw out any aspect of it that implies it is not in need of saving. It thus has to posit the Judaic as a lack – insufficient and partial – and as an excess to be cast out, to inscribe it as outside. (Jill Robbins, *Prodigal Son/Elder Brother*, 10)

Christian cultural discourse has always had a complex relationship with the Jewish other who is irrevocably inscribed within Christian history and scripture. Despite varied histories of Christian persecutions – crusades, Inquisitions, pogroms, and holocausts that sought to erase the presence of actual Jewish people in Christian cultures – it has always been impossible to erase Jewish presence from the integral structure of Christian theological discourse. In this system, the Jew is a figure who, though "other," always has the capacity for conversion into

32

Christian self; likewise, Christianity's reliance on the Hebrew Scriptures insists that Jewish history can never be totally rejected, but rather can be read as "pre-history," the roots, if not the revelation, of Christian identity. As Jill Robbins suggests above, Jewish identity in a Christian hermeneutic must be simultaneously "saved" and "cast out," understood as incomplete, yet always with the potential to become complete through Christian conversion – a conversion enacted both on Jewish individuals as well as the historical narratives and individuals of the Jewish Scriptures.

One discursive method Christian culture uses to construct this complex relationship between Jewish and Christian identity is Christian typological exegesis, a hermeneutic system of reading which casts Jewish identity and Judaic history/knowledge as both a metaphor for "a kind" of Christian identity, as well as a simultaneously "lacking" form of identity. This typological understanding of Hebraic figures and events from Hebrew Scriptures was crucial in the early codification of Christian identity in the New Testament and other Christian texts, but its rhetorical power extends to many other interpretative moments in Christian cultures. George Landow has noted that in Victorian England, typological exegesis was perhaps the most important cultural exegetical mode of analysis, and he notes how Victorian literature in particular relies on typological allusions and ways of reading; other scholars have described a typological paradigm in many Victorian texts without necessarily seeing the roots of this paradigm in Christian discourse.[1]

The passage above from John Keble's final lecture in his *Praelectiones Academicae* (*Lectures on Poetry*) uses standard typological analysis to construct a relationship between Jewish poets/prophets of the Old Testament and a theory of poetry. Keble's approach, both to poetry and the role of the Hebrew poets, is typical of larger Christian theological analysis, which claims the Hebrew poets and prophets as having access to a certain degree of divine truth, while also not quite perceiving the "fuller revelation which was to come." To create such a reading, a Christian typologist must value the words of the Jewish poet/prophet, but simultaneously divorce those words from their historical context of meaning, as well as from the particular (Jewish) body from which they emanate. As Keble puts it, these Jewish prophets have "a kind of relationship" with "the dispositions and tone of mind of those whom we honour pre-eminently as poets or at least as disciples of the poets" (474). With his emphasis on "dispositions and tone of mind," Keble successfully abstracts prophetic/poetic identity from the historical bodies of Jewish people, and extracts that disembodied essence in order to link it to the role of the Christian poet. Keble thus "saves" the words of the Hebrew poet/prophet while also insisting on their ultimate insufficiency that marks, in his mind, a specifically Jewish prophetic/poetic identity.

As we will see in this chapter, this simultaneous invocation and dismissal of Jewish poetic/prophetic identity is essential to the project Keble and other Christian critics and clerics undertake in the Victorian period: to recast the very genre of poetry as an explicitly Christian theological endeavor. Yet before turning to the specific texts of Victorian theological poetics, let me suggest what this analysis has to do with a study of women poets, who are rarely, if ever, explicitly invoked by the male clerics and critics who arbitrate the discourse on theological poetry. When we juxtapose the passage from George Bethune's evaluation of Elizabeth Barrett Browning's poetic talent – taken from his 1848 anthology of British women poets – against Keble's estimation of Hebraic prophecy, it becomes clear that women poets in Victorian England were subject to a very similar process of evaluation as the Hebrew prophets of the Old Testament were in Victorian Christian theology.[2] Bethune begins by suggesting that Barrett Browning "has drunk true inspiration," but as his passage continues, he delimits the power of the inspiration by suggesting that though she may speak a certain kind of "bold and adventurous" truth gleaned from her ability to enter the seemingly divine realm of "cloud and ... mist," she nevertheless "utters what she herself has but dimly perceived."

Like Keble's reading of the significance of Hebrew poets, Bethune seems to suggest that Barrett Browning has "a kind of relationship" to poetic truth, but it is not the relationship of true poet/prophet. Bethune attempts to "save" some aspect of Barrett Browning's value as a poet, but he ultimately works to inscribe her prophetic abilities as "dimly perceived"; that is, to use Robbins' description of Jewish identity in Christian culture, they are described as "a lack – insufficient and partial" and simultaneously as "adventurous" and "enthusias[tic] – that is, as "an excess." In short, Bethune attributes to Barrett Browning a kind of prophetic identity that parallels quite precisely the identity granted to Jewishness in Christian epistemology, and his passage is also paradigmatic of the ways women's poetic authority was repeatedly diminished by a mainstream Victorian literary establishment.

In this chapter, I explore some texts of Christian androcentric Victorian poetic theory, with an eye to how a specifically Christian theological poetic theory constructs femaleness and Jewishness within its parameters. I argue that as Victorian poetics grew increasingly theological in nature, male Christian critics and clerics constructed difference within their poetics as "a lack – insufficient and partial – and as an excess to be cast out, to inscribe it as outside" – a lack which applied to both the Jewish and female other, in differing kinds of theoretical contexts. Yet as I will suggest, these seeming parallel discourses about Jewishness and femaleness did not in fact remain on parallel (separate) trajectories. When we examine some of the dominant Christian critics of the day, we find constant intersections, collisions, contradictions, and elisions between the languages of femaleness and Jewishness. As the discourse on Jewishness became a central and contested site for figuring androcentric poetic identity, it was likewise a crucial and contested site to which women poets turned in their own bids for poetic authority. We cannot understand fully why and how women poets repeatedly engaged with figures of Jewish identity in their poetry until we see that these women poets were in dialogue with the hegemonic discourses on religion and gender that pervade Victorian theological poetics.

What makes this a particularly useful analysis for nineteenth-century England is that by the early part of the nineteenth century, the somewhat abstracted or theoretical invocations of Jewishness and femaleness became increasingly manifest – or shall we say embodied – in the somewhat coincidental emergence of the Jewish community and women poets in English culture. Women poets emerged as important in their own right in the Romantic age, but by 1830, poets like L. E. L. and Felicia Hemans had come to dominate the poetic markets, and the figure of the "poetess" was a clearly recognizable cultural icon – and one that ruptured certain major assumptions of English poetic identity.[3] The rise of the figure of the woman poet coincided with a period of national debate on theories of Jewish identity galvanized by the re-evaluation of Jewish civil and political disability that occurred from 1830 to 1858.[4] Though Jews were only readmitted to England in the seventeenth century, two hundred years had brought their community – and the attendant national and parliamentary debates around "the Jew Bills" – into the English spotlight in and around the same historical moment that the figure of the woman poet was increasingly visible.[5] Here, I propose not to link the *reasons* for the historical emergence of both the Anglo-Jews and the woman poet as newly viable forms of English identity, but rather explore some of the potential ideological *consequences* of that convergence as they emerge in many different commentaries on the nature of the poet and poetry in Victorian poetic discourses.

As Michael Ragussis, Bryan Cheyette, and others have charted in recent work on Jewishness and English literary history, Jewishness emerges
as central category of concern in English society, letters, and politics in
Victorian England, and Jewishness is a concept that gets explored and
exploited in terms of race and sexuality, as well as religion. Most studies of
Jewishness in Victorian England however, have completely ignored the
specific dimensions of poetic discourse, while most critics of Victorian
poetry have likewise remained remarkably unobservant of the perva-
siveness of a Jewish discourse that emerges – in a variety of ways – in
Victorian literary theories about poetry. In part, this "unseeing" is related
to the fact that few, if any, scholarly studies of Victorian poetry read the
work of non-Christian authors, and thus the dominant critical method
for generating theories of Victorian poetry naturalizes the idea that all
Victorians were, in one way or another, Christian. Without fully naming
the anti-Judaism that structures most Victorian poetic discourse, recent
scholarship has been unable to see the Jewish other in the texts and
margins of Christian Victorian poetics and poetry, by men and women.

The historical presence of the Jewish other on English shores (rather
than the other as experienced through foreign colonialism) made
"the Jewish question" pertinent to many different kinds of Christians.
Thus, while denominational differences between different strains of
Anglicanism, Nonconformist Protestants, and even Roman Catholics
may have created different specific concerns with the "problem" of
Jewishness, here I hope to suggest a broader frame for this analysis, one
that examines the larger parameters of Christian identity within a group
of thinkers who were aligned to differing degrees within Anglican institutions. As Gavin Langmuir has suggested, any Jewish presence in a
Christian culture often galvanizes crises in Christian self-identification.
Describing the early decades of Christianity's codification, Langmuir
writes:

Jews and Judaic religions posed a problem for Christian religiosity and Christian
religions that Christians could not avoid, for it was the result of tensions within
the religiosity of Christians and between Christians. They could not help asking
and trying to explain why the vast majority of Jews had been unwilling to accept
the Christians' belief about Jesus . . . Jews were thus the very incarnation of
disbelief in Jesus. And because they were, not only could they inspire doubts
but Christians who were seriously bothered by their own doubts could hardly
avoid thinking of Jews. (*History, Religion, and Antisemitism*, 284)

While Langmuir's point applies specifically to the first centuries of
Christianity, it seems to be applicable to any period in which Christian

doubt is galvanized through the presence of actual Jewish people. This continued persistence of Jewish identity and belief in the Diaspora always poses a problem for Christianity, calling into question the assumed universality of Christian truth. And in Victorian England, the notion of "universal" Christian truth and the authority of the national Church was already under attack on a variety of fronts: in the successful Nonconformist challenges to Anglican supremacy, the sharp rise in Roman Catholicism, the contested response of the Oxford Movement to claim the Anglican Church as the authentic Church, and finally increasing dissemination of historical Biblical criticism, Darwinist and positivist intellectual challenges to religious faith itself. Against this backdrop of religious turbulence, the increased economic and political success of the Jewish community and the very public debates about Jewish political enfranchisement were necessarily causes for Christian scrutiny. Configuring the poet as an agent of Christian theology was one way dominant critics broadly identified as Anglican maintained the hegemony of Christian identity in an historical moment when religious diversity threatened the English national Church quite dramatically.

As Jewish people became a commonplace aspect of urban life and an increasingly national presence in the much publicized debates about Jewish political enfranchisement in Parliament, the ideological and cultural meaning of Jewishness was explored in a variety of literary contexts – including poetry. While Jewishness in recent scholarship has generally been approached through its relationship to Victorian racial discourse, I want to place special emphasis here on the *theological* roots of anti-Judaism, rather than anti-Semitism *per se*. I would contend with Langmuir – as well as Christian theologian Rosemary Radford Ruether – that the racialized (anti-Semitic) discourse of the Jew remains inseparable from its theological manifestation in Christian discourse, anti-Judaism.[6] This theological emphasis has everything to do with the generic context of women's poetry with which I am concerned in this project.[7] Because poetry – up until the *fin-de-siècle* – retained a powerful connection to religious and theological discourse in English literary history, it is in poetic discourse that theological attention to Jewish difference is most crucial.

"TOSSED TO AND FRO": GENDERED CROSSINGS IN PROPHETIC/POETIC IDENTITY

Vates means both Prophet and Poet; and indeed at all times, Prophet and Poet, well understood, have much kindred of meaning. Fundamentally indeed they are still the same; in this most important respect especially, That they have

penetrated both of them into the sacred mystery of the Universe, what Goethe
calls "the open secret!" . . . But now I say, whoever may forget this divine mystery,
the Vates, whether Prophet or Poet, had penetrated into it; it is a man sent
hither to make it more impressively known to us. (Thomas Carlyle, "The Hero
as Poet," 69)

She is no Sibyl, tossed to and fro in the tempest of furious excitement, but ever
a "deep, majestical and high souled woman" – the calm mistress of the highest
and stormiest of her emotions . . . To herself she seems to be uttering oracular
deliverances. Alas! "oracles speak," and her poetry, to all effective utterance of
original truth, is silent. (George Gilfillan, "Female Authors," 360)

The Romantic theorists of the early nineteenth century claimed the
figure of the poet as prophet in response to the more socio-political and
"rational" approach to poetry of the earlier eighteenth-century neo-
classicists.[8] Thus, by the time Thomas Carlyle writes in the 1840s, the
notion that the poet was a prophet was a commonplace idea; Carlyle
links both poet and prophet to the "Vates," a figure who has access to
the "sacred mystery of the Universe." With this characteristically broad
definition, Carlyle thus escapes from defining any specific theological
context from or to which the poet/prophet must speak. While his definition of the poet carries with it many entangled roots in religious discourse,
Carlyle remains uninterested in defining a specific creed that might
specify what the actual prophetic content might look like. But of course,
the prophets whom he uses as examples, and indeed, most prophets in
general, do speak from specific historical and religious contexts, the most
common and obvious reference being to Mohammed, the prophets
from classical Greek literature, or those from the Hebrew Scriptures.[9]

The Victorian poetic theorists I explore in this chapter – John Keble,
John Henry Newman, Eneas Dallas, Matthew Arnold, and Stopford
Brooke – offered a quite different definition of poetry and the poet,
one which counters the Romantic and Carlylean view of a universalized
poet/prophet figure by situating the poet/prophet within a specific theological identity; in so doing, they revise theories of the poet as prophet
that have been more emphasized in scholarly accounts – and especially
feminist accounts – of nineteenth-century literary history. Though the
point of this chapter is to suggest the influence of this paradigm I term
"theological poetics," it is important to look briefly at the poet as prophet
paradigm because it was the context through which most public criticism
of women poets was conducted.

As I have already demonstrated at the start of this chapter, women
poets were generally excluded from the title poet/prophet in dominant

criticism; this expulsion is replicated in the passage, cited above, by George Gilfillan on Felicia Hemans. Hemans is cited for thinking herself a prophet, but producing work that is devoid of "original truth," and Gilfillan makes his claims with full acknowledgment of the poet as prophet paradigm. From his passage, and countless others in this period, we learn how gender identity becomes intimately connected with a poet's ability to interact with "the divine." For Gilfillan, Hemans lacks some essential quality of poetic/prophetic identity, and it seems related to the fact that she remains a "deep, majestical and high souled woman" rather than one who can, like the Sibyl of Greek myth, allow herself to be "tossed to and fro in the tempest of furious excitement." In short, it seems that embodying woman-ness too fully exempts one from prophetic identity; thus, because Hemans, in Gilfillan's view, is a "calm mistress of . . . her emotions" she can not really be a prophet in the tradition of a Sibyl – that is, she does not have an authentic connection to the "sacred mystery of the Universe."

I have isolated this idea of the prophet as one who is "tossed to and fro" in the title of this section because I think it quite accurately describes the dynamics of gender identity in the rhetoric of the poet as prophet. In short, the poet/prophet is a man who manages to combine qualities associated with both men and women in one prophetic identity, a figure, not unlike that of the mythical Tiresias, who is "tossed to and fro" between different gendered identities as a condition of prophetic identity. Because Victorian culture relied so heavily on a system of separate gendered spheres which demarcated all kinds of human experience, this construction of the poet as one who can move between different realms of experience and identity served as a distinct challenge to those explicitly gendered identities – at least in terms of male poets who were "allowed" to negotiate the gendered crossings that Romantic poetic theory constructed. As Wordsworth put it in his famous "Preface to Lyrical Ballads" (1802 version), the poet is able to combine "a more lively sensibility, more enthusiasm and tenderness" (e.g. qualities coded female) with "a greater knowledge of human nature, and a more comprehensive soul" (qualities coded male) (255). Looking back at these dominant Romantic theories, we see clearly how Romantic male poets, according to critic Marlon Ross, "make women . . . an extension of themselves" (*The Contours of Masculine Desire*, 5), and in so doing appropriate the realm of the heart for their own poetic uses.[10] As a figure who could (apparently) transcend the boundaries of gendered identity, the male poet was a special "universal" figure indeed in Victorian England; as a figure who remained bound by the walls of sensibility, domesticity, sympathy, and feeling, the woman poet was often perceived as a much more limited creature.

This gendered discourse of separate spheres insisted that women were suited to a particular kind of poetry, one which did not require them to transcend gendered identity as male poets might, as is clear from the following passage from Frederic Rowton's introduction to his volume on women poets.

Man is bold, enterprising, and strong; woman cautious, prudent and stead-fast. Man is self-relying and self-possessed; woman timid, clinging and dependent. Man is suspicious and secret, woman confiding. Man is fearless; woman apprehensive. Man arrives at truth by long and tedious study; woman by intuition. He thinks; she feels. He reasons; she sympathizes. He has courage; she has patience. The strong passions are his: ambition, love of conquest, love of fame. The mild affections are hers: love of home, love of virtue, love of friends. Intellect is his, heart is hers . . . (Rowton, *The Female Poets of Great Britain*, lii)

The passage sets up a system of separate complementary gendered roles which concludes by granting to men "intellect" and to women "the heart." Thus, in this context, the figure of the heart becomes a metonym for femininity or femaleness, a sign of heightened sensibility and emotion, and even symbolic of a specific connection to the body which stands in opposition to the more abstracted intellect, which is cast as a specifically male quality. In an ideology understood to be structured exclusively on gendered dualism, "the heart is [certainly] hers."

Yet, there is an implicit contradiction at work in this definition of the heart and its poetic role as only "hers" in Victorian culture. Indeed, literary criticism on Romantic poetics has repeatedly demonstrated that for the Romantics – and I would add critics like Carlyle and others who clearly call on Romantic poetics – the realm of the heart always is a very necessary attribute for male poetic identity. As Alan Richardson has aptly written of the Romantic male poets, "where male writers had relegated sympathy and sensibility to their mothers, wives, and sisters, they now sought to reclaim 'feminine' qualities through incorporating something of these same figures" (Richardson, "Romanticism and the Colonization of the Feminine," 15). Women poets, on the other hand, were understood to excel only at the poetry of the heart. But as I demonstrated above, it is not the realm of the heart *per se* that was understood to limit women's poetic identity; rather, it was the fact that women could not claim the necessary male attributes of poetry the way male poets appropriated female qualities. Thus, women poets come to be defined by dominant male critical culture as embodying only one side of the poet/prophet equation. In his Introduction to *The British Female Poets* (1848) George Bethune writes:

The last hundred, especially the last fifty years, have demonstrated, that as there are offices necessary to the elegant perfection of society, which can be discharged only by the delicate and more sensitive faculties of woman, so her graceful skill can shed charms over letters, which man could never diffuse. In all pertaining to the affections, which constitute the best part of human nature, we readily confess her superiority; it is, therefore, consistent with her character that the genius of woman should yield peculiar delight when its themes are love, childhood, and the softer beauties of creation, the joys and sorrows of the heart, domestic life, mercy, religion, and the instincts of justice. Hence, her excellence in the poetry of the sensibilities. (iii–iv)

The characteristics with which the female poet is associated – sensibility and "heart" – are crucial aspects of poetic identity; yet within the prophetic paradigm, these qualities are only cast as transcendent and participating in "true poetry" when they are extracted from female bodies, and located in the identity of the male poet.

Because the model of the poet/prophet has been understood as such a powerful paradigm in nineteenth-century England, much feminist criticism of the nineteenth-century woman poet has used it as the basis for understanding the ways women poets have been read within Victorian culture. In particular, the identification between the woman poet and the realm of the heart has been a touchstone for feminist criticism of Victorian women poets, and if we were to generalize, it would be safe to say that feminist critics have tended to reconstruct women's literary history and female poetic identity by arguing that women poets of the nineteenth century needed to "transcend" the heart, the realm of domesticity and sensibility to which male critics of the day would relegate women. Women could not afford to remain only in the realm of the heart, feminist critics have argued, but rather had to challenge what Deirdre David has called "the intellectual patriarchy" and thus claim the realms of intellect and philosophy in order to emerge as authoritative poets themselves.

Likewise, Angela Leighton's *Victorian Women Poets: Writing Against the Heart* offers the most in-depth analysis of the figure of the heart in Victorian women's poetry, suggesting that women's poetry of this period

grows out of a struggle with and against a highly moralized celebration of women's sensibility. Through Hemans and L. E. L., sensibility becomes, not only profitable and fashionable again in the 1820s and 30s, but it also accrues certain

strongly prescriptive, gender specific values of sincerity and purity... Without
the heart to guarantee femininity, feeling and truth, the imagination enters a
world of skeptically disordered moral and linguistic reference. While the aesthetic possibilities of such disorder are seductive, the moral cost, especially for
women, is high. (3)

Leighton's important book follows the assumption of most feminist critics of Victorian women poets which reads women poets as having to
"struggle with and against" the terms of gendered identity – sensibility
and heart – which are bequeathed to them by dominant Victorian
gendered and literary ideology. That is, women need "the heart" to
"guarantee femininity, feeling and truth" in their perceived poetic identity, but if they conform to that realm alone, Leighton suggests, they
lose access to a "seductive world of skeptically disordered moral and
linguistic reference" (3). And while Leighton is clearly describing the
ways women poets were perceived in their day, her terms suggest that
within a more contemporary feminist poetics, women poets must also
transcend this realm of the heart in order to emerge as legitimate artists
within the terms of present-day feminist aesthetics. With this emphasis
on women "challenging" the realm of the heart, many feminist critics of
women's poetry have remained less interested in those poets who seem
to overtly claim the realm of sensibility, which includes the realm of
religious/sentimental poetry. Relying on a set of aesthetic values that
replicate androcentric poetic evaluation, much feminist criticism of
Victorian women's poetry has thus replicated some of the same assumptions generated by the androcentric Victorian critics who base their
theories of poetry on the paradigm of the "poet as prophet." But this
poet as prophet model, while clearly an important paradigm for poetic
identity in this early nineteenth-century period, was not the only poetic
paradigm available to poets or the reading public. In the next section,
I explore an alternative understanding of poetic identity operative in
this period as well, one in which the symbol of the heart carries a set of
associations with much more potential power and authority than it does
in the poet as prophet model of poetry. Understanding the significance
of the specifically Christian heart sheds new light on the ways femaleness
and Jewishness were linked in Victorian poetics.

RECONFIGURING THE HEART: POETRY AS THEOLOGY

Ye are our epistle written in our hearts, known and read of all men: Forasmuch as
ye are manifestly declared to be the epistle of Christ ministered by us, written not
with ink, but with the Spirit of the living God; not in tables of stone, but in fleshly

tables of the heart. And such trust have we through Christ to God-ward . . . Who also hath made us able ministers of the new testament; not of the letter, but of the spirit; for the letter killeth, but the spirit giveth life. (2 Corinthians 3: 2–6, King James Version)

It (the heart) does not altogether lose its physical reference, for it is made of "flesh" (2 Cor. iii. 3), but it is the seat of the will (e.g. Mk. iii. 5), of the intellect (e.g. Mk. ii. 6, 8) and of feeling (e.g. Lk. xxiv. 32). This means that the "heart" comes the nearest of the New Testament terms to mean "person." (C. Ryder Smith, quoted in Douglas, ed., *The New Bible Dictionary*, 509)

The ideology of separate spheres has been identified as one of the primary systems for categorizing human experience in Victorian England, and as we saw in the previous section, was especially used to categorize poetic identity for men and women. In that system, the realm of the heart is a female realm to which male poets must lay claim for their own complete poetic identity; the heart is one part of a poetic identity, and must be complemented by the other side of the equation: intellect or philosophy/theory. The passages quoted above suggest a different system of organization for kinds of identity and experience in explicitly Christian culture. Paul's Second Letter to the Corinthians reminds us that the heart, rather than being associated with a limited form of female identity exclusively, is also a term used repeatedly in the Christian Scriptures as a sign of complete Christian identity – often in contradistinction to the incomplete heart which is the sign of Jewish difference. In that scheme, the "fleshly tables of the heart" are the markers for an explicit Christian identity, demarcated from the "tables of stone" which represent Judaism; in addition, the heart becomes aligned with the figure of the life-giving Christian "spirit" in and against the figure of the "kill[ing]" Jewish "letter." In this theological system, the heart is not "hers" alone; it is also Christ's.

These categories of Christian and Jewish difference are the defining qualities of identity in the New Testament; like the Victorian ideology of separate spheres, the distinctions between the sphere of spirit and the sphere of law are all-encompassing. Indeed, we can see how important the realm of the heart can be in an explicitly Christian epistemology from C. Ryder's Smith's analysis of the symbol of the heart in Christian thought. Ryder suggests that in an explicitly Christological context, the heart signifies not a piece of a complete identity, but rather a complete identity in itself, linked to "will" and "the intellect" as well as "feeling." When Smith writes that "the 'heart' comes the nearest of the New Testament terms to mean 'person,'" we see the important rupture an explicitly Christian context offers to the idea of the supposedly female "heart"; instead of being one side of a complementary formula, the figure of the heart is the ideal symbol for the complete Christian self. And in nineteenth-century (Christian) England, both sets of organizing principles – gendered difference and religious difference – were simultaneously operative, intersecting in complex ways that are only perceivable when critics look beyond the monological parameters of gender discourse.

John Henry Newman's 1829 essay "Poetry, with Reference to Aristotle's Poetics" in the *London Review* offers a glimpse into how this alternative configuration of the symbol of the heart affects constructions of gender and poetry. After the bulk of the essay, which explores Aristotle's doctrine in relation to modern poetry, Newman turns to a "fresh position," arguing that "poetical talent" can be defined as "the originality of right moral feeling." In the following passage, Newman locates "a poetic view of things" as a specifically Christian characteristic, and writes:

> With Christians, a poetical view of things is a duty, – we are bid to colour all things with hues of faith, to see a divine meaning in every event, and a superhuman tendency . . . It may be added, that the virtues peculiarly Christian are especially poetical: – meekness, gentleness, compassion, contentment, modesty, not to mention the devotional virtues; whereas the ruder and more ordinary feelings are the instruments of rhetoric more justly than of poetry – anger, indignation, emulation, martial spirit, and love of independence. (23)

What is important in this description of the "poetic view of things" is that the very impulse to poetry is named as an explicitly Christian set of attributes. Calling this poetic view a Christian "duty," Newman goes on to align the poetic instinct with a set of terms – "meekness, gentleness, compassion, contentment, modesty" – which are terms generally read as female in Victorian culture. Yet, rather than naming those qualities as marked by gendered female identity, Newman marks them as "peculiarly Christian." On the other side of the generic equation for Newman are qualities of "rhetoric" which mirror (with the possible exception of "emulation") characteristics often defined as male in Victorian notions of gendered identity. Significantly, they are also terms which are linked with common anti-Judaic descriptions of "Old Testament Judaism" as bound to the "letter" of the law (rather than spirit), and linked to images of "revengeful" and "cruel" religious visions of God.

Newman's passage could be read in terms of the gendered discourse surrounding the different poetic aptitudes of men and women. But it is crucial to see that Newman is not constructing a theory of gendered poetic identity, he is constructing a theory of theological poetic identity, one that is also structured dualistically, positioning that which is Christian and "poetical" as the highest form of identity, and that which is not Christian as "other" to true poetry. When we conjoin this theological value system with the gender value system of Victorian England, we see that which is feminized in a Victorian gendered ideology is that which is idealized and universalized in Newman's Christian poetics. Likewise, that which might be masculinized in a gendered economy of meaning is seen as less valuable, and indeed perhaps linked to Judaism in this Christian poetics. Highlighting the complex intersections between gendered and religious discourses of "the heart," Newman's 1829 essay helps to initiate a trajectory of theological poetic criticism that, while it rarely addresses the "problem" of the woman poet specifically, nevertheless is of vital importance for understanding the cultural context in which Victorian woman poets wrote.

These intersecting figures of religious and gendered identity occur frequently in the early poetic theory of the Oxford Movement theorists John Keble and John Henry Newman, as well as in the later writings of the critics Eneas Dallas, Matthew Arnold, and the Reverend Stopford Brooke. One of the salient features of this trajectory of Victorian criticism was that commentators emerge from backgrounds in which men (*sic*) freely moved between realms of religion and literature as if they were already coexistent discourses; it may be significant that all these literary men were affiliated with the Anglican Church, either loosely or quite explicitly, if only because such affiliation gave them more claim to cultural capital in Victorian England. John Keble was thus not only one of the founders of what we consider a religious movement (the Oxford Movement); he was also Professor of Poetry at Oxford, and wrote a volume of poetry, *The Christian Year*, which outsold all books of poetry in his era.[11] Newman was a tutor in Oxford and Vicar of St. Mary's Church but he was also a publishing poet and critic. Stopford Brooke was the Chaplain to the Queen and Vicar of St. James who gave three years' worth of Sunday lectures titled *Theology in the English Poets*. Arnold, also Professor of Poetry at Oxford (and son of the one of the most famous Broad Church clerics of the century, Thomas Arnold) wrote extensively on the relationship between poetry and religion in his era. Eneas Dallas was a journalist and author of extensive literary criticism who was overt about his Christian allegiance. These biographical facts support Steven Prickett's statement that: "[t]he nature of literary criticism (and the kinds of sensibility it implies) cannot be understood in the nineteenth century without reference to contemporary theology, just as contemporary theology cannot be understood without reference to the literary criticism of the period" (*Romanticism and Religion*, 7). Rereading their poetics with an eye to how they implicitly or explicitly construct gendered and religious difference, some fascinating implications emerge for the ways women poets of both Jewish and Christian affiliation might have been able to imagine their poetic identity within and against these critical perspectives.

In his role as Professor of Poetry at Oxford, Keble concluded his *Lectures on Poetry* (*Praelectiones Academicae*, 1832–41) with lecture XL, the final section of which urges the young men in his audience to recognize the important role poetry can play in religious education. Keble discusses "the hidden tie of kinship" between "Poetry and Theology" (479) and writes: "Only then will Poetry be fitly followed and studied, when those who love it remember that it is a gift to mankind, given that, like a high born handmaid, it may wait upon and minister to true Religion; and therefore it is to be honoured, not with lip service, but really and truly, with all modesty, constancy and purity" (484). Keble sets up a relationship of essential relatedness between poetry and religion in terms of a servant/master relationship. Poetry is figured like a subservient woman who is nevertheless "high born" and thus deserving of a reverence not always associated with the figure of a handmaid because she serves the highest of all masters, religion. With this figure of poetry as a "handmaid" to religion, we encounter a radical departure from the construction of the poet as prophet, or poetry as a form of prophecy. For in Keble's formulation, poetry is not the unique utterance of the "divine mystery"; poetry is defined as an essential tool and aid for religion, explicitly Christianity.[12] In this figure of poetry as "ministering" to religion, the divine agency of the poet is severely curtailed in comparison to a Carlylean model of the poet as a prophet, and is distinctly feminized – though of course in a manner totally abstracted from any relationship to real women.

When poetry itself becomes a "handmaid to religion," it would seem that this poetic realm might be more hospitable to a Victorian construction of the woman poet, because in this theological poetics, the poet is no longer a unique figure who must engage with a direct knowledge of the divine. Indeed, as the following passage from the same lecture suggests, poetry can emerge not from a triumphant meeting of an individual "Vates" man and the divine, but rather, poetry is defined as that which mediates the universal experience of "helplessness" which attends any human reflection on the divine.

Now, partly the very nature of religion in itself, partly the actual confession of all who can be supposed to have the faintest sense of true piety, impress on us the fact that nothing takes such entire possession of the human heart, and, in a way, concentrates its feeling, as the thought of God and an eternity to come: nowhere is our feeble mortal nature more conscious of its helplessness; nothing so powerfully impels it, sadly and anxiously, to look round on all sides for remedy and relief. As a result of this, Religion freely and gladly avails itself of every comfort and assistance which Poetry may afford. (480)

Where Carlyle would have his poet/prophet meet God "face to face" as it were, for Keble, poetry becomes that which can mediate the "entire possession of the human heart" when "possessed" by "the thought of God and an eternity to come." In this sense, the poet's agency is considerably reduced, while poetry is nevertheless a crucial support for the practice of religion. No longer is it only the poet who has direct access to the divine mystery; rather, for Keble, "all who can be supposed to have the faintest sense of true piety" must face their "helplessness" in the reckoning of God. In Keble's system, it is not the power of the intellect or "more comprehensive soul" (Wordsworth) that guarantees either poetry or prophecy; instead, it is the "possession of the . . . heart" which indicates true piety and poetry.

Finally, in a related passage from *Tracts for the Times*, Keble makes clear that only Christ is the ideal poet, as we see from Keble's description in Tract 89 ("On the Mysticism attributed to the Early Fathers of the Church," 1840).

If we suppose Poetry in general to mean the expression of an overflowing mind, relieving itself, more or less indirectly and reservedly, of the thoughts and passions which most oppress it: – on which hypothesis each person will have a Poetry of his own, a set of associations appropriate to himself for the works of nature and other visible objects, in themselves common to him with others: – if this be so, what follows will not perhaps be thought altogether an unwarrantable conjecture; proposed, as it ought, and is wished to be, with all fear and religious reverence. May it not, then, be so, that our Blessed Lord, in union and communion with all His members, is represented to us as constituting, in a certain sense, one great and manifold Person, into which, by degrees, all souls of men, who do not cast themselves away, are to be absorbed? And as it is a scriptural and ecclesiastical way of speaking, to say, Christ suffers in our flesh, is put to shame in our sins, our members are part of Him; so may it not be affirmed that He condescends in like manner to have a Poetry of His own, a set of holy and divine associations and meanings, wherewith it is his will to invest all material things? (Keble, *Tracts*, 144)

Where in the poet as prophet paradigm it is the male poet who "absorbs" all aspects of identity to emerge whole, here it is Christ, not the mortal male poet, who is figured as having "a Poetry of His own" which he "condescends" to offer just as he offered his own body as a redemptive substitute for fallen Christians. Christ's "Poetry," that is, is the holiest form of poetry as it stands for his very existence and, like Christ's body, conveys upon "material things" a "set of holy and divine associations." Because no human can actually replicate Christ's identity, human poetry is only a shadow or mirror of that originary poetic body, and the poet merely imitates Christ in the creation of poetry. With this emphasis on a universalized Christian identity, the poet is no longer a "special" man with unique access to the divine, since that role has been claimed by Christ himself; on some level, Keble's (and for that matter Newman's) idea of poetry suggests that anyone who is a Christian may be "especially poetical." In the poetry as theology paradigm, the idea of human poetry takes on a certain quality of humility, removed from the realm of the "special man" and available to anyone who emulates Christ. Likewise, theology itself is also transformed from a high intellectual "science" into something quite personal and local – and thus feminized.

We can observe the radical difference between Keble and Newman's theories of poetry as a sort of heartfelt "overflow" of Christian instinct against the notion of theology as science if we turn briefly to a much cited statement by John Ruskin in *Sesame and Lilies* (1865 / 1871). In the essay "Of Queens' Gardens," Ruskin details the many disciplines to which women's education should be open, yet concludes the section on women's education with a lengthy passage about women and (Christian) theology:

> There *is* one dangerous science for women – one which let them indeed beware how they profanely touch – that of theology. Strange, and miserably strange, that while they are modest enough to doubt their powers, and pause at the threshold of sciences where every step is demonstrable and sure, they will plunge headlong, and without one thought of incompetency, into that science in which the greatest men have trembled and the wisest erred. Strange, in creatures born to be Love visible, that where they can know least, they will condemn first, and think to recommend themselves to their Master by scrambling up the steps of His judgment-throne, to divide it with him. (83)

For Ruskin, theology is the highest "science" and thus not suited to women's special purposes on earth. Ruskin links women to the discourse of the Christian heart when he terms them "Love visible"; with this phrase, he reassociates women with the figure of the Christian body while disassociating them from the capacity to "know." Because for Ruskin theology was a science, perhaps the highest science of all, it was easy to exclude women from its bounds; relying on a gendered ideology, he assumed women did not have the intellectual capacity to engage with that science. Indeed, when Ruskin poses the rather threatening and strangely physical image of women "scrambling up the steps of His judgment-throne, to divide it with him," he exposes the potential danger of any theological model which might authorize that which is female to engage with Christian theology. However, where Ruskin upholds this boundary by denying to women the possibility of engaging with theology, critics who reject the idea of theology as a science and associate theology with the realm of feeling offer some fascinating discursive openings through which women poets could claim legitimate poetic identity.

In 1871, almost simultaneous with Ruskin's *Sesame and Lilies*, the Reverend Stopford Brooke, "Chaplain in Ordinary to her Majesty the Queen and Minister of St. James Chapel," began a series of lectures on Sunday afternoons in London's St. James chapel titled *Theology in the English Poets*.[13] These lectures were subsequently published in 1874, and the volume had gone through four editions by 1880, suggesting their popularity. At the very start of this volume, Brooke clarifies his use of the term "theology."

The Poets of England ever since Cowper have been more and more theological, till we reach such men as Tennyson or Browning, whose poetry is overcrowded with theology. But the theology of poets is different from that of Churches and of Sects, in this especially, that it is not formulated into propositions, but is the natural growth of their own hearts. They are, by their very nature, strongly individual; they grow more by their special genius than by the influence of the life of the world around them, and they are, therefore, sure to have a theology – that is, a Doctrine of God in his relation to Man, Nature and their own soul – which will be independent of conventional religious thought. (1–2)

Countering Ruskin's explicit construction of theology as a science, Brooke draws on the tradition of Keble and Newman in order to offer a very different understanding of theology. In the passage above, Brooke offers a very particular notion of the "theology of poets" as "different from that of Churches and of Sects" in that each individual male poet develops a "Doctrine of God in his relation to Man, Nature, and their own soul" which may not necessarily conform to institutionalized theological doctrine.[14] Calling this poetic theology "the natural growth of their own hearts," Brooke's formula for theological poetry implicitly links the male poet to the discourse of the heart generally associated, as we have seen, with the woman poet in the earlier part of the century.

Brooke seems to go further than Keble or Newman in his idea that
theology itself is a deeply individual and personal language; thus, Brooke
works to disassociate the theology of the heart not only from Ruskin's
notion of "science" but also the idea of institutional creed and doctrine.
Writing about poets, Brooke states:

For in their ordinary intercourse with men they were subject to the same in-
fluences as other men, and if religious, held a distinct creed or conformed to a
special sect; and if irreligious, expressed the strongest denial of theological opinions. It is plain that in ordinary life their intellect would work consciously on the
subject, and their prejudices come into play. But in their poetry, their imagination worked unconsciously on the subject. Their theology was not produced as
a matter of intellectual coordination of truths, but as a matter of truths which
were true because they were felt; and the fact is, that in this realm of emotion
where prejudice dies, the thoughts and feelings of their poetry on the subject
of God and Man are often wholly different from those expressed in everyday
life. (2–3)

Brooke argues that "the realm of emotion" offers a site where "prejudice
dies" and he sets this realm of feeling clearly against an "intellectual coordination of truths." Thus Brooke reconfigures the idea of great male
poetry from the Romantic construction of a combined relationship between feeling and intellect, and constructs a realm of male discourse
that lets male poets speak the way women poets were supposed to speak,
uttering "truths which were true because they were felt." But at the moment Brooke names these "felt truths" theological, he makes a clear challenge to the Ruskinian idea of theology as an objective science. Brooke
recasts not only the idea of poetry here; more radically, he takes the
idea of theology from a supposed "male" realm of academic science and
"Churches and . . . Sects," and transforms it into the realm of personal
emotion.

Offering a more radical view of both poetry and theology than Keble,
Newman or Ruskin, Brooke reconfigures the idea of theology in order
to define poetry. He argues that in poetry, "[w]e see theology, as it
were, in the rough; as, at its beginnings, it must have grown up in the
minds of earnest and imaginative men around certain revealed intuitive
truths, such as the Being of God or the need of redemption" (2). What
Brooke does with this definition, in essence, is to naturalize the process of
Christian theology; for indeed, it is important to note that all the poets
he explores are Christians who, though perhaps differing in some ways,
would certainly understand the ideas of "the Being of [Christ]" and the
"need of redemption" in particularly Christian ways. Because, not surprisingly, Brooke only examines the work of the so-called "major male

poets," his generalizations about poetry work to naturalize the idea that the theology of the heart is a male Christian discourse. However, when we juxtapose his rhetoric of this theology of the heart against those commentators who speak specifically of women's poetry, we begin to see how the two discursive registers have in fact begun to replicate each other; as the discourse of gendered poetic identity and religious poetic identity collide, the poetic heart is revealed as an idealized realm that privileges female and Christian identity.

Given this context of theological poetics – as it emerges from commentators like Newman, Keble, and Brooke, I would suggest that "writing against the heart" (the subtitle of Leighton's book on Victorian women poets) may not have been the primary strategic approach for women poets to take in Victorian England. Instead, we might speculate that Christian women in particular learned to galvanize many of the assumptions about poetic identity rooted in what might be termed the "poetry as theology" discourse I have charted above. Claiming this kind of heartfelt Christian poetic authority through the discourse of the heart, Christian women poets could claim a complete poetic identity, rather than one understood to be "lacking." And, once this discourse of the poetic Christian heart is revealed as a central discourse for many Victorian literary theorists of poetry, the dynamics of religious, gendered, and literary identity shift in other directions as well. In the following section, I explore how this paradigm of poetry as theology situates poetic identity along another discursive register, namely that of Jewish difference.

For, as numerous New Testament passages suggest, this figure of the Christian heart was not necessarily gender-coded – that is, "woman" does not serve explicitly in the position of "other" in the idealization of the Christian poetic heart. Instead, it is the unconverted Jew who becomes associated with the "lack" of the other, and this lack is constantly described through images of the "hardened," "uncircumcised," and faithless Jewish heart. For example, in Hebrews 4:12, Jesus states that that those who refuse his covenant are analogous to those Jews who rebelled in the Jewish Exodus: "Their hearts are forever astray; they would not discern my ways." Paul then expands this exhortation to the Hebrews, writing "See to it, my friends, that no one among you has the wicked and faithless heart of a deserter from the living God." In short, the figure of the stony, hardened, impatient, ruthless, and insincere Jewish heart becomes a cornerstone of anti-Semitic and anti-Judaic imagery in Christian culture. Because Christian poetic theory relied on an explicitly Christian model of the poetic heart, this figure of Jewish difference becomes an important – if vexed – figure in much Victorian poetic theory. The impact of a Christian theological model of poetry is particularly evident in the repeated references to Jewishness in the work of J. B. Selkirk, Eneas Dallas, and Matthew Arnold, critics who call on Jewish identity as a pivotal trope for the constructing English poetic identity.

THE SWEET SINGERS OF ISRAEL: JEWISHNESS IN VICTORIAN POETICS

With what grander poetry could the religious instinct ally itself than the exultant raptures of Isaiah? Where can finer fellow-feeling for humanity be found than in the penitential pathos of the sweet singer of Israel, with that ever fresh-hearted faith in the final issue, which so strongly characterizes the deepest and darkest of its sorrows? Our indebtedness to Hebrew poetry withdrawn, it would be impossible to form any adequate conception of what civilization would have been. (Selkirk, *Ethics and Aesthetics of Modern Poetry*, 161–2)

Any discussion of the role of Jewishness in Victorian poetics must begin by acknowledging a distinct trajectory of criticism that idealized Hebrew Biblical poetry. Though Keble and most other Christian clerics who invoke Jewish superiority in poetry often go on to recast that superiority so that it might not threaten Christian transcendence, the passage from critic J. B. Selkirk above demonstrates the important philo-Judaic discourse that emerged in eighteenth- and nineteenth-century discussions of poetry, a discourse that repeatedly emphasized the perfect poetry epitomized by "the sweet singer of Israel." This "sweet singer" was generally understood to be King David in his assumed authorship of the Psalms, but the image extends to other Hebrew poets of the Bible and classical Judaism. Selkirk's image of the "fresh-hearted faith" of Hebrew poets offers a particular contrast to the idea of the faithless Jewish heart of much Christian theological discourse. Resisting the typological impulse to diminish this "Israelite" poetry as not fully Christianized, Selkirk and others repeatedly suggest that Hebrew poetry contains the roots of Western civilization, and that the Hebrew poets represent the highest model of poetic identity available.

Prior to Keble's (and Newman's) work in the 1820s and 1830s, there had already been a history of linking Jewishness to poetic identity in the Romantic literary studies of Biblical poetry typified by Bishop Lowth and Johann Gottfried Herder. The work of these two influential eighteenth-century Biblical scholars combined to make the term "Hebrew poetry" a commonplace of nineteenth-century literary criticism. Bishop Robert

Lowth's *Lectures on the Sacred Poetry of the Hebrews* were delivered in Latin at Oxford between 1741 and 1750 while Lowth was Professor of Poetry; these lectures were published in English in 1787 and the importance of this text can be marked by the fact that it then was continuously published until 1847. Johann Gottfried Herder's "The Spirit of Hebrew Poetry," originally published in Germany in 1782–3, was translated into English in 1833. Both works sought to analyze and explain Hebrew poetry from the Bible, and both contributed to the definition of this poetry as a "sublime" form.

Indeed, this influential work of Lowth and Herder helped to link the very definition of true poetry to theories of Hebrew language, Hebraic identity, and the Old Testament. David Norton has suggested that Lowth's lectures "make an argument for the supremacy of the Hebraic poetry" and that Lowth's work, in arguing that the Jewish prophets must also be considered exemplary poets, "drastically widened the sense of poetry in the [Old Testament]" (Norton, *A History of the Bible as Literature*, 61, 65). Likewise, Herder is, according to Norton, "an important model of a theological aesthetic" which displays a "critical intelligence unhampered by doctrine" (202); in short, it seems Herder was the most able of the Christian Biblical scholars to consider Hebrew poetry on its own merits without casting it within a more standard Christian typological devaluation. Frank Manuel suggests that it was Herder who became the "standard bearer of the new doctrine" which defined "the creative core of ancient Judaism as its poetic nature." Manuel argues that when translated, Herder's work could be read as "an emotionalized and romanticized religion of Israel" (*The Broken Staff*, 263). In other words, his poetics derived from Hebrew poetry maintained a much more open and flexible stance toward Jewishness, able to see in it a poetic "spirituality" that is often denied to Judaism by Christian detractors. Thus, before Jewish people gained a real visibility in the mid-nineteenth century, Christian England formed much of its philo-Judaic imagery from this idealization of the mythic Biblical Hebrew poet.[15] Yet, as we move to critics from the latter half of the nineteenth century, we can see a subtle shift in the ways Hebrew poetry is represented. Often drawing on certain links between Christianity and poetry, critics like Eneas Dallas and Matthew Arnold emphasize the "other" role Jewish identity plays in a theologically based poetics.

Eneas Dallas' excessive, almost Carlylean rhetoric might seem to position him as an inheritor of Carlyle's poet as prophet model, yet closer examination reveals that in many sections of his work, *Poetics* (1852), it is Keble and Newman's models of poetry as theology upon which he bases his poetics – despite the fact that Dallas was not specifically associated with their religious movement, Tractarianism. In his conclusion, Dallas attempts to explain poetry's import to present-day life; he acknowledges that "the influence of poesy over our practice is not great in degree" (*Poetics*, 293). But while he names poetry's minimal effects on daily lives, Dallas also suggests that even the most limited form of poetic influence is "of a higher order" (293) than any other kind of influence on human practice. To explain his theory of the special influence of poetry as like "the work of love" (293), Dallas creates an analogy between the relative power of Old and New Testament covenants, using the Psalmists as the symbol for Judaism, which he then goes on to compare to Christianity. Dallas writes:

> Under the reign of Law, in so far as it agreed with that title, obedience was enforced by the spur of conscience, as is shown in the Psalms, where one can not but be struck with the conscious integrity which the sweet singers of Israel carry about with them, and which in the kingdom of Love, where, in so far as it answers to the title, obedience wells up without effort, is but little known; and of John the Baptist, the last prophet of the Law, and the herald of him who was to make the eye itself full of light, the Saviour said, "Among them that are born of women there hath not risen a greater than John the Baptist; notwithstanding he that is least in the kingdom of heaven is greater than he." It is even so. Great as are the deeds of the law, the least work of love is greater. (293)

This excessive exercise in comparison argues that despite the power of the Psalms, true poetry operates analogously to Christianity rather than Judaism. Dallas uses this complex passage as part of his argument that poetry has an influence much like Christianity, in which "the least work of love" is nevertheless of crucial import to daily life. In this passage, Dallas describes Judaism through a particular Christian lens, claiming it is governed by the "obedience" born of "conscious integrity" that he sees in the "sweet singers of Israel" (the Psalmists); this form of "conscious integrity" is contrasted against a different kind of Christian "obedience" that "wells up without effort" in the later "kingdom of Love" or Christianity. By the end of the passage, Dallas can conclude that "Great as are the deeds of the law, the least work of love is greater," and so even the "least work of poetry" is greater than other forms of writing.

With the belief that the processes of poetry and Christianity are essentially linked, Victorian theological poetic theory repeatedly engaged with Jewish difference as part of the process of constructing the English Christian poetic self, yet always with an explicit need to disassociate this theory of poetry from actual Jewish people. Dallas' construction of poetry in this passage is thus another indication of the essential role the Judaic plays in English literary consciousness; though he is clearly interested in describing poetry in explicitly Christian terms, Dallas, and others, can never fully erase that "trace" of Jewishness which is fully embedded in the discourse of Victorian Christian poetics. Of course, these traces of Jewishness in poetic theory never actually refer to embodied Jewish people, but rather to the historical Jew who lurks in every invocation of Christian history and "Old Testament" text. However, the presence of an actual Jewish reading subject who might offer a self-interpretation of Jewishness threatens the "logic" of this theory of poetry. As Jill Robbins explains, in an explicitly Christian epistemology, "Judaic exegesis" must be denied any context of Jewish "self-understanding," that is, an interpretation that is rooted in a specifically Jewish epistemology, because

the self-understanding of Judaic exegesis would give lie to the figural assertion that the Old Testament discredits its own authority and transfers it to the New. It would disrupt the dyadic and hierarchical oppositions such as carnal and spiritual, literal and figurative, that structure every figural claim . . . For if the book the Jews carry is not an Old Testament but a Hebrew Bible, then the figural discourse would collapse. Thus Christian hermeneutics has to suppress the self-understanding of Judaic exegesis. But it cannot, as it were, suppress it enough. It cannot suppress the Judaic without leaving a trace, as when it *in*scribes it as outside. (Robbins, *Prodigal Son / Elder Brother*, 12)

Robbins' theory helps explain not only why references to Jewishness become necessary aspects of Christian literary theory; the passage above also highlights the potential "collapse" of this literary theory at the moment when actual Jewish people claim their own poetic identity in England. A poet who was Jewish, that is, could rupture in all the "hierarchical oppositions such as carnal and spiritual, literal and figurative, that structure every figural claim" of Christian theology and in our case, a Christian poetics; a Jewish poet, offering a "self-understanding" of Jewish identity, becomes an oxymoron for Christian theological poetics.

We can observe the danger a Jewish identity poses to this understanding of Christian poetry by examining Matthew Arnold's essay "Heinrich Heine" (1863), an essay which introduces many ideas and terms that Arnold will later pursue in the more famous *Culture and Anarchy* (1869). While other critics have termed the Heine essay "baffling," "uncomfortable," and "incoherent," when we read it from the perspective of Christian poetics I have been exploring in this chapter, the essay becomes quite legible, fitting nicely into not only Arnold's larger critical method, but also into Victorian theories of poetry as Christian theology.[16] Indeed, the Heine essay exposes the radical disjunction that typology creates between an ahistorical, abstracted, and figural Jewish identity and an historical, local, and literal Jewish identity; thus, the essay constructs the essential otherness of Jewishness through an attendant explanation of the nature of Christian poetry.

Arnold begins his essay by suggesting that his goal is to "mark Heine's place in modern European literature, the scope of his activity, and his value" ("Heinrich Heine," 117). In this context of defining Heine's "value" in "European" culture, Heine's Jewishness is not initially a problem for Arnold.[17] Indeed, though Heine – like Benjamin Disraeli – converted to Protestantism, Arnold reads Heine as "Hebrew" in racial, cultural, and religious terms.[18] The issue of Heine's Jewishness first appears in a reference to "race" at the start of the essay; later, Arnold lauds Heine for being able to represent the "things of the Hebrews" as relevant to non-Jews, that is, Arnold praises Heine for his ability to make Jewish experience "universal," a quality that makes him exceptional in Arnold's eyes: "By his perfection of literary form, by his love of clearness, by his love of beauty, Heine is Greek; by his intensity, by his untameableness, by his 'longing which cannot be uttered,' he is Hebrew. Yet what Hebrew ever treated the things of the Hebrews like this? – " (128). Arnold goes on to quote long passages of Heine's work with little or no interpretation, ostensibly indicating their "universal" meaning. Arnold's methodology suggests that Heine's words have significance for all readers – even those words that come out of quite specific moments in Jewish history, as many of Heine's poems do. Yet, as he reads Heine as a poet who gives access to universal truths, Arnold is faced with a knotty problem at the end of the Heine essay: how to claim this non-Christian writer as eternally valuable, when in a Christian epistemology, the contemporary Jew cannot claim eternal value?

Thus while the essay sets itself up as a testament to Heine's value as a "main stream" (108) poet who is "incomparably the most important figure" in "the European poetry of that quarter of a century which follows the death of Goethe" (132), Arnold's essay ends on a profoundly ambivalent note. It is Heine's moral *"dis*respectab[ility]" (131) that Arnold seems compelled to address at the end of the essay, and this moral "lack" is rhetorically linked to Jewishness in a number of complex ways. Arnold ends the essay with references to Heine's "moral" disease, naming Heine's "crying faults," a list of character traits that have echoes of certain anti-Semitic stereotypes – including "unscrupulous passion," "want of generosity," "sensuality," and "incessant mocking" (132) – a list of traits that echoes those characteristics Newman, in the 1829 essay, had listed as essentially non-poetic, and non-Christian. After building this list of Heine's faults, Arnold concludes by interpreting Heine through the New Testament, where he suddenly is recast as an incomplete figure of "lack" – namely, as a Jew.

> Well, then, look at Heine. Heine had all the culture of Germany; in his head fermented all the idea of modern Europe. And what have we got from Heine? A half result, for want of moral balance, and of nobleness of soul and character. That is what I say; there is so much power, so many seem able to run well, so many give promise of running well; – so few reach the goal, so few are chosen. *Many are called, few chosen.* (132)

At the moment when he evokes Matthew 22:14, Arnold recasts his historically and nationally specific evaluation of Heine into an ahistorized, Christian moral and theological realm.[19] Calling on the reference to chosenness in the context of Matthew's gospel, Arnold implies the impossibility of Jewish transcendence in a Christian system. In choosing this allusion to end his essay, Arnold suggests that though Heine can be understood as a great European poet in a specific historical period, Heine's "eternally needful moral deliverance" (132) remains a mark of his Jewishness which can never be "chosen" or canonized within a Christian literary evaluation.

Arnold's Heine essay is the forerunner to his *magnum opus, Culture and Anarchy*; indeed, the patterns for interpreting ultimate "Hebraic" lack which emerge in *Culture and Anarchy* are already established in the Heine essay. Thus, just as he must disassociate the "Jewish" poet from any final claim to eternal poetic greatness, so too does Arnold, in *Culture and Anarchy*, repeatedly claim "the Hebraic" as an essential quality of English culture, while simultaneously disassociating this idealization of the Hebraic from any connection to Judaism or Jewish people. When Arnold writes in *Culture and Anarchy* that "the habits and discipline received from Hebraism remain for our race an eternal possession" (37), his rhetoric of possession replicates a process of Christian typology, which "extracts" a Hebrew essence out of actual Jewish history in order to reclaim that essence as part of Christianity. Indeed, Arnold is scrupulous in *Culture and Anarchy* in constructing "Hebraism" as a metaphor for middle-class English Protestant identity, severing the term from any relation to real Jews. For Arnold, Hebraism has neither any historical or contemporary connection to actual Jewish bodies; indeed, it is the perhaps the clearest example we have in Victorian poetics of the ways the idea of the Hebraic can be totally abstracted and extracted from any relationship to Jewishness *per se* – despite the fact that when Arnold was writing, the Anglo-Jewish community had a very distinct presence in English culture – and indeed Arnold's own consciousness.[20]

The idealization of the Biblical Hebrew poet by Christian culture is only possible when the work of contemporary Jewish poets – who from a Jewish perspective could be seen as the truest heirs to the Jewish Psalmists and prophets of the Bible – are excluded from incorporation in this Christian poetic canon. In a sense, it is a discursive pattern we already saw in relation to theories of the poetic heart; there, as here, the theory is able to idealize the potential "otherness" of the Jew/female only when there is no possibility that the Jew or female will actually intervene in this poetic system as subject in his/her own right. In fact, Arnold pursues this link between the disembodiment of both Jewishness and femaleness in a quite bizarre passage from *Culture and Anarchy* which brings together the discourses of sexuality, poetry, and Christian anti-Judaism while offering a final repudiation of the Hebraic when it is literally attached to Jewish bodies. In his reading of the following passage, Michael Ragussis notes that on a literal level, Arnold is "speaking against a bill that, on the authority of the Hebrew Scriptures, would allow a man to marry the sister of his deceased wife" (*Figures of Conversion*, 223). Yet I want to argue that this passage provides crucial clues to Arnold's understanding of the relationship between the abstracted term "Hebraism" and that which is Jewish, as well as clues to his understandings of femaleness and poetry. Arnold writes:

And, immense as is our debt to the Hebrew race and its genius, incomparable as is its authority on certain profoundly important sides of our human nature, worthy as it is to be described as having uttered, for those sides, the voice of the deepest necessities of our nature, the statutes of the divine and eternal order of things, the law of God, – who, that is not manacled and hoodwinked by his Hebraism, can believe that, as to love and marriage, our reason and the necessities of our humanity have their true, sufficient, and divine law expressed for them by the voice of any Oriental and polygamous nation like the Hebrews? Who, I say, will believe, when he really considers the matter, that where the feminine nature, the feminine ideal, and our relations to them, are brought into question, the delicate and apprehensive genius of the Indo-European race, the race which invented the Muses, and chivalry, and the Madonna, is to find its last word on this question in the institutions of a Semitic people, whose wisest king had seven hundred wives and three hundred concubines? (*Culture and Anarchy*, 183–4)

Here, "the Hebrew race" is owed "a debt" for "having uttered . . . the law of God"; however, this reverence for Hebraism becomes a distinct problem as soon as one is "manacled and hoodwinked" by it. To be "manacled" to Hebraism suggests an image of bodily connection, to be "hoodwinked" is to believe that which is false; with this phrase, then, Arnold is saying is that Hebraism is only valuable when explicitly disassociated from its embodiment (literally) in the bodies of Jews, and when the literal beliefs of Judaism do not "hoodwink" believers with their apparent falseness.[21]

In this passage Arnold maintains poetry and "the feminine ideal" as the central elements of his highest forms of culture, while simultaneously asserting that Jewishness offers the antithesis of these ideals. Hebrews, metonymized as "the voice of any Oriental and polygamous nation" are set in opposition to the "Indo-European race . . . which invented the Muses, and chivalry, and the Madonna" – that is, a formulation of Western Christian culture defined by those cultural institutions that explicitly regulate womanhood, and I would argue, implicitly regulate the institution of English poetry. "The Muses" are obviously linked to poetry, understood as a mysterious female essence which galvanizes and supports male poetic inspiration; similarly, "chivalry" operates, in part, as a literary process which objectifies idealized female images and provides poetic subject matter in both idyll and sonnet forms. Finally, in the institution of Christianity, "the Madonna" stands as the most powerful figure of the idealized, paradoxically chaste mother, who is the centerpiece of countless objectified works of Christian art and poetry. What happens then, in this extraordinarily loaded passage, is that the idea of the Jew – both in the form of King David as well as any person "manacled and hoodwinked by . . . Hebraism" – is cast as the complete other to all of Christian poetic and artistic culture.

Arnold's insistence on delimiting the power of the Hebraic poetry is given an ironic twist at his criticism of the Jewish king, David, who was considered the highest of poets. Discrediting his marriage practices as immoral and non-Christian, Arnold likewise discredits his poetry, just as he discredited Heine's "eternal greatness" through a critique of his "moral disrespectability." It is no coincidence, I think, that Arnold's most venomous moment of attack on Hebraism occurs at the moment an actual Jewish law is proposed for the jurisdiction of Christian women's bodies. For it is at this moment that Hebraism becomes aligned with the apparently monstrous effects of Jewish sexuality, so that David, once read as "sweet singer of Israel" must be ironically recast as a symbol of the corrupt Jewish community, "whose wisest king had seven hundred wives and three hundred concubines." At the moment David becomes "manacled" to his Hebraism, he can no longer be an idealized figure for Christian poetic identity. It is this potential for rupturing the basic binary oppositions that structure literary Christian identity that link both the Jew and the woman poet in Victorian culture. Because both femaleness and Jewishness exist as abstracted and essentialized figures in the construction of Victorian poetry, the moment in which real women and real Jews assert poetic identity is potentially a moment of acute crisis in Victorian culture.

I would go further to suggest that the images of Jewishness and femaleness so prevalent in Victorian poetics are not random or unmotivated concerns at this historical moment. On the contrary, the concerns with Jewishness and femaleness are inextricably linked to the historical moment in which a Jewish community and a female literary community came into their own in English history. If – speaking generally – eighteenth-century Biblical and literary theorists could idealize Hebrew poetry and the feminization of the Romantic poet, they did so in an historical context which did not yet have to reckon with a powerful tradition of women poets, nor an emerging Anglo-Jewish political consciousness. By the mid-Victorian period, that idealization of Jewishness and femaleness in literary theory would have had profoundly different resonances. In short, the threat was that Jews and women could now provide "self-understanding" of the systems which had abstracted and idealized them as sources of poetry, and with this self-understanding, women/Jewish poets serve to rupture many of the binary oppositions upon which Victorian culture based its theories of religious and gender identity. When Victorian England was faced with the actual rising Jewish community, Jewishness, perhaps even more acutely than femaleness, comes to represent otherness in Christian theological poetics; further, Jewishness becomes a trope which Christian women poets can also construct as "other" to their own literary identity.

Clearly, the roles femaleness and Jewishness play in Victorian poetics are complex, and it would be impossible to construct a theory of one meaning that emerges from this particular intersection between religious and gendered identity in Victorian poetic theory. As both feminist studies and Jewish studies have repeatedly demonstrated, the figures of Jew and woman have always absorbed any number of projected meanings in patriarchal Christian cultures; in my varied readings of Victorian poetic theory, I have tried to suggest that the patterns which mark the

interpretation of Jewishness in Christian theology – namely, the simultaneous idealization and discreditation of Jewishness – parallel the ways
femaleness is constructed in Victorian poetics, as that which is both
essential and ultimately lacking. However, these roles are never static
or simple in design; there are also moments in Victorian poetic theory in
which discourses of femaleness and Jewishness collide rather than par-
alleling each other, creating strange moments where Christian women
theologians do battle with Christ, or where the Jewish King David is denied poetic power on the basis of his relations with women. Depending
on one's larger theological position then, the "sweet singers of Israel"
have a range of potential referents in Victorian poetics. Yet regardless of
the varied permutations, Jewishness and femaleness emerge as central
tropes through which Victorian poetics were imagined. In the chapters that follow on Elizabeth Barrett Browning and Christina Rossetti,
I will suggest that these Christian women poets likewise engaged in the
discourse of Christian poetics, and in so doing necessarily called on
discourses of Jewishness as an inherent part of their literary identity.
The Anglo-Jewish poets Amy Levy and Grace Aguilar were also acutely
aware of the powerful role this Christian poetics played in their cultural
moment, and their poetry both responds to and challenges the Christian
approaches to Jewishness as these women sought to claim their Jewish
voices within the English literary tradition.

CHAPTER 3

Elizabeth Barrett Browning and the "Hebraic monster"

"HEBREW ROOTS ENOUGH ... TO FRIGHTEN": THE DOUBLE
EDGE OF HEBRAIC KNOWLEDGE

Although she [Miss Barrett] has read Plato, in the original, from beginning to
end, and the Hebrew Bible from Genesis to Malachi (nor suffered her course to
be stopped by the Chaldean), yet there is probably not a single good romance
of the most romantic kind in whose marvellous and impossible scenes she has
not delighted ... All of this, our readers may be assured, that we believe to be
as strictly authentic as the very existence of the lady in question, although, as
we have already confessed, we have no absolute knowledge of this fact. But lest
the reader should exclaim, "Then, *after all*, there really may be no such person!"
we should bear witness to having been shown a letter of Miss Mitford's to a
friend, from which it was plainly to be inferred that she had actually seen and
conversed with her. (Richard Horne, *A New Spirit of the Age*, 339–40)

So he has exalted me personally with all manner of devices ... & with the aid of
"charming notes to fair friends", – & Hebrew roots & Plato enough to frighten
away friends fair and brown ... the circumstance of your name being mentioned
(as it is once) in connection with me, goes very far to reconcile me to my position
as an Hebraic monster who lives in the dark. Also, I shall appear much tamer
for it in the eyes of the public. (Elizabeth Barrett Browning to Mary Russell
Mitford)[1]

In 1844, Richard Hengist Horne published a volume of essays titled *A
New Spirit of the Age*, a work modeled on William Hazlitt's 1825 volume *The
Spirit of the Age*. Horne, like Hazlitt, compiled essays which described "a
set of men ... [who] have obtained eminent positions in the public mind"
(xix) in the fields of arts, letters, politics, and science. Horne includes seven
women in his list of approximately thirty-eight figures; in the chapter
titled "Miss E. B. Barrett and Mrs. Norton," Horne compares the two
women poets by noting that Norton "is well known, personally, to a large
and admiring circle" while Barrett "is not known personally, to anybody,
we almost said" (338). Horne's play on proving the actual existence of

Barrett Browning[2] was in fact quite an excessive rhetorical maneuver, since Elizabeth Barrett Browning was a good friend of Horne's and a virtual co-editor of *A New Spirit of the Age* with Horne.[3]

Nevertheless, most of Horne's essay focuses on the reclusive "unknowability" of Barrett Browning, and with this focus, Horne emphasizes Barrett's scholarly capacities over any specific poetic talent, describing her as having exhaustive knowledge of all kinds of literature. However, he seems to want to reassure his readers that she is not only a scholar; after mentioning her abilities to read "the Chaldean" (an especially obscure Semitic dialect in the Bible), Horne works to counter the apparently troubling evidence of Barrett Browning's classical and Hebraic studies with assurance to his readers that "although" she reads Hebrew and Greek, "yet" she also delights in "romance of the most romantic kind." His sentence structure alone suggests that these two kinds of reading are opposed to each other, and it also suggests his own anxiety, or his projection of his audience's anxiety, about the true identity of a Victorian woman who might read Hebrew without necessarily enjoying "romance."

The second passage above, excerpted from two letters of Barrett Browning's to her long-time correspondent Mary Russell Mitford, describes the poet's disappointment with Horne's essay, going so far as to express fears that Horne's description might damage her critical reputation.[4] Though she refused to tell Horne of her own unhappiness with his comments, Barrett Browning maintained repeatedly to Mitford that her central problem with Horne's description was that he neglected to mention her poetry with any specificity. Instead, as she puts it, he focuses on her "Hebrew roots and Plato enough to frighten . . . friends"; thus, in Barrett Browning's eyes, Horne turns her into an intellectual recluse separated from any true poetic identity, and even more "frightening," a woman with scholarly ties to "Hebrew roots." Barrett Browning's ultimate description of the way Horne represents her is the fascinating figure of an "Hebraic monster who lives in the dark." With this term, she explores the potential pun on this notion of "Hebrew roots" as not only referring to grammatical terms, but perhaps also implying a certain notion of heredity or identity. Having Hebrew "roots," it seems, may turn one into "Hebraic monster" instead of a Christian woman poet.

Barrett Browning's comment that Horne implies some essential relationship between her and Hebraic identity is further confirmed by perhaps the strangest passage in Horne's essay. Continuing his play on "proving" "whether such an individual as Miss E. B. Barrett had ever really existed," Horne writes:

neither the poetry, nor the prose, nor the delightfully gossiping notes to fair friends, nor the frank correspondence with scholars, such as Lady Jane Grey might have written to Roger Ascham — no, not even if the great grandson of some learned Jewish doctor could show a note in Hebrew (quite a likely thing really to be extant) with the same signature, darkly translated by four letters, – nay, though he should display it as a relic treasured in his family, the very pen, with its oblique Hebraic nib, that wrote it – not any one, nor all of those things could be sufficient to demonstrate the fact that such a lady had really adorned the present century. (*A New Spirit of the Age*, 338)

Horne creates a figure of the "great grand-son of some learned Jewish doctor" to stand as a potential future witness to Barrett Browning's existence. The scenario Horne suggests here is that her Hebrew knowledge would allow her to communicate with "real Jews"; the Jewish grandson, cast as a "true" possessor of Hebrew language and those related hereditary "roots," claims connection to Barrett Browning herself by way of a Hebrew letter, and he cherishes the pen with which she wrote this letter like a "relic"; with this term, Horne creates a daring analogy: just as Christ's body parts, garments, and objects he ostensibly touched, are considered relics by Christians, so too are objects that Barrett Browning touched revered by Jews. Culminating this strange set of images, Horne describes how Barrett Browning's own signature would look in Hebrew – "darkly translated by four letters"; here, Horne suggests, that with her ability to write in Hebrew, Barrett Browning's own identity/name becomes dangerously close to that of a "dark" Jew herself.

Ultimately, Horne discredits this fantasized "evidence" of Barrett Browning's Jewish correspondence; the evidence provided by this Jewish grandson is not "sufficient" to "prove" her existence. Instead, Horne decides that the only incontestable proof of Barrett Browning's existence is a letter of "Miss Mitford" which Horne himself has seen, "in which it was plainly to be inferred that she had actually seen and conversed with her."[5] It is the comforting reference to Miss Mitford, rather than to a Jewish reader of Hebrew letters, that ultimately confirms Barrett Browning's "actual" existence for Horne and his Victorian (Christian) readership. With the final reference to Miss Mitford, Horne reclaims Barrett Browning from her unknowable Hebraic identity and instead links her to arguably one of the century's most "womanly" Christian literary figures.[6] What Horne's bizarre essay cannot quite contain is its anxiety about that juxtaposition between this eminent Victorian Christian woman and her relationship to the Hebraic – both its language and people.

Although Barrett Browning demonstrates her own awareness of how disruptive the idea of a Hebrew-reading woman could be to the Victorian reading public, she nevertheless quite consciously displayed her Hebrew knowledge at important moments in her own early writing career, risking the danger of being seen as an "Hebraic monster" in order to garner a particular kind of intellectual and theological authority. Using her access to Hebrew and figures of Jewishness, Barrett Browning reconstructed the terms upon which Christian women poets were identified, combining both intellectual and theological authority with certain qualities more consistent with Victorian representations of Christian womanhood. Her explicit reconstruction of the image of the Victorian woman poet also threatened to place Barrett Browning herself as an outsider in the world of women's literature – the very issue with which Horne's essay repeatedly struggles.

In fact, it is precisely Barrett Browning's "otherness" that prompts Horne's final comparison of her work with the very different poetic style of Mrs. Norton in his essay; it is one of the few places he actually, if obliquely, refers to Barrett Browning's poetry. Horne writes

[Mrs. Norton] writes from the dictates of a human heart in all the eloquence of beauty and individuality; the other [Barrett Browning] like an inspired priestess – not without a most truthful heart, but a heart that is devoted to religion, and whose individuality is cast upward in the divine afflatus, and dissolved and carried off in the recipient breath of angelic ministrants. (*A New Spirit of the Age*, 343)

Horne's term "priestess" separates Barrett Browning from Norton, who writes religiously from the realm of the "human heart." Further, Mrs. Norton's association with her female and religious "heart" also maintains a certain construction of her physical femaleness, her "beauty and individuality," whereas Barrett Browning loses her physical markers of femaleness as well as her individuality, "dissolved and carried off in the . . . breath of angelic ministrants." Horne's passage suggests that by carrying a certain prophetic identity, Barrett Browning may be understood to lose her female identity – a pattern we saw quite clearly articulated in the dual gendered identity that marks the poet as prophet discourse discussed in chapter 2. Putting sections of Horne's essay together, it seems Barrett Browning's "difference" comes both from her strange "Jewish" associations as well as from her status as a "priestess." In what follows, I will suggest that Barrett Browning actually conjoined these two representations to create a prophetic female poetic identity through reference to Jewish identity and "the Hebraic" throughout her poetry.[7]

The idea that Barrett Browning was somehow "different" from other woman poets of her day has been pursued by many contemporary critics, though none have explored how her status as poet was affected by her literary concern with Jewish figures and Hebrew language. Much has been made, however, of Barrett Browning's unique education and somewhat isolated early adult years of invalidism; as Dorothy Mermin writes, these early factors offered "the advantage . . . of differentiating her from the common run of women poets and protecting her from such easy [critical] scorn" that was, as we saw in chapter 2, so often directed at women poets in this period (*Elizabeth Barrett Browning*, 47). Linda Lewis notes that while there were many women who followed Barrett Browning in the path of religious poetry – including Felicia Hemans, Mary Howitt, Jean Ingelow, Dora Greenwell, and Christina Rossetti – few "studied theology," or "position[ed] themselves as priestess/prophet/sage" (*Elizabeth Barrett Browning's Spiritual Progress*, 213), even as many did pursue specific theological concepts that concerned Barrett Browning. Like Mermin, Lewis notes that most of these poets lacked the depth of Barrett Browning's education in classical and Biblical languages, the theology of Greek Christian poets, Tractarians, and Church fathers, and so most did not venture into the scholarly, intellectual turf that she (and I would add George Eliot) were somewhat uniquely able to explore as highly educated women.[8]

Indeed, unlike many of her counterparts, Barrett Browning went further than simply arguing that her spiritual authority came from her unique moral superiority of womanhood. Rather than identify herself, or all women, as having a particular "spiritual" aptitude because they were women, Barrett Browning sought to reclaim poetry itself as a specifically religious endeavor, clearly galvanizing the powerful links that were re-emerging in Victorian poetics between poetry and religion as discussed in chapter 2. In the Preface to her 1838 volume *The Seraphim*, Barrett Browning wrote: "'An irreligious poet,' said Burns, meaning an undevotional one, 'is a monster.' An irreligious poet, he might have said, is no poet at all" (*Poetical Works*, 80).[9] Rewriting Burns' quote, Barrett Browning suggests that without a means to combine the poetic with the religious, one is not a poet at all. Indeed, it seems possible that this earlier reference she picks up from Burns about a "monster" informed her own later comment about Horne representing her as an "Hebraic monster"; in both cases, she is commenting on a figure of a poet who is not explicitly linked to religion and poetics simultaneously. Paying attention to Barrett Browning's references to Jewishness and the Hebraic in her early work up until *Aurora Leigh*, I argue that Barrett Browning sought to transform the potentially monstrous implications of her Hebraic knowledge into a specific poetic and theological authority.

Recent scholarship has begun to analyze some of the more specific contours that shaped Barrett Browning's own religious identity. Linda Lewis' 1998 book, *Elizabeth Barrett Browning's Spiritual Progress*, offers our most detailed look to date at Barrett Browning's particular brand of Christianity, a Christianity loosely associated with various groups. Lewis notes that the Barrett family attended Congregationalist (Dissenting) chapel, that Barrett Browning was married in an Anglican church, baptized her child in a French Lutheran church, attended Catholic Mass at St. Peter's when in Rome, and also read extensively in the works of Swedenborg (9–12). In her own words, according to Lewis "she claimed membership in Christ's invisible Church as referred to in Scripture" (13), and thus she seems to have avoided any easy alliance with a particular Christian institution, although she was most obviously connected to Christian identity in the broad terms I outlined in chapter 1. In many ways, it seems possible that Barrett Browning's lack of specific institutional affiliation may have enabled the quite original Christian theological work she sought to perform in her poetry.

The first part of this chapter explores how Barrett Browning displayed her study of Hebrew in order to construct herself as a serious scholar of Biblical texts, and likewise a poet with a serious theological mission. With this strategy, Barrett Browning refused to relinquish her Christian female identity to the claims of the Christian heart only, and instead repeatedly demonstrated her theological and scholarly tools, which she in turn used to claim a literary authority with male critics and poets, notably Milton and Samuel Johnson. Along with her strategic display of Hebrew knowledge, however, this chapter also charts another dimension to Barrett Browning's "possession" and "display" of things Hebraic. For, in many ways, Barrett Browning's "possession" of the Hebrew language mirrors her own larger typological "possession" of the Hebrew Scriptures and the Jewish historical figures who people those Scriptures. Using the Jewish/Hebraic woman as a model for female prophetic voice and religious agency, first in her early works "The Virgin Mary to the

Child Jesus," and "A Vision of Poets," and then most notably in her most important work, *Aurora Leigh*, Barrett Browning claimed a particular model of Jewish poet/woman as integral to her construction of authoritative Christian female poetic identity. Barrett Browning's interactions with both the Hebrew language and Hebrew scriptural text and characters were crucial aspects of her theory of Christian female poetic identity; ultimately, however, she suggests that this idealized Hebraic identity must be appropriated and repositioned within a Christian framework in order to attain true Christian womanhood.

Of course, claiming a relationship to the Hebrew Scriptures, or "Old Testament," was commonplace for most Christian writers of the day; however, there were any number of ways writers of the period constructed their particular understanding of Hebrew texts and narrative. In this and the following chapter, I compare the typological approach of two of the most important Christian women writers of the period, Elizabeth Barrett Browning and Christina Rossetti. Read together, chapters 3 and 4 argue that for these women, the discourses of the Jewish/Hebraic and discourses of sexual difference were constantly colliding. For both Barrett Browning and Rossetti, the figure of the Jewish/Hebraic woman embodied a certain sexual autonomy as well as political/religious authority. What differentiates Rossetti's and Barrett Browning's interests in the Jewish/Hebraic woman, however, are their evaluations of this Jewish female sexual and religious agency in relation to Victorian culture's alternative construction of Christian womanhood. As I argue in the next chapter, Rossetti refused to idealize the somewhat tantalizing stereotypes of Hebraized female identity, finding them instead to be a dangerous temptation that could lead women away from the ideals of true Christian womanhood; in her poetry, she seeks to erase and expunge Jewishness from her vision of the complete Christian self. Barrett Browning, on the other hand, found this stereotype of the Jewish woman's sexual and political agency ultimately liberating, and made it an essential ingredient of her vision of Christian womanhood, a necessary phase of spiritual development, though never, of course, an end point in itself. Her reliance on the relationship between Jewish and female prophetic identity is thus the flip side of her fears about Hebraic monstrosity, offering her a way to reconstruct and idealize exactly the formulation that was potentially threatening to more conventional models of female authorship in her day.

Barrett Browning's idealization of the Hebraic, both linguistic and figural, was not without its complications, however. For if, as the opening of this chapter argues, Barrett Browning's own authorial identity was both potentially bolstered and tainted by the association with things Hebraic/Jewish, so too did the figural use of Jewish Biblical woman both solve and create new problems for her. On the one hand, it was easy for Barrett Browning and indeed other Christian women writers to claim that "Old Testament" figures like Miriam, Deborah, Hannah, and Esther were exemplary models for women's public and literary identity. These women, often explicitly named as leaders, poets, and prophets in the Hebrew Scriptures, could quite easily be claimed as forerunners to the Christian women poets and leaders emerging in Victorian England. Yet whenever these Hebraic woman were idealized as model female poets and leaders, attendant theological and theoretical questions emerge: what did it mean when Christian women found it somehow easier to construct an authoritative female poetic identity out of the Old (potentially Jewish) rather than New (clearly Christian) Testament? In short, the idealization of the Jewish scriptural woman threatened to expose the deep conflicts that the ideology of Christian womanhood created for woman poets. The task for Barrett Browning and other Christian women writers was to figure out how to claim and use these Hebraic materials without relinquishing their own specifically Christian authority. Deeply aware of how a close alliance with Hebraic and Jewish identity might threaten the very existence of a Christian woman poet, Barrett Browning sought to tame the Hebraic monster even as she repeatedly invoked the Hebraic as an essential ingredient in her construction of the Christian female poet.

BARRETT BROWNING'S HEBRAIC DISPLAY: THE AUTHORITY OF HEBREW LANGUAGE

it was not entirely out of devotion to her future husband that she wished to know Latin and Greek. Those provinces of masculine knowledge seemed to her a standing ground from which all truth could be seen more truly . . . Perhaps even Hebrew might be necessary – at least the alphabet and a few roots – in order to arrive at the core of things and judge soundly on the social duties of the Christian. (George Eliot, *Middlemarch*, 64)

Barrett Browning's desire to learn Hebrew was not especially unique for her time, though her ultimate achievement to do so was – at least for women. George Eliot gets at the heart of the importance of Hebrew to Victorian Christians, as well as women's limited access to the language, in the passage from *Middlemarch* (1872), above, in which Dorothea muses that knowing Hebrew would allow one to "arrive at the core of things and judge soundly on the social duties of the Christian." Knowing Hebrew was often considered the highest proof of serious exegetical ability, and until mid-century, when it was found to be linguistically connected to other human languages, Hebrew was considered unique as the language of God.[10] Even after the reverence for Hebrew was, according to Maurice Olender, replaced by a reverence for Sanskrit in the nineteenth century, Hebrew maintained a certain heightened mystique for Christians, in part because of the "mysterious" nature of Hebrew voweling.[11] Olender points out that from the medieval period onward, questions about the actual "language of God" and what language was the originary one spoken in the Garden of Eden were repeatedly posed by Christian exegetes and theologians (Olender, *The Languages of Paradise*, 1–6). As discussed in chapter 2, Herder and Lowth contributed to a body of scholarship which claimed the essentially "poetic" nature of Hebrew.

Barrett Browning engaged in her study of Hebrew around 1832, taking as her task the reading of the Hebrew Bible in the original.[12] After this time, and until the 1844 volume, we find a number of places in her earlier works in which Barrett Browning uses actual untranslated (though often transliterated) Hebrew words, disrupting English with a completely different language in the same way that she and others more commonly used Greek within their English texts.[13] Unlike her seemingly more conventional interest in the typological and thematic invocations of Hebrew scriptural characters and events, which I discuss in a later section, when Barrett Browning allows the actual Hebrew characters into her text, they create strange moments for a reader, moments in which Barrett Browning insists on her primary, exceptional Hebrew knowledge, emphasizing her own theological authority and using it to justify certain moments when she believes her work to be possibly radical in intention or interpretation.

Barrett Browning's earliest public manifestations of her Hebrew knowledge occur in her 1838 *The Seraphim and Other Poems*, her first volume after her commencement of Hebrew studies. "A Supplication for Love" opens with a epigraph from an "extempore Discourse" preached at Sidmouth, 1833, placing it near the start of the poet's interest in Hebrew.[14] The poem is divided into four separate "Hymns," the last of which is titled "The Measure" and which begins with two quotations, one from Isaiah, "He comprehended the dust of the earth in a measure" and the other from Psalm LXXX, "Thou givest them tears to drink in a measure"; after each epigraph, the Hebrew letters for the term "measure" שָׁלִישׁ (shalish) indicate that both Biblical references use the same Hebrew word. Then, Barrett Browning includes a remarkable footnote with these

Hebrew references, stating: "I believe that the word occurs in no other part of the Hebrew Scriptures." This assertion implies, of course, that the author has read all of the Hebrew Scriptures quite carefully, and so the poem takes on the quality of being based in quite specialized scholarly knowledge.

More importantly, the knowledge of the original language allows her to linguistically connect the passages quoted – a connection which is at the heart of the poem's content. The poem links the two concepts of dust (first epigraph) and tears (second epigraph) through the Bible's shared use of the term for "measure," as is clear from the opening stanza, which reads

> God, the Creator, with a pulseless hand
> Of unoriginated power, hath weighed
> The dust of earth and tears of man in one
>   Measure, and by one weight:
>   So saith his holy book.
>   (*The Seraphim, Poetical Works*, lines 1–5)

The poem continues the play between the balance of "dust and tears," ending with the idea that in our death "[t]hese tearful eyes be filled / With the dry dust of death." Barrett Browning's poem centers on the use of the Hebrew term "measure" as that which equalizes our suffering with our life on earth. With her recourse to the original Hebrew, Barrett Browning offers a particularly compelling authority for her interpretation of what "saith his holy book."

Her 1844 volume, *Poems*, which included the important "A Drama of Exile," continues her display of Hebrew, while also invoking the Hebraic through a complex use of the figure of "exile." In the preface that she wrote for a later edition of her work, Barrett Browning makes clear that what was at stake for her in this volume was both her position as woman writer and her claim to authoritative scriptural interpretation. Of this volume, Dorothy Mermin has written that "She had justified her emulation of Aeschylus in *The Seraphim* by the fact she was a Christian. Now, more daringly, she attempts to amplify Milton on the basis of her experience as a woman" (*Elizabeth Barrett Browning*, 87). In this important preface, however, Barrett Browning invokes not only her "experience as a woman," but also her experience as a scholar of Hebrew.

In that preface, she directly addresses her fear that readers and critics would think she was too bold in her revision of Milton's *Paradise Lost*.

Writing about the "pleasure" she took in exploring "the idea of exile," Barrett Browning then states:

But when all was done I felt afraid, as I said before, of my position. I had promised my own prudence to shut close the gates of Eden between Milton and myself, so that none might say I dared to walk in his footsteps. He should be within, I thought, with his Adam and Eve unfallen or falling, – and I, without, with my EXILES, – *I* also an exile! It would not do. The subject and his glory covering it, swept through the gates, and I stood full in it, against my will, and contrary to my vow, till I shrank back fearing, almost desponding... (*Poetical Works*, 102)

In short, the passage chronicles her own refusal to remain "an exile" from the worlds of both Biblical exegesis and literary ambition. Though she attempts to "shut close the gates...between Milton and myself," Barrett Browning cannot separate herself from her fascination with the theological subject of "exile." Barrett Browning goes on to rhetorically resolve her dilemma by claiming first, that "Milton is too high" for her to really be a direct threat to his interpretation, and second, that her revisionary impulse is equivalent to "what the Greek dramatists achieved lawfully in respect to Homer" (102).

Many feminist critics have commented on the significant issues about women writers and the anxiety surrounding female literary authority that this passage raises.[15] However, there is a later paragraph in this preface that also responds, somewhat less directly, to Barrett Browning's particular problem of positioning herself as an innovator of Milton's scriptural interpretation. Commenting on the fact that "A Drama of Exile" is set in a period of time from "evening into the night," Barrett Browning writes:

If it should be objected that I have lengthened my twilight too much for the East, I might hasten to answer that we know nothing of the length of mornings or evenings before the Flood, and that I cannot, for my own part, believe in an Eden without the longest of purple twilights. The evening, ערב [erev] of Genesis signifies a "mingling," and approaches the meaning of our "twilight" analytically. Apart from which considerations, my "exiles" are surrounded, in the scene described, by supernatural appearances; and the shadows that approach them are not only of the night (*Poetical Works*, 103).

By returning to the Hebrew root for evening, ערב (erev), Barrett Browning attempts to support her own claim for a lengthy twilight and thus finds textual support for her own representation of Adam and Eve's experience against potential critics. The issue she raises is how we might know how long evening is in "the East"; to help answer this question, she turns to the Eastern language, Hebrew, to examine the roots of the term, erev. Interestingly, it is not completely clear how her citation of the Hebrew root actually helps her argument. This passage seems to say that though her rendition of the evening is potentially radical in its length, it is an image based on scholarly scriptural evidence, as gleaned from the original Hebrew root for "evening," which also means "mingling"; further, she suggests that the "shadows" of her depicted evening are also from "supernatural appearances." If Barrett Browning names herself as "exile" from the land of literary genius in the first passage, then, her later passage seems to reinstate her right to – with Milton – reinterpret the Bible on the basis of her Hebrew knowledge.

In another important poem in the 1844 volume, Barrett Browning draws not only on the authority her Hebrew studies grant her, but also makes a more specific connections between the use of Hebrew language, the religious covenant of Judaism and the "Old Testament," and the very sources of poetic inspiration. In "A Vision of Poets," Barrett Browning creates a poet who wanders out one night, feeling particularly unappreciated by the world, who is privy to a divine vision which shows that poets are the closest beings to God. Eventually, the poet is given a vision of an angel who stand before God playing an organ; around the angel are gathered a crowd of Western culture's most famous poets, a list that begins with Homer and moves chronologically through both English and European poets, ending with Coleridge. The list only includes one woman poet, Sappho and, somewhat surprisingly, the Hebrew scriptural poets are not included in this list – surprising given Barrett Browning's interest in them in the 1838 preface.[16]

Yet, the exclusion of the Hebrew poets *per se* does not preclude Barrett Browning's idealization of the Hebraic as an essential aspect of all poetic endeavor. Thus, as the poem continues, she makes a few crucial references which locate Hebrew as the language of divine blessing for poets. The angel at the divine organ before the altar of God is described as having "eyes[that] were dreadful, for you saw/ That *they* saw God – his lips and jaw, /Grand-made and strong, as Sinai's Law" ("A Vision of Poets," *Poetical Works*, lines 253–5). This angel, linked specifically to Sinai and thus the Hebrew Scriptural/Jewish covenant rather than New Testament law, is the agent of the organ-instrument which serves, through a complex technical metaphor, to combine the work of poets with the work of God. The lady/spirit who leads the poet to this altar describes the workings of this organ as follows:

Hearken, O poet whom I led
From the dark wood. Dismissing dread,
Now hear this angel in my stead.

His organ's clavier strikes along
These poets' hearts, sonorous, strong,
They gave him without count of wrong, –

A diapason whence to guide
Up to God's feet, from these who died,
An anthem fully glorified.

Whereat God's blessing . . . IBARAK יברך
Breathes back this music – folds it back
About the earth in vapoury rack,

And men walk in it, crying "Lo,
The world is wider, and we know
The very heavens look brighter so."

(lines 439–53)

The angel plays an organ whose clavier "strikes along these poets' hearts" and they, thus aroused into a song, create a collective "diapason" (harmony/tune) which is received by God and then sent back to earth having been enfolded with God's blessing, יברך "Ibarak," which is the Hebrew word for blessing.[17] Barrett Browning thus creates an image of sacred poetry which emerges from the union of human poets and a divine (Hebrew) blessing from God. With this use of a Hebrew term actually inserted in the poem, Barrett Browning suggests that Hebrew is the immortal language of God that still "breathes" in all poetic utterance, and so implicitly, she takes a stand about Hebrew as the originary "holy" tongue of poetry. Significantly, it is specifically a "lady" with prophetic powers who repeats God's Hebrew word, thus making the visionary representative of all religious verse a Hebrew-speaking woman.

The combined imagery of the female muse figure who describes God's blessing in Hebrew along with the description of the angel who is "grand-made and strong as Sinai's law" situates the agents of poetry in relation to Hebraic/Jewish identity.[18] Yet by the end of the poem, Barrett Browning transforms this relationship between poetry, Hebrew blessing, and the Jewish covenant, reconfiguring poetry as a specifically Christian activity and likewise recasting the imagery of the poem from Hebraic to specifically Christian. In the "Conclusion" of the poem, the poet-pilgrim has died, and the unnamed speaker encounters the poet's son gathering palm branches for his father's grave; though "[t]he world . . . had

been somewhat slow / In honouring his living brow" (lines 874–5) now
it seems he will be celebrated with palms, reminiscent of Palm Sunday.
This son speaks in what the speaker notes is a strangely adult mode,
and is described with obviously Christ-like imagery, coupled with some
typological Mosaic imagery – as when the child describes his father's last
words, and then his own actions in response to those words:

> "Come and kiss me!" So the one in truth
> Who loved him best – in love, not ruth
> Bowed down and kissed him mouth to mouth.
>
> And, in that kiss of Love, was won
> Life's manumission. All was done –
> The mouth that kissed last, kissed *alone*.
>
> But in the former, confluent kiss,
> The same was sealed, I think, by His
> To words of truth and uprightedness.
>
> (lines 964–72)

The image of being kissed "mouth to mouth" has many echoes, in par-
ticular that of the death of Moses in Deuteronomy. Though the King
James Version describes his death by the "word of the Lord," Barrett
Browning knew (as she demonstrates in "the Virgin Mary to the Child
Jesus," discussed below) that an alternative translation of the Hebrew
is "mouth" instead of "word"; likewise, she clearly had access to Jewish
midrashic sources which said that Moses died with the "kisses of the
Lord" on his mouth.[19]

In the stanzas above, this notion of dying with a "mouth to mouth" kiss
is transferred from a Mosaic context into a specifically Christ-like kiss at
the moment the speaker asks the son who it was who offered this kiss:
"'*I*,' softly said the child; and then, / '*I*,' he said louder, once again; / '*His*
son*, – my rank is among men'" (lines 325–7). This child merges his
own Christ-like identity with his father's and his last words complete the
ultimately Christian positioning of these figures: "'Glory to God – to
God!' he saith, / KNOWLEDGE BY SUFFERING ENTERETH, / AND LIFE
IS PERFECTED BY DEATH" (lines 333–5), emphasis Barrett Browning's).
This last phrase, along with the son's kiss, represents the specifically
Christian blessing that now transcends and replaces the earlier Hebrew
"Ibarak" blessing of the poet's vision. That "Sinaitic" blessing was an
imperative part of the poet-pilgrim's journey, but as is typical for Barrett
Browning, it represents a crucial phase in the poet's development, rather

than an end-point for the poem. Ultimately, this is a Hebrew blessing that inspires a particularly Christian poet whose son recognizes in himself and his father specifically Christian virtues and the rhetoric of suffering.

While Barrett Browning demonstrated her Hebrew skills in only a few places in her poetry, these moments of Hebraic display are often coincident with very important statements about religious or literary authority. In the examples above, Barrett Browning turned to Hebrew words in order to confirm her knowledge of Scripture, and to support her interpretations in light of potential criticism; in "A Vision of Poets" she goes further, linking Hebrew (and thus knowledge of Hebrew) to the very roots of poetic identity. Barrett Browning pursues her emphasis on the role Hebraic identity plays in the formation of the Christian poet in two major works, the dramatic monologue "The Virgin Mary to the Child Jesus" (1838), and her *magnum opus*, *Aurora Leigh*.

KISSING MOSES/KISSING CHRIST: THE JUDAIZING OF THE VIRGIN MARY

It was subsequent to my writing the poem called *The Virgin Mary to the Child Jesus* that I read in a selection of religious poetry, made by Mr. James Montgomery, a lyric of the sixteenth century upon the same subject,[20] together with an observation of the editor, that no living poet would be daring enough to approach it. As it has here been approached and attempted by the "weak'st of many," I would prove by this explanation, that consciously to impugn an opinion of Mr. Montgomery's, and to enter into rivalship with the bold simplicity of an ancient ballad, made no part of the daringness of which I confess myself guilty. (Preface to first edition of *The Seraphim*, *Poetical Works* 79–80)

"The Virgin Mary to the Child Jesus" was first published in *The Seraphim and Other Poems* (1838). In this poem, Barrett Browning reconstructs the image and voice of perhaps the most important, and most traditionally silent of Christian female figures, the Virgin Mary. She creates a strongly voiced, proud mother and female prophet, who, like Barrett Browning herself, displays her own Hebraic knowledge as part of claiming her centrality to religious history. In many ways, this poem serves as a precursor to the relationships Barrett Browning will establish between the figure of the Jewish woman prophet Miriam and her poet-heroine, *Aurora Leigh*. Yet where the latter poem seeks to rewrite the Jewish figure of Miriam in order to construct a Christian poet-heroine, in this earlier poem, Barrett Browning revises the most important woman in the New Testament narrative by emphasizing her Jewish identity.

Despite its provocative subject matter, the poem has been almost universally ignored by critics in Barrett Browning's day, as well as our own.[21] While critics have not found this poem to be important, it is clear that Barrett Browning was concerned enough about the poem's "daringness" to make explicit mention of it in her preface to *The Seraphim* volume, cited above. Barrett Browning, referring to herself as "the weak'st of many," suggests (somewhat unconvincingly) that although she is guilty of "daringness" in attempting such a poem, she asserts no competitive spirit with a similar sixteenth-century lyric as an impetus for writing. Her self-consciousness of the "daringness" of the poem itself and her desire to justify her own motives in attempting such a poem suggest the high stakes involved for women when they challenge hegemonic representations of scriptural figures. And indeed, this poem is daring in that Barrett Browning envisions the Virgin Mary as a prophet/poet who claims her Jewish roots as the source for her powerful voice.[22]

The epigraph for "The Virgin Mary" is from Milton's "Hymn on the Nativity" and thus sets up an overt contrast with other poetic representations of Mary as silent object. The epigraph reads "But see the Virgin blest / Hath laid her babe to rest." In Milton's poem, these lines are one of only two references to Mary's role – the other brief reference occurs in the prologue to the poem and refers to Mary as the object of a prepositional phrase that calls Christ "Of wedded maid and virgin mother born." Milton's lines present Mary as the object of male narrational gaze and minimize her active role in Christian history. Barrett Browning's poem explores the moment Milton's lines describe, depicting what Mary might say at the moment Jesus is asleep, and opening a space for Mary, rather than Jesus, to claim a central role of Christian history; the poem ends at the moment Jesus wakes, replacing Mary's vocal agency. As I will argue here, one source of Mary's vocal authority comes from her power over the sleeping Jesus, and her ability to protect him, indeed control him in this earlier phase of his life. Finally, as the poem is set long before Christ's Resurrection, it also covertly poses the problem of Mary's specific religious affiliation; at this point in history, both she and Jesus are in fact Jewish, as the poem itself seems to emphasize.

The poem opens with an emphasis on Mary's vocal/linguistic control over Jesus, as well as an assertion of a maternal ownership over Jesus.

> Sleep, sleep, mine Holy One!
> My flesh, my Lord! – what name? I do not know
> A name that seemeth not too high or low,
> Too far from me or heaven.

My Jesus, *that* is best! that word being given
By the majestic angel whose command
Was softly as a man's beseeching said,
When I and all the earth appeared to stand
In the great overflow
Of light celestial from his wings and head.
Sleep, sleep, my saving One!
("The Virgin Mary to the Child Jesus," I: 1–11)

Here Mary asserts her ability to command her baby's actions in her repeated imperative "sleep"; she also claims her own unique maternal relationship with Jesus through repeated personal pronouns, "my" and "mine." This privileged relationship is also evident in the double meanings implied in the phrase "my flesh, my Lord"; as Jesus' natural mother, Mary alone can claim him as flesh, just as she was one with his body throughout her pregnancy. Jesus is, however, also simultaneously "her Lord," and the conjunction of these ideas suggests Mary's quite particular relationship to Christ: she is the only human woman to have a profoundly physical relationship with the Lord, as manifest in Jesus' human body. When she adds the question "what name?," Barrett Browning extends to Mary not only a physical relationship, however, but also a powerful linguistic presence. This right of naming is not usually granted to her in Biblical representations, which grant to the angel Gabriel the "naming" of Jesus; in Luke 1: 31, for example, the angel tells Mary "and thou shalt call him Jesus." Though Barrett Browning's Mary eventually settles on the "word . . . given by the majestic angel," her line "My flesh, my Lord – what name?" suggests that she, as mother, retains the right to make a final choice of the "best" name for her child, and so positions her as a speaker with both spiritual and linguistic authority.

The poem continues to link Mary's spiritual power to her linguistic power. In the fourth section Barrett Browning makes an explicit connection between the physical bond between mother and child and Mary's own vocal/prophetic (poetic) agency. The connection is enabled through the figure of a kiss, a kiss which Mary apparently gives to Jesus in the section directly preceding this one (III) when she says: "suffer this mother's kiss." Inserting a specific physical action into her dramatic scenario, Mary then muses on the relationship between kissing her son and her own prophetic identity. Section IV begins:

The slumber of His lips meseems to run
Through *my* lips to mine heart, – to all its shiftings

Of sensual life, bringing contrariousness
In a great calm. I feel I could lie down
As Moses did, and die,* – and then live most.
I am 'ware of you, heavenly Presences,
That stand with your peculiar light unlost,
Each forehead with a high thought for a crown,
Unsunned i' the sunshine! I am 'ware. (IV: 1–9)

The emphasis in this figure is on lips – lips that receive both divine language as well as divine kisses. The first lines emphasize the fleshly connection between Mary and Jesus through their lips; the ability to kiss Jesus' lips links Mary to Moses – as her crucial footnote explains.

The footnote for line five, "It is a Jewish tradition that Moses died of the kisses of God's lips" (*Poetical Works*, 241), is an imperative piece of information needed by any reader who seeks to understand Mary's reference to Moses, and Barrett Browning's insertion of this information suggests she knew that most Christian readers would not know this scriptural allusion. This tradition is evident only through an understanding of the intricacies of Hebrew translation, since the King James translation of this section represses this "kissing" tradition in its translation: "So Moses . . . died there in the land of Moab, according to the word of the Lord" (Deut. 34: 5). But in Hebrew, the literal translation of this passage is "by the mouth of the Lord," and this is apparently the source of the midrashic commentary which says Moses dies with God's kiss. By imposing this knowledge on her characterization of Mary, Barrett Browning reminds her readers that Mary also would have known Hebrew tradition since she was of Jewish origin. Indeed, by highlighting Mary's knowledge of Jewish tradition, the poem asks us to consider whether, at this particular moment, Mary speaks as a Jewish mother or the first Christian convert.

While the answer to this question remains much more ambiguous than it will be, for example, in Amy Levy's dramatic monologue "Magdalen" (see chapter 6), Barrett Browning is nevertheless positioning Mary as having a unique status not only in relationship to Jesus, but also in Christian history. As she creates a metaphoric identification with Moses as she kisses Jesus, Mary positions herself at the center of religious history, as leader and spiritual prophet. From a typological perspective, this comparison is especially radical, since conventionally it is Moses who is considered the precursor for the Christian messiah. Yet, here, as the mother of Jesus, the poem seems to say Mary is like Moses, the father-mother-nurturer of the Jewish people and Judaism; she is even more like

Moses in her ability to call up the knowledge of Jewish interpretation of a "divine kiss."

Directly after this mention of the kiss, Mary asserts her ability to sense and speak to "the heavenly Presences" around them, and her repeated "I am 'ware" suggests her own heightened ability to perceive divine beings.

> ... I bear, I bear,
> To look upon the dropt lids of your eyes,
> Though their external shining testifies
> To that beatitude within, which were
> Enough to blast an eagle at his sun:
> I fall not on my sad clay face before ye, –
> I look on His. I know
> My spirit which dilateth with the woe
> Of His mortality
> May well contain your glory.
> Yea, drop your lids more low.
> Ye are but fellow worshippers with me!
> Sleep, sleep, my worshipped One!
>
> (IV: 14–26)

The repetition of "I bear, I bear" and the enjambment on this phrase emphasizes both Mary's own act of giving birth, as well as, in the next line, that she can "bear" to look upon the "unseen" "Presences" to whom she speaks. Mary is remarkably uncowed by their presence; indeed, she asserts her own equality with such "heavenly Presences" by stating "I fall not on my sad clay face before ye," since, with the birth of Jesus, those Presences "are but fellow worshippers with" her, and she goes so far as to command those Presences to "drop [their] lids more low" in the presence of the son only she can claim as her own.

In the next sections of the poem, Barrett Browning pursues the idea of Mary's privileged relationship to divinity, and explores her own "pride" in relation to the role she plays in this religious drama. Section VI begins with a statement that she is "not proud"; however, by the end of the passage, Mary turns this idea around considerably:

> I am not proud – meek angels, ye invest
> New meeknesses to hear such utterance rest
> On mortal lips, – "I am not proud" – *not proud!*
> Albeit in my flesh God sent his son
> Albeit over him my head is bowed
> As others bow before Him, still mine heart
> Bows lower than their knees ...   (VI: 1–7)

By exploring the potentially loaded issue of Mary's pride in being chosen the mother of God, Barrett Browning challenges the Christian assumption of the Virgin's silent passive humility; her repetition of "not proud" points to the irony of such a statement, just as her statement that her heart bows lower than anyone else to her Son suggests a certain ironic pride in her own humility!

The poem points to Mary's pride at other moments as well. Section VIII begins with Mary's ability to command nature and the heavens: "Art Thou a King, then? Come, His universe, / Come crown me Him a King! (VIII: 1–2) Here, the "crowning" is done in the context of a command from Mary, who uses the phrase "crown ME a King," which grammatically, poetically, and metrically positions herself at the center of the divine Christian and Jewish narratives of redemption.[23] Mary's linguistic power culminates in Section X, when she explicitly names herself a prophet; in essence, the entire poem, from her identification with Moses to her imperatives to the "Heavenly Presences" leads to this short, powerful section, which also initiates a shift in mood and subject. In the section directly preceding, Mary notes that her child – unlike other babies – "wear[s] /An aspect very sorrowful"; she opens the next stanza as follows:

> And then the drear sharp tongue of prophecy,
> With the dread sense of things which shall be done,
> Doth smite me inly, like a sword! a sword? –
> (That "smites the Shepherd.") Then I think aloud
> The words "despised," – "rejected" – every word
> Recoiling into darkness as I view
> The DARLING on my knee.   (X: 1–6)

Here, quite clearly, Mary claims herself as a prophet; significantly, the figure of the tongue, linking back to repeated images of voice and language throughout the poem, now becomes a "drear sharp tongue" which "smite[s] [her] inly" rather than an instrument of her triumph or power. Though perhaps implicit in so many depictions of the Virgin as sorrowful, Barrett Browning makes explicit that Mary's sorrow is rooted in her power of prophecy about her son's death, not merely her maternal suffering.

Through a variety of statements and rhetorical strategies, then, Barrett Browning rewrites many of the conventions that have often governed the representations of the Virgin Mary. The structure of the dramatic monologue itself is yet another way the poem resists constructing Mary as a speaker offering a conventional devotional address to Jesus. The sleeping child as auditor becomes an opportunity for parental projection through speech; the auditor/baby, that is, is both present and absent because of his state of sleep.[24] And when the sleeping infant auditor of a dramatic monologue is in fact Jesus himself, the boundaries between dramatic speech, apostrophized lyric, and devotional poetry become blurred as Barrett Browning's poem poses a number of generic questions about what it means to "speak" poetically to God. For, at some point in this poem a reader must wonder how aware Jesus is at this particular moment in his history; does he hear all as he will in his post-ascension state as auditor for all Christian devotional lyric? Or does this monologue represent a very particular moment of speech, in which Mary maintains her linguistic and prophetic power over Jesus at perhaps the only moment when he can not yet hear all – as a sleeping infant? Throughout the poem Mary's speech makes a number of self-reflexive comments about language: "[w]hat is my word," (VIII: 6), "what name," "Then I think aloud." Likewise Jesus is repeatedly figured as "speechless" (II: 2 and IX: 4) and "noiseless" (III: 12). Barrett Browning's dramatic monologue thus highlights how different Mary's situation is from any conventional Christian speaker; her language takes on specific power because it is directed not at a Jesus who knows her heart simply because of his divine status. Instead, Mary's concern with her own language suggests that her utterance has importance on its own, as well as in relation to Jesus.

If Section X makes clear Mary's role as a prophet, Section XI offers the most explicit example of Mary's claim to religious authority through her status as Jesus' mother.

> It is enough to bear
> This image still and fair –
> This holier in sleep
> Than a saint at prayer;
> ⋯
> Awful is this watching place,
> Awful what I see from hence –
> A king, without regalia,
> A God, without the thunder,
> A child, without the heart for play;
> Ay, a Creator, rent asunder
> From His first glory and cast away
> On His own world, for me alone
> To hold in hands created, crying – Son!
>
> (XI: 1–4, 11–19)

This final image of Mary, echoing God's language of calling Jesus "Son," and holding the baby, is the most disruptive moment in the poem from a traditional Christian perspective. Even as she describes Jesus as a "Creator, rent asunder/From His first glory" she herself becomes both a motherly creator of the "Creator" as well as "created" herself; she is the only human figure who can – like God – claim Jesus as "Son." Her emphasis on "me alone" erases God "the Father" from the equation, depicting Jesus as an object that Mary "alone" can hold in her hands and claim as Son.

We might imagine this as a quite dramatic ending to a poem that has repeatedly asserted Mary as a vocal and physical presence who has a certain amount of control over her baby, over the divine beings who surround her, and who identifies herself as prophet. But the final stanza of the poem enacts a dramatic revision of the previous images of Mary; as is a pattern in many of the poems I discuss in this chapter, the end of the poem repositions this radical representation of Jewish prophetic womanhood with more conventional Christian representation. In this last stanza, Barrett Browning acknowledges the problem inherent in imagining Mary as a linguistic, creative prophet in her own right, a problem because in a Christian epistemology Jesus must be eventually claimed as the primary agent of salvation, not to mention the supreme poet/speaker.

And so, in the last section (XII) of the poem, Mary prepares for her own silence as she notes that Jesus seems to wake from "hearing" a tear that has not even dropped on him:

> That tear fell not on Thee,
> Beloved, yet thou stirrest in Thy slumber!
> Thou, stirring not for glad sounds out of number
> Which through the vibratory palm-trees run
> From summer wind and bird,
> So quickly hast thou heard
> A tear fall silently?
> Wak'st Thou, O loving One? – (XII: 1–8)

At this moment in the poem, Barrett Browning reconfirms that even as infant, Jesus "hears" Mary's suffering. However, this ending seems to offer a number of pointed contradictions if we are to take the previous dramatic scenario of the poem seriously. For Mary has repeatedly insisted that she speaks out loud, and the lines directly before this last stanza seem to imply a thunderous cry of "Son"; it is not, it seems, words that awaken Jesus, but rather the hearing of a tear drop. With this image of Jesus responding to her body rather than her words, Barrett Browning's Mary re-emphasizes her more conventional physical self over her linguistic self; indeed, these lines seem to negate the power of her own previous words, even as other lines reassert the fact that she has been speaking. For example, the speaker makes a metrical pun in the line "Thou, stirring not for glad sounds out of number," since that line itself is "out of number," or rather extends the pentameter by one feminine ending. Calling attention to her own poetic sounds, Mary is nevertheless transformed from a figure of linguistic power into a silent nurturing mother who can only refer to her quite powerful prophetic poetry as "out of number" sounds. This ending of the poem suggests that it was perhaps only when Jesus slept that Mary could realize her own creative/prophetic agency.

"The Virgin Mary to the Child Jesus" offers another example of how Barrett Browning called on Jewish identity as a source for authorizing female prophetic/poetic speech. Barrett Browning's poem elevates Mary's agency at the moments she is connected to Jewish tradition; it is the initial relationship of the lips that Mary establishes between Moses, herself, and Jesus that enables the powerful speech of the poem itself, whereas her recognition of Jesus' awakening at the end of the poem initiates her transformation into a more familiar, silent, suffering Pietà. As a representative of Jewish knowledge and Mosaic connection, Mary is a prophetic poetic speaker; as the symbol of originary Christian womanhood, Mary is a silent mother. As in "A Vision of Poets" Barrett Browning chooses to initially identify prophetic and poetic production with a specific Jewishness which is eventually replaced; while this pattern is perhaps normative for many Christian interpretations of Jewishness in a theological discourse, here we see how Barrett Browning conjoins the theological and poetic discourses in her construction of a specifically religious, female poetic speaker.

Barrett Browning returns to her interests in women's poetic identity in her most important work, *Aurora Leigh* (1856), and she goes even further in linking this female poetic identity to Jewishness through her central use of the figure of Miriam. However, in *Aurora Leigh*, she refuses to totally silence her Christian woman poet at the end of the poem as she does in "The Virgin Mary to the Child Jesus" – since to do so would be to undermine a central thesis of *Aurora Leigh*: women can be great (Christian) poets. While the discourse of poetic identity remains a subtext in the earlier poem, in *Aurora Leigh* the nature of woman's poetic identity is made central, and so requires Barrett Browning to devise a different set of strategies with which to reconcile the idealized relationship between her Christian heroine and a figure of Jewish prophetic identity. By the end of *Aurora Leigh*, Barrett Browning enacts a complex narrative of conversions which extricates her ideal Christian woman poet from the potential "monstrosity" of her Hebraic roots, even as she speaks the transfigured terms of Hebrew text.

MARRYING OFF MIRIAM: CHRISTIAN CONVERSION IN *AURORA LEIGH*

But sit in London, at the day's decline,
And view the city perish in the mist
Like Pharaoh's armaments in the deep Red Sea, –
The chariots, horsemen, footmen, all the host,
Sucked down and choked to silence – then, surprised
By a sudden sense of vision and of tune,
You feel as conquerors though you did not fight,
And you and Israel's other singing girls,
Ay, Miriam with them, sing the song you choose.

(Aurora Leigh, III: 195–203)[25]

Miriam, called a prophetess, appears after the passage of the Red Sea as heading the women of Israel in that responsive song in which the glorious deliverance was celebrated (Exodus xv. 20–21). The next occasion in which she is mentioned presents a dark contrast to that earlier day of joy. Miriam, by whom the Lord had spoken, and whom he had sent before his people unites with Aaron in jealous murmuring against Moses. Her sin is immediately visited with frightful punishment. She is struck with leprosy; and Aaron as the priest has to look on his accomplice, and officially pronounce her unclean; and consequently for seven days, till healed and cleansed by the mercy of God, she is excluded from the camp (Numbers xii; Deut. xxiv.9). It must have read an impressive lesson to Israel that God will by no means spare the guilty (Rev. John Ayre, *The Treasury of Bible Knowledge*, 600).

The moment in which Barrett Browning's poet-heroine, Aurora, claims Miriam as the mother of women's "song" in *Aurora Leigh* is a moment of great triumph, both in terms of the epic's narrative structure, as well as in terms of Aurora's personal development as poet/narrator. "[H]appy and unafraid of solitude" (III: 169) Aurora has set herself up as a successful, independent woman writer in London. When she likens herself and other women writers to Miriam and "Israel's other singing girls," she invokes the Hebraic type for female, prophetic agency – and she invokes literary and theological authority for women writers. But to invoke this particular image of Miriam is to tell only half of Miriam's story. As *The Treasury of Bible Knowledge* points out all too clearly, Miriam's moment of religious agency and leadership is short-lived in the Hebrew Scriptures. Indeed, God and the patriarchs of Israel condemned Miriam, striking her with leprosy and ejecting her from the Israelite community. The language of *The Treasury*, "plain, popular information . . . for general readers" (xiv) casts Miriam's demise as a moral lesson about the "guilty" who challenge patriarchal authority. Miriam's fall is a far one: from divine poet to unclean woman. Choosing to use her as the idealized model for her figure of the Victorian woman poet posed some particular theological and narrative complications for Barrett Browning's "novel-poem."

In what follows, I suggest that in *Aurora Leigh* Barrett Browning not only rewrites Biblical ("Old Testament") narrative, but also constructs a specifically woman-centered Christian typological practice. Barrett Browning's simultaneous goals of authorizing women's poetry and revising heterosexual Christian relationships require a complicated narrative of conversions: in short, Miriam/Aurora must be "converted" from her initial identification with an overly independent (Jewish) prophetic woman into a transcendent Christian wife – all while still maintaining her poetic voice. In turn, Romney, her male counterpart, must transform his misguided typological relationship to Moses in order to emerge as a "true" Christian husband. Recognizing the central roles Jewish figures play in the narrative structure of the poem, I argue that Barrett Browning actually critiques the conventions of traditional Christian typological practice, while enacting a revised form of "feminist typology" in order to construct a specifically Christian female poetic identity. Thus, *Aurora Leigh* solves the problem that "The Virgin Mary to the Child Jesus" could not fully escape, namely, how to appropriate the apparent prophetic power of Hebraic women in the service of constructing a authoritative, vocal, specifically Christian female poet.

Barrett Browning's feminist critics have proven most adept in charting the chronological changes in the poet's representations of women.[26] Almost all of her critics agree that *Aurora Leigh* represents the poet's most articulate expression of female poetic agency, but the poem remains a site of controversy as feminist critics struggle to decide if the poem's ending is essentially radical or conservative in relation to feminist politics.[27] On the one hand, readers like Cora Kaplan, while acknowledging the poem's "difficulties" particularly in its representation of the lower classes, nevertheless state that the poem can be read as "radical and rupturing, a major confrontation of patriarchal attitudes unique in the imaginative literature of its day" (Kaplan, Introduction, *Aurora Leigh*, 35). But other readings of the poem find this a text that finally "submits" to patriarchal ideology; thus, for Deirdre David, the conflation of Aurora's sexual identity with her poetic creativity impinges upon the poem's more radical assertions about women's poetic authority, and so the poem is read as "a coherent expression of Barrett Browning's conservative sexual politics . . . [where] woman's art is made the servitor of male ideal" (David, "'Art's a Service,'" 164). Alicia E. Holmes offers the most in-depth analysis of the Miriam/Moses subtext in *Aurora Leigh*, suggesting that Barrett Browning "appropriated the most highly authoritative text, the Bible, to legitimize women's literary authority" ("Elizabeth Barrett Browning," 605). Further, Holmes points out Barrett Browning's omission of Miriam's less "rosy" Biblical ending, finding the ending of the poem "interrupts the implication of the possibility for women of freedom outside of marriage, causing the novel to be liberating in the discreet, but oppressive overall" (604). In my reading of this poem, which expands on Holmes', I suggest that her critical formulation misses one central component, namely that Barrett Browning seeks to construct a specifically Christian female poetic identity in this poem, and that her commitment to Christianity and to a specific dynamic of Christian Biblical interpretation – typology – complicates how we might understand the idea of "liberation" or "oppression" in this poem.

In *Victorian Types, Victorian Shadows*, George Landow suggested that Barrett Browning "founds a theory of the arts upon typology" (6), and Landow uses *Aurora Leigh* as a paradigm for Victorian typological practice. The most common form of Christian typology interprets the Hebrew Scriptures from a Christian point of view; the Hebrew type gains its significance in its relation or prefigurement to an anti-type, namely events, people or concepts from Christ's life and gospels.[28] Of course, the Talmudic tradition in Judaism had always interpreted Hebrew Scripture for the use of the present community, so it is important to see that the act of interpreting Hebrew scriptural event for new situations is not what distinguishes Christian typology as a practice. What is different in a specifically Christian practice is that the Hebraic event, figure or idea is removed from its literary and historical context in Hebrew Scripture and Jewish epistemology, and read within a completely different hermeneutic frame, that of Christian revelation. As theologian Rosemary Radford Ruether writes:

Christianity confronted Judaism with a demand for a conversionist relation to its own past that abrogated that past, in the sense that the past itself no longer provided a covenant of salvation. Christianity did not ask Judaism merely to extend itself in continuity with its past, but to abrogate itself by substituting one covenantal principle from the past for another provided by Jesus. (*Faith and Fratricide*, 80)

Ruether's emphasis on "abrogation" is crucial here, for the term makes explicit the annulment of the Jewish covenant that Christian typology insists upon; though the notion of a "Judeo-Christian" tradition is based upon the idea that Christianity and Judaism are connected doctrinally and historically, Ruether's description reminds us that Judaism and Christianity are based on completely different relationships to the Divine, completely different notions of that covenant, and thus completely different hermeneutic codes.

More importantly, Christianity does not merely assert the possibility of reading Jewish history from a Christian perspective; the typological impulse goes further in insisting that Hebrew history has no independent significance without the larger context of Christianity. Thus, typology sets up a relationship between Hebrew history and Christianity that might be termed "significance through relationship"; in such a relationship, Judaism, as represented in the "Old Testament" is an important element of Christian history and identity, but only so far as Judaism/Jewishness maintains a relationship with Christian interpretation. At the moment Judaism asserts itself as significant outside or separate from Christianity, it is no longer significant or meaningful from a Christian perspective.

This typological assumption of "significance through relationship" has an implicit connection to discourses surrounding gender in the nineteenth century, a discourse that Barrett Browning invokes throughout *Aurora Leigh*. In terms of Victorian poetic discourse, as I argued in chapter 2, the prophetic model of poetic identity also insisted that women poets were not "significant" poets because they could not establish a relationship with masculine qualities of intellect and philosophy. Without relationship to maleness, that is, women were unable to articulate (according to dominant male theories) a complete poetic nature, and remained restricted to the realm of the heart. However, within a specifically Christian discourse, this realm of the heart could be understood as a complete religious and poetic identity. By claiming themselves as specifically Christian poets then, Victorian women poets could galvanize the discourse of the Christian heart, and at least begin to rewrite the terms of prophetic poetic identity which insisted they were incomplete. Thus, the discourses of Jewish identity in a Christian epistemology and female identity in a patriarchal epistemology overlap at the moment both are perceived as "significant through relationship."

In *Aurora Leigh*, Barrett Browning demonstrates a specifically female Christian typological perspective, which maintains the notion that Jewish/female identity can only be significant when in relationship, or union, with Christian/male identity. Yet, Barrett Browning also seeks to implicate men in this relational Christian identity. In order to reconstruct the conventional understanding of women's poetic identity, she maintains her investment in Christian typological practice, but insists that it is a practice that must be revised from its traditional male-centered forms of reading. In short, she argues for the centrality of both Hebraic and female identity, as well as Christian and male identity, but insists that each must find union with each other – as initiated by Christ's union with his Church, often figured as the Bridegroom and the Bride, respectively. Nevertheless, as she maintains an investment in the figure of significance through relationship/union, Barrett Browning refuses to grant to men the higher position in the relationship; her poem thus repeatedly seeks to critique male-centered Christian typology, while nevertheless maintaining a profound commitment to Christian typology as it is reformulated from her feminist perspective. Recognizing this complex intersection Barrett Browning creates between Christian typology, gender discourse, and feminist poetics, it becomes easier to see the poem as one that challenges Christian patriarchal discourse while simultaneously reclaiming Christian discourse in service of a specifically female poetic authority. The Jewish woman prophet/poet Miriam is the figure upon which Barrett Browning's argument about Christian women's poetic identity hinges. Thus, while those critics who examine Miriam's role in this poem tend to find her "a model" for the woman poet in this poem, I will argue that Barrett Browning ultimately rejects the Jewish Miriam as a viable model, and instead insists that it is only through Miriam's Christian/typological conversion that a ideal woman poet emerges in *Aurora Leigh*.[29]

In order to fully contextualize Barrett Browning's revision of Miriam's identity, it is important to situate Miriam and other Jewish women prophets in a larger Victorian discourse about Jewish women artists. The

Jewish woman was constructed by Victorian Christian England from two sources: one, as already mentioned, was the powerful, prophetic figures of the Hebrew Bible, women like Miriam, Deborah, Esther, Jael, Rachel, and Hannah who – in a variety of ways – are often interpreted as agents of prophetic, poetic, religious, and political power in Jewish history. Yet this "mythic" understanding of the Jewish woman was joined to a more contemporary stereotype of Jewish female identity: the growing cultural stereotype of the Jewish woman as performer in the Victorian public sphere. Ann Pellegrini traces the ways nineteenth- and early twentieth-century Jewish women performers were linked to "sexual promiscuity" and likewise notes how the Jewish woman performer emerges "[in] the novels of "Eliot, James and Proust . . . as exotic and erotic spectacle" ("Whiteface Performances," 110).[30] Perhaps the most famous Jewish actress/performer was Rachel, who appears as the model for the Jewish woman performer in many Victorian texts; we see traces of her in Bronte's famous Vashti chapter in *Villette*, in Eliot's multiple Jewish singers and actresses in *Daniel Deronda*, and more directly in Matthew Arnold's poems about the actress herself. All these examples attest to the ideological weight the image of the Jewish woman performer had in this period; she was repeatedly invoked as a figure quite other to the model of the Christian "angel in the house" who was marked for her sexual passivity, rather than the erotic and public power associated with the Jewish female performer.[31]

Combining this figure of the woman performer with her Biblical counterpart, the Jewish woman emerges as a figure who embodied many qualities that Christian women artists often sought but could not safely claim and simultaneously maintain their relationship to values of Christian womanhood. For the construction of the ideal Christian woman was based on qualities antithetical to displays of artistic power, sexual autonomy, and public sphere agency. Thus, Christian women poets like Barrett Browning, Christina Rossetti, and Felicia Hemans often projected onto Jewish women the ability to, as Rossetti puts it in her Esther sonnet, "take [their lives] . . . in [their] hand" (see chapter 4), or as Barrett Browning writes, "to sing the song [they] choose." It should be noted, of course, that these stereotypical images of Jewish female autonomy were rarely claimed as "true" by Jewish women writers of the day, as Amy Levy's novel of Jewish womanhood, *Reuben Sachs*, makes all too clear.[32]

Looking briefly at Felicia Hemans' use of Miriam as the archetype for the Jewish woman performer highlights some of the particular ways

Barrett Browning adapts Miriam for her own uses in *Aurora Leigh*. In Hemans' sonnet "The Song of Miriam," a poem I suspect was an important source for Barrett Browning's figuration of Miriam in *Aurora Leigh*, Miriam becomes the role model for not only women's public performance, but indeed all poetry. Hemans isolates Miriam at the moment where Miriam sings her song of praise to God after the "parting" of the Red Sea in Exodus 15: 20–1. Hemans' sonnet provides a gloss on the meaning of Miriam's song:

> A song for Israel's God! Spear, crest, and helm,
> Lay by the billows of the old Red Sea,
> When Miriam's voice o'er that sepulchral realm
> Sent on the blast a hymn of jubilee.
> With her lit eye, and long hair floating free,
> Queen-like she stood, and glorious was the strain,
> E'en as instinct with the tempestuous glee
> Of the dark waters, tossing o'er the slain.
> A song for God's own victory! Oh, thy lays,
> Bright Poesy! were holy in their birth:
> How hath it died, their seraph-note of praise,
> In the bewildering melodies of earth!
> Return from troubling, bitter founts – return,
> Back to the life-springs of thy native urn![33]
> ("The Song of Miriam," lines 1–14)

For Hemans, Miriam's hymn in Exodus is a moment of divine song, and Miriam is represented as a powerful player in that central moment in Jewish political and divine history. In the culminating sestet of the sonnet, Hemans considers the significance of Miriam's song for contemporary poetry, suggesting that Miriam's song is the "holy" birth of poetry, and she exhorts contemporary poets to model their song on her precedent. Miriam's voice becomes – for Hemans – a symbol of the very roots of "true" poetry even as other details in Hemans' poem, Miriam's "lit eye, and long hair floating free," offer images that call on the stock figure of the Jewish female performer who displays a distinctly sexualized and erotic spectacle.

Barrett Browning's figuration of Miriam in *Aurora Leigh* initially echoes much of Hemans' imagery. But though it seems Barrett Browning, like Hemans, sets up Miriam as the model for all poetic production, examining the Miriam narrative throughout *Aurora Leigh* more closely reveals Barrett Browning's critique of Hemans' idealization of Miriam as poetic model. Barrett Browning's first allusion to Miriam in *Aurora Leigh* occurs in Book II. Barrett Browning initiates her exploration of how typology might mean differently for men and women by having Romney invoke Miriam in order to deride the role of poetic women. He argues:

> . . . Who has time,
> An hour's time . . . think! – to sit upon a bank
> And hear the cymbal tinkle in white hands?
> When Egypt's slain, I say, let Miriam sing! –
> Before – where's Moses?   (II: 168–172)

Romney minimizes Miriam's role at the Red Sea by describing simply a "cymbal tinkl[ing] in white hands."[34] This diminution symbolizes a larger typological point; in Romney's eyes, "Egypt" is a symbol for the "oppressors" of British social reform; thus, he suggests that Victorian culture is still "enslaved," still waiting for a Moses to save it, rather than a Miriam. Romney's point in this allusion is twofold, designed to claim that a woman poet cannot be a significant leader, as well as to identify his own role as that of a potential Moses.

Aurora goes on to extend Romney's initial allusion to Miriam and Moses, but she sharply questions Romney's own aspirations to Moses' role as the savior of England. She transforms his question "Where's Moses?" from a repudiation of women poets into a comment on Moses' humble beginnings.

> Ah, exactly that.
> Where's Moses? – is a Moses to be found?
> You'll seek him vainly in the bulrushes,
> While I in vain touch cymbals. Yet concede,
> Such sounding brass has done some actual good . . .
>   (II: 172–6)

What Aurora does in this passage is to galvanize other aspects of the Mosaic narrative that include Miriam as a central figure. There is no Moses to be found in contemporary life; he remains hidden in the "bulrushes," and her reference to Moses' infancy reminds the listener/reader of the primary moment of his "saving" in Biblical tradition which was enacted by women – indeed, by his older sister, Miriam, herself.[35] Aurora's image calls on the figure of Moses at his most vulnerable, and compares it to an image of Miriam, singing at her most powerful moment; her figure insists that poetry and women have the ability to create significant social and moral good, and further, that women are often the ones responsible for men's ability to become leaders.

In citing the "vain" search in the bulrushes, Aurora also makes a pun about the motives behind typological comparison: Romney's male vanity, she implies, motivates his desire to model the contemporary savior on an Hebraic man. This notion of Romney's vanity – indeed his hubris in believing he can be the Moses for the century – suggests the potential moral danger men can make in typological comparisons that do not recognize how Moses must be a type for Christ, not for a mere human reformer like Romney. His own typological identification with Moses demonstrates Romney's ignorance regarding typological identification with Biblical characters; rather than model himself on a Moses, he should be seeking union with Christ, who is the only true anti-type for Moses. Aurora's response suggests that this initial argument between Romney and Aurora is about two issues: their potential marriage and "correct" typological comparison.

From Aurora's point of view, Romney's "incorrect" typology exposes his vanity, while her "feminist" typological vision allows her to position Miriam as an equally important figure to Moses, and at the center of her own interpretation of Biblical narrative. The feminist and Christian discourses also collide in Romney's comments, as it turns out that Romney's argument for a marriage in which woman is "helpmeet" to man hinges on denying to women any significant role in the Christian narrative. He tells Aurora:

> Women as you are,
> Mere women, personal and passionate,
> You give us doting mothers, and perfect wives,
> Sublime Madonnas, and enduring saints!
> We get no Christ from you, – and verily
> We shall not get a poet, in my mind. (II: 220–5)

Romney's "We get no Christ from you" is Barrett Browning's clearest demonstration of the faults in Romney's (chauvinist) typological interpretation. His statement insists that since the aim of most conventional typology centers around finding a correlation to Christ's life, women are inevitably excluded from this goal because of their sexual difference from Christ. But Romney once again exhibits his larger misunderstanding of typological significance, since it is not the human individual who provides "a Christ" – indeed, this is almost blasphemy; there can only be emulation of Christ's example, or a union with Christ rather than an identification with his actual identity. Further, Romney's statement rejects the possibility that women's roles in society can be modeled on Christ, since the only available figures of women in Christian narrative, in his mind, are the Madonna, "saints," "mothers, and . . . wives."

There is an implicit contradiction in Romney's reasoning (and a pun from Barrett Browning) in the use of the term "get," since a "Madonna" did "get" a Christ according to Christian doctrine. But for Romney, "getting a Christ" refers to finding the man who will become the savior of England; his desire to be the next Christ limits his ability to see the mythic origins of Jesus in Mary's body just as it limits his ability to see how a woman can be central to acts of Christian salvation. Finally, Romney's words assert a link between Christian agency, gender, and poetry; just as we will "get no Christ" from women, so will we "get no poets." Romney assumes that the poet must be able to transcend the "personal and passionate" which mark women's expression for him. Romney's speech makes plain the roles relegated to women in Christian history, and they are exactly those roles which Aurora refuses to adopt throughout the poem; at this point in the poem, her defense is to identify herself with a Hebraic female prophet, a woman whose varied roles in the Hebrew Scriptures stand in stark opposition to Romney's assumptions about women. Indeed, Aurora's affinity to Miriam demonstrates her obvious rejection of Christian womanhood, figured in the terms "sublime Madonnas," "doting mothers," and "perfect wives"; Miriam was neither mother, nor wife, but rather sister of a prophet, and so she is not easily figured within conventional Christian typology.[36] Standing outside of Romney's system of Christian typological interpretation, Aurora's identification with Miriam lets her maintain an autonomous female artistic identity, albeit one that remains linked to Jewish identity and has no clear relationship to Christian identity or narrative.

The implicit question the text leaves unanswered at this moment is how we are to understand Aurora's self-identification with Miriam. On the one hand, because Miriam has no real New Testament counterpart, Aurora's comparison with Miriam does not implicate her in any misguided Christian typology; her self-identification with Miriam stands outside conventional typological interpretation. On the other hand, Miriam's resistance to Christian typological interpretation threatens to position Aurora as likewise outside of the realm of Christian interpretation, leaving the idea of the woman poet – the figure Barrett Browning seeks to authorize in this poem – "outside the camp," as it were. Aurora has used this Biblical figure to readjust Romney's incorrect chauvinist interpretations about women's identity and so clearly make a "feminist" argument; what remains unclear is whether Aurora can combine her interpretive practice in order to make equally "correct" Christian interpretations of her own life.

Book II ends with a seeming rupture of any romantic connection between Aurora and Romney; they have disagreed on the meaning of marriage and gender roles just as they have disagreed on the correct interpretation of Biblical figures and narratives. Book III finds Aurora alone, yet also at her most successful professional moment as a woman poet, and it is at this moment that Aurora reclaims the figure of Miriam, again recasting Romney's derisive use of the Biblical poet/prophet into Aurora's most triumphant image of the contemporary female poet. In discussing how urban life suits a poet's purposes, Aurora explains:

> No one sings,
> Descending Sinai: on Parnassus-mount
> You take a mule to climb and not a muse,
> Except in fable and figure: forests chant
> Their anthems to themselves, and leave you dumb.
> But sit in London at the day's decline,
> And view the city perish in the mist
> Like Pharaoh's armaments in the deep Red Sea, –
> The chariots, horsemen, footmen, all the host,
> Sucked down and choked to silence – then, surprised
> By a sudden sense of vision and of tune,
> You feel as conquerors though you did not fight,
> And you and Israel's other singing girls,
> Ay, Miriam with them, sing the song you choose.
>   (III: 190–203)

This apocalyptic passage is at the heart of Barrett Browning's ideas about poetic production, and it represents the culmination of her inclusion of the Hebraic into her feminist poetics. Pointing to the two central traditions of literary and theological authority – Moses' transcription of God's word on Sinai and the classical source of poetic inspiration, Mt. Parnassus – Aurora suggests that they do not finally symbolize the sort of poetic inspiration she seeks. Or rather, Aurora debunks the myths of artistic identity that underlie these conventional representations of linguistic triumph. When Moses "descends" Sinai, he has just conversed with God, and thus is the prophet of the divine word, but this interaction has not resulted in his own poetic production; rather, he carries the tablet "written by the finger of God" (Exodus 32: 16) – not his own finger; in that sense, Moses is not really a type for a human poet, but rather a conveyer of God's word. Similarly, the female "muses" of classical poetry exist only in "fable and figure"; the truth of climbing Parnassus is that one needs a "mule" because it is hard work. Aurora also rejects the claim that nature can be a poetic source; for her nature has its own language, which is not available for human use.

Finally, having rejected the conventional models of poetic inspiration, Aurora locates true poetry within human culture. What is striking about her comparison of her own identity to "Israel's singing girls" is that their "song" is born out of a moment of intense social and political conflict, which the simile compares to a vision of the city. Further, the moment of Miriam's song is a moment of worship and praise to God; this particular Biblical moment combines political triumph with divine praise, thus locating the poetic as simultaneously religious, de-naturalized, and female. The poet is related to the position of women in the idea that s/he "did not fight" – poets and women, remaining outside direct physical action, are nevertheless of central importance to society through their acts of artistic vision and moral inspiration.[37]

Thus, in the middle of her autobiographical narrative, Aurora positions herself as a Hebrew woman, a woman recently released from the "slavery" of her confining past, a woman suddenly freed to sing as a prophet and in full possession of creative agency. From a twenty-first-century secular feminist perspective, this vision of Aurora as Miriam is powerful and transformative. But this seemingly emancipated identification with Miriam becomes increasingly problematic for Aurora as the poem continues. On the one hand, the pressures of the marriage plot are unresolved, and on the other, the pressures of a specifically Christian revelation/transformation have yet to be revealed. The use of the two types, Miriam and Moses, will not really provide the figurative closure the poem seeks, since to carry Miriam's mythic narrative to conclusion would place her as Moses' antagonistic sister, as well as an "unclean" woman expelled from the Hebrew camp. The poem must also bridge the differences in Romney's and Aurora's interpretations of the Bible, "healing" Romney's diseased vision of himself as a Mosaic successor, while simultaneously showing Aurora the potential joys of Christian marriage.

Thus, as the poem moves toward closure in Books VIII and IX, Barrett Browning must revise Miriam's narrative in order to contain the threat that Miriam (and women poets) pose to Christian patriarchy, while nevertheless finding a place for the woman poet within a revised, woman-friendly Christianity. Likewise, a revised Romney must emerge if he is to remain Aurora's counterpart, one who becomes the Christian husband who can accept the idea of a poetic and prophetic wife as well as realign his own misguided vision of his Christian role. The three competing discourses of this poem – generic (novelistic) closure, female poetic identity, and Christian typology – must be realigned from this mid-point moment of apparent female poetic triumph for Aurora; as the Hebraic Miriam, Aurora has typologically connected herself to a Biblical figural identity which threatens to leave her unmarried, condemned by God, and Jewish. If the first parts of *Aurora Leigh* call on patterns of Old Testament figures to authorize Aurora's claims to poetic identity, the latter half of the poem seeks to revise that model of the woman poet into a more explicitly Christian identity. The realignment Barrett Browning proposes, however, is ingeniously subtle as it also suggests what a specifically feminist Christian typological practice might look like.

This revision of both Aurora's and Romney's identity is signaled in Book VII by a revision of the typological conversation about marriage that marked Book II. The need for such revision was signaled by Aurora's explicit comment on her earlier conversation with Romney; in Book VIII she offers this retrospective analysis:

> We both were wrong that June-day, – both as wrong
> As an east wind had been. I who talked of art,
> And you who grieved for all men's griefs . . . what then?
> We surely made too small a part for God
> In these things.   (VIII: 552–6)

This then, becomes the frame through which Aurora and Romney re-configure their younger selves; in their first conversation about marriage, Miriam, and Moses, they did not place their arguments in a "correct" religious interpretative framework. As they seek to name the God with whom they credit their redemption, both Aurora and Romney reassert their relationship to a specifically Christian God, and thus must necessarily realign their typological identifications.

When Aurora and Romney are reunited in Book VIII, Miriam is explicitly invoked once more by Romney, but his new idealization of her role suggests that he has reconceived his initial typological practice. Blind, ruined, and refreshingly self-critical, Romney offers a new characterization of his past self:

Oh, deserved,
Deserved! that I, who verily had not learnt
God's lesson half, attaining as a dunce
To obliterate good words with fractious thumbs
And cheat myself of the context, – I should push
Aside, with male ferocious impudence,
The world's Aurora who had conned her part
On the other side the leaf! ignore her so,
Because she was a woman and a queen,
And had no beard to bristle through her song,
My teacher, who has taught me with a book,
My Miriam, whose sweet mouth, when nearly drowned
I still heard singing on the shore!   (VIII: 323–35)

Romney understands not only Aurora's poetic contributions, but also his own sexism in his previous refusal to grant her poetic authority. He attributes his previous "blindness" to "male ferocious impudence" and understands how he had falsely imagined maleness – figured as a "beard" – as a prerequisite to song. But the most interesting moment of his figure comes at its conclusion, when Romney positions himself as "nearly drowned" while Aurora/Miriam is "singing on the shore." With the enjambment on "nearly drowned," Romney now understands his own typological identification with the Red Sea narrative in two possible ways; either he casts himself as an Egyptian, an oppressor, hearing the victorious song of Miriam and the Israelites right before he drowns, or conversely, Romney maintains his identification with Moses, but now suggests that Miriam reached the shore before Moses, and that Moses was saved by her singing, by her poetry.

In the first possible reading, Romney addresses the political discourse about gender identity, linking the figure of dominant Egyptian (slave-holding) identity to his own dominant male identity in England. Here, then, Romney implies his own recognition that women in England, like Jews in Egypt, can be seen as oppressed groups, and further, that the oppressors (men, Egyptians) will not succeed in keeping women (Jews) enslaved because of the powerful voice of a Miriam (a female poet). This reading, which asserts the possibility that Romney identifies with a drowned Egyptian suggests a complete renunciation of his earlier identification with Moses, and indeed, a refusal to see himself as one of the "chosen people" at this point in his life; with this reading, Romney offers a rethinking of his ideas about gender identity in particular.

But if these figures of Romney-as-Egyptian-oppressor and Aurora-as-"free"- Jewish-Miriam were maintained, these figural identifications would inhibit any "new" heterosexual Christian union at the end of the poem. It is not enough that Romney recognize himself as patriarchal oppressor and submit to Aurora's earlier vision of him. The demands for closure – and heterosexual union – must also allow him to become transformed into a Christian husband who can create an alliance with Aurora. Here, then, the second reading of these lines can be galvanized, suggesting that Romney as "nearly drowned" is still identified with Moses, but a Moses cast in a new, feminist typological vision. Miriam is cast as the "saving sister" reinhabiting her identity as the savior of Moses not only in his infancy, but also later in his life at his first moment of community leadership. As the nearly drowned Moses, then, Romney recognizes his potential to have become an oppressive Egyptian enemy, but also casts himself as a potential leader dependent on the work of women, dependent, that is, on the poetry of his sister, Miriam.[38]

However, as an independent professional woman, sister to Marian and surrogate provider for Marian's child, Aurora has yet to take her place in either the heterosexual or Christian contexts with which the poem is deeply implicated. To remain allied with the Biblical Miriam – even in Romney's new positive understanding of her role – means that Aurora will remain a woman who stands outside of Christian heterosexuality, as well as a poetic woman who risks a "correct" relationship to God's authority. Only through marriage, it seems, can Romney and Aurora can save each other from their previously flawed understandings of their own social, artistic, and religious roles, understandings of their identities that were intrinsically "incomplete" because of their reliance on Hebrew types. Through marriage, that is, they can imitate not specific Biblical characters, but rather let their marriage serve as an act of union like the one Christ enacts with his Church. Union, rather than metaphorical identification, Barrett Browning argues, is the best way to locate oneself within Christian epistemology.

In order to enact this Christian union, however, Aurora and Romney must both relinquish their reliance on Hebraic identity, and Barrett Browning's strategy for their conversion is both fascinating and brilliant, as she circles around the problem that her Hebraic figures now pose for her Christian closure. Her process of conversion is initiated by the most explicit reference to Jewish practice in the whole poem, where Barrett Browning links Romney's identity with that of a cantor in an "old Jewish temple";

> And then calm, equal, smooth with weights of joy,
> His voice rose, as some chief musician's song
> Amid the old Jewish temple's Selah-pause,
> And bade me mark how we two met at last
> Upon this moon-bathed promontory of earth,
> To give up much on each side, then, take all.
>
>   (IX: 843–8)

Romney's voice is compared to that of the "chief musician's song amid the old Jewish temple's Selah-pause," once again locating the source of prophetic song in Hebrew culture.[39] This reference also refers to the practice of actual "old Jew[s]," rather than abstracted Biblical "Hebrews," and so implicitly points to the ongoing nature of Jewish practice – as well as pointing to the historical destruction of the Jewish Temple and the later dominance of Christianity. By placing Romney as a priest in the Temple when he is blind, Barrett Browning insists he has a limited vision which needs assistance. However, the comparison of Romney to the Hebrew high priest becomes a potentially dangerous admission for such a typologically charged text, since the reference to an unconverted Jewish identity signals – from a Christian perspective – that God's kingdom is not yet achieved on earth. Significantly, this reference – this moment when the Jewishness of Miriam and Moses is closest to being named, and when the Christian typological perspective comes closest to being ruptured – initiates the final expulsion of the Jews, or rather Old Testament identification, from the figural landscape of *Aurora Leigh*.

Thus, as Barrett Browning reconciles the lovers, she also transforms this union into a moment of Christian revelation, necessitating that Romney's "Jewish" voice be "converted" as it gradually begins to speak Christian doctrine.

> "Beloved" it sang, "we must be here to work;
> And men who work can only work for men,
> And, not to work in vain, must comprehend
> Humanity and so work humanely,
> And raise men's bodies still by raising souls,
> As God did, first."
>   "But stand upon the earth,"
> I said, "to raise them, – (this is human too,
> There's nothing high which has not first been low,
> My humbleness, said One, has made me great!)
> As God did, last."

"And work all silently
And simply," he returned, "as God does all;
Distort our nature never for our work,
Nor count our right hands stronger for being hoofs.
The man most man, with tenderest human hands,
Works best for man, – as God in Nazareth."
                                                  (IX: 849–63)

The "voice" is referred to in the abstract, as Aurora describes how "it sang" to her; this abstraction enacts the distance needed to transform the threatening image of Romney in an "old Jewish temple." Aurora's voice joins in this passage, uniting their two voices in prophecy of future Christian work; Romney then makes the final pointed allusion to "God in Nazareth," significantly refiguring God as Jesus. The conversion of the Jews is completed in this passage, as the figure of the "Jewish" voice is recast as a Christian, speaking in tandem with "his Miriam" who likewise goes on to acknowledge her own willingness for conversion, both Christian and wifely. Yet it is here that I would resist a reading that aligns Aurora with "oppression"; within a Christian formulation, this is the moment in which she is "freed" through her union with Christian identity, freed to become a Christian woman poet/prophet in the ways Miriam could never fully realize in the Biblical ending of her story.[40] What Barrett Browning suggests is that Aurora's initial identification with Miriam's autonomy as a single woman artist is a misreading, one that does not account for her later chastisement by God. The only way for Miriam to escape this divine rejection – in Barrett Browning's poem – is to claim her place in a new covenantal union with Christ and Romney.

In his final description of their Christian marriage of joint work, Romney offers his final reformulation of Aurora/Miriam's identity as a woman poet. After a long passage on how their work will now be a collaboration, "Commended . . . [by] all true workers and true lovers born" (IX: 927–8), Romney says to Aurora:

Now press the clarion on thy woman's lip
(Loves holy kiss shall still keep consecrate)
And breathe the fine keen breath along the brass,
And blow all class-walls level as Jericho's
Past Jordan,
                              . . .
                    The world's old;
But the old world waits the time to be renewed. . .
                                                  (IX: 929–42)

Romney explicitly calls on Aurora's language from Book II, when she described the work of the woman poet's "touching cymbals" as a contrast to Romney's own "vain" search for Moses "in the bulrushes"; in that passage she has asked Romney to "concede, Such sounding brass has done some actual good," and he does exactly "concede" that point here when he describes the potential good work Aurora can do by "breath[ing] the fine keen breath along the brass." Stating clearly their final commitment to "renew" the old world in order to "make all new" (IX: 949) in their emulation of Christ, Romney and Aurora release their previously exclusive ties to the Old Testament figures that have governed much of their relationship.

This commitment to a new, specifically Christian identity is signaled at the moment Aurora cries "My Romney" (IX: 950), enacting the final conversion of the poem. She claims him, accepts him possessively just as he had claimed her as "my Miriam," avoiding any comparison to Moses (and thus her identity as Miriam) that had marked their previous flawed Hebraic identification. This reformulation of their typological identities is confirmed in the last lines of the poem, which refer to the text of Revelation 21: 1–20 – a New Testament text describing the building of the New Jerusalem which is an exact reference to the Old Testament text Exodus 28: 17–20, describing Aaron's breastplate. In Revelation, John describes his vision of God on the heavenly throne, a God who announces he will "make all things new," and commands John to "write" (verse 5). Finally, one of the seven angels tells John he will show him "the bride, the Lamb's wife" (verse 9), and this "bride" turns out to be the "new Jerusalem" whose walls are comprised of the same stone that made up Aaron's breastplate in Exodus. The reconstructed Jerusalem is the "bride" of Jesus in this passage, and so with this reference, Barrett Browning places the marriage at the end of the poem in a specifically Christian typological context, a context which insists that Old Testament/Jewish covenants and identity will be reappropriated into Christian revelation, just as the figure of Miriam and Moses have been reconstituted in the images of Christian husband and wife in the poem itself. If the poem has linked the discourses of marriage (and thus sexual difference) and Biblical typology throughout the poem, then the ending of the poem reasserts this link, demonstrating that the marriage of Romney and Aurora is in fact the most appropriate typological identification for Christian men and women, as well as a signal for the marriage of Old and New Testament text that dominates the ending of the poem.

Michael Ragussis has argued that the genre of the comic novel and its reliance on the marriage plot is intrinsically linked to tropes of Christian conversion. Through a reading of *The Merchant of Venice*, and Maria Edgeworth's novel *Harrington*, Ragussis thus reformulates a theory of comic structure, asking: "Does woman occupy the same position as the Jew in an institution that legitimates and facilitates the transfer of her property and her personal identity? Is marriage a kind of conversion?" (*Figures of Conversion*, 78). I would argue that Barrett Browning's uses of Jewish text and figures in *Aurora Leigh* anticipate these questions, albeit from a specifically Christian perspective, as it explores the relationships between female poetic identity, interpretations of the Hebrew Scriptures, and tropes of Christian marriage. Calling on Old Testament (Jewish) figures as the major figural identities for Aurora and Romney in the text, Barrett Browning creates a meta-commentary on the correct uses of textual Jewishness from a Christian perspective. Ultimately, the text argues that figural identification with Hebrew scriptural characters is fraught with problems for Christian women, and the narrative of Miriam exemplifies the dangers of Christian women's over-identification with Jewish Biblical women.

Barrett Browning needs Miriam as a figure of Biblically sanctioned poetic authority for women, but the contradictions this typological identification poses for a Christian feminist, as outlined above, insist that she re-evaluate patterns of Christian typology and re-evaluate a theory of feminist practice/poetic which posits the Miriam figure as a potential ideal. To reconsider the questions about whether this is ultimately an oppressive or liberatory text for women, then, we must first recognize the larger Christian interpretative frame which surrounds this poem and Barrett Browning's approach to women's poetic identity. Assuming, perhaps, the poem to be "conventional" in its religious/Christian doctrine, critics have instead emphasized the poem's interest in a discourse of gendered otherness without linking these representations to the discourse of Jewish and Christian identity which runs throughout the poem. While the richness of *Aurora Leigh's* imagery does indeed call for many other kinds of analyses than the one I perform here, I do think that removing the idea of "feminist poetics" from the overt Christian impulse of this poem can produce readings that may distort Barrett Browning's theology considerably.[41]

If we put Barrett Browning's particular approach to Jewish identity in context with that of Christina Rossetti in the next chapter, the comparison between each woman's approach to Hebrew scriptural materials illuminates many of their theological differences. Rossetti takes a rather aggressive approach to Jewish text and identity in her theological poetics, consistently rejecting Hebraic identity, constructing it as a dangerous site for Christian women. For Rossetti, women and Jews, both contemporary and Old Testament, are always constructed as figures of lack, and both can only find "completion" through Christ which will abolish both gender difference and Jewish difference from the world. Barrett Browning, as I argue in this chapter, takes a quite different typological approach, celebrating and integrating the Jewish/Hebraic as an essential part of her larger vision of Christian female identity, yet while she sees the value in Jewish/Hebraic identity, it is a value that is only realized when understood as linked to Christian identity. In part, this link between Jewish/Christian relationship and male/female relationship is generated from the idea that in a Christian perspective, Judaism maintains its significance through a relationship to Christianity, rather than having any true identity outside of a larger Christian narrative; this notion of significance through relationship has everything to do with the ways femaleness was constructed in Victorian England, as both Rossetti and Barrett Browning clearly understood. Thus, each poet's construction of Jewish identity and its relationship to Christian identity remains deeply tied to each poet's different constructions of heterosexual identity.

When Barrett Browning jokingly termed herself a potential "Hebraic monster," she acknowledged the anxiety that attended the Victorian Christian women's "possession" of Hebrew and "the Hebraic" in an attempt to position themselves in relation to Hebrew history and Hebraic scriptural authority. In this fascinating turn of phrase, she also acknowledged the problematic gender categories that might emerge for a Christian woman overly identified with Jewishness in Victorian society. In many ways, this notion of the female "Hebraic monster" is the flip side to the image of "Israel's singing girls" she calls up in *Aurora Leigh;* in each image, Jewish identity emerges as central trope through which to understand her identity as female poet. Yet for Barrett Browning, the Hebraic monster and Miriam were also marked by their exceptional status, figures made tantalizing by their apparent self-sufficiency; more troubling, however, was how both figures remain removed from any quality of Christian union which was so central to her theological understanding of true Christian self and work. We might speculate that within a formulation of gender identity so closely linked to a theory of Christian union, Barrett Browning's own marriage to Robert Browning was instrumental in her own construction of her identity as a Christian woman poet.

Or perhaps it was this marriage, which released her from the excessive dominance of her father, that also initiated a new theological understanding of the significance of Christian union. Just as Aurora's marriage to Romney helps "correct" her over-identification with the figure of the Jewish Miriam, Barrett Browning's marriage to Robert Browning may have helped transform her public persona from that of a potential "Hebraic monster who live[d] in the dark" into one of Victorian England's most famous Christian women poets.

CHAPTER 4

Christina Rossetti and the Hebraic goblins
of the Jewish Scriptures

"A LINE DRAWN SOMEWHERE": ROSSETTI AND
THE CONSTRUCTION OF DIFFERENCE

Does it not appear as if the Bible was based upon an understood unalterable distinction between men and women, their position, duties, privileges? Not arrogating to myself but most earnestly desiring to attain to the character of a humble orthodox Xtian, so does it appear to me; not merely under the Old but also under the New Dispensation. The fact of the Priesthood being exclusively man's, leaves me in no doubt that the highest functions are not in this world open to both sexes: and if not all, then a selection must be made and a line drawn somewhere. (Letter, cited in Bell, *Christina Rossetti*, 111–12)

When as samples of Old Testament servants of God we select some (since we cannot discuss all), who evidently and eminently have prefigured Christ, at the least in some point of their career, we shall many times find them characterized by that very uncompletedness (if I may term it so: for I mean a very different thing from the defect named incompleteness) which we have been considering. (Christina Rossetti, *Seek and Find*, 147)

Christina Rossetti (1830–94) is perhaps the most famous and anthologized of all women poets of her day. Cast as the master craftswoman of tightly wrought, highly symbolic poems, the deeply devout spinster, Rossetti carries one of the most powerful reputations of all Victorian women poets, and likewise embodies some of the most stereotypical myths of the Victorian woman artist.[1] Rossetti published four separate books of poetry; in addition her poetry was reprinted in three different collections during her lifetime and countless others after her death. Along with her poetry, Rossetti wrote a number of books designed specifically for children, as well as five books of prose on religious and theological topics, all published by the Society for the Promotion of Christian Knowledge.[2] Though her reputation dropped in the modernist backlash against the Victorians, Rossetti's status in the British literary canon – feminist and otherwise – has never been seriously in doubt, and she was – unlike so many women poets – equally revered by literary culture in her own day as well as ours.[3]

Rossetti's critical and historical success is surely related to the fact that her work has appeal to critics from a broad spectrum of methods and theoretical schools. Rossetti's poetry (and less read prose, for that matter) has important things to say to those who would situate her as primarily a devotional poet, a woman poet, a pre-Raphaelite poet, an Anglican poet, an ascetic poet, a feminist poet or an anti-feminist poet. Not surprisingly, critics seeking to align Rossetti with one or another movement focus on certain poems exclusively; in particular, a split is often made between those poems which are read as "devotional" because they have explicitly religious content, and those which get read as "secular" because they offer content that appears to be non-religious, concerned with nature, artistic tradition or gender.[4] This critical compartmentalizing of her work, however commonplace in literary criticism, has served to obscure certain connections between gender identity and religious identity in Rossetti's poetics, a poetics I will argue has profound concerns with the figure of the Jewish other, and the otherness of Judaic text.[5]

The passages I have chosen as epigraphs sketch out the discourses of difference with which I am concerned in this chapter. As the famous letter to Augusta Webster cited above suggests, Rossetti was quite clear that there were "unalterable distinction[s]" between men and women in their roles on earth as articulated by the Bible. In the passage above, Rossetti is critical of women's subordination on earth, but clearly accepts it as the order of things in her role as a "humble orthodox Xtian"; in that role, she sees a clear demarcation – "a line drawn somewhere" that differentiates the roles and identity of the sexes. Yet her qualification "in this world" suggests that in the "next" world this hierarchy of sexual difference might be dissolved. Though Christian conversion does not entail a literal conversion of a female body into a male body, Rossetti suggests that when Christian salvation is obtained, women might escape the religious and political subordination placed on them in Victorian England.

If the letter to Augusta Webster makes clear that Rossetti saw gender identity as needing a differential "line drawn somewhere" between female and male identity, the passage from her devotional and exegetical prose work *Seek and Find* (1879), makes clear that Jewishness – as represented by the Hebrew Scriptures – constituted for Rossetti another central paradigm of difference. In *Seek and Find*, one of Rossetti's prose works published through the Society for the Promotion of Christian

Knowledge (an explicitly Christian conversionary institution) Rossetti explores the identity of "Old Testament servants of God" as existing in a state of "uncompletedness" which she differentiates from "incompleteness." This distinction between that which is essentially and eternally in a fixed state of "incompleteness," and that which maintains the potential (grammatical and literal) to become complete – "uncompletedness" – is deeply important in Rossetti's theo-poetics. If Rossetti's categorization of "Old Testament servants of God" – Jews of the Hebrew Scriptures – maintains a possibility for "completedness" through the subsequent narrative of Christ, then Rossetti's representations of unconverted Jewish identity remain figures of deficiency in much of her writing. Just as "a line [must be] drawn somewhere" to determine gendered difference in this world only to be dissolved in the next (Christian world), so too, it seems, must a line be drawn between Old Testament Jews who can be read as potentially Christian/complete in the future, and those who remain in a state of incompleteness, namely those "real Jews" who persistently refuse to acknowledge Christ as messiah. Understanding the distinctions in Rossetti's quite particular interpretations of Jewish difference reveals, ultimately, an acute anti-Judaism as a central aspect of her poetics; in addition, it becomes clear that there were very specific connections between her theories of Jewish and female difference.

Rossetti's attitudes toward Jewishness remain almost remarkably untalked about in critical circles; in general, the poems have been linked either to discourses of gender identity or Christianity without connection to the discourse of Jewishness. Because no critical attention has been played to figures of Jewishness in Rossetti's theology, the lack of attention to Rossetti's understanding of religious difference also affects the way critics have interpreted her theories of gendered difference. Thus, her critical heritage has been unable to articulate a cohesive pattern for her theories of theology, gender, and poetry. Feminist critics in particular have been at a loss to explain how Rossetti's devout religious identity can coincide with a woman's artistic and imaginative self – as I explored in chapter 1 of this book. Angela Leighton has written, in reference to the letter to Augusta Webster cited above, that "[Rossetti's] sympathies, as so often in her writings, run against her religious interests. She concludes [the letter], defensively and illogically, 'I do not think the present social movements tend on the whole to uphold Xtianity' . . . But meanwhile, the grounds of her opposition have slipped from under her racing, forward thinking pen" (Leighton, *Victorian Women Poets: Writing Against the Heart*, 128). Leighton's comments on Rossetti's "forward thinking pen" rely on her assumption that Rossetti's "domestic devotion and religious fervor" are only a "public facade ... behind which her imagination had plenty of room to play" (129). In Leighton's formulation, Rossetti's religious beliefs have little or no bearing on her theories of women's identity, poetry or indeed her poetic imagination. Linda Peterson takes a different approach to Rossetti's interest in female identity, art and religion; Peterson writes that Rossetti uses female figures in her poetry to suggest that women are "faithful readers of the scriptures. Because they are so, they can become fulfillments – and fulfillers – of biblical types and allusions ... Rossetti ... makes her women active and original typologists of everyday life" ("Restoring the Book," 223). Peterson's argument suggests that Rossetti was clearly concerned with the position of the "other" (female) readers of Scriptures, and my readings expand on the idea that Rossetti was deeply concerned with the reading practices of not only women, but also Jews, in their identity both as sanctioned "Old Testament" prophets and as real Jewish people in Victorian life.

Revealing the anti-Judaism that structures Rossetti's women-centered approach to typology, it becomes clear that she used her imaginative and artistic powers in the service of her specific commitments to Christian theology, rather than despite that religious commitment.[6] I argue that through her own Christian understanding of Jewishness, both Biblical and contemporary, Rossetti came up with a way to understand difference itself, and it is this model of difference that helps construct her complex notion of female identity as well. This chapter begins by exploring *Seek and Find* and the relationships between Rossetti's theology of Jewish and gendered difference; from these texts I then turn to poems which explicitly take up allusions to the Hebrew Scriptures, and are rarely read in current Rossetti criticism. By looking first at Rossetti's less read poetry and prose work which make explicit how she constructs Jewish identity, I will go on to see how this paradigm operates in two of her most canonized works – *Goblin Market* and the sonnet sequence "Monna Innominata," suggesting that Rossetti's understanding of gender identity was always imbedded within a discourse of religious (Christian/Jewish) difference.[7]

"MAGNIFY MINE OFFICE": JEWISHNESS AND FEMALENESS
IN *SEEK AND FIND*

One recurring problem in Rossetti criticism is that little of the work examines Rossetti's prose and poetry simultaneously, and so critics rely on brief comments in letters or biographical material to provide a larger context in which to place Rossetti's poetry.[8] In what follows, I use Rossetti's comments on both gendered and religious difference from her prose work

Seek and Find (1879) as a frame with which to consider some of her poetry on similar topics. *Seek and Find* was the second in the list of devotional prose works that Rossetti wrote in the last twenty years of her life and was the first to be published by The Society for the Promotion of Christian Knowledge (SPCK); it reflects her increasing emphasis on so called "devotional" prose writing in the latter part of her career. Although P. G. Stanwood has suggested that "little about *Seek and Find* is original apart from its ingenious structure and telling arrangement of biblical texts" ("Christina Rossetti's Devotional Prose," 234), I would argue it is in fact this "ingenious" structure of *Seek and Find* that works to recast the very idea of "originality" within a Christian framework.[9] Rossetti's approach in this text challenges how we might conceive of "originality" in an explicitly religious world view; the alternation between Rossetti's own glosses and her use of scriptural evidence implies that no human idea is ever purely original but is rather always contained within the totality of God's creation and God's word – and in the case of *Seek and Find*, Anglican liturgy itself. *Seek and Find* thus serves as a testament to how women writers assert alternative interpretations of Scripture even as they use Scripture to support and authorize their ideas.

The title itself is suggestive of the ways Rossetti imagines her authorial role; rather than creator or original translator, she typifies herself as a Christian thinker who "seeks" understandings of a given issue/topic, and can be assured of "finding" that answer in Scripture and Christian doctrine. *Seek and Find* is thus basically a series of what seem to be free associations Rossetti makes between Biblical passages from an Anglican devotional text, the Benedicite, and her own Biblical and metaphorical glosses.[10] The volume is divided into two larger sections, titled "The First Series: Creation" and "The Second Series: Redemption"; each of these larger sections is divided into chapters which take their titles from the actual words which make up the text of the Benedicite: for example, sections are headed: "All Works," "Showers and Dews," "Israel," and "Servants of the Lord."

Significantly, with the exception of one key passage I will examine later, Rossetti rarely mentions that she is a woman author in this text. Even her "Prefatory Note" skirts the issue of gender:

In writing the following pages, when I have consulted a Harmony it has been that of the late Rev. Isaac Williams.

Any textual elucidations, as I know neither Hebrew nor Greek, are simply based upon some translation; many valuable alternative readings being found in the Margin of an ordinary Reference Bible. (3)

If we compare this preface to any of Barrett Browning's, it is clear that Rossetti constructs her authority in a manner almost antithetical to her poetic predecessor; where Barrett Browning repeatedly asserts her own learning in Hebrew and Greek as a source of authority, Rossetti denies her ability to read in the original languages. Associating herself with Isaac Williams, Rossetti situates herself in association with a prominent Tractarian writer and simultaneously as "any" Christian who has access to an "ordinary Reference Bible."[11] But if her critics associate Rossetti and her ideas with those of the Tractarians (often one way critics thus deny to her an "original" theology), it is important to note that all of those theologians were part of a major religious movement primarily located in the all-male institutions of Oxford University. Clearly without any of the institutional privileges that accompanied real "membership" in this group, Rossetti thus claims her authority to write and speak precisely because she only has access to that which any Christian might claim: an ability to read an "ordinary Reference Bible." Indeed, unlike Barrett Browning and more like Grace Aguilar, Rossetti separates herself from scholars, positioning herself as a universal Christian "everywoman" "seeking" and "finding" ways to understand the natural and divine world through recourse to authorized Scripture.[12]

Though not explicit about her female authorial identity in the text, Rossetti does pay special attention to various tropes of femaleness as they emerge in Scripture, both Old and New Testament. An example of her complex use of Biblical female imagery occurs in the Second Series section, "Ice and Snow":

Symbols, parables, analogies, inferences, may be fascinating, must be barren, unless we make them to ourselves words of the wise which are as goads (Eccles. XII. 11). Let us imitate the practical example of that virtuous woman who "is not afraid of the snow for her household: for all her household are clothed with scarlet" (Prov. XXXI. 10–31); and copying her we shall become trustworthy, loving, prudent, diligent . . .
Yet so long as each one of us gives all diligence to make her own personal calling and election sure (2 St. Peter I. 10), it will do us no harm to recognise in this saintly spouse a figure of the Church: that great Mother and Mistress (Gal. IV. 26) who because her whole family was washed and beautified in the blood of Christ (Rev. VII. 13, 14) has no need to fear any transitory creature . . . (223–4)

Rossetti begins by commenting on how to understand "symbols, parables, analogies, inferences" correctly: by connecting them "to ourselves . . . [as] words of the wise"; thus, her discussion of "Ice and Snow"

immediately goes to the use of the term "snow" in the passage on the virtuous woman in Proverbs. The first point is to find a literal and "practical"
understanding of snow for women; if one has been "trustworthy, loving,
prudent, diligent" (and "clothed" a household sufficiently) there is no
need to fear snow – or its metaphorical meaning of earthly challenges.

After exploring the particular, literal meaning of her passage, Rossetti
allows that this figure of the virtuous wife also has a larger, more "universal" meaning. Here, she continues to offer instruction on the proper
ways to interpret Scripture in the realm of one's own life, suggesting
that finding a more figural meaning is only sanctionable ("will do . . . no
harm") after the literal or "plain" meaning of the text is identified. By the
end of the passage, Rossetti moves to the more universalized symbolic
understandings of this "spouse," as a "figure of the Church," that is, as a
figure with much larger implications than simply a literal wife; instead,
the "wife" becomes symbolic for the Church, and all Christians. With
this attention to exegetical technique, she illustrates how devout women
make their own kinds of meaning from Biblical texts. Indeed, Rossetti
emphasizes the importance of female imagery throughout this passage
with the use of terms like "barren" as well as her use of the feminine pronoun "her." That pronoun suggests that for her all Christians reading
this passage are female or at least feminized in their role in emulating
the "virtuous woman."

Of course, this symbolic use of female identity as a figure for a religious community itself is a strategy that occurs in both Hebrew and
Christian Scriptures. In both cases, the governing figure is of heterosexual marriage; in the Hebrew Scriptures, the Israelites are figured in a
conjugal relationship to God, and similarly in the New Testament, as we
see above, the Church (community of Christians and/or the institution of
the Anglican Church itself) is understood to become Christ's bride, with
Jesus figured as the Bridegroom.[13] In these spousal metaphors, maleness
is always linked to the divine role, while femaleness is always linked to the
non-divine human community. Thus, as many before me have argued,
maleness is reserved in these systems for whatever term is understood
to be transcendent and dominant. What is interesting about this rather
common strategy of feminizing an entire religious community, however,
is that by making the heterosexual relationship a metaphor for the relationship between the human (female) and divine (male) attributes, the
discourse of gender difference between actual women and men on earth
is erased. By figuring the entire earthly Christian community as female,
then, Rossetti can pass over the limitations placed on actual women,

suggesting that symbolically at least, all Christians are positioned as figurative women. It is a formula which only functions, however, when there are no actual men in the picture to disrupt the construction of an idealized female Christian realm.

Indeed, we can see how much more complicated the issues of gender identity and Christian symbolism become when Rossetti does try to include the hierarchical relationship between mortal (as opposed to divine) men and woman, specifically in *Seek and Find*. In the First Series chapter titled "Sun and Moon," Rossetti explores a number of approaches to gendered difference; the chapter opens with the passage from Genesis 1: 16: "God made two great lights; the greater light to rule the day, and the lesser light to rule the night." Rossetti then writes:

Both lights great: one exceeding the other: both good. Such a gradation of greater and less, both being acceptable to Him Who made them, pervades much if not the whole of the world in which we live: sun and moon, man and woman; or to ascend to the supreme instance, Christ and His Church. I, being a woman, will copy St. Paul's example and "magnify mine office" (Rom. XI. 13). (29–30)

The tension in this passage comes from Rossetti's rapidly shifting examples of the concept of "greater or less." In the first sentence she begins by claiming "both" as great, then "one" as better, then "both" again as "good." She summarizes this pattern by stating that though there is "gradation," both elements are "acceptable to Him Who made them." This explanation of difference becomes infinitely more complicated at the moment Rossetti identifies herself: "I, being a woman" and then connects this assertion of identity to a specific moment in Paul's Epistle to the Romans.

This allusion to Paul and his "magnif[ied] . . . office" implicitly adds Jewish difference to the list of hierarchies "sun and moon, man and woman . . . Christ and His Church" examined in this paragraph. Chapter 11 from Paul's Epistle to the Romans concerns Paul's plea for the Gentiles' conversion; the verse to which Rossetti alludes, combined with the subsequent verse that completes Paul's sentence reads: "For I speak to you Gentiles, inasmuch as I am the apostle of the Gentiles, I magnify mine office: If by any means I may provoke to emulation *them which are* my flesh, and might save some of them" (Romans 11: 13–14, King James Version). Throughout this Epistle, Paul uses his own past identity as Jew in conjunction with his present identity as a Christian to explain the difference between the Jewish and Christian covenant. Arguing that God has not "cast away his people," Paul argues that the conversion of the Gentiles is also a way to promote Jewish conversion. In this context, Paul asserts his authority to speak by claiming a dual identification: he is a Jew in "flesh," even as he speaks as a Christian who has transformed himself from a Jew inwardly. Thus, he is both Jew and not Jew in his identity as a Christian speaking to Gentiles, and he acknowledges that his doubled identity offers him a "magnified" speaking power.

When Rossetti compares herself to Paul in her specific discussion of gender difference, she makes a clear link between the apparent lesser position of a woman, and Paul's previous "lesser" position as a Jew. Rossetti thus links Jewish and female identity as analogous "lesser" states which can "magnify" themselves. In Paul's case, magnification comes from Christian conversion; to follow the rhetorical logic of Rossetti's assertion, her "magnification" from the lesser state of woman also comes from her identification with Christianity. With her own doubled identity as woman in flesh and Christian in spirit, Rossetti can likewise claim authority to speak to those who are not women, just as Paul claimed his magnified authority to speak to Gentiles. However, Rossetti's analogy – between her "lesser" position as woman, who magnifies her identity, as it were, through her Christian belief, and Paul's once "lesser" position as Jew who magnifies his identity through Christian belief – cannot be carried to its logical completion because the premise which makes it possible – the figure of conversion – cannot generally function in a system of sexual identity.[14] To really emulate Paul as she describes, Rossetti would have to undergo a similar conversion to become a man from having been a woman, just as he became a Christian from a Jew.

Rossetti's subsequent passage recognizes this potential problem in her logic, and to help resolve this contradiction, she introduces a new hierarchy with which to recast her discussion of sameness and difference in gendered and religious terms.

Probably there were in his day persons who rated the Apostle of the Gentiles, as such, far below the Apostle of the Jews (1 Cor. IX. 1–6; Gal. II.8), and one aspect of truth may have been honoured by such an estimate: yet was not the estimate exhaustive, for it was not one which embraced the entire field of God's Love towards His human family. (*Seek and Find*, 30)

Here, directly following her own admission of her "lesser" gender, Rossetti explores the interpretative problem of assigning value to any kind of hierarchical value to individuals. Thus, she suggests that one level of "estimation" might consider Paul as one "who rated . . . far below" Peter "the apostle of the circumcised" (Galatians 2: 8), yet she suggests that such an hierarchical classification only has "one aspect of truth" since it does not take into account "the entire field of God's Love towards his human family." In other words, whenever the notions of greater and lesser are attached, whether to sun and moon, man and woman, Paul and Peter, or even Jew and Christian, such an hierarchy does not fully consider the implications of God's love, which in its ostensible universality erases all attribution of hierarchy itself.

Directly after posing this statement about the falseness of hierarchy in God's scheme, Rossetti returns to the problem of female difference in the next paragraph, and offers a new idea on the subject of female identity, this time considering women's link to Christ.

In many points the feminine lot copies very closely the voluntarily assumed position of our Lord and Pattern. Woman must obey: and Christ "learned obedience" (Gen III.16; Heb. V. 8). She must be fruitful, but in sorrow: and He, symbolized by a corn of wheat, had not brought forth much fruit except He had died (Gen. III. 16, St. John XII.24). She by natural constitution is adapted not to assert herself, but to be subordinate: and He came not to be ministered unto but to minister; He was among His own "as he that serveth" (1 St. Peter III.7; 1 Tim. II. 11,12; St. Mark x. 45; St. Luke XXII. 27). Her office is to be man's helpmeet: and concerning Christ God saith, "I have laid help upon One that is mighty" (Gen. II.18, 21, 22; Ps. LXXXIX. 19). And well may she glory, inasmuch as one of the tenderest divine promises takes (so to say) the feminine form: "As one whom his mother comforteth, so will I comfort you" (Is. LXVI. 13). (30–1).

In this passage, Rossetti tries to resolve the problem that her comparison with Paul raised, namely, how can a woman ever be as complete a Christian as a man, given that Christ was a man on earth? Her solution, of course, is to invoke Christ's identity as symbolically female. This overt connection between Christ and the "feminine lot" privileges women as the true "imitators" of Christ; Rossetti lists the assumed qualities of female character – "obedience," non-assertiveness, the ability to "minister" and "mother" – as parallels between Christ and women. But by connecting women's identity as passive helpmeet to Christ's identity as "minister," or by universalizing the idea of the "good wife" to describe all Christians, Rossetti must deny the other more traditional construction of Christ as one who took the form of a human man, an aspect of Christ's identity she often obscures.

Having claimed Christ as essentially female, Rossetti constructs what is often understood as lack into completeness, but the formulation only holds if all references to Christ's human maleness are erased from the equation. In the final passage in this chapter of *Seek and Find*, Rossetti moves back to her discussion of the relative merits of "sun and moon" and in so doing returns to the "problem" of an hierarchical understanding of gender difference, still trying to come to a resolution.

It used to be popularly supposed that "the moon walking in brightness" (Job XXXI, 26) is no more than a mirror reflecting the sun's radiance: now careful observation leads towards the hypothesis that she may also exhibit inherent luminosity. But if our proud waves will after all not be stayed or at any rate not be allayed (for stayed they must be) by the limit of God's ordinance concerning our sex, one final consolation yet remains to careful and troubled hearts: in Christ there is neither male nor female, for we are all one (Gal. III. 28). (31–2)

Rossetti asserts that the woman, here figured by the moon, has an "inherent luminosity" and so suggests that women have their own particular virtues that are not comparable or dependent on the relationship to men.[15] But if her subsequent statement addresses those "careful and troubled hearts," the obliqueness of this term does not really specify who these hearts might be. Given the context it seems they could be anyone who is troubled by the "problem" of women's rights in Rossetti's historical moment. Rossetti's conclusion to the problem, that "we are all one" in Christ, suggests that for Christians, the relative evaluation of men and woman's identity is a moot discussion, and she insists on shifting the terms of the argument to the moment of salvation when gender will apparently be abolished as a category. Finally, with her allusion to Galatians 3: 28, Rossetti makes one more implicit connection between religious and gendered difference; the passage to which she refers offers an extended Biblical discussion about the position of Jews in Christianity. The entire verse she paraphrases reads: "There is neither Jew nor Greek, there is neither bond nor free, there is neither male nor female: for ye are all one in Christ Jesus." Thus, through a Biblical passage on the meaning of Jewish identity, Rossetti finds answers for her questions about female identity.

Summarizing how Rossetti constructs gender and religious difference in *Seek and Find*, I want to emphasize how her total investment in a Christian epistemology that asserts that we are all "one in Christ" means that the entire concept of difference is recast for Rossetti. Perhaps the clearest articulation of the "difference" between Jews and Christians occurs in the First Series chapter titled "Servants of the Lord" cited at the beginning of this chapter, a passage which gains a certain clarity after the previous examination of Jewish and gendered difference in the other passages:

When as samples of Old Testament servants of God we select some (since we cannot discuss all), who evidently and eminently have prefigured Christ, at the least in some point of their career, we shall many times find them characterized by that very uncompletedness (if I may term it so for I mean a very different thing from the defect named incompleteness) which we have been considering. (147)

Rossetti's distinction between the idea of "incompleteness" and "uncompletedness" is a significant moment in her negotiations with the entire problem of both gendered and religious difference. The terms are distinguishable through temporal implications: "uncomplet*ed*ness" gives a temporal quality to the state of "lack," which allows for the future possibility of becoming completed. "Incompleteness," on the other hand, has no temporal component, implying instead a permanent quality of lack. The "Old Testament servants of God" are not in a state of permanent lack, nor are they "other" to some understanding of Christian identity; instead, they have potential, through the process of Christian interpretation, for "completedness," or total Christian identification. Though she repeatedly imagines Jews and certain women as deficient identities, essentially incomplete at any given present moment, both have (through Christian belief and a typological insertion in Christian narrative) the ability to achieve totality, completeness, and equality.

For Rossetti, Christian identity could eradicate difference, otherness, and deficiency in the world to come, if not in the earthly realm. In such a model of personal transformation, which we might identify as archetypally Christian in construct, the one category that remains totally other is comprised of those figures that refuse spiritual transformation, namely, unconverted Jews living in contemporary (as opposed to Biblical) society, who insistently assert their "incompletion" in their refusal to convert from "uncompletedness." It is this mistake of claiming one's limited, partial identity as somehow "complete" that likewise threatens women who seek "equality" or "completion" on earth; they, like Jews, are missing the larger Christian picture that Rossetti suggests is visible to the 'humble orthodox Xtian." This concern with the lack that marks Jewish identity is replicated in Rossetti's concerns about the Jewish texts that are imbedded in the Christian Bible, and she gives special attention to the texts of Hebrew prophecy in a number of her poems.

"AS A TALE ENDS THAT IS TOLD": ROSSETTI'S DIALOGUE
WITH HEBREW PROPHECY

"By the Waters of Babylon B.C. 570" and "Christian and Jew: A
Dialogue" are not poems that have received much attention in Rossetti
scholarship, nor do they appear in any recent anthologies. Both poems,
however, are extremely important because they indicate the complexity with which Rossetti approached Hebrew prophetic texts. In "By the
Waters of Babylon B.C. 570," Rossetti produces a dramatic monologue
in the voice of a Jew during the Babylonian captivity, a poem which –
without careful analysis – might indeed seem to "paraphrase the Bible"
(see chapter 1). Yet with closer attention, it becomes clear that Rossetti is
exploring the dynamics of Jewish prophecy from a specifically Christian
perspective by imbedding this "Jewish" voice within a larger Christian
authorial structure. "Christian and Jew: A Dialogue" takes a similar
interest in issues of Jewish and Christian voice as it reworks the words
of the Hebrew prophet Ezekiel in subtle and very radical ways to highlight the hegemony of Christian belief. Understanding the ways Rossetti
constructs Jewish/Hebraic prophetic texts in these two lesser-known
poems is crucial to understanding her concern with Jewishness in *Goblin
Market* and "Monna Innominata."

There are a number of references throughout "By the Waters of
Babylon B.C. 570" that suggest Rossetti is offering her version of
Jeremiah's Lamentations. The reference to the "foes" who "hiss" refers to
the enemies of Judah in Lamentations 2: 15–16; the lengthy description in lines 52–60 of the defilement of the speaker's "daughters,"
"sisters," and "wives" echoes Jeremiah's repeated figures of Israel as
a fallen and captive woman;[16] in Lamentations 5: 1 the speaker implores
God to "remember" just as Rossetti's speaker does in line 81 of her
poem. These are only a few of the allusions to Lamentations; Rossetti's
interest in this particular moment of Jewish history suggests that she
closely identifies Hebraic identity with this moment of the fall into captivity, a moment that seems to call for the redemption which Christian
epistemology would claim only Christ brings to Jewish history.[17]

Rossetti calls on the structure of Lamentations in which the speaker
alternates between a description of his own personal suffering and the
collective suffering of his people. Her poem begins:

> Here, where I dwell, I waste to skin and bone;
>   The curse is come upon me, and I waste
>   In penal torment powerless to atone.

> The curse is come on me, which makes no haste
>   And doth not tarry, crushing both the proud
>   Hard man and him the sinner double-faced.
> Look not upon me, for my soul is bowed
>   Within me, as is my body in this mire;
>   My soul crawls dumb-struck, sore bestead and cowed.
>   . . .
>   So we the elect ones perish in his ire.   (lines 1–9, 12)

The shift from first person to the collective "we" in line 12 echoes
Jeremiah's construction of his voice as both the voice of Jews in general and the voice of one particular Jew and allows Rossetti to cast her
own speaker as a representative male Jew. But whereas many of these
images come straight from Jeremiah's text, Rossetti's manipulation of
poetic form works to emphasize certain aspects of this Jewish condition. The enjambments on "waste," "proud," and "bowed" highlight
the mythic crimes of the Jews in their "wastefulness" of God's grace and
natural bounty and their "pride" which is at the root of their loss of God's
love.

While she sets up certain parallels with Jeremiah's voice in Lamentations, Rossetti also transforms many of the key themes in Jeremiah's
text to fit her particular vision of Jewish identity. Rossetti represents the
subjectivity of the Jew through repeated images of the speaker's belief
that God has forsaken him and his people, and further that their remorse
is all in "vain."

> Vainly we gird on sackcloth, vainly kneel
>   With famished faces toward Jerusalem:
>   His heart is shut against us not to feel,
> His ears against our cry He shutteth them,
>   His hand He shorteneth that He will not save,
>   His law is loud against us to condemn . . .
>   (lines 13–18)

These lines echo many of the sentiments from Lamentations, but
Rossetti's version transforms Jeremiah's construction of the Jewish relation to God quite significantly. While Jeremiah repeatedly recounts
God's refusal to "hear" and "rescue" the Jewish people because they
have transgressed his covenant, Jeremiah – from a Jewish perspective –
also maintains a belief in God's eventual forgiveness in lines like "For the
Lord will not cast off for ever" (Lamentations 3: 31), or more explicitly in
3: 21 when Jeremiah states he can "recall" the knowledge of his own past

suffering which was once alleviated, so that "therefore [he] has hope" for the future; Rossetti's speaker seems, on the other hand, to have no hope of redemption within a Jewish framework.

Rossetti's reworking of Jeremiah's text repeatedly emphasizes the loss of connection between God and the Jewish speaker, a revision that becomes most evident by comparing the poem's last eleven lines to the end of Lamentations. The last verses of Lamentations in the King James translation end as follows:

19. Thou, O Lord, remainest for ever; thy throne from generation to generation.
20. Wherefore dost thou forget us for ever, *and* forsake us so long time?
21. Turn thou us unto thee, O Lord, and we shall be turned; renew our days as of old.
22. But thou hast utterly rejected us; thou art very wroth against us.

Jeremiah emphasizes the ongoing nature of Jewish history, symbolized by God's unchanging presence from "generation to generation." The change in the Jewish condition can result only if God "turns" Jews back to righteous ways so that they "shall be turned"; redemption is figured as an activity which God controls. For Jeremiah, the process of redemption is not figured as a "conversion" or "turn" of Jewish identity, but rather as a shift in God's attitude toward the Jewish people as they remain Jewish in perpetuity.

Not surprisingly, Rossetti's text revises this understanding of the ongoing nature of Jewish history and identity. The last lines of her version of Jeremiah's text read:

> Yet now, before our sun grow dark at noon,
> Before we come to nought beneath Thy rod,
>   Before we go down quick into the pit,
>   Remember us for good, O God, our God: –
> Thy name will I remember, praising it,
>   Tho' Thou forget me, tho' Thou hide Thy face,
>   And blot me from the Book which Thou hast writ;
> The name will I remember in my praise
>   And call to mind Thy faithfulness of old,
> Tho' as a weaver Thou cut off my days
>   And end me as a tale ends that is told.
>
> (lines 78–88)

Rossetti removes the sense of hope that Jeremiah insists on in his text; in this poem the Jew has no ability to imagine redemption from his current position as "fallen." Even as her Jew states that he will "remember"

God's "name" twice, this action is rendered "in vain" by the repeated dependent clauses "Tho' Thou forget me, tho' Thou hide Thy face" and most significantly "Tho' as a weaver Thou cut off my days / And end me as a tale ends that is told." These final lines echo Lamentations 3: 53–4, in which Jeremiah refers to the way his enemies "cut off [his] life, and then states "I am cut off"; it is a present-tense utterance that does not suggest a permanent removal from God. Rossetti's transformation of the line offers a radical revision of Jeremiah's own notion of God's eternal presence in his life. For Rossetti has her speaker state that it is God, not the "enemies," who "cut[s him] off"; thus, where Jeremiah's text emphasizes the ongoing emotional relationship – in this case anger – that insists there is still some kind of connection between God and the Jews, Rossetti reorganizes these relationships to emphasize a total break and end in that Jewish / God relationship, figuring Jewish history and identity as something "end[ed]" because it has been "told."

Rossetti's last image of the Jew as "end[ed] . . . as a tale ends that is told" emphasizes how the structure of the dramatic monologue situates the speaking voice of the character within the absorptive poetic agency of the seemingly absent (Christian) author/poet. That is, there is an implicit connection between the Christian absorption of Jewish history and Rossetti's own authorial absorption of Jeremiah's voice into her dramatic monologue. In both cases Jewish history and Jewish identity are "end[ed]" at the moment their "tale" is told. The specific title of this poem situates a Jewish end in the Babylonian captivity, and with Rossetti's complex revision, her Jewish speaker becomes a prophet not of Jewish redemption, but of the future destruction of Judaism, an historical narrative that this speaker states will "end" like a story or tale, superseded by the "tale" or narrative of Christianity. When Rossetti has her Jewish speaker include a passing reference to a future messiah "One shall fill thy seat/Born of thy body, as the sun and moon/Stablished for aye in sovereignty complete" (lines 73–5), she intends her audience to read this in a standard Christian way, as a reference to Jesus Christ. From this perspective, when her Jewish speaker thus prays "O Lord, remember David and that soon!" (line 76) he becomes a "naive" Christian prophet, but only to a Christian reader who recognizes what his apparently "ignorant" reference to Jesus means. The dramatic monologue provides the perfect structure for the presentation of a "naive" speaker from Jewish history; indeed, Rossetti seems to be adopting the strategy Robert Browning used in many of his dramatic monologues, spoken in the voices of the unconverted who shared Christ's historical moment.[18]

Rossetti returns to an exploration of Jewish/Christian relationship in her poem "Christian and Jew: A Dialogue." In this poem, also rarely explored in Rossetti criticism, Rossetti creates a dialogue to represent what Jewish and Christian identity might look like, or rather sound like, in conversation. Significantly, unlike "By the Waters of Babylon B.C. 570," this poem resists location in a particular historical time period, suggesting that the individual speakers in the poem engage in a timeless dialogue between Judaism and Christianity; however, as the poem progresses, it becomes clear that both participants do not share equally in linguistic, indeed prophetic, speaking power.

The opening stanza gives a general indication of the essential theological difference between Jews and Christians, as well as their relationship to each other; the quotation marks are only marks in change of voice, as the poem begins in the voice of the Christian, then alternates with the Jew.

> "O happy happy land!
> Angels like rushes stand
>   About the wells of light." –
>   "Alas I have not eyes for this fair sight:
> Hold fast my hand." –   (lines 1–5)

This stanza creates a pattern repeated for the next four stanzas; the Christian asserts an ability to "see" and "hear" certain visionary sights and sounds in Paradise; the Jew, however, seems to lack the sensory ability to perceive what the Christian can, stating "Alas, I have not eyes for this fair sight" (line 4); "I cannot see so far" (line 9); "I look in vain above / And miss their [seraphim's] hymn" (lines 15–16); and finally, in response to the Christian's joy in hearing the angels' song: "I do not hear them, I" (line 21). In all these instances the Jew is figured as "lacking" the sensory ability to perceive the joys of Christian redemption; as the first stanza suggests, the Jew is dependent ("hold fast my hand") on the Christian's more powerful vision, hearing – and speaking.

With the Jew's apparent inability to perceive and speak of Paradise, the Christian voice takes over this dialogue in stanzas 5–8, offering a richly imaged description of Christian redemption in Heaven, where it seems that being "elect" is linked with one's ability to "sing to the Lord" in the eighth stanza; the Christian voice states:

> "Sing to the Lord,
>   All spirits of all flesh, sing:
> For He hath not abhorred

Our low estate nor scorn'd our offering:
Shout to our King." –   (lines 38–42)

The phrase "Sing to the Lord" offers many Biblical echoes, not least
of which is Miriam and Moses' song at the Red Sea – "Sing ye to the
Lord." But in "Christian and Jew: A Dialogue," it is the mark of the
"saved" Christian to be able to offer song; the Jew, on the other hand,
is marked throughout the poem by a far less skillful – and passive –
vocal agency. One of the most interesting ways Rossetti represents the
difference between Jewish and Christian speech in this poem is in how
she designates which speaker gets to say what passages from what Biblical
texts. In response to the Christian's elaborate and optimistic description
of Paradise, the Jewish speaker responds in language that echoes the
prophetic texts of the Jewish prophet Jeremiah as well as Lamentations,
both of which repeatedly liken the condition of Israel to that of a fallen
woman.

> "But Zion said:
>   My Lord forgetteth me.
> Lo, she hath made her bed
>   In dust; forsaken weepeth she
>   Where alien rivers swell the sea.
>
> "She laid her body as the ground,
>   Her tender body as the ground to those
> Who passed; her harpstrings cannot sound
>   In a strange land; discrowned
>   She sits, and drunk with woes." –
>   (lines 43–52)

Here, where the Jewish voice is given an opportunity to describe Jewish
identity in relation to God, it calls on the metaphor of the fallen woman's
body, a common trope for Jewish prophetic anguish. This figure casts
the Jewish community in terms of a "forsaken" feminized body, as well
as one whose "harpstrings cannot sound."

Rossetti's choice to link Jewishness with an explicitly female image
from the Bible is reflective of the ways Jewish identity and female identity get linked as "lesser" in other of her writings as well. The poem creates
an image of Jewish weakness and fallenness, as well as a feminized passivity for the Jewish voice; the Christian voice of this poem is, by comparison, powerful and morally superior, and not associated in any way

with femaleness. As the poem closes, the spiritual limitation of the Jew is reflected as a vocal limitation when the Christian says to the Jew: "Be not afraid, arise, be no more dumb;/Arise, shine/For thy light is come" (lines 55–7). This attribution of "dumbness" is particularly interesting in a poem that is termed "a dialogue," for the idea that the Jew has been "dumb" contradicts that fact that there has been a Jewish speaker throughout the poem! The problem, of course, is that the Jew remains unable to speak the language of Revelation about which the Christian speaker has so much to say.

The final stanza of the poem completes the erasure of Jewish prophetic authority and voice by rewriting a passage from Ezekiel. The direct scriptural source for this passage is Ezekiel 37, in which God sets Ezekiel down in a "valley full of bones"; the passage Rossetti invokes reads (King James Version) "And he said to me, Son of Man, Can these bones live? And I answered, O Lord God, thou knowest" (Ezekiel 37: 3); the entire passage serves as part of an extended lesson to Ezekiel about the power of God's ongoing covenant with the people of Israel. Rossetti offers her own complex re-enactment of this passage in her last stanza; following the dialogic structure of the poem, the quotation marks here indicate that the Jew speaks the first line, and the Christian responds:

> "Can these bones live?" –
>   "God knows:
> The prophet saw such clothed with flesh and skin,
> A wind blew on them and life entered in,
> They shook and rose.
>   Hasten the time, O Lord, blot out their sin,
>   Let life begin."   (lines 58–64)

Rossetti's recasting of this prophetic moment actually rewrites the original text quite radically. In the Biblical text of Ezekiel, it is God who asks "Can these bones live"; in giving that line now to the Jew in the poem, Rossetti totally transforms the rhetorical context of the scriptural scene. For when God asks Ezekiel this question in the Biblical text, it is necessarily a rhetorical question; God poses it merely to set the stage for his subsequent "raising" of the bones to life. But when the Jew in "Christian and Jew: A Dialogue" addresses this question to the Christian, it becomes a seemingly genuine question from a bereft Jewish speaker who must turn to the Christian voice for any access to God; further, in this rhetorical setting, the phrase "these bones" seems self-referential, rather than referring to an abstracted valley of unidentified bones. Further, in the Biblical passage, it is Ezekiel, the Jewish prophet, who answers God's question with "O Lord God, thou knowest." In Rossetti's version, how-ever, when the Christian says "God knows," there is an echo of Ezekiel's Biblical words, but Rossetti's text implies that the Christian also knows the answer God speaks, that is, has access to God's knowledge; it is only the Jew in the poem who does not know the "truth." Playing with the different voices in the text of Ezekiel allows Rossetti to recast divine au-thority as always related to the Christian's voice, while the Jew, ironically, speaks God's words in total ignorance – much in the way classic Christian typology recasts the Jewish authority of Hebrew prophets into claiming a specifically Christian authority. In both "By the Waters of Babylon B.C. 570" and "Christian and Jew: A Dialogue," Rossetti constructs the Jew/Hebrew as a distinct other who can rarely be granted a voice and identity outside of a connection to Christian structures or narratives.

These poems which draw on Jewish prophetic texts help us understand the ways Rossetti conceptualized Jewish difference both historically and theologically. What can we glean from this writing about Rossetti's at-titudes and constructions of an unconverted Jewishness which was an increasingly present identity/community in her own historical moment? Though both these poems seem particularly concerned with an ab-stracted and Biblical Jewishness, Rebecca Crump, the modern editor of Rossetti's complete poems, identifies "Christian and Jew: A Dialogue" as written in 1858, the very same year Jews won the right to sit in Par-liament; "By the Waters of Babylon B.C. 570" was composed in 1864. When we situate these poems in that historical moment, then, it is hard to ignore the connection between Rossetti's exploration of Jewish identity and the rise of a politically empowered Jewish identity – a literal Jewish voice in England. For Rossetti, Jewishness belongs in the past of what was for her a profoundly Christian present; the idea of an ongoing, un-converted Jewish presence in Victorian England must have been a quite troubling idea from her theological perspective. At the moment when a Jew could be seen as a literal subject and "political representative" of England, there were distinct theo-literary efforts – as I also explored in chapter 2 – to recontextualize Jewishness as silent, non-prophetic, and non-authoritative – an effort in which Rossetti clearly participates in the poems and texts explored above, as well as in *Goblin Market*, explored in the next section.

GOBLIN MARKET: ROSSETTI'S REWRITING
OF HEBREW PROPHECY

Ho, every one that thirsteth, come ye to the waters, and he that hath no money;
come ye, buy, and eat; yea, come, buy wine and milk without money and without
price. (Isaiah 55: 1)

> "Come buy," call the goblins
> Hobbling down the glen.
> "Oh," cried Lizzie, "Laura, Laura,
> You should not peep at goblin men."
> (*Goblin Market*, lines 46–9)

In *Goblin Market* (1859), Rossetti brings together ideas about Jewish
Biblical prophecy with a larger commentary on the meaning of contemporary Jewish identity in a Christian culture; in so doing, she creates a
lush theological fantasy of Jewish erasure. Yet the clear echoes between
the texts of Jewish prophecy, specifically Isaiah, and this poem have
never been revealed in the seemingly endless commentary on this poem.
Goblin Market has more often been examined as part of a "women's literary tradition," as a poem explicitly concerned with women's experience
and the female poetic identity. For many critics, it represents Rossetti's
most original treatment of themes that recur often in her poetry: sibling
relationships, female experience, and redemptive Christian narratives.[19]
Reading *Goblin Market* in context with the texts of the previous section,
I will argue that the construction of a redemptive "heroic" female identity is completely dependent on a bifurcated and ultimately anti-Judaic
and anti-Semitic construction of Jewish/Hebraic identity. Read with the
texts of Jeremiah and Isaiah in mind, the temptation the goblins offer
in this poem is not merely luscious fruit, or female sexuality, or artistic
knowledge, as other critics have suggested. Rather, Rossetti is showing
how the prophetic work of the Hebrew Bible and its potential maintenance of Jewish identity offer a dangerous temptation for Christian
women. The narrative of the poem works to explore the nature of that
temptation, and the ways women can be "saved" from using the "fruits"
of the Hebrew Bible in the wrong ways.

The plot of the poem tells of two sisters who hear the goblin's call
"come buy" and taste the lusciously described fruits of the goblin market.
Only one sister, Laura, succumbs to the goblins, paying for her fruit
purchase with a lock of blonde hair. After her initial taste of goblin fruit,
she has an insatiable desire for more, yet she can no longer see or hear
the goblins or their wares. Gradually, she loses all her orientation to

the domestic world of the sisters, and starts to "dwindle," much like Jeannie, a woman whom we are told is now dead from having consumed the goblin fruits. Finally, Lizzie, the sister who warned Laura about the goblin threat, goes to purchase fruits for her sister, only this time, she uses a coin, signifying a very different relationship to the wares of the goblins. The goblins refuse her money, enact a sort of rape/attack in which they try to force her to eat fruit, and Lizzie returns home intact, but with fruit smeared all over her. She urges her sister Laura to consume the fruit from off her body, and as Laura does so, this second taste of goblin fruit causes a violent, near-death reaction in Laura, who "falls" into an ambiguous life/death state. Lizzie "ministers" to her through the night, and Laura awakens, cured of the goblin disease. The poem ends with the sisters telling their children of the story from their past, and noting that the goblins are a part of "not-returning time" – that is, are no longer a threat to the domestic and woman-centered world the poem depicts.

Perhaps the least-known and most important Biblical reference in this poem is to the Hebrew Scriptures: the goblin's refrain "Come buy" is a direct reference to Isaiah 55, cited at the start of this section, words the prophet speaks in his specific historical context to urge the "fallen" Israel to remember the commandments of God's covenant with the Jewish people.[20] Isaiah, in his specifically Jewish context, uses the symbols of "wine and milk" as that which Jews can figuratively buy without money thanks to God's redemptive concern; in short, Isaiah promises a special economy of spiritual sustenance for Jews based on their return to and maintenance of the original covenant with God at Sinai. Rossetti uses this refrain "Come buy" as a signal phrase through which to identify the goblins with Isaiah's text, though she changes the context of its utterance considerably.

Rossetti takes the notion of a special economy of redemption implied in Isaiah's metaphor, and with her figure of the "goblin market" recasts that (Jewish) economy as a dangerous and corrupt form of moral exchange. In her poem, the false redemption promised from the "goblin" economy is integral to the ultimate "saving" of the fallen sister, but it is a redemption that can only be realized by a symbolically Christian revision of the goblin economy; thus, Lizzie, the symbolic Christian, must interact with the goblin fruit just as Christian theology interacts with Jewish text, finding a "new" use/interpretation for the materials (fruits/texts) of the "goblin market" in order to create true redemption for her sister. The narrative of *Goblin Market* suggests that the antidote to Judaism relies on the fruits of Hebrew Scripture reclaimed and reinterpreted through a specifically

Christian female redemptive act, a "female" act of "ministering" that we know from reading *Seek and Find* that Rossetti connects specifically to Christ.

Rossetti conjoins a number of different Hebrew scriptural references in the poem to create her incredibly layered understanding of the role of Hebrew prophecy in Christianity. For example, she replaces the "wine and milk" of Isaiah's "come buy" passage with a rich array of fruits. This fruit signals more than just a reference to the Garden of Eden apple; indeed, this fruit is symbolic of the special temptations she sees for women in reading the Hebrew Scriptures; it is the fruit of the sexually tantalizing Song of Songs, the aesthetic pleasure of Jewish redemption in the Hebrew Psalms, and the lush language and imagery of Isaiah and Jeremiah which often calls on explicitly sexualized female imagery.

Another structural link between *Goblin Market* and the texts of Jeremiah and Isaiah is the use of "daughters" as the central players in this narrative. Rossetti takes the figures to which Jeremiah addresses himself in Lamentations, "O daughter of Jerusalem" and "O virgin daughter of Zion," and literalizes these metaphorical addressees in her figures of Lizzie and Laura. In writing this sibling narrative, Rossetti also explores the richness of the Biblical narratives of redeemed/fallen siblings; in particular, she links these metaphors to the idea of the Christian Church as the saved younger sibling to Judaism's lapsed elder position. And Rossetti was clearly a careful reader of Hebrew prophecy; when we look more closely at Jeremiah's use of the daughter metaphor for the Jewish community, it seems to take on two slightly different configurations, both of which Rossetti uses. For Jeremiah, Israel is figured alternately as a fallen woman or "harlot" (Lamentations 1: 8–9 and elsewhere) or, at other moments, the figural emphasis is on Israel as a raped or attacked woman who is repeatedly oppressed and ridiculed by "enemies"; the dual figuration of the raped or fallen woman blurs the distinctions between a chosen moral fall and victimization. The two sisters absorb these dual roles in Rossetti's poem; Laura is both a "fallen" woman in her buying of goblin fruit with her hair (body), and also a victim of goblin mocking; Lizzie resists these roles, refusing to choose a moral fall, and refusing victimization by not allowing the goblins to "have their way with her," that is, eat the fruit herself.

Laura's suffering from the goblins' fruit creates her internal "dwindling" – a loss of physical and thus spiritual vitality. The goblin fruits – on their own – offer only a very temporary gratification that soon becomes akin to a disease. Thus, after her first taste, the fruits themselves lose their ability to invigorate her; though at one point she sets a "kernel stone" of one of the fruits to grow, it bears "no waxing root." Given Rossetti's alignment between the goblins and the language of Isaiah and Jeremiah, the disease of goblin fruit seems to be a commitment to a specifically Jewish system of moral deliverance. Judaism, aligned with the goblin market, is figured as a corrupt, diseased religious system, an economy of moral allegory that seems especially dangerous for women. The work of the poem *Goblin Market* is to redefine Laura's spiritual orientation away from the goblin world of the Judaic into a specifically Christian understanding of spiritual life where Jewishness/goblin-ness is ultimately reinterpreted not as tantalizing, but as threatening, and then erased as a sign of "not-returning time."

Rossetti thus calls on and rewrites the texts of Jeremiah and Isaiah repeatedly in order to reconfigure Jeremiah's Jewish perspective into a Christian one. For example, Jeremiah describes the "enemies" of the daughter of Judah in Lamentations 2: 15–16

All that pass by clap their hands at thee; they hiss and wag their head at the daughter of Jerusalem, saying, is this the city that men call The perfection of beauty, The joy of the whole earth?

All thine enemies have opened their mouth against thee: they hiss and gnash the teeth; they say, We have swallowed her up; certainly this is the day that we looked for; we have found, we have seen it.

Jeremiah describes the enemies of the daughter of Jerusalem with threatening characteristics of "hissing," "gnashing," "wag[ging] heads," and "swallowing"; Rossetti takes that imagery of the "enemy" in her description of the goblins' attack on Lizzie:

> Their tones waxed loud,
> Their looks were evil.
> Lashing their tails
> They trod and hustled her,
> Elbowed and jostled her
> Clawed with their nails,
> Barking, mewing, hissing, mocking
>   . . .
> Held her hands and squeezed their fruits
> Against her mouth to make her eat.
>
> (lines 396–402, 406–7)

By figuring the goblins as "Barking, mewing, hissing, mocking" Rossetti adds to the suggestion that they speak the words of the Jewish prophets ("come buy"); she also aligns them with the role of "enemy" in the Biblical texts, an enemy that in Jewish historical context is of course not Jewish, but rather representative of Babylonian captors, namely gentiles. The goblins are thus symbolic figures who speak the language of Jewish prophets and yet behave analogously to the "enemies" of the Jews in Jeremiah's texts. Through this complex use of Biblical text in representing the goblins, Rossetti discredits that language of those Hebrew prophets as precisely those voices who threaten, rather than "save" a seemingly "lost" religious individual or community.

By recognizing the complex rewriting of Hebraic texts Rossetti enacts in this poem, the strange narrative complexities of *Goblin Market* become much easier to decode. For example, if the goblins are described in the same terms as false prophets in Jeremiah's texts, these characteristics are also evident in Laura's goblin "disease"; she too is found "gnash[ing] her teeth for baulked desire" (line 267) when she cannot get access to more goblin fruit, and this imagery illustrates that in her desire for goblin fruit, she verges on becoming a kind of goblin/false prophet herself. When she returns from her first foray into the market, she does indeed speak the language of the tempting fruit, much like a prophet, telling her sister "have done with sorrow; / I'll bring you plums tomorrow" (lines 169–70) and thus trying to "tempt" her sister as the goblins tempt. The work of the poem, and specifically Lizzie's narrative, is to realign Laura's misguided relationship to Hebrew texts – a relationship women seem prone to, as the mysterious reference to Jeannie suggests.

Lizzie successfully subverts the goblin Judaic economy by refusing to "trade" in their preferred currency; Lizzie refuses to use her body as barter, opting for a coin instead. Lizzie's refusal to swallow the goblin fruit, as the goblins want, mirrors the insistent resistance to Jewish self-understanding that Christian readers enact on Jewish texts: she will not consume the fruits as the goblins would have her do, nor do Christian readers ingest Jewish prophecy as Jews would. The goblins reject her form of barter, an action which suggests a certain perversity in their system: they deal, it seems in the bodies (hair) of young women rather than with the more "normal" currency of a coin, and in so doing, they demonstrate that their system only works on literal physical terms rather than through symbolic substitution (money in the form of coins). This representation of Judaism parallels the critique often created by Christian interpreters who cast Judaism as conforming to "letter of the law" rather than "spirit," and likewise seeks to show that Christianity grasps the true symbolic meaning of Hebrew text without a literal Jewish reading. The images of barter and commercial exchange also, of course, invoke familiar anti-Semitic stereotypes of Jewish avarice.

This recasting of the meaning of Jewish prophecy is evident both in terms of form and content in *Goblin Market*. When Laura first eats the goblin fruit, she is struck by the sweetness of the fruits she has "bought." They are not only tantalizing to look at; they taste better than any fruit she has ever eaten. Yet, after that first taste, she cannot hear the language of the goblins nor gain access to their falsely appearing fruit; the promises of goblin fruit, it seems, are short-lived and false. When Lizzie the redeemer becomes the subsequent victim of goblin violence, Rossetti's language again echoes that of Lamentations 1: 15, which describes how "the Lord hath trodden the virgin, the daughter of Jerusalem, as in a winepress"; however, in Rossetti's version it is goblins, not "the Lord" who smash fruit against Lizzie's body, making "wine" out of the fruit and so transforming its original materiality. The importance of this wine is that it alone can become the antidote to Laura's disease; in having the goblin fruit (Jewishness) transformed through personal suffering, Rossetti clarifies that the texts of Jewish prophecy – the fruit – are indeed a necessary ingredient for Christian salvation; however, they are a material that must be radically transformed from raw fruit to wine in the process of Christian redemption.

When Laura has her second taste of goblin fruit, significantly transformed by its connection with her sister's body, her "lips be[gin] to scorch" as "that juice was wormwood to her tongue" (lines 493–4); as well, she "gorge[s] on bitterness without a name" (line 510). The language Rossetti chooses here comes directly from Jeremiah's description of suffering, remorse, and punishment he attributes to being "under the wrath of God" in Lamentations 3; the text reads: "He hath filled me with bitterness, he hath made me drunken with wormwood" (3: 15); similar imagery appears in Jeremiah 23: 15, where the prophecy concerns the Lord's punishment of false prophets: " I shall give them wormwood to eat, and bitter poison to drink." If Laura's reaction to the second taste of goblin fruit makes her like Jeremiah's description of the suffering, fallen prophets and communities, Rossetti suggests that the "solution" or "cure" for such suffering is to undergo the death-to-life Christian conversion process that Lizzie enables for her sister. She is cured of her addiction to goblin fruit, and thus symbolically cured of her misreading of Jewish prophetic text in her Christian-coded rebirth. Where Jeremiah councils that the Jews should return to the original covenant with God and know that Jewish salvation will arrive, Rossetti suggests that such patient waiting for salvation from those goblin fruits only leads to a "dwindling" death; what can cure such spiritual disease, it seems, are the fruits ingested in a new form.

Yet perhaps most remarkable in Rossetti's rewriting of Jewish prophetic text is the way she suggests that once redemption is won through the refiguration of Jewish text/goblin fruit, there is no longer any need for the goblin market in a larger Christian world view. In the poem's ending, Rossetti enacts a strategy of the "ended tale" similar to the one she used in "By the Waters of Babylon B.C. 570." After Lizzie refuses to be tempted, thus testifying to her incorruptible Christian identity, the goblin men disappear:

> At last the evil people
> Worn out by her resistance
> Flung back her penny, kicked their fruit
> Along whichever road they took,
> Not leaving root or stone or shoot;
> Some writhed into the ground,
> Some dived into the brook
> With a ring and ripple,
> Some scudded on the gale without a sound,
> Some vanished in the distance.
>
> (lines 437–46)

The goblins' erasure from the narrative leaves the female Christian world of Lizzie, Laura, and their children completely free from threat. But the goblins are not only erased physically; at the end of the poem, when Laura recounts the story of their past, the goblins exist exactly like the "tale that is told" in "By the Waters of Babylon B.C. 570." In the closing frame of the narrative, Rossetti writes:

> Laura would call the little ones
> And tell them of her early prime,
> Those pleasant days long gone
> Of not-returning time . . .
>
> (lines 548–51)

As the goblin threat becomes a narrative of "not-returning time" so also is Jewish history reduced to that which cannot return, nor exist in the present of Christianity. This complete erasure of the threat of the *present* Jew/goblin represents the flip side of Christian conversion, which can only recognize the figure of the converted Jew, and for which the figure of a present Jew represents an essential questioning of Christian "truth."

Finally, it is crucial to see that Rossetti's reimagining of religious history does not remain limited to understanding Jewishness as an abstracted narrative of "not-returning time." Or rather, *Goblin Market* contains its own subtle critique of Jews living in Rossetti's contemporary world; thus, along with their alignment with Biblical Jewish prophets, the goblins carry distinct anti-Semitic characteristics often attributed to Jews in Rossetti's own historical moment.[21] In this context, the fact that these goblins cry "Come buy" is more than an echo of Isaiah's text; that phrase also implicitly connects the goblins to a world of commerce conventionally associated with the contemporary Jews of London. Todd Endelman cites Robert Southey's complaint of "Hebrew lads who infest you in the streets with oranges and red slippers, or tempt schoolboys to dip in a bag for gingerbread nuts" to suggest the degree to which Jews were derogatorily associated with street-hawking. Endelman also cites an anonymous review in *Gentleman's Magazine* of Milman's *History of the Jews* that notes how difficult it was for an Englishman "to separate the idea of Jews from pedlars who cry 'old clothes,' hawk sealing wax, and have a peculiar physiognomic character." The goblins in Rossetti's poem thus combine identifying characteristics of "Old Testament" Jewishness as well as contemporary Victorian anti-Semitism, and thus Rossetti includes the possibility that contemporary Jews also interact in a more literal material economy which may mirror their spiritual corruption.

Goblin Market thus explores the role of Jewishness in multiple forms – both as historical religious prophecy and contemporary Jewish identity – and "argues" through a fantasy narrative that both Hebrew prophecy and Jewishness can be forgotten; now that a better use for "goblin fruits" has emerged, the original system of the goblin market can be relegated to "not-returning time." When "[c]urious Laura ... wonder[s] at each merchant man" (lines 69–70) she signals the problem contemporary Jewishness poses to a Christian world view: how is it that Jews can persist as "merchant men" given the moral insufficiency of their spiritual covenant? Aligning these "merchant men" with a Svengali-like sexuality that likewise threatens Christian chastity, and then using the language of Hebrew prophecy to depict this goblin world, Rossetti negotiates the complicated figures of the goblin men so that they can be constructed as enemies to women's chastity and moral redemption at any given moment – that is, until one woman/Christ, manipulates their ultimate dispersal. Rossetti renders the narrative of Jewishness as a fairy tale of "wicked, quaint fruit-merchant men, / Their fruits like honey to the throat / But poison in the blood" (lines 553–5), and creates an idealized female world freed of goblin-Jewishness at the end of her poem.

The idea that the texts of Hebrew prophecy can be read as "honey to the throat" and "poison in the blood" underscores the link between sexuality and aesthetics in this poem, the final point I want to turn to in this reading of the poem. Indeed, as we look back through Rossetti's work, we can see that she is clearly drawn to the rich language and imagery of the Hebrew Scriptures – and particular Hebrew prophecy. Isaiah, Jeremiah, Ezekiel, The Song of Songs, and of course the Psalms, are all lush, highly metaphoric texts to which Rossetti repeatedly refers in her poetry. Likewise, as we saw in chapter 2, there was a cultural discourse Rossetti must have been aware of that claimed the poetry of the Hebrew Scriptures was the highest form of poetry ever written. Understanding that the goblin "fruits" represent the fruits of Hebrew prophecy/poetry helps explain why these fruits are so delicious, but ultimately corrupt and corrupting. Indeed, the rather flat and prosaic ending of *Goblin Market* – a closure that disappoints so many feminist critics and my students in its seeming re-establishment of the domestic order cleansed of the lush goblin market – signals the poem's recognition that the aesthetic pleasure and moral promises available from the Hebrew Scriptures may not be particularly healthy for Christian women. Some of the unhealthful quality of this goblin fruit is clearly related to women's relationship to male sexuality. In making the goblins the only repository of masculinity in the poem – albeit a "queer" sexuality (line 94), Rossetti conflates unconverted Jewishness with a dangerous masculine sexual presence that is remarkably absent from the redeemed world of the poem's conclusion, which offers many "children" to the sisters with no evidence of husbands. Indeed, their motherhood seems best understood in terms of "virgin" birth, and thus represents a particularly Christian understanding of female sexuality.[22] Yet while clearly setting up a parallel to Mary's identity, this ending of *Goblin Market* also suggests some deeper connection Rossetti is making between the dangerous poetry of the Hebrew Bible and the danger of an overtly sexualized female identity which abounds in Hebrew scriptural text.

For what Rossetti illuminates in her reading of Hebrew prophets is that these texts are full of complex, often sexualized, sometimes violent, sometimes triumphant images of femaleness that are almost always linked to heterosexually constructed desire.[23] Further, the metaphoric references to women in the Hebrew Bible are always dependent on heterosexually imagined relationships with the masculine divine, and so women are repeatedly figured in terms of sexuality, either fallen or chaste. Thus, what makes the Hebrew Scriptures dangerous for Rossetti, is that they appear to offer women a certain kind of powerful religious identity, but one that is often predicated on the expression of their sexual body, reproductive body, or their married body. Institutionalized Jewish and Christian readings have rendered these female images and texts "safe" by insisting on their intrinsically metaphorical, that is, poetic nature. Rossetti, however, remains suspicious that these representations and their poetic implications for women can ever be "safe"; in *Goblin Market*, she exploits that relationship between images of female sexuality and the Hebrew prophetic texts to create a lush fantasy of the temptations Christian women face when reading the Hebrew Bible, and she offers a Christian revision of female identity which for her remains chaste and unconnected to any form of masculinity. In her sonnet sequence "Monna Innominata," she also takes up the relationships between poetry, heterosexuality, and religious discourse, yet she does so without the enabling frame of fantasy which guarantees *Goblin Market*'s "happy ending."

"IF I MIGHT TAKE MY LIFE SO IN MY HAND": "MONNA INNOMINATA" AND THE HEROIC JEWISH WOMAN

In the "Monna Innominata" sonnet sequence, Rossetti re-approaches the problem of Christian female agency, and she adds a new term to her set of concerns. Her repeated epigraphs from Dante and Petrarch, as well as her famous Preface, explicitly position the sequence in relation to male-dominated literary history, and the context of heterosexual romance which generates so many of the poetic conventions in the sonnet sequence. Rossetti replaces her fantasized female Christian world, where men exist only as goblins/Jews, with a far more "realistic" discourse of Christian heterosexual poetry, even though Rossetti changes the conventional terms of the sonnet sequence by having the woman, rather than the male poet, speak. Rossetti displays her interest in Jewishness through the figure of Esther whom she invokes in the eighth sonnet. This Sonnet 8 of "Monna Innominata" offers Rossetti's most explicit exploration of an actual Jewish historical woman, and so deserves attention in this study for that quality alone. But explicating the Esther sonnet is also crucial for constructing a larger reading of "Monna Innominata," which Rossetti termed a "sonnet of sonnets," suggesting that the position of each sonnet corresponded to the position of lines in traditional Petrarchan conventions. Thus, traditionally, the eighth sonnet should be the one in which the "turn" of the sonnet, or in this case sonnet sequence, should occur.

Given this important position in the sequence, it is significant to note that the Esther sonnet has been either ignored or named "puzzling" and "perplexing" by even the most adept of Rossetti's critics. Anthony Harrison situates this sonnet in the sequence as part of the movement toward union between the lovers as "happy equals" and writes: "Sonnet 8 perplexingly reinforces the speaker's hope for such a union by prefacing a prayer for God's sanction of her earthly love with an elaborately sensualized rendition of the Book of Esther" (*Christina Rossetti in Context*, 154). Harrison suggests that Rossetti offers a critique of the objectification to which Esther makes herself subject, and sets the speaker against this willingness to "trap" and "vanquish," realizing her objective is based on the "false values" of the "cultural ideology of romance" (181); it is worth noting that Harrison almost always refers to Sonnet 8 as "perplexing" (154, 180). William Whitla has approached Sonnet 8 from a different perspective; while he seems to pay the least attention to this sonnet of them all in his reading of the sequence, he sees the poem as "describ[ing] not so much an event or action as a ceremonial occasion involving the risk of death" ("Questioning the Convention," 124) where Rossetti "makes her temptress the instrument of divine will, the means of saving Israel" (125). But Whitla also leaves his reading full of unanswerable problems: "All that is clear is that the speaker is appealing to the power of Love beyond herself . . . the subject of the speaker's prayer, its content and goal, is never stated here (except that it is 'for my love'). Further, even the prayer is conditional: 'if I might'" (125). While both Whitla and Harrison's readings offer intricate and useful scholarly interpretations, their failure to consider the full implications of the Esther analogy leaves their readings unable to account for the total shift in mood and theme of the sequence which this sonnet initiates.

Ironically, Rossetti's Preface to the sequence has been read more fully and often than the Esther sonnet. As William Whitla suggests, this Preface has also been consistently misread due to its highly cryptic rhetorical and grammatical maneuvers (85–92). After suggesting that the most famous women of the sonnet tradition, Beatrice and Laura, are "resplendent with charms, but . . . scant of attractiveness," Rossetti writes: "one can imagine many a lady as sharing her lover's poetic aptitude, while the barrier between them might be one held sacred by both, yet not such as to render mutual love incompatible with mutual honor"

(*Complete Poems*, II: 86). What Rossetti proposes is that she will explore how one might "imagine" "mutual love" "rendered" *compatibly* with "mutual honor" by a talented female poet who also holds the "barrier" between her identity as a Christian woman and her identity as a lover "sacred." This passage echoes those in *Seek and Find* which carefully alternate between statements of sameness and difference between the sexes; thus here, the lady can "share" her lover's "poetic aptitude" while still upholding a "sacred barrier" between them; the repetition of "mutual" is countered by the idea of "incompatibility." Likewise, the Preface echoes Rossetti's own statements (to Augusta Webster) about women's rights where she asserted her own belief in female "inferiority" with her desire "to attain to the character of a humble orthodox Xtian."[24] Rossetti carefully negotiates the suggestion that a woman can have an "equal" share of "poetic aptitude" while still upholding the ideology of Christian sexual difference that grants men higher authority in realms religious, poetic, and sexual. It is "poetic aptitude" that seems to mediate these various contradictions for Rossetti, since it through poetry that one *might* "render" the delicate balance of "love" and "honor."

In the next paragraph of the Preface, Rossetti speculates that "[h]ad such a lady spoken for herself," as opposed to being the object of poetic description, her poetry would have created a "more tender, if less dignified" portrait than one drawn by a friend. Then, Rossetti critiques Barrett Browning as the "Great Poetess," suggesting that if she had been "unhappy instead of happy" her sonnets too would have been "worthy to occupy a niche beside Beatrice and Laura" (*Complete Poems*, II: 86). Encoded in Rossetti's idea of "unhappy and happy" is a reference to female sexuality; since the writing and publication of *Sonnets from the Portuguese* were imbedded within the very public awareness of the Brownings' marriage, Rossetti alludes to the fact that Barrett Browning was freer to explore an active female sexuality in a sonnet sequence than an unmarried Victorian woman could ever be. Indeed, Barrett Browning's sonnets are quite sexually suggestive; this different approach to issues of sexuality and religion may reflect the different perspectives Rossetti and Barrett Browning held within Christian discourse; Rossetti's devout High Anglicanism seems to have led her to more ascetic leanings than Barrett Browning's more eclectic and less strict interests in Dissenting, Swedenborgian, and even spiritualist religious positions.[25] Not surprisingly, Barrett Browning's triumphant vision of the married Christian woman poet at the end of *Aurora Leigh* offers a sharp conflict to Rossetti's imagined "silent" ending for her poet woman in "Monna Innominata."[26]

Assuming that the sequence does indeed replicate the structure of a Petrarchan sonnet, it becomes possible to locate certain themes in each group of sonnets as they correspond to traditional line groupings in Petrarchan sonnets.[27] The first group of four sets out the problem that the lovers cannot be together, as well as the fact that the speaker sees the world completely in terms of her lover; she claims him as "my world of all the men / This wide world holds; O love, my world is you" (1: 7–8); likewise, she marks the day of their meeting as "a day of days" that structures her entire personal history, though she terms herself "blind to see and to foresee" the true significance of that event (2: 6–10). The last two sonnets in this group explore the impossibility of the lover's union in conventional Petrarchan terms, acknowledging that "only in a dream we are at one" (3: 9) while simultaneously insisting that love can remove any notion of "difference" in their capacity for love and poetry. What these first four sonnets seem to argue is that the female speaker risks losing herself – and specifically her religious commitments – in a context of romantic heterosexual love which blinds her to larger Christian truth.

The second sequence begins to incorporate a religious element, as the speaker tries to maneuver between her allegiance to God and the subsequent sexual renunciation that she believes such a vow entails. It is in these next four sonnets that the speaker introduces the problematic nature of her particular position as woman/lover. In Sonnet 5 she asks that "God be with" her lover (5: 2) and suggests the many positive results that can come of her lover's devotion to God, most particularly that God will "perfect you as He would have you be" (5: 8). But directly after stating that the male lover can be "perfected" through Christian devotion, the speaker poses a central problem when she asks "So much for you; but what of me, dear friend?" (5: 9). Her question suggests that while Christian devotion can bring the man immense satisfaction and "perfection," it has different possibilities for a woman. The speaker realizes that her position as Christian woman guarantees none of the same privileges as for the man; for him, loving God "setteth [him] free" and makes him "perfect," while all she is sanctioned to do is "love without stint . . . to love you much and yet to love you more" (5: 10–11). Thus for her there is no attainment of perfection, but rather only unending giving of love. The speaker explains this apparent difference in their relationship to God in the last line, by quoting the Biblical injunction that "woman is the helpmeet made for man," thus apparently accepting the role assigned to her in Genesis.

But her desire to uphold God's law becomes an increasing obstacle in her love for the man, and Sonnet 6 insists (despite the fear of the man's "rebuke") on figuring a reconciliation of her dilemma between her sexual and spiritual desire. Sonnet 6 ends in a tautological dilemma: "I cannot love you if I love not Him, / I cannot love Him if I love not you." With this statement, the speaker seems headed for potential conflict and crisis; in Sonnet 7 she states "My heart's a coward tho' my words are brave," suggesting her inability to act in the interest of her "heart" or desire; the sonnet ends with her finding "comfort in his Book, who saith / Tho' jealousy be cruel as the grave / And death be strong, yet love is strong as death." The attribution of jealousy suggests the lover's impatience with her repeated vows of devotion to God, which keep her from consummating her desire sexually; there is some implication that the lover is also getting impatient with her. Thus, Sonnets 1–7 have offered, as good Petrarchan sonnets do, the establishment of a problem or idea, and a conflict or alternative idea which the eighth line (or in this case sonnet) should both summarize and "turn" to a new issue of solution.

Sonnet 8 is set up to resolve the tension between sexual desire and spiritual desire from a woman's point of view, and it opens by referring to that which the speaker has "found" in God's "Book" – (referred to in the previous sonnet) – which is significantly not a book of the Christian New Testament, but rather of the Old Testament, the Hebrew Book of Esther. In the Book of Esther, Esther is the woman who, having been deemed the most beautiful woman in King Ahasueras' kingdom, replaces Vashti, the previous queen, who was banished because she refused to display her beauty before the king and his men when commanded. The Esther story thus immediately invokes a complex narrative of women's objectification, oppression, and competition. Esther's bravery is legendary on account of the risk she takes in appearing before the king even though not summoned by him, an act often punishable by death; she comes to him to ask protection for all the Jews in the land who are being persecuted by the king's minister, Haman. Esther utters her famous line: "I, if I perish, perish" at the moment she decides to appear before the king unbidden. After her characteristic epigraphs from Dante and Petrarch, these too are the opening lines of Rossetti's eighth sonnet:[28]

> "I, if I perish, perish." – Esther spake:
> And bride of life or death she made her fair
> In all the lustre of her perfumed hair
> And smiles that kindle longing but to slake.
> She put on pomp of loveliness, to take
> Her husband thro' his eyes at unaware;
> She spread abroad her beauty for a snare,
> Harmless as doves and subtle as a snake.
>
> (8: 1–8)

Rossetti's description of the sexually vanquishing Esther bears little resemblance to the Biblical language, which offers none of the physical details Rossetti provides.[29] For Rossetti's speaker, Esther is a strangely ambiguous character in these opening descriptions, powerful yet sneaky, manipulating her beauty "for a snare" as she engages the language of her sexual body in order to appeal to her husband. Rossetti combines some of the Biblical language of Esther with conventional images of the "captivating lady" of the sonnet tradition; as depicted by male speakers, that powerful lady is usually seen as cold and heartless in her rejection of the "poor" male suitor/poet. Read into that poetic context of sexual favors between lovers, Esther's seductive actions seem familiar and appropriate; however, when read from the perspective of Christian female honor, her overt sexuality seems condemnable.

Yet Rossetti transforms the private context of Esther's narrative in the following sestet, where Esther's "vanquishing" actions are both summarized and then recontextualized out of the world of private romance, and into public Jewish history:

> She trapped him with one mesh of silken hair,
> She vanquished him by wisdom of her wit,
> And built her people's house that it should stand: –
>
> (8: 9–11)

In the summary of Esther's power, Rossetti focuses on her body (metonymized by her hair, as in both *Goblin Market* and Hemans' Miriam sonnet), and the "wisdom of her wit"; the "trapping" actions that might seem condemnable in a context of Christian honor are thus sanctioned, here, because Esther acts in a larger moral, political, historical, and ultimately divine context: to "buil[d] her people's house that it should stand." In contrast to the speaker's self description in Sonnet 7: 9: "My heart's a coward though my words are brave," Esther's earthly desires and her religious goals are linked; Esther's words and actions are brave and divinely sanctioned, whereas the speaker sees the disjunction between the language of desire she produces in her poetry and her own actions, or rather lack of ability to act on her desire.

Rossetti's understanding of Esther's Jewishness is that as a Jewish woman, she always has a public, communal identity; the love that Esther acts on is for her people, rather than for an individual man; thus that crucial detail is inserted: she is represented as battling ("trapping" and "vanquishing") with the king, her sexual object, in the name of the Jewish people. It is this recognition of Esther's combined political and sexual agency that initiates the speaker's longing for an analogous way to imagine her own artistic and sexual identity. She ends the sonnet by comparing herself directly to Esther:

> If I might take my life so in my hand,
> And for my love to Love put up my prayer,
> And for love's sake by Love be granted it!
>
> (8: 12–14)

With the phrase "If I might take my life so in my hand," the speaker creates a connection between the sanctioned female spiritual activity of "prayer" and Esther's sexualized "saving" of her people. But the phrase also begins to reveal the deep differences between Esther and the poem's speaker. Whereas Esther "takes her life in her hand" through her public and political actions – appearing unbidden before the king, orchestrating the ultimate saving of all Jews in the kingdom – the speaker can "take her life in her hand" either through the act of prayer, by writing, or by threatening her Christian life by acting on the desire of her body, "her hand." But, even as the metonym "hand" attempts to bridge the gap in Esther's and the speaker's access to female agency, when the speaker asks "if [she] might" make this connection to Esther, the conclusion the sonnet leads to is that in truth, this Christian woman can never really be like Esther at all.

Indeed, these last statements of analogy between the Jewish Esther and the Christian female poet speaker remain conditional, as Whitla points out. The "if" clause is never resolved, the subsequent "then" clause being exactly that which must be withheld by the chaste Christian female speaker. For what the Esther sonnet reveals is that to gain a unified, theologically sanctioned gendered identity, Rossetti's Christian speaker would have to be a Jewish woman, a woman who does not subscribe to constraints of Christian individuality, honor, and chaste love, and likewise a woman – like Esther – who is given an active and public role of leadership in her people's religious fate. Indeed, it is important to note that the Book of Esther ends with Esther specifically writing a decree in the name of the Jewish people, and thus taking on a very public and literate leadership of her own. Choosing Esther as the potential model for her poetic speaker, Rossetti has intentionally chosen a woman who has power through the word – both her own historical words and the Biblical words about her – as well as her body. But if finding Esther's example of female agency and heroic action in "his Book" (sonnet 7: 12) seems to offer a potential model for the speaker's own actions and texts, she is ultimately faced with an unresolvable contradiction: how can the Christian female poet fully identify with the radical reformulation of female sexual and spiritual agency that Esther symbolizes when she has dual commitments to the sonnet tradition and Christian virtue? When the speaker of this sonnet attempts to identify with Esther, therefore, what becomes evident is not the similarity in their respective positions, but rather their radical difference. Esther's model also makes evident the discourse of oppression that underlies the historical narrative of the Jewish people in the Book of Esther and elsewhere, and this subtext of Jewish oppression also complicates the Christian poet/speaker's identification with her. For, while Esther may in fact be figured like a sneaky "captivating" lady in the conventions of the sonnet tradition, her identity as a Jew during a period of Jewish captivity and potential persecution makes actions that might seem condemnable from the perspective of Christian gender relations completely justifiable.[30] But Rossetti's Christian female speaker has no larger affiliation with oppression outside the discourse of gender, and so has no larger justification to "vanquish" her lover.

Instead, the larger message of this sequence suggests that the act of imagining a Christian woman as an agent of her own sexuality, or as a politically powerful player in her people's history are as impossible as imagining herself to be a Jew. The Jewish woman's capacity to suspend the values of sexual chastity in the name of a larger spiritual mission is shown to be impossible for the Christian woman, whose private body is constructed as the site of Christian virtue itself.[31] And it is with this realization of the impossibility of the comparison she sets up in the sonnet that Rossetti brilliantly dissolves the conventional structure of the sonnet; thus, the eleven lines concerning Esther, and the subsequent three lines that provide the strange closure to the sonnet disrupt the traditional structure of octave and sestet over which the speaker/poet had previously exhibited total control – and toward which she had seemed to make a distinct poetic commitment. But the Esther sonnet exposes too many contradictions for the Christian female speaker/lover, and so the speaker relinquishes formal control, problematizing her own commitment to the conventions of male poetry at the moment the contradictions in her position seem unresolvable.

After indulging in the fantasy of being an Esther, a woman who at least in Rossetti's reading can use her body in the name of God, the Christian speaker begins her next sonnet as follows:

Thinking of you, and all that was, and all
That might have been and now can never be,
I feel your honoured excellence, and see
Myself unworthy of the happier call:
For woe is me who walk so apt to fall,
So apt to shrink afraid, so apt to flee,
Apt to lie down and die (ah woe is me!)
Faithless and hopeless turning to the wall.

(9: 1–8)

The "now" of the second line suggests that something significant has happened to negate the possibility of what "might have been" and so supports the reading of Sonnet 8 as finally accepting the impossibility of reconciling "mutual love" and "mutual honor" from the perspective of a Christian woman. There also seems to be a play on sexual language here; when she calls herself "unworthy of the happier" call, she rejects sexuality through an ironic play on the idea of a religious "call" and "worthiness." Likewise, the speaker's aptness "to fall" and "lie down and die" suggests a possible tendency toward sexuality that she chooses to curb. The subsequent lines reinscribe the speaker's resignation to her own position of "lack," subordination, and passivity; likewise, the lines offer a sharp contrast to the previous figuration of Esther, who in fact refused quite explicitly to "lie down and die." This sonnet thus initiates the closure of the sequence; from this moment in the sequence, the poet speaker renounces the possibility of "happiness" (sexual gratification) in an attempt at true Christian devotion to God. She also renounces the very act of poetry by the end of the sequence in her emphasis on "silence." It is the realization that she can never be like the Jewish Esther in Sonnet 8 that thus initiates the speaker's final realization of the incompatibility of the terms woman, poet, and lover in a Christian tradition.

Putting the "Monna Innominata" sequence, and particularly the Esther sonnet, in context with *Goblin Market* suggests that these two poems offer two very different negotiations with the Hebrew Bible, Jewishness, and femaleness. For while both poems attempt to construct a "complete" heroic female Christian identity by transforming figures of Jewishness, *Goblin Market* posits the possibility of such an heroic Christian woman in the form of Lizzie, while the "Monna Innominata" suggests the complete impossibility of such an heroic Christian woman. One of the major differences in these poems is that while they both engage with the texts of the Hebrew Scriptures, *Goblin Market* enacts a conventional typological conversion of Jewish identity which critiques the figuration of femaleness in the Hebrew Bible; the Esther sonnet, on the other hand, reverses this typology, figuring the Hebraic woman as the idealized example of female sexual/religious agency – and ultimately rejecting that model as one that cannot be realized by any devout Christian woman. Likewise, the difference between the two poems is marked by totally different generic contexts, and a very different approach to Christian masculinity; *Goblin Market* creates a Christian female heroine through the construction of a fantasized female world where Jewish and male identity are effectively erased, repressed, and expunged. By removing the discourse of sexual difference from the fantasy world of *Goblin Market*, Rossetti is able to imagine how female heroism might operate within a Christian framework. But when the problem of sexual difference is reintroduced in the sonnet sequence, the strategies of typological conversion and erasure of difference are no longer possible.

Rather than producing "standard" theological readings of either Esther or Jeremiah, Rossetti's poetic imagination rewrites these texts to produce poems that offer "tantalizing" ideas and images for and about women, while also remaining deeply committed to Christian epistemology. Both poems suggest that Rossetti's representations of women and understanding of femaleness are deeply tied to her concerns with Jewishness, the Hebrew Bible, and Jewish women. It is because the Hebrew Scriptures provide figures of women that stand as heroes, prophets, and divine agents that Christian women like Rossetti and Barrett Browning could turn to these figures as sanctioned sources of female agency in *Aurora Leigh* and "Monna Innominata." But as my readings of the Esther sonnet and *Goblin Market* suggest, these identifications with Hebraic women were fraught with contradictions for Christian women. Barrett Browning resolves these contradictions by refusing to sanction the idea of "woman as helpmeet" to man; instead, she posits that both men and women must undergo a "conversion" process analogous to her Christian conversion of her Hebraic types. For Barrett Browning, the Christian typological hermeneutic "resolves" the tensions of sexual difference and religious difference simultaneously, so that she can assert the possibility of a female "heroic" identity at the end of *Aurora Leigh*. But Rossetti refuses a critique of male Christian identity, and insists that woman's equality is not attainable on earth; for her, women need Christian salvation as much as the Jews of the Hebrew Scriptures, both existing in a state of "uncompletedness" that can only be mediated through Christian conversion. For Rossetti, Christian women who seek to claim their completedness on earth, as equals to Christian men, run the risk of being like misguided Jews, who likewise claim their moral system as "perfect" already, and not in need of the redemptive work of Christ. One danger, Rossetti suggests, is that both Jews and contemporary Christian women might believe their own context to be complete; a further danger is that Christian women might misread Jewish text and its examples of women as having meaning outside the encompassing frame of Christian belief.

From these varied readings of Rossetti's poetic and prose texts, it becomes clear that her own constructions of Christian female identity and the relationship this identity had to poetry were deeply influenced by her theological understanding of Jewishness. Though "Monna Innominata" speaks to the complications writing posed to Rossetti as a devout Christian woman, it is important to note that Rossetti always wrote and continued to write as a devout Anglican woman. Her texts did not emerge despite that religiosity, but rather because of her own individual theological explorations of literature, Christian redemption, Jewish difference, and women's experience. Rossetti's sometimes troubling representations of Jewishness and the Judaic clearly affected her poetic, aesthetic, religious, and gendered values as they emerge in her poetry and prose; yet my hope is not to undermine her achievements for contemporary readers, but rather demonstrate their immense complexity. Untangling these intersecting relationships between her theology and her poetics, we are better able to rethink the ways women writers have used their own particular religious perspectives to construct their creative texts.

CHAPTER 5

"Judaism rightly reverenced": Grace Aguilar's theological poetics

INTRODUCTION: FROM "PECULIAR" TO "ELOQUENT": POETRY AS THEOLOGICAL STRATEGY

A lady, and that too young a lady, whatever the advantages of quick perception conceded to her sex, is, by the iron rule of custom, limited to fewer opportunities of acquiring that information and experience, which might restrict a too apt disposition to generalize from few facts. The notions which many form of Talmudic study, or of traditional doctrine, are founded not on what they sift from them, but on what they are told concerning them. The book before us bears evident traces of the peculiar readings of its fair writer, not designedly or even avoidably peculiar, so far as she is concerned . . . We will now turn to the more agreeable task of pointing out the many beauties that the work contains. Miss Aguilar is a poet, and of no mean grade . . . and wherever she quits the province of schoolmen and pours forth her own pious sentiments of the heart's duties, and the soul's destiny, she is fervid, eloquent and truthful. (Review of Grace Aguilar's *The Spirit of Judaism*).[1]

We want Jewish writers, Jewish books . . . There is none now, and the fault is our own! We make no effort to enlighten our neighbors as to the true spirit of the hope that is in us, though no struggle is too great to obtain a proper position and estimation in the Christian world. I am writing warmly, bitterly, perhaps you will say, though I hope not; but the subject ever makes my heart beat, and my temples throb, with the vain yearnings to perceive the true spirit of Hebrew patriotism awakening in our people – that they would but feel; it is not enough to make the *Jew* respected, but to have JUDAISM rightly reverenced: and to do this, there must be a JEWISH LITERATURE, or the Jewish people will not advance one step. (Grace Aguilar, *The Jewish Faith*, 264–5)

It would not be an exaggeration to say that Grace Aguilar (1816–47) was the most important Jewish woman writer in nineteenth-century England. Her prolific publishing history – all before her premature death at age thirty-one – included works of liturgy, theological prose, Jewish history, historical novels, domestic moral tales, short stories, and poetry. Yet Aguilar has remained virtually unexamined in recent feminist literary and theological scholarship; though mentioned in many of the "great woman writer" anthologies and coffee-table books, there has been only limited scholarly inquiry into the specific dynamics of her theology, and almost no exploration of her poetry; happily, more attention has quite recently been paid to her fiction.[2] In this chapter, I explore some of the unique strategies Aguilar used to construct both religious and literary authority for herself in the heterogeneity of Anglo-Jewish and dominant Christian Victorian culture, focusing in particular on her use of the first-person lyric as a response to her particular theological concerns and cultural position as a devout Anglo-Jewish woman. Because her position as a woman necessarily limited her authority in Jewish theological circles, Aguilar turned to the literary forms of hegemonic Christian culture to find a subject position that could escape the "censorious" eye of Rabbinical authority; however, as a devoutly Jewish woman, Aguilar could never fully lay claim to the title "woman poet" as it was constructed in Victorian England, since, as we saw in chapter 2, this identity was generally predicated on a Christian religious identification. That Aguilar achieved the incredible success she did while negotiating her complex subject positions is a testament to the literary strategies she instituted; Aguilar's ability to combine discourses of Judaism, Romanticism, and "the poetess" marks her as a crucial figure not only in Anglo-Jewish literary history, but also in Victorian literary history.

We can better understand why poetry was such an important discourse for Aguilar when we examine the tensions that were raised in a review of her very first book of prose, *The Spirit of Judaism* (1842). Written when she was twenty, and then rewritten at age twenty-six, this book takes up an overtly theological project: exegesis of the most important Hebrew declaration of faith, the Shema; thus, the book clearly makes generic claims to "theology" in its most traditional sense. Yet, after this volume, Aguilar never again published (in her lifetime) a work in quite so conventional a theological form, even though she was writing prayers, Biblical interpretations, and exegetical tracts all her life.[3] A review of *The Spirit of Judaism* from the British journal *The Voice of Jacob* clarifies why Aguilar might have turned from more conventional theological writing to literary genres; opening the review with a lengthy passage about the lack of Jewish leadership in the current moment, the reviewer goes on to suggest that the existence of Aguilar's theological writing is evidence of this dire condition of Jewish leadership. The male reviewer offers a quite derogatory evaluation of Aguilar's ideas about religious tradition and Talmud, suggesting they are "generalized from few facts" and thus exhibit the "peculiar readings of [their] fair writer"; it is a quite typical dismissal of women's religious authority, a dismissal which explicitly names theology as "the province of schoolmen." However, the reviewer continues, when she "quits" that "province," Aguilar can be praised, associated with a more sanctionable role for a woman, that of the poetess.

For the male reviewers of Aguilar's theological writing, the genre of lyric poetry was a more suitable place for a young woman; turning to the poetic element of *The Spirit of Judaism*, these reviewers see Aguilar not as "peculiar," but rather as "fervid, eloquent and truthful." Clearly, the male Jewish reviewer calls on the emerging discourse of the poetess in this reference, seeking to align Aguilar with what must be termed a Christian tradition of female writing, rather than a tradition of Jewish theological leadership. And while Aguilar seems to have taken the advice of this reviewer by choosing to publish in her lifetime only in genres other than conventional theology after this book, I argue that Aguilar's use of lyric poetry allowed her to offer her own specific set of theological ideas while escaping the criticism of Rabbinical authority. Responding pragmatically to the critique of her theological authority, but never relinquishing her powerful vision of a spiritual Judaism, Aguilar constructed her own unique religious and literary identity with and against the "provinces" of the traditional Jewish male Torah scholar/Rabbi and the emerging figure of the (Christian) woman writer.

The second passage above, quoted from Aguilar's *The Jewish Faith: Its Spiritual Consolation, Moral Guidance, and Immortal Hope* (1846), demonstrates how important literature was to Aguilar's larger religious project. Presented as a series of letters between an older Jewish woman and a young Jewish girl on the verge, it seems, of Christian conversion, *The Jewish Faith* uses fictional characters to generate epistolary theological prose. With these fictional letters, Aguilar creates the authoritative voice of a Jewish woman who serves as theologian, teacher, and spiritual guide to a young Jewish woman. In the midst of her detailed explanations of Jewish devotional practice, Jewish theology, and Jewish history, the older woman asserts – with "temples throb[bing]" – the imperative need for a "Jewish literature" that can explain and justify Judaism to both Jewish and Christian readers. Here and elsewhere in her work, Aguilar insists that the "right reverence" of Judaism can only occur when both Christians and Jews can understand "the true spirit of . . . hope" that is in Jewish people and Judaism itself. Noting elsewhere that Christian books were always "infused" with the doctrine of Christianity, Aguilar critiques the notion that Christian literature is "universal" – that is, without its own prejudices. She argues that there must be a Jewish literature that can challenge the dominance of Christian anti-Semitic and anti-Judaic representations, create positive Jewish self-identity, and encourage more accurate theological understandings of Judaism within Victorian culture.

Aguilar's desire to produce literature that promotes a new understanding of Judaism was in response to her awareness of the hegemony of Christianity in her culture, and she paid special attention to the needs of Jewish women in her writing, knowing that they were often readers of Victorian novels and poetry written from Christian perspectives. Aguilar understood that the explicit association between true womanhood and Christianity often depicted in the literature of the day could have a particularly detrimental effect on Jewish women's connection to Jewish spirituality and practice. Aguilar exploits the emerging cultural power of the "spiritual" woman writer and the discourse of theological poetry while also offering conscious resistance to the ways Christian women writers appropriate Jewish/Biblical women in the service of their own Christian and artistic authority. Although Aguilar often made explicit links of her own to this tradition of woman's writing, she could never fully align herself with the category of the "authoress" because it was an identity that, in her mind, was too closely tied to the literary marketplace and thus not seen as "holy."

Indeed, in her short story "The Authoress," Aguilar quite explicitly addresses the concerns she has about women writers. Early on in the story, her heroine, Clara, must use her writing as a source of necessary income after her father's death. Later, however, she and her mother come into some money, and Clara rejoices that "now . . . I may concentrate my energies to a better and holier purpose than the mere literature of the day; now I may indulge in the dream of effecting *good*, more than the mere amusement of the hour; now I am no longer *bound*" (231; emphasis in original). When she speaks of being "bound," Clara makes an interesting twist on the usual notions of women's being bound in a domestic, female space; on the contrary, it is not the domestic space that "b[i]nds" her, but rather having to rely on the public literary marketplace; she is ostensibly "freed" at the moment she can concentrate on the production, of religious texts, rather than commercial texts. Examining an explicitly Christian woman in "The Authoress," Aguilar hints at how she would like to revise the relationships between gender, literary production, and religious texts in Victorian England; that she chose to write in the context of Christian England is of course not surprising, since she was clearly aware the figure of the "authoress" was understood to be a Christian woman in her culture. The story acknowledges, I think, that the figure of a Jewish "authoress" would have been somewhat of an anomaly to her larger audience of either Christians or Jews.

Aguilar's self-conscious references to the discourse of the "poetess" and "authoress" in her fiction and poetry allowed her to link her own literary identity to that of Christian women writers; her challenge, of course, was to co-opt some of the cultural authority of the poetess without relinquishing her specific Jewish identity and voice. Thus, while she explicitly cites figures like Felicia Hemans, Mary Howitt, Caroline Bowles, and Joanna Baillie as examples of a "spiritual tradition" of writing with which she associates herself, Aguilar's work also offers a subtle critique of the assumption that women's spirituality – and poetry – are rooted in Christian identity.[4] Because lyric poetry was explicitly linked to Christian theological discourse, as we saw in chapter 2, finding a way to claim poetry for her specifically Jewish needs was crucial to Aguilar's larger literary project.[5]

BACKGROUNDS: BIOGRAPHICAL AND CRITICAL

Aguilar was born in 1816 in the Hackney district of London and died in Germany (having gone there for health reasons) in 1847.[6] Her mother and father were both of Sephardic origin, their respective families having escaped from Portugal and Spain; as Beth-Zion Lask Abrahams points out, Aguilar's family seems to have practiced traditional Jewish observance, her father, Emmanuel Aguilar, serving actively in the Sephardic community and particularly in the Spanish and Portuguese Synagogue. In 1828, the family moved to Devonshire, apparently because of the ill health of Aguilar's father. This move to a rural setting made an important rupture in the twelve-year-old girl's world view; Aguilar's few chroniclers have cited this move as a formative moment for her ideas about the relationships between Christianity and Judaism, as well as Christians and Jews. Abrahams explains Aguilar's tolerance for Christianity as a rational, logical response to these early experiences with "gentle Christian society." Apparently, Aguilar attended Protestant services quite frequently, "altering those parts of the prayer-book where she could not join to her belief" (Abrahams, "Grace Aguilar," 139), and Aguilar often recounts in later writings the value of attending Christian services as a way of clarifying one's own Jewish identity. However, these moments in Christian worship services were clearly vexed for Aguilar as well; many unpublished poems in the manuscript copy books in University College Library (London) describe the conflicts and despair Aguilar experienced when she chose not to follow a dear friend into Protestant church services; Aguilar states explicitly in the poem that if she did enter the church, people would assume she was abandoning her Judaism.

Clearly, the rural isolation of Devonshire, and the lack of a strong Jewish community insisted that Aguilar seek attachments in her local community, in which Church worship was most likely a major social and cultural, as well as religious activity. Balancing her devout Jewish identity in such a world was obviously a complex and formative experience.[7] She portrays some aspects of this experience in her work of epistolary prose, *The Jewish Faith*, where she creates the fictional character of an isolated young Jewish girl, Annie Montague, who writes letters to her older Jewish woman friend, Inez. In her depiction of a young girl who veers close to believing that "the Christian is the most spiritual" religion, Aguilar explores the experience of living as a minority in majority Christian culture; like her fictional creation Annie, Aguilar's experiences with a brand of rural Protestantism seem to have given her an early understanding not just of the principles of Christian doctrine, but also evidence for the ways Christian literature, theology, and interpretation represented – or misrepresented – Jewish identity and history.[8]

Aguilar's family differed from that of her fictional Annie, however, in that it is clear that Aguilar's parents instilled in her a very positive sense of Jewish identity. Aguilar was educated mostly by her mother, according to Abrahams, who also notes Aguilar's constant literary and scholarly activity from an early age. Later in life, Aguilar opened a boarding school for boys with her mother; the advertisement in the *Voice of Jacob* states they would receive instruction in "Religion, the English and Hebrew Languages, Writing, Arithmetic, Geography and History" (Abrahams, "Grace Aguilar," 141), suggesting the breadth of both Aguilar's and her mother's education. It seems both her parents were invalids of sorts, and Aguilar's writing took on an important economic role in the family. Abrahams speculates that the delayed publication of some of her non-Jewish writing, like *Home Influence* (1847), written ten years before it was published, may have been prompted by strained economics after her father's death in 1846 ("Grace Aguilar," 144). In June of 1847, Aguilar left England to seek the German spas on the advice of her doctors; she died in Frankfurt-on-Main in September of that year.[9]

Aguilar's publishing history is extraordinary under any circumstances; that she herself was sick for much of her life makes it that much more remarkable. She published an anonymous volume of poems titled *The Magic Wreath* in 1835; in 1838 she translated Orobio de Castro's *Israel Defended* from the French, a translation that was commissioned by Moses Moccatta, one of the century's most prominent and influential Anglo-Jews. Her first original work published under her own name was *The Spirit of Judaism*, written in 1837 but published in 1842 (the original manuscript was lost in a transatlantic crossing and rewritten); the book was edited by Isaac Leeser, a prominent Philadelphia Rabbi whose works Aguilar read and admired. Aguilar sent Leeser the manuscript of her book, asking that he edit it; Leeser published the volume, but only after adding extensive commentary and "corrections," none of which Aguilar saw before the text was published. The fact that Aguilar wrote a fiery and irate response to Leeser's review of her next work, *The Records of Israel*, suggests she was all too capable of defending herself when given the opportunity.[10]

Between 1843 and her death in 1847 Aguilar published *The Records of Israel* (*2 Tales*) (1844), *The Women of Israel* (1845), *The Jewish Faith: Its Spiritual Consolation, Moral Guidance, and Immortal Hope* (1846), *The History of the Jews in England* (1847), *and Home Influence: a Tale for Mothers and Daughters* (1847). After her death in 1847, Aguilar's mother became her official editor, and continued publishing her daughter's work posthumously. Not all of Aguilar's texts took up Jewish themes; she wrote a Scottish historical romance titled *The Days of Bruce: A Story of Scottish History*, published in 1852. Her novel *Home Influence* was republished in 1849 by Aguilar's mother and is prefaced with Aguilar's own reassurance to Christian readers that it is a "simple domestic story, the characters in which are all Christians, believing in and practicing that religion" (cited in Galchinsky, *The Origin of the Modern Jewish Woman Writer*, 174). *Home Influence* had gone through twenty-four editions by 1869, rivaling its nearest counterpart in women's "moral sphere" writing, Sarah Lewis' *Woman's Mission* (1839). The sequel to *Home Influence*, *A Mother's Recompense* (1851) was also non-Jewish in content. In addition, a volume of prayers, sermons, and exegetical writing was published by her mother; titled *Essays and Miscellanies: Choice Cullings from the Manuscripts of Grace Aguilar*; this volume suggest that Aguilar was writing conventional theology throughout her life, even though not choosing to publishing it. Aguilar's most famous fiction of Jewish content, published after her death, was the novel *The Vale of Cedars; or The Martyr* (1850), and the collection of stories *Home Scenes and Heart Studies* (1853). Many of Aguilar's works went through numerous editions and some were translated into German, Italian, Yiddish, and Hebrew. At her death in 1847 her obituary appeared in British periodicals as far ranging as the

London Athenaeum, *The Jewish Chronicle*, and *The Art Union*, as well as in American and German presses.

Throughout all of her life, Aguilar was also writing and publishing poetry in a wide variety of British and American journals. Aside from her volume *The Magic Wreath*, the manuscript copy books in University College Library record her poetry from about 1833 to 1839, often copied in books complete with handwritten sample cover pages and tables of contents; she was clearly aiming for publication. This early poetry takes up historical narratives and romance as well as dedicatory and personal poems; as she gets older, her interest in devotional poetry increases, and it is this later poetry that is easiest to find in published sources, especially Leeser's journal, *The Occident*. Abrahams offers an interesting anecdote about Aguilar's publication efforts after 1842:

> Quantities of verse, some written a long time earlier, are now to be met with in both the general and the Jewish press. One sees also Grace's own new assessment of her new [successful] position, such as her irritation when the *Voice of Jacob* failed to publish a contribution from her pen as soon as it was received. It was promptly dispatched and published in the Christian *Ladies Magazine*. The same effusion was sent to Leeser's *Occident* in Philadelphia and found ready publication. ("Grace Aguilar," 143)

What we learn from these anecdotes is that Aguilar fully intended her poetry to be read by Christian and Jewish audiences; just as her theological goal was to reach both Christian and Jewish audiences in the name of having "Judaism rightly reverenced" by both groups. And indeed, Abrahams also points out that Aguilar may have been more fully appreciated by Christian audiences than Jewish ones. A strange series of editorials in *The Jewish Chronicle* after Aguilar's death cites the lack of respect Aguilar was given by prominent Anglo-Jewry (with the exception of the Moses Moccatta commission mentioned above), a fact that may also account for the mixed reception her early theological works received from an Anglo-Jewish community.[11]

This appreciation by Christian audiences and her obvious interest in reaching such an audience has had the effect in critical literature of casting Aguilar as too interested in Christianity, a critique which has thus led to an implicit questioning of her Jewish identification. Abrahams criticizes her theology in *The Spirit of Judaism* as representing a form of "Jewish Protestantism drawn from her early association with non-Jewish acquaintances" and likewise notes that "The concentration on spirituality and religious submissiveness does not in her case go together with profound knowledge of Rabbinical Judaism ... a great deal of her Jewish knowledge was derived largely from the Christian studies of Jewish learning, rarely the original sources, and certainly never from a direct study of the Talmud or Codes" ("Grace Aguilar," 142). Abrahams' criticisms here are intriguing, since it is hard to imagine where she thought Aguilar would have gotten a "profound knowledge of Rabbinical Judaism" or access to "direct study of the Talmud or Codes" as a Jewish woman in the nineteenth century; that is, for both Abrahams and the Jewish men who reviewed her work above, Aguilar's theological authority was always suspect because of her apparent lack of scholarly Jewish learning.[12] Such a critique, however, misses the fact that Aguilar fervently believed that only through active "defensive" engagement with Christian culture could Jews and Judaism advance in Diaspora life; she took on this project of advancing Jewish learning despite the fact that she was excluded from traditional Jewish theology. If she sought strategies that could speak conclusively and inclusively to Christian readers, it was always part of a project of advancing Judaism and the Jewish people, a rhetorical strategy, I would argue, rather than ideological commitment to Christian/Protestant doctrine.

Yet I think the claim – or accusation – of "Jewish Protestantism" is more complex than it may appear; in many ways, such a claim also defuses the radical nature of Aguilar's Jewish theological critique, a critique that actually seems to anticipate many later ideas of twentieth-century Jewish feminism. For when Abrahams names Aguilar's "Jewish Protestantism," she seems to respond to Aguilar's claim that "private spirituality" can create a substantive relationship between the individual and God, one not dependent on halakha (traditional Rabbinical interpretation of Jewish law). Yet, later feminist approaches to Judaism have raised quite similar concerns with the role of "tradition" in Jewish women's religious practices and experiences. In her 1989 article "Creating a Jewish Feminist Theology," Ellen Umansky titles one section "Delineating the Problem: Personal Experience versus Tradition" and writes that any Jewish feminist would have to decide which voice to listen to: "her own voice or the voice of Jewish tradition" (189). Umansky goes on to suggest that the Jewish feminist theologian will have to redefine the term "theology" itself, constructing a specifically feminist understanding of a "responsive" Jewish theology that

need not be a commitment to the norms of that tradition but to its sources and "fundamental categories" of God, Torah, and Israel. Jewish feminist theology then, is a theology that emerges *in response* to Jewish sources and Jewish beliefs. These responses are shaped by the experiences of the theologian as woman and as Jew. What may emerge is a transformation not only of Jewish theology but of the sources the feminist uses in transmitting her visions. ("Delineating the Problem," 195)

From this understanding of Jewish theology, I think it clear that Aguilar maintains an unwavering commitment to Judaism; she constructs a theology that makes a commitment to "God, Torah, and Israel" while never fully deferring to the "normative" scholarly traditions of Jewish commentary. If we call Aguilar's emphasis on the individual's relationship to the Bible and God "Jewish Protestantism," I think we exclude the possibility of asserting – as Aguilar did repeatedly – that Judaism offers a profound system for deeply personal interactions with God, Torah, and Jewish history. To a priori assume that such an emphasis is "Protestant" is, on some level, to reify the anti-Judaic (and likewise anti-Catholic) premises that were also part of the Protestant Revolution. Instead, we might more productively locate Aguilar's emphasis on the individual and private relationships to God, Torah, and Jewish history as a sustained and detailed theology which sought to offer nineteenth-century Jewish women full subjectivity within Judaism; in so doing, Aguilar rewrites the notion of theology itself long before a Jewish feminist movement theorized such a position.

REORGANIZING PUBLIC AND PRIVATE: AGUILAR'S ALLIANCE WITH ROMANTICISM

Exposing a work, which has long been the darling object of an author's cares, the treasured subject of his secret thoughts, the companion of private hours, to the eye of a censorious world, must ever be attended with many varied and conflicting feelings, more particularly if that treasured subject be theology ... the condemnation or approval of peculiar sentiments and feelings, may be attended with a degree of pain, which, however, can at length become indifference; but when it is the deepest, dearest, most precious feelings of the heart included in that one word, Religion, – indifference can never blunt the pain, or ease the trembling doubt which ever attend their exposure to the world. (*The Spirit of Judaism*, 9)

Understanding Aguilar's conceptualization of public and private realms within Jewish life and practice is one key to understanding her larger poetic project and achievement. As we turn more specifically to examine how Aguilar's theology was expressed in her poetry, it becomes clear that Romantic poetic discourse offered to Aguilar a number of poetic

models – as well as theories of experience – that conformed to her own
religious thinking. She developed this strain of her theology in her very
first work, *The Spirit of Judaism* and she continued to develop it in her
theological writing that was only published after her death.[13] In *The Spirit
of Judaism*, Aguilar challenges the authority of traditional Jewish scholarship and commentary in order to make a claim for a more personal and
"spiritual" approach to Jewish theology. In order to reorganize the relative weight granted to scholarly versus experiential authority in Jewish
theology, Aguilar first offers a quite unique interpretation of theology
itself, cited above. If a work of theology is traditionally defined as the
very public and scholarly work of an educated man, Aguilar's opening
paragraph (above) essentially redefines the meaning of "religion" and
"theology" as a deeply private activity that encompasses very personal,
and conventionally female, "feelings of the heart." With this definition,
she reverses the conventional notion of theology as that which is a highly
public treatise designed to regulate individual private devotions, and
points toward the poetic theology of thinkers like Stopford Brooke and
John Keble. In *The Spirit of Judaism*, Aguilar articulates her suspicion of
"mere declamatorial eloquence . . . by those who can glibly and smoothly
give them vent in words" (9) and so she raises a theme that recurs in
much of her other writing: a suspicion about the authenticity of those
who speak or write for publication or fame only.[14] Indeed, as the passage
above suggests, for Aguilar, it is the very notion of public "exposure"
that threatens the development of a personal theology, an exposure to
the "censorious world" – a term that seems to encompass any number
of potential audiences who might critique her claim to authority.

Explicitly in *The Spirit of Judaism*, and implicitly in her poetry, as we
shall see, Aguilar argues that the hierarchy which grants more value to
the public (religious) life needs to be reversed. And in taking on the
relative weight of public and private devotion in Judaism, Aguilar necessarily addresses issues of gendered authority in Judaism as well. In
nineteenth-century Judaism, the study of literary and oral literature was
only available to men; women were completely excluded from Talmudic
study and commentary. Likewise, within Jewish law, women were ex-
empt from the obligations of public prayer; this exemption stems from the
Talmudic principle that "women are free from commandments that must
be performed at specific times" (Gordis, *The Dynamics of Judaism*, 180). In
Women and Jewish Law, Rachel Biale analyzes the larger patterns of inclusion and exclusion in the mitzvot (commandments) applied to women
regarding public prayer and Torah study and concludes:

The exemptions substantially exclude women from the realm of public religious life. At best, women remain passive participants in public prayer and reading of the Torah. In the final analysis the status of women in relation to the mitzvot is a result of the position of women in traditional Jewish society: they have no public role and their proper sphere is the home. The private nature of women's prayer is a result of the same exclusion of women from public life. (40)

Aguilar's own distrust of the public realm of Jewish practice, as well as the public secular realm, made it impossible for her to solve the problem of Jewish women's religious agency by making claims for women's public rights in Judaism. Instead, she claims the private sphere as the essential realm of true Jewish practice.

Making her claims in the name of the individual's spiritual agency, and within a historical context of lapsing spiritual commitment in the nineteenth-century Anglo-Jewish community, Aguilar's argument is one primarily concerned with Jewish spiritual renewal, an argument with which her editor, Rabbi Isaac Leeser, often takes issue. Consider this paradigmatic moment from *The Spirit of Judaism*, where Aguilar asserts a core tenet of her theology, followed by her own, and Leeser's footnotes to the comment.

were the Jewish religion studied as it ought to be by its professors of every age and sex; were the BIBLE, not *tradition*,* its foundation and defense; were its spirit felt, pervading the inmost heart, giving strength and hope, and faith and comfort: we should stand forth firm as the ocean rock, which neither tempest nor the slow, still, constant dripping of the waters can bend or shake ... the more we studied of their belief, the more we should feel the veil cast upon them is indeed of God.* (27–8, emphasis in original)

In many ways this short passage captures a number of major themes of *The Spirit of Judaism* and later work. Aguilar puts a major emphasis on the study of the Bible by all Jewish "professors of every age and sex," – a nice turn on the notion of profession – while de-emphasizing the role of "tradition." The passage is imbedded in a larger point about the benefits in Jewish/Christian theological dialogue; there can be no danger in such dialogue, Aguilar argues, provided that the Jewish participant has the right Jewish "spirit ... pervading the inmost heart." It is this heartfelt spirit that provides the best defense against the ever-present Christian "tempest" – or her more unusual image, the "slow, still, constant dripping" which stands for the constant and subtle erosion of Jewish faith which might occur when living in a completely Christian culture.

There are two footnotes attached to this passage, one Leeser's, the other Aguilar's. Aguilar inserts her footnote to the end of the above passage, noting that her point "is not mere fanciful hypothesis of the author alone; it owes its foundation alike to constant observation and personal experience" (28). This seems a curious moment to assert this authority of experience unless Aguilar recognized the danger of her position; indeed, Aguilar's use of the forms of scholarly evidence here to claim a certain personal authority for her ideas was well placed, as Leeser does indeed question her point most forcefully, in his own footnote (which takes up close to a full page of text) to the phrase "not tradition"; part of it reads:

It is useless to say, that the Scriptures speak for themselves; they assuredly do so to the person who has received instruction; but it requires no argument to prove that difference of education makes people take a different view of the sacred Text ... Certainly the Scriptures should constitute the daily exercise of every Israelite; but the interpretations, dogmas and opinions of our ancients should not be neglected; ay, tradition is the firm support of the Unity of God. (28)

When Leeser states that "difference of education makes people take a different view of the sacred Text," he highlights one of the major points of difference between Aguilar and himself, for in fact their difference in Jewish education does determine their "different view" – not of the Scriptures, but of the centuries of Jewish learning ("the ancients") to which women have been barred. As Michael Galchinsky has written: "If there was a difference between Aguilar's version of reform and Jewish men's, it was that hers was motivated by an acute awareness that she had been excluded from many of the primary texts of her tradition because of her gender" (*The Origin of the Modern Jewish Woman Writer*, 145). Their very different awareness of traditional Jewish learning also affects the way these two thinkers understand the very definition of Jewish identity; Leeser writes that it is "the received mode of interpretation which forms the characteristic distinction between us and others" (*The Spirit of Judaism*, 27); Aguilar, on the other hand, locates the most profound source of Jewish difference in the individual's particular and personal embrace of Torah.

Aguilar's interest in validating the "private" dimensions of Judaism has also provoked complex responses from Jewish literary critics who try to account for the degree of Aguilar's Jewish observance through the texts of her theology. As we already saw, one such critique positions Aguilar as a "Jewish Protestant." A more complex reading comes from Aguilar's most important contemporary criticism, Michael Galchinsky's *The Origin of the Modern Jewish Woman Writer: Romance and Reform in Victorian England*.[15] Linking her domestic and spiritual Judaism to the theology of the male Jewish reformers of her day, Galchinsky argues that Aguilar's relative historical success as a writer emerges from her ability "to bargain," to construct ideological "trade-offs [that] enabled her work to appeal to groups on every side" (187). He writes:

Conversionists could see her as a "Jewish Protestant," while Jews could laud her as a moderate reformer with strong traditional leanings. In the 1860s, when women's rights debates grew strong, Aguilar's work could appeal both to feminists and to anti-feminists. Feminists could support her work as a Jewish woman's groundbreaking act of self-representation and advocacy, a stage on the way to liberation, while anti-feminists could support it as a model of modesty and domesticity. (187)

Galchinsky's analysis notes the multiple subject positions Aguilar was able to occupy in Victorian England and appreciates the complexity of her literary and religious identities. In particular, he notes Aguilar's repeated rejection of a public female sphere, writing that: "Aguilar's genuine commitment to assigning women to the sphere of the domestic was in conflict with her genuine desire to have her ideas on the separation of spheres known and acknowledged by the public" (159). Through careful analysis of her fiction, Galchinsky theorizes that Aguilar's writing struck "bargains" between the already established Victorian paradigms of gender and separate spheres, and he reads Aguilar as advocating that Anglo-Jews should restrict their expressions of Jewish difference to the private sphere, and appear as fully assimilated "liberal" Jews in public. This private sphere, for Galchinsky, is thus differentiated from conventional Christian Victorian domestic ideology in its ability to foster specifically Jewish worship and cultural identity. Yet Galchinsky nevertheless associates Aguilar's "private" realm with a sphere of domesticity that replicates paradigms of Victorian Christian culture, and thus in his theory, it is a realm that excludes the production of literary or theological texts which are assumed to exist within the binary opposite of the "public and male" realm.

With her overt concern with women's spiritual lives, and with an emphasis on the link between the spiritual and domestic sphere, Aguilar can often appear complicit with reigning discourses of Victorian separate gendered spheres. Indeed, Aguilar remained, I think, remarkably uninterested in promoting women's access to public literary voices and public religious spaces, despite her own role as one of the most public Jewish voices of her day, and I want to suggest that this seeming contradiction which Galchinsky also notes in Aguilar's literary persona can be understood more clearly in light of her larger theological project. For while Aguilar clearly subscribes to a "separation of spheres" for men and women, what has been missed in most analyses of Aguilar's work is how her theology reorganizes the very meaning of those public and private spheres within Judaism, and likewise, creates a different trajectory for public and private gendered spheres than that of conventional Christian culture. Aguilar seeks to realign traditional forms of Judaism which place highest value on the communal devotional practices of the synagogue and the traditions of male Rabbinical scholarship. In place of an emphasis on the public, communal, and scholarly aspects of Judaism, Aguilar's theology suggests that it is the private, individual aspects of Jewish worship that are at the core of Jewish religious identity.

Thus, while we may be tempted to read her theology as one that ultimately reinscribes women's disenfranchisement from public space, it is important to see that within Aguilar's theological vision of Judaism, public speech, communal public worship, and the traditions of a "professional" male Rabbinate are all highly problematic forms of Jewish practice which impinge on the possibility of individual spiritual connection with God; thus, her goal is not to claim women's rights in what she sees as the problematic public space of institutionalized worship, but rather to position the private and individual as the central theological power in Judaism. By reworking the hierarchy of public and private devotion, Aguilar insists that women can claim full agency as Jewish devotional subjects, in contradistinction to various traditional practices and precepts that, in the nineteenth century, tended to position women as second-class citizens within Jewish law.

From this abbreviated reading of the issues of religious authority in Aguilar's earliest theological writing, we can begin to see why Romantic poetic theory and poetic texts proved so attractive to Aguilar in her larger theological project. Aguilar's attitude to Rabbinical scholarship puts her in a position analogous to the ways first-generation Romantic poets positioned themselves *vis-à-vis* traditions of literary/scholarly authority. Just as the hegemonic Romantic poets defined their poetic project against the courtly and scholarly conventions of the eighteenth-century neo-classicists in order to represent the philosophical truths of common experience, Aguilar defines her theological project against the traditions of Jewish scholarship in order to represent the truth of women's

Jewish experience. In Romantic poetics, authoritative privilege is granted to the expression of personal, private experience which can claim authority not on the basis of scholarly learning (as in an eighteenth-century model of poetry), but rather in its relative freedom from the weight of traditional literary learning.

Aguilar turns specifically to Wordsworth to authorize her theories of women's spirituality in two places in her prose writing, and these examples help demonstrate how important Romantic ideology was to her larger project in defining women's religious identity. The last lines of the story "The Authoress" read:

as Lady Granville, the authoress, continues her path of literary and domestic usefulness, proving to the full how very possible it is for woman to unite the two, and that our great poet * is right when, in contradiction to Moore's shallow theory of the unfitness of genius to domestic happiness, he answered – "It is not because they possess genius that they make unhappy homes, but because they do not possess genius enough. A higher order of mind would enable them to see and feel all the beauty of domestic ties." ("The Authoress," 243–4)

Footnoting "the great poet" as Wordsworth, Aguilar makes her final claim to the premier male poetic authority of the day as one who upholds the importance of uniting "genius" with women's domestic lives. The "authoress" becomes the model rather than the aberration for domestic happiness.

The use of Wordsworth in "The Authoress" remains, however, within a completely Christian context; more radical, I think is Aguilar's use of Wordsworth as a primary "proof text" in a fascinating passage from the conclusion of *The Women of Israel*, her most theologically charged work after *The Spirit of Judaism*. As part of an extended peroration on Jewish women's spirituality, Aguilar writes:

She [the Jewish woman] will look on the meanest flower, the humblest bird, even as on the loftiest things of nature, with that peculiar feeling which the poet describes in those exquisite lines:

> "Thanks to the Human heart by which we live,
> Thanks to its tenderness, its joys and fears,
> To me, the meanest flower which blows can bring
> Thoughts that do often lie too deep for tears." *

because she feels them the work of her Father in heaven, created as much for her individual joy and thanksgiving, as for the multitudes, who in the Past and the Present and Future have gazed, and will still gaze upon the same.

This is to be spiritual; this is to be an Israelite; this is to be WOMAN. We are quite aware that many of our English readers will exclaim "Why this is to be a Christian!" and refuse to believe that such emotions can have existence in a Jewish heart. While our Jewish readers will, in consequence, refuse to seek its attainment, because if it resemble Christianity it cannot be Jewish; both parties choosing to forget that the SPIRIT of their widely different creeds has exactly the same origin, the word of God; whence all of Christianity, save its doctrine of belief, originally came … (*The Women of Israel*, 564)

This remarkable passage, with a footnote which acknowledges Wordsworth as the author of the famous lines from the "Intimations of Immortality" ode, accomplishes a number of important goals for Aguilar. It invests the Jewish woman with the same capacity for "peculiar feeling" as the Romantic poet, and it identifies this "peculiar feeling" with the apprehension of nature which produces "thoughts that do often lie too deep for tears." Yet, these thoughts about and emanating from natural observation are also fully linked to a specifically Jewish woman's spiritual identity. While the above passage does not exhort the Jewish woman to acts of poetry, nor does it name her as a prophet, it does suggest that her capacity to recognize God in nature is *just like* that of the Romantic poet. Further, this natural element is something which transcends historical cultural specificity, and so can provide a link between those "in the Past and the Present and the Future" just as it links Jewish and Christian women who can recognize this spirituality in nature as a link between their "widely different creeds."

Romantic poetic theory provided Aguilar with that which she could not find in her limited access to traditional Jewish philosophy, namely, a culturally sanctioned form and process for claiming individual spiritual experience as a source of philosophical and religious authority.[16] Thus, Aguilar's poetry is important in how it rewrites conventions of post-Romantic lyric poetry in order to represent the "private" experience of a Jewish woman as spiritually authoritative in a heterogeneous Victorian culture of Christian and Jewish readers. Her poetry – calling on mainstream Christian literary conventions – offers covert resistance against the exclusive male Rabbinical ownership of Jewish theology while simultaneously speaking in the hegemonic poetic language of early nineteenth-century England. Using this explicitly literary discourse, Aguilar could appear to be following the prescriptions of her Rabbinical reviewers who wished her to focus not on the "province of schoolmen," but on the province of poetry. Further, lyric poetry was also a genre, unlike traditional theology, that would allow Aguilar to accomplish one of her most important goals: namely, to reach both Christian and Jews in order to have "Judaism rightly reverenced."

AGUILAR AND ROMANTIC POETIC MODELS

Aguilar's early experiences in rural Devonshire contributed to a unique aspect of her Anglo-Jewish literary identity: her concern with nature poetry. While other Anglo-Jewish women writers who followed her, in particular Amy Levy and Emily Harris, tended to emphasize the importance of the urban setting in Jewish experience, perhaps in recognition of the Jewish exclusion from English pastoral traditions,[17] Aguilar's somewhat unusual life experience in rural England allowed her to participate in the Romantic tradition of nature poetry, most clearly seen in her series of poems titled "Communings With Nature." In this sequence, Aguilar calls on nature imagery to depict specifically Jewish experience, using imagery familiar to Romantic poetics, but using these nature poems to repeatedly praise God from a Jewish perspective. The "Communings With Nature" sequence is made up of six lyrics, respectively titled: "Night," "Ocean," "Hymn to Summer," "Autumn Leaves," "Autumn Winds," and "The Evergreen."[18] Each poem explores the particular natural phenomena of the title; in "The Evergreen," Aguilar makes her most pointed use of Romantic conventions of nature poetry for a specifically Jewish subject.

"The Evergreen" becomes a symbol of the "changeless" nature of Jewish identity through the ages; as such, this poem works to recast negative Christian stereotypes of Judaism, and to claim the natural world as rich with Jewish meaning. Opening with a question to the evergreen, "Why art thou sad and lone?" the stanza goes on to articulate the conventional response to the evergreen: "We leave thee as a thing of gloom, / That hath no gleesome tone." The rest of the poem goes on to reevaluate the beauty and worth of the tree that is often ignored in more conventional representations of the English landscape, or alternatively associated with gloomy or gothic settings. The second stanza makes an explicit connection between the evergreen's difference from other natural forms and its seemingly "unpoetic" identity:

Thou art so changeless, that we deem
No poesy dwells in thee,
No vision'd love, no shadowy dream
Shrin'd in thy leaves may be.

(lines 5–8)

The changelessness of the evergreen seems to make it less suited to the more conventional narratives of "poesy" which Aguilar names as "vision'd love," or "shadowy dream"; whereas other symbols of nature are often celebrated in traditional nature poetry for their changing seasonal shapes and forms, and thus likened to changing human emotional states or transitory heterosexual romance, the evergreen is a somewhat unconventional figure in that poetic tradition. Pointing out how in each season, spring, summer, and autumn, the evergreen is "pass[ed] by" (line 18), Aguilar suggests that only in winter does the evergreen seem to be appreciated.

> In winter's storms, – ah, there alone,
> When all is bleak and bare,
> We love to list thy changeless tone,
> To feel – our friend is there.
>
> And still thou smilest, – man's neglect,
> Rude storm, and blighting blast,
> Thine upward growth have never checked,
> Nor lain thee with the past. (lines 21–8)

Aguilar explores the evergreen as an important symbol of permanence despite "man's neglect," or the "blighting blast." As she demonstrates how the evergreen has persisted despite different forms of human and natural persecution, Aguilar begins to connect the evergreen with specifically Jewish identity; this identification is more explicit in the ninth stanza:

> Emblem of God's omnific love,
> His never-changing care!
> Fair shrub, His faithfulness to prove,
> Thou'rt scatter'd ev'ry where.
>   (lines 33–6)

At the moment the evergreen is defined in relation to God's "never-changing care," as well as described as "scatter'd everywhere," the metaphoric identification with the Jewish people is made; what the poem suggests is that only in learning to appreciate the special virtues of "changeless" constancy can one fully appreciate the evergreen/Judaism; likewise, even through neglect and crisis, Jews, like the evergreen, remain an emblem of God's "never-changing care." The evergreen is ultimately figured as a symbol – like so many other aspects of nature for Aguilar – for the permanence of God's love for the Jewish people.

Like her other theological work, this poem works to correct a vision of Judaism for both Jews and Christians, so that they can, as the last stanza asserts, "feel how much of poesy lies / In thy still changeless shrine. . ." Indeed, this poem offers a clear response to a Christian notion that God indeed did change his feelings toward Jews by instituting a second covenant in the form of Jesus; using the seemingly innocuous form of a Romantic nature poem, Aguilar manages to make a strong claim for the spiritual authority of Judaism's permanence despite Christian detractors. Further, by the end of the poem, the reader is asked to reconsider how the very notion of "poesy" and its conventions may encompass specifically Christian biases that cast the evergreen as "other," seemingly unpoetic. This tribute to the evergreen is thus a claim, albeit a subtle one, for understanding that Judaism is as beautiful and worthy of poetry as Christianity. Finding in the evergreen the quality of "poesy," Aguilar challenges traditions of English nature and devotional poetry that privilege specifically Christian symbols of resurrection and rebirth as signifiers of "the poetic."

Aguilar also asks her readers to self-consciously reflect on conventions of Romantic poetry in her poem "Angels: Written While Watching At Past Midnight, Alone By the Bedside of a Beloved Friend."[19] The title echoes Coleridge's "Frost at Midnight" lyric, which is also set at midnight with "the inmates of [his] cottage all at rest." In his poem, Coleridge observes a flicker of soot in a fire and uses that as a figure for "the idling Spirit" that has a seemingly universal presence. He contextualizes this figure of the film in supernatural folklore, including a footnote to this passage: "In all parts of the kingdom these films are called strangers and supposed to portend the arrival of some absent friend." His poem then muses on his own past childhood, and then on his son's future life in nature as a way of being with God, and offers a final merging of spiritual and natural forces in a powerful image of the "secret ministry of frost" which can transform dripping eaves drops into "silent icicles / Quietly shining to the quiet Moon."

Aguilar picks up on the figure of the "fluttering" supernatural presence in a remarkably similar setting of watching her sick mother sleep "after midnight." Like Coleridge, she senses "beauteous forms" which offer to her "a deeper quivering sense" (1–2). Yet, as the poem goes on, these beauteous forms are identified as "angels," and in a footnote like Coleridge's, Aguilar also identifies her source of these fluttering forms; where Coleridge links them to supernatural portents of pagan folklore, Aguilar terms them "Meek messengers of Heaven" (9) in her poem, and she adds a footnote that reads: "The Hebrew word מלאך [melach] translated angel, signifies lit. *messengers,* applied to whatever is sent by God to execute his will, from לאך Arabic,[20] to send or employ." Later in the poem she names those that "link this earth with heaven" (27) with another footnote to the Genesis story of Jacob's dream about angels, suggesting the angels in her poem are rooted in this Biblical reference. This footnoting strategy is familiar in much of Aguilar's verse; as I explore later in relation to her devotional verse, she is always careful to note Biblical passages as coming from Hebrew Scriptures, in order to suggest how figures of spirituality are located in Judaism, not only Christianity.

Thus, in "Angels" Aguilar takes the Romantic poetic model of the philosophical contemplation of natural phenomena, and transfers the genre into a scriptural context that explains the specifically Jewish theological concept of unseen divine beings. Significantly, she also relocates the poetic interchange from father to son to mother and daughter, highlighting the importance of women's private spiritual communication. Aguilar ends her poem much like Coleridge, with an image of the upward reflection of earthly forms to heaven.

> In ev'ry balmy sleep, that seals yon sufferer's aching eyes,
> In ev'ry smile, that on her lip, in cradled slumber lies,
> In ev'ry soothing thought that comes, to check the watcher's tear,
> Angels of Heav'n! – spirit forms! I know that ye are near;
> Oh linger round me! still oh still, my silent watch to share,
> And upward! upward on your wings my fainting spirit bear.
>
> (lines 29–34)

Where the Romantics turn to nature and the self as a source for contemplation of the supernatural, broadly and non-doctrinally conceived, Aguilar takes the same contemplative, domestic situation but transforms the poem into a contemplation on specific divine beings of angels that offer her a connection to God.

Both "Angels" and "The Evergreen" thus make claims on specific Romantic genres and styles; claiming this discourse gave Aguilar a particular kind of cultural authority through which to explore issues of Jewish experience, identity, and faith. Both poems allow her to enter into a discourse on various theological concepts – the relationship of Judaism to nature, exploration of the nature of divine beings – without ever having to make claims of Rabbinical authority. Further, Romantic discourse gave her a certain literary authority with a Christian literary audience steeped in the assumptions and values of Romantic verse. Indeed, in both

"Angels" and "The Evergreen," it is important to note that neither poem insists on an identification with Jewish experience as essential to constructing meaning. As we will see in the later work of Amy Levy, Jewish identification in these poems becomes a matter of an audience's perception; Aguilar's achievement in these lyrics is in finding a poetic voice fully participating in the conventions of a Christian literary tradition that can nevertheless speak to and about Jewish epistemology to those who can find it; it is, we might say, a lyric identity that can pass as non-Jewish, but maintains a Jewish perspective within Romantic conventions.

THE POLITICS AND POETICS OF ANGLO-JEWISH DEVOTIONAL LYRIC

This emphasis on the dual requirements of her audience becomes clearer in Aguilar's more specifically devotional poetry. In her series "Sabbath Thoughts," Aguilar's lyric strategies become more pointed in their refutation of the authority of scholarly theology; likewise, they counter more forcefully Christian misconceptions about Judaism. And in taking up what are even more theologically based questions in these poems, Aguilar finds her most effective means of combining the ostensible "province of schoolmen" with the poetic identity of the poetess who "pours forth her own pious sentiments of the heart's duties, and the soul's destiny." Indeed, these poems in particular also serve to critique that province of the scholar – and the poet, as ultimately misguided approaches to spiritual agency. Finally, if these poems seek to challenge certain presuppositions about the nature of a male, Rabbinical scholarly address to God, they also serve to challenge the conventionally assumed seamless relationship between the English devotional lyric and the assumption that such lyrics always emanate from a Christian perspective. In their use of a subtle dialogic structure which constructs a possible skeptical reader, Aguilar can address Christian detractors of Judaism who deny to it a deeply spiritual and personal quality of faith – as well as encourage Jewish readers to adopt a more direct religious relationship with God.

Aguilar confronted a knotty problem in seeking to write Jewish devotional verse in English: namely, how to write explicitly Jewish devotional poems within a tradition that claimed devotional verse as part of a "universal" (read: Christian) tradition. "Sabbath Thoughts" might best be described as devotional lyrics which – in the tradition of English Protestant devotional poetry and the Biblical Psalms – allow for religious questioning and musing within a specific theological perspective. The six poems that make up this sequence explore a variety of states of devotion, and are often subtitled to explain their situation: "Written on the Close of a Peculiarly Blessed Day of Rest," "Parting From Friends" or "Written During Illness." While it is a common technique of Romantic poetry to "situate" the poet's musing, Aguilar seems particularly concerned with placing these poems within a proper theological and personal context, a concern that might be of more urgency for a poet writing of Jewish religious experience to an heterogeneous audience.

We can see this concern for theological clarity in two of these poems which seem particularly concerned with issues of audience and authority. In "Sabbath Thoughts I,"[21] Aguilar begins with an epigraph from Proverbs, "[t]he heart knoweth its own bitterness, and a stranger intermeddleth not with its joy." This epigraph sets the stage for a poem that takes up the theme of being alienated from and misunderstood by a human audience; it also inserts the notion of "the stranger" as a figure for a human audience, as opposed to a figure of a familiar, understanding reader. This idea that audience is ultimately alienated from our deepest selves is pursued as the poem opens by arguing that God is the only ideal audience for "reading ... our inmost soul"; indeed, the poem seems to make a subtle argument against the false pretense that human audiences can understand "our secret selves" (lines 63). The first two stanzas read

> Yes! better far our God should read,
> And God alone – our inmost soul,
> That He alone can see it bleed
> 'Neath its dark veil of stern control;
> 'Tis best that man can never know
> One half the spirit's joy or woe.
>
> For did earth give us all we seek,
> A perfect sympathy and love –
> Did man console in accents meek –
> Oh, should we ever look above?
> Contented to the earth we'd cling,
> And clip the spirit's soaring wing!
>
> (lines 1–12)

This sense of the poet's isolation from the human audience is of course a commonplace of Romantic poetry, but I think it takes on a special significance in the context of the Anglo-Jewish woman writer, whose search for a receptive and authorizing audience remains doubly challenged by the cultural constraints of both patriarchy and anti-Semitism. If these initial lines reject the possibility of human "sympath[etic]" response, they likewise initiate a subtle critique of secular Romantic poetry which assumes others can "read . . . our inmost soul." The lines suggest that such a state of alienation is "best" because if one could be understood on earth one would have no reason to turn to God.

Later in the poem Aguilar continues with the idea that the deepest spiritual or emotional conditions are "unreadable," indeed unspeakable:

> We cannot give our sorrows speech –
> When all within is dark and drear,
> And none may mark the spirit's tear . . .
>
> (lines 28–30)

As Aguilar negates the possibility of speaking one's truest feeling, she also negates the power of human language, both written and spoken. The issue becomes not only that "none (human) can read" or hear the "spirit's veiled recess" but also that this spirit "can scarce define its own distress" (line 66). Distress, sorrow, the secret veiled self do not show themselves through any humanly discernible linguistic "mark," but

> . . . God will deign
> To hear each throb of agony,
> And trace unto its source the tear
> Which falls, when none to mark are near.
>
> (lines 63–6)

Aguilar devalues the conventional modes of Jewish male theological discourse, namely, reading and writing, as suitable modes for communing with God. The poem asserts that spiritual communication is extra-linguistic; however, Aguilar calls on the language of scholarship to describe this connection with God. Thus, God becomes the scholar "trace(ing) unto its source the tear"; Aguilar suggests there is a degree of male hubris in taking up the acts of "reading" and "tracing" in which God excels. Though there is no mention of the speaker's gender in this poem, Aguilar suggests here, as in *The Spirit of Judaism*, that God weighs the silent "lowly" prayer of women equally with the scholarly public learning of men. Aguilar thus uses the poem to reconstruct what might be understood as "representative" experience in Judaism. Recasting the significance of reading, writing, and human interpreting, Aguilar puts emphasis on individual prayer as the most important act of communication.[22]

If Aguilar devalues the trappings of scholarship in relation to Jewish devotional acts, she does again turn to the specifically scholarly technique of the footnote to help situate her larger theological concepts in relation to specifically Christian readers. Using this technique, somewhat unusual in the space of the lyric poem, Aguilar is able to make claims that resonate with both Jewish and Christian readers without relinquishing her commitment to Judaism. This footnoting strategy ensures that her Jewish readers will be able to claim her description of spirituality as explicitly Jewish, yet it also serves to assure a Christian reader that there are common themes that bind Jewish and Christian belief. Thus, in "Sabbath Thoughts I" she writes:

> No earthly forms the void can fill,
> Which thirsts to drink th'immortal spring –
> No earthly balm the heart can still,
> Which droops to clasp his Saviour's wing.*
> Then blessed be that lonely hour
> Which first proclaims a Father's power.
>
> Come then, and seek the Fount of love,
> Whose living waters all may share;
> The Friend who sits enshrined above,
> Will all our sorrows soothe and bear;
> Come but to Him, and He will give
> Us fitting grace, for heav'n to live.
>
> (lines 37–48)

Aguilar articulates a vision of an all-loving God using terms that would surely resonate with a Christian audience; her references to the "Saviour," "the Friend," and the "Fount of Love" are images found repeatedly in both Christianity and Judaism, though generally more associated with the Christian rhetoric of God/Jesus as "Love." Aguilar is careful to address this assumption that she must be referring to a Christian God; thus, the asterisk after the term "Saviour" offers a footnote that identifies the source of that idea in "Psalms XCI; Isaiah XLI 26, LX 16, LXIII 8." Guiding the reader to a number of specific passages in Psalms and Isaiah, the footnoting strategy reinforces that the figure of "Saviour" is an image from Hebrew Scriptures, not the New Testament. Thus, while this poem makes no overt statement of having a Jewish speaker, it manages to construct devotional images that can be claimed as "representative" from both Jewish and Christian perspectives.[23]

In "Sabbath Thoughts VI," subtitled "Written During Illness," Aguilar's own poetic voice more actively argues with Christian theories of Judaism.[24] The poem opens as if in conversation with a reader who seems to offer repeated, albeit silent opposition to the speaker's claims; recognition of this dialogic context transforms what seems like a deeply personal lyric into a larger meditation on the perception of Jewish religious identity in Christian history. The first stanzas read:

> Oh, do not think because I weep
> And smiles a while are flown,
> And thoughts of darkness o'er me creep,
> My God hath left me lone;
>
> That His deep love is vain to hush
> This wildly yearning heart,
> That to the dreams which o'er me rush,
> He cannot peace impart;
>
> That 'tis but vain, religious balm,
> Which joy my soul had stored,
> And fruitless all, the hope, the calm,
> Found in His precious word.   (lines 1–12)

These opening verses detail the speaker's depth of faith despite her bodily suffering, yet rather than stating this faith in positive terms, Aguilar casts this meditation against a reader who clearly might "think" that this Jewish speaker's despondency – physical and emotional – is in fact a sign that "God hath left" the speaker "lone." Anticipating the reaction of this reader, Aguilar is thus able to voice and refute traditional Christian anti-Semitic charges that the Jews have been left by God and replaced as the chosen ones through the intervention of Christian history, and that they will remain eternally bereft of God's redemption unless they convert.

Aguilar repeats again and again in this poem that the reader is not to interpret her religious crisis as a sign of God's rejection, finally explaining her position in Stanza seven:

> No! no! 'tis only for a little while,
> He turns away His face,
> And once again His cheering smile,
> My yearning soul shall trace;
>
> And 'tis His love, which lays me low,
> And bows my soul to dust,
> And bids the tear of anguish flow
> To mark if still I trust:
>
> If still, though comfortless, I turn,
> And pine, and long for Him,

> And loving mercy still discern,
> Though mortal sight be dim, –
>   (lines 25–36)

The speaker's emphatic "No! No!" is the culmination of the running refutation of the hidden auditor's response, and in this section of the poem the most important explanation for suffering from a Jewish perspective is made, namely, that suffering is the larger test of faith God asks of Jews throughout post-exilic history.

As if to enact this faith, the second half of the poem addresses God directly. Shifting the address away from the skeptical auditor, this second part of the poem retains its concern with Jewish/Christian relations by having its Jewish speaker insistently refuse the choice to "leave" her vision of God for a different kind of freedom.

> Heed not my crying, Lord! 'tis well,
> Or Thou wouldst let me free,
> Better in chains with Thee to dwell
> Than free, apart from Thee.
>   (lines 49–52)

The image of captivity initiates the poem's shift from the individual Jew to historical figures of Jewry. Here, the figure of freedom is associated with conversion, which might bring a relief for the cultural suffering of the Jewish community, but only at the cost of losing the Jewish God. Rather than seek such false freedom, the speaker instead argues there is a clear reason for her own, and by extension, the Jewish people's, suffering; referring to her "hours of pain," the speaker states:

> They call me for a while from earth,
> And all her pleasant dreams,
> And if they check the voice of mirth,
> And joy's too dazzling gleams:
>
> Oh, 'tis to hold commune with Thee,
> To feel I am Thine own,
> Thy "still small voice" would silent be
> In festal halls alone.   (lines 57–64)

Suffering is valuable here because it insists on a turning away from earthly pleasure to God, and likewise enables the speaker to hear God's "still small voice" which would not be audible in the context of festivity. The quoted passage, signficantly from the King James translation of 1 Kings 19: 12, positions the speaker as analogous to the prophet Elijah in his ability to hear God's voice in the midst of his suffering over Israel's faith-lessness; with this reference, the speaker suggests that it is her personal suffering that allows her – like the prophet – to hear God's "still small voice."

With her specific link to the Biblical prophet, Aguilar's speaker makes perhaps her most daring association; as Elijah is the (bereft) spiritual leader of that community, so too does Aguilar's speaker imply that her own experiences of suffering give her larger spiritual insights which might be prophetic for her community, though she does not fully spec-ify who that community might be. Indeed, as with her other devotional lyrics, the poem seeks to maintain a participation in a seeming uni-versal devotional experience – one that could be apprehended by a Christian or a Jew, at least. Thus, if one of the claims of Christian discourse is that it counters and transcends the particularity and thus "narrowness" of Judaism's emphasis on a "chosen" people, Aguilar counters those derogatory claims of Jewish particularity by suggest-ing that her Judaism also participates in a universally accessible di-vine experience – and that she herself, in her suffering, is a conduit for such a message. Yet "Sabbath Thoughts" does not necessarily pro-claim what the content of this prophetic message might be for those reading it; on the contrary, the poem maintains an explicit interest in the process of creating connection to God, rather than naming the spe-cific content of that communion. As she delineates the personal dy-namics of Jewish faith, Aguilar also fulfills her own commandment for a "Jewish literature," a literature that can counter the hegemony of anti-Judaic and anti-Semitic representations, and likewise reclaim the discourse of spirituality from a wholly Christian association. Writ-ing devotional lyrics under her own clearly Jewish signature, Aguilar inserts herself into a tradition of poetry that assumed the poet to be Christian; she claims the very space of the English lyric for Jewish ex-pression rendered universally meaningful.

If lyric poetry is the site where Aguilar emphasizes the potential "same-ness" of Jewish and Christian spirituality, her midrashic explorations of Biblical women in *The Women of Israel* is the site where she explores more specifically the differences between Jewish and Christian women, as well as between Jewish women of different historical eras. In *The Women of Israel*, she delineates her approach to history while also offering an im-portant sub-argument about the role of poetry and prophecy in Jewish women's history. In particular, Aguilar argues that the differing historical circumstances facing Jewish women, combined with their own personal devotional spirit, determine the authenticity of their poetry. Understanding Aguilar's sense of Jewish history is one way to understand her theory of women's poetry, and to explore, in more detail, her understanding of Jewish women's changing relationship to that "still small voice" of prophetic knowledge.

"THE HIGH-SOUNDING RELIGION OF FLOWING VERSE": AGUILAR AND THE POETRY OF BIBLICAL WOMEN

Looking back at the devotional and nature lyrics discussed above, it is worth noting that Aguilar rarely claims any exalted poetic or prophetic powers of apprehension for herself. Unlike Barrett Browning's triumphant claims to prophetic utterance in *Aurora Leigh*, or Rossetti's self-conscious exploration of the Christian woman poet in "Monna Innominata," Aguilar seems averse to highlighting her own individual artistry in her poetry, and rarely writes about the act of writing poetry as a subject in its own right. Likewise, her claims to prophetic authority seem rather limited compared to other women poets; her alliance with the "still small voice" of God is emblematic of a quiet poetic humility rather than a bold claim of access to God's word. This lack of a public self-reflexive poetics, coupled with her obvious endorsement of the private sphere and suspicion of the public, could easily result in Aguilar's work being dismissed by feminist theologians and critics alike. In this section, then, I suggest the complexity which marks Aguilar's interpretations of women's poetic agency, and emphasize her desire to challenge the terms through which Christian women claimed a superior moral and feminist political position – often on the basis of their religious identity as Christians. Aguilar understood quite acutely the different kinds of prophetic and poetic power that were granted to Jewish and Christian women in Victorian England, and thus she was a far more cautious advocate and very different kind of poet than her more audacious Christian sisters; in particular, she was extraordinarily attuned to the vicissitudes of history, and how historical and cultural context affect poetic and prophetic utterance.

One of the main arguments of *The Women of Israel* is to show contemporary Jewish women – whom Aguilar saw as disenfranchised from their own spiritual traditions – that they can model themselves on the examples of Biblical Jewish women, and that they can thus find personal connection to Jewish history. Yet with this argument, Aguilar comes up against a sharp contradiction: how can she construct Biblical women prophets as models for contemporary Jewish women when many of the women from Jewish history had far more religious agency and power in their historical moments than any Jewish woman in Victorian England? In particular, she comes up against the problem of Biblical female prophecy, and how to render powerful figures like Miriam and Deborah identifiable to contemporary Jewish women without insisting that women must act in the public spheres of politics or religious institutions as those Biblical women did. Her approach thus differs from that of Hemans' or Barrett Browning's use of Miriam as powerful woman poet and prophet who thus sanctions their own entry into the public literary and religious sphere (see chapter 3).[25] In *The Women of Israel*, Aguilar examines the roles and identities of Biblical Jewish women and maintains the suspicion of public religious voices she constructed in *The Spirit of Judaism*. This persistent devaluation of the public sphere of religious action creates her theory of women's prophetic/poetic agency – a theory that implicitly critiques the models of public authorship often associated with Christian women of her day.

The Women of Israel opens with an explicit critique of how Christian women wrongly appropriate the idea of true womanhood as a specifically Christian virtue. Placing herself in a line with Christian women who have preceded her in producing texts about Christian womanhood, Aguilar asks if these texts provide "woman of every race, and every creed, [with] all sufficient to teach her her duty and herself?" (2). She goes on to answer:

We would say she had; yet for the women of Israel still something more is needed. The authors above mentioned are Christians themselves, and write for the Christian world. Education and nationality compel them to believe that "Christianity is the sole source of female excellence." To Christianity alone they owe their present station in the world: their influence, their equality with man, their spiritual provision in this life, and hopes of immortality in the next. Nay more, that the value and dignity of woman's character would never have been known, but for the religion of Jesus; that pure, loving, self-denying doctrines, were unknown to woman; she knew not even her relation to the Eternal; dared not look upon Him as her Father, Consoler, and Saviour, till the advent of Christianity . . . We feel neither anger nor uncharitableness toward those who would thus deny to Israel those very privileges which were ours, ages before they became theirs; and which, in fact, have descended from us to them. Yet we cannot pass such assertions unanswered . . . (2).

Thus, *The Women of Israel* claims Judaism as a women's religion in a distinct challenge to Christian claims that "Christianity is the sole source of

female excellence." In her detailed study of every Jewish woman in the
Bible, Talmud, and even later Jewish history, Aguilar argues that true
womanhood actually resides in Jewish women; along the way, she offers a fascinating and complex subtext about authentic poetic/prophetic
speech. The difference between Aguilar's readings of Biblical women and
Christian women's readings is perhaps most evident in their readings of
Miriam's character and role.

Aguilar's chapter on Miriam is lengthy, but it does not focus much
attention on her powers of poetry or song; on the contrary, the section
casts Miriam as a false prophet/poet.[26] Aguilar begins her exploration of
Miriam by noting her connection to saving Moses as an infant, and then
turns to "her sharing the holy triumph of that brother, and responding,
with apparently her whole heart, to the song of praise bursting forth from
the assembled Israelites" (189). After quoting the Biblical passage from
Exodus that begins "And Miriam the prophetess," Aguilar writes:

> The Hebrew word הנביאה, [hanavayah] here used, and translated prophetess,
> means also, a *poetess*, and the wife of a prophet, and is applied sometimes to a
> singer of hymns. In this latter meaning, and perhaps, also, as a poetess, it must
> be applied to Miriam, as she was neither the wife of a prophet, nor, as in the
> case of Deborah, and afterward Huldah, endowed by the eternal with the power
> of prophecy itself. She appears to have been one of those gifted beings, from
> whom the words of sacred song flow spontaneously. The miracles performed
> in their very sight were sufficient to excite enthusiasm in a woman's heart, and
> awaken the burst of thanksgiving; and Miriam might have fancied herself at
> that moment as zealous and earnest in the cause of God as she appeared to be.
> But for true piety, something more is wanted than the mere enthusiasms of the
> moment, or the high-sounding religion of flowing verse. By Miriam not being
> permitted to enter the promised land, it is evident that she "had not followed
> the Lord fully," but had probably joined in the rebellions and mumurings which
> characterized almost the whole body of the Israelites during their wanderings
> in the wilderness. (189)

Aguilar begins her exploration of Miriam's significance by noting the
linguistic connection between the Hebrew term for prophetess and poetess, but by the end of her passage, she has discredited any notion that
Miriam is a true prophet or poet. Aguilar's theological connection to
the entire narrative of Jewish history insists that she cannot ignore the
second half of Miriam's story, in which she is accused of claiming false
prophetic powers, punished with leprosy by God, and ejected from the
camp of the Israelites for a week (Numbers 12). Where Barrett Browning,
as we saw in chapter 3, evades direct reference to Miriam's Biblical end,

Aguilar raises this conclusion to Miriam's Biblical fate in the same paragraph that she discusses her Song at the Sea, immediately insisting that Miriam's moment of song/poetry must be examined in terms of her larger historical narrative; in so doing, Aguilar suggests that rather than being aligned with God's power, Miriam is in fact shown to be one who "had not followed the Lord fully."

Aguilar essentially accuses Miriam of being a woman who is caught up in "mere enthusiasms of the moment," and thus her poetry is not authentic, but rather "the high-sounding religion of flowing verse" that does not reflect "true piety." Her act of poetry is not significant as an artistic triumph, but rather important in how it masks her problematic inner character. Aguilar's reading suggests that Miriam's very interest in public performance, and in calling attention to her prophetic powers may be a sign of her flawed spiritual character – her sense of "presumptuous self-importance" (*The Women of Israel*, 192). Aguilar's explanation for Miriam's actions is that she was jealous of Moses' wife Zipporah being raised above her; Aguilar goes into an extended analysis of how single women are prone to such feelings "of secret and unconfessed jealousy" unless they are "taught from earliest years to find and take pleasure in the resources *within*" (190). Thus, Miriam's actions represent how "most women, unenlightened by that pure spirit of religious love" (190) would act, and so she is interpreted by Aguilar as "one of the most perfect delineations of woman in her mixed nature of good and evil" (189). Rather than idealize Miriam as a prophetess who teaches women about public religious power, Aguilar instead casts Miriam as an example of a woman too caught up in her inner emotional life to distinguish between true piety and a personal desire for "elevation."

Miriam comes to represent a potentially dangerous model for Jewish women in Victorian England, a model of a woman who gives into "[P]resumption, jealousy, the scorn of individual blessings, in the coveting of others" (194). Yet, Aguilar's disavowal of Miriam's prophetic and spiritual leadership ends on a fascinating note; in an almost paradoxical twist, she ends up arguing that Miriam's ultimate punishment is a sign of women's high place in Judaism.

As women of Israel, the history of Miriam is fraught with particular interest, from its so undeniably proving that woman must be quite as responsible a being as man before the Lord, or He certainly would not have deigned to appear Himself as her judge. Were woman unable of herself to eschew sin, Miriam's punishment would have been undoubtedly unjust. Nay, were she not responsible for her *feelings* as well as acts, God would not thus have stretched forth His avenging hand . . . Were woman in a degraded position, Miriam, in the first place would not have had sufficient power for her seditious words to be of any consequence; and in the next, it would have been incumbent on man to chastise – there needed no interference of the Lord. We see, therefore, by the very sinfulness of Jewish women, as recorded in the Bible, undeniable evidence of their equality, alike in their power to subdue sin, and in its responsibility before God. (195)

Aguilar sees God's punishment of Miriam as a sign of respect for Miriam's identity – otherwise, she reasons, why not simply have Moses chastise her? Indeed, Aguilar goes further to state that "the Eternal graciously pardoned [Miriam] at the word of Moses, is not proof that Miriam needed the supplication of man, to bring her cause before the Lord, but simply that intercession from the injured for the injurer, are peculiarly acceptable to Him, and will ever bring reply" (195). Miriam is punished, it seems, not because she is a woman making claims to prophetic power, but because she is a misguided individual who stands equally before the Lord to be judged.

What Aguilar resists in her reading of Miriam, and indeed the other women prophets she examines, is any indication of "exceptional" character; in short, all of Aguilar's work in *The Women of Israel* is designed to show how, though important figures in their own right, Biblical women were no more "exceptional" than any Jewish woman of the nineteenth century. What differentiates Biblical women from contemporary Jewish women, Aguilar repeatedly argues, is that they lived in a time when Judaism was practiced freely, so women had more religious freedom than in the Diaspora. With her desire to render female heroines prophets just like any Jewish woman, Aguilar must dismantle certain assumptions about prophets; unlike the Romantic assumptions of the prophet as a special man, Aguilar suggests that what empowered these prophetic women was not their special-ness, but rather their historical context combined with personal devotion.

If Aguilar uses Miriam to warn women about projecting a public spiritual identity on faulty emotional premises, she turns to Hannah and Deborah to show the proper mode for women's poetic and prophetic acts. Thus, after narrating Hannah's story of childlessness, and her despair, Aguilar notes that "the condition of married women among the Jews, in the time of Judges, must have been perfectly free and unrestrained" (240). Aguilar quite specifically links Hannah's ability to go to the Temple and "pour out her gratitude to her God" to the freedom for women that marks that historical era of Judaism for Aguilar; this point about "equal access" to Temple prayer is designed to counter Christian claims that women were always more degraded in Judaism than in Christianity. Within that context, Hannah's initially silent prayer, and subsequent "song of gratitude" take on a specific role in Aguilar's analysis of women's poetic and spiritual voice. Aguilar interprets Hannah's silent prayer as follows:

We find her rising up after they had eaten and drunk in Shiloh, and without even imparting her intentions to her husband, much less asking his consent, going perfectly unattended and unrebuked to the temple of the Lord. There, in bitterness of soul weeping, she prayed unto the Lord of Hosts; and, in perfect accordance with Mosaic Law, which expressly provided for such emergencies, she vowed a vow, that if the Eternal would in His infinite Mercy remember His handmaid, and grant her a male child, she would devote him unto the Lord all the days of his life . . . (240–1)

Aguilar is careful to contextualize Hannah's act of going to the temple as an independent act of devotion "in perfect accordance with Mosaic Law," and she points out that Hannah made no deferential request to her husband about this act. Yet if Hannah follows Mosaic law in her act of making a vow, her act of prayer is perceived by the High priest Eli as a strange transgression; Aguilar notes it "must have been an aggravation of [Hannah's} sorrow to find herself so misunderstood by one, who, as a high priest, she might have with some justice believed would have required no explanation on her part" (241). Here, as in the poetry discussed in the previous section, Aguilar offers a subtle critique of the misguided "professional" man who regulates Jewish devotion without a deeper spiritual understanding of those individual acts.

The language Aguilar uses to describe both Hannah's acts of prayer and her later "hymn of thanksgiving" signals Aguilar's specific notions of prayer and poetry in this passage. Of Hannah's first "silent" prayer, Aguilar writes: "But she prayed not aloud, nor in any stated formula of prayer; she prayed merely as the heart dictated: 'she spoke in her heart,' as we have it in the touching language of Scripture – only her lips moved, but her voice was not heard" (241). This idea of "speaking in her heart" of course relates back to Aguilar's own lyric poetry of prayer, which as we saw in "Sabbath Thoughts" sequence, insists that speaking through the heart to God is a more powerful mode of speech than human words or "marks." Yet as she goes on to describe Hannah's subsequent song of gratitude, Aguilar casts its significance not only as spiritually valuable, but also as having literary and intellectual value.

The prayer, or rather hymn, of thanksgiving in which Hannah poured forth her gratitude to her God in a strain of the sublimest poetry and vivid conception of the power and goodness of Him whom she addressed, is a forcible illustration of the *intellectual* as well as the spiritual piety which characterized the women of Israel, and which in its very existence denies the possibility of degradation applying to women, either individually, socially, or domestically. Their intellect must have been of a very superior grade; while the facility of throwing the aspirations of the spirit into the sublimest poetry, evinces constant practice in so doing, and proves how completely prayer and thanksgiving impregnated their vital breath. (243)

Here, Aguilar counters the construction of the poetess as one whose talents go beyond the "pour[ing] forth her own pious sentiments of the heart's duties, and the soul's destiny" – as the *Voice of Jacob* reviewers termed Aguilar's own poetic talent. Aguilar is careful here to assert that Hannah's poetry requires an intellect of "a very superior grade." Further, she suggests that such poetic skill is not the result of a one-time inspirational moment, but that such skill "evinces constant practice in so doing" – thus suggesting that poetry and prayer is part of Jewish women's collective identity, and that Hannah's words are "a forcible illustration of the *intellectual* as well as the spiritual piety which character-ized the women of Israel" (Aguilar's emphasis). Thus, in contradistinction with Miriam's "high-sounding religion of flowing verse," Aguilar terms Hannah's prayer "a transcript of the swelling gratitude of a truly pious heart, as her prayer before had breathed its bitterness of grief. . . Hannah was . . . one of the most perfectly spiritually pious characters of the Bible. There was no self-exaltation in her song of praise"(243). Unlike Miriam's song, Hannah's prayer is "sublimest poetry" because it is directed to God rather than at a human audience.

When Aguilar comes to the prophetess Deborah, she is faced with a character who seems to combine both a very public identity, and a deep piety. She is neither a Miriam or a Hannah, and thus Aguilar's reading of Deborah's significance in Jewish history reflects the tension in her theories of public and private, poetic and prophetic utterance by women. In her discussion of Deborah, Aguilar again emphasizes how Deborah's roles as prophet and judge indicate the high status Judaism afforded to women at her historical moment, noting that:

Had there been the very least foundation for the supposition of the degrading and heathenizing the Hebrew female, we should not find the offices of prophet, judge, military instructor, poet, and sacred singer, all *combined* and *perfected* in the person of a woman; a fact clearly and almost startlingly illustrative of what must have been their high and intellectual training, as well as natural aptitude of guiding and enforcing the statutes of their God, to which at that time women could attain. (203–4)

The subtext to this passage relates to Aguilar's introductory remarks regarding how later history may be responsible for the lower status of women in Judaism; Deborah stands for that which "at that time women could attain," and so there is an implicit contrast between Aguilar's contemporary moment and Deborah's. What Aguilar emphasizes is the fact that Deborah must have been well educated, a condition Aguilar hopes to see replicated for women of her own day.

When Aguilar turns to describe Deborah's poetic talents, she ranks them as of the highest quality, as well as noting that such poetry is an indication of the high position of women in this historical moment:

> We next find Deborah exercising that glorious talent of extempore poetry only found among the Hebrews; and by her, a woman and a wife in Israel, possessed to an almost equal degree with the Psalmist and prophets, who followed at a later period. Her song is considered one of the most beautiful specimens of Hebrew poetry, whether read in the original, or in the English version. We find her taking no glory whatever to herself, but calling upon the princes and governors, and people of Israel, to join with her in "blessing the Lord for the avenging of Israel." (206)

Deborah thus combines Miriam's claim to public voice and authority with Hannah's "glorious talent" for poetic speech; the key indication that validates Deborah's poetic identity is that, like Hannah, she "tak[es] no glory whatever to herself"; thus, her song, unlike Miriam's, is not designed to generate fame for herself, but rather glory for all the people of Israel, whom she "bids ... speak" throughout her song. In her close reading of Deborah's song, Aguilar makes a subtle note about the "correct" attitude of the prophetess, writing: "The simplicity and lowliness of the prophetess's natural position, is beautifully illustrated by the term she applies to herself – neither princess, nor governor, nor judge, nor prophetess, though both the last offices she fulfilled – 'until that I, Deborah, arose, until I arose a MOTHER in Israel'" (207, emphasis in original). In what may be an implicit allusion back to Miriam's "problematic" character, Aguilar emphasizes Deborah's self-effacement and her identification with her own domestic role, noting that Deborah "asked no greater honor or privilege for herself individually, than the being recognized as the mother of the people whom the Lord alone had endowed her with power to judge" (207). Likewise, Aguilar echoes her themes from the short story "The Authoress" when she links Deborah's public, political, and prophetic acts to her domestic role: "To a really great mind, domestic and public duties are so perfectly compatible that the first never need be sacrificed for the last" (209). However, Aguilar is forceful in her claims that Deborah is also a powerful public leader, writing that her poem is "one of the sublimest strains of spiritual fervor in the Bible; and mark forcibly, by her conduct, both as prophetess and judge, that in Deborah, even as in Gideon, David, and the prophets of later years, God disdained not to breathe His spirit, but made WOMAN His instrument to judge, to prophesy, to teach, and to redeem" (emphasis in original, 207).

Given this description of Deborah's power in realms not only maternal, but also political, public, prophetic, and poetic, Aguilar has a harder time identifying Deborah as a model for contemporary Jewish women. Given the very extreme difference in women's roles that mark their respective historical periods, it is easier to understand why Aguilar focuses on Deborah as a mother – at least one role her contemporary readers can emulate. But as she concludes her section on Deborah, Aguilar repeatedly notes a number of differences that mark Deborah from contemporary women. She writes: "In a *practical* view, perhaps, the character of Deborah cannot now be brought home to the conduct of her descendants, for woman can no longer occupy a position of such trust and wisdom in Israel; but *theoretically*, we may take the history of Deborah to our hearts, both *nationally* and individually" (emphasis in original, 208).

Aguilar's comparison ultimately serves as a critique of the current conditions for Jewish women, and Aguilar thus refuses to suggest that contemporary Jewish women can attain the roles and power Deborah did. Her reasoning is based on a pragmatic assessment of the historical conditions of contemporary Anglo-Jewish life:

To follow in the steps of our great ancestors is not possible now that the prophetic spirit is removed from Israel and the few public offices left us fall naturally to the guardianship of man . . .

Deborahs in truth we cannot be, but each and all have talents given, and a sphere assigned them, and, like her, all have it in their power, in the good performed toward man, to use the one, and consecrate the other to the service of their God. (210–11)

Here is Aguilar's clearest statement that women of her day can not "follow in the steps of [their] ancestors." Her acknowledgment that "Deborahs in truth we cannot be" is the moment in which Aguilar names overtly the very clear differences between her own sense of religious and poetic agency, and the agency and religious power which Christian women of the day claim for themselves when they more easily connect their own poetic acts to the women prophets of the Bible. As a Jewish woman living in a society that still denied political enfranchisement to Jews, Aguilar could have no illusions that a Jewish woman could claim "a prophet's place" in Victorian England.

Having clearly stated that "Deborahs in truth we cannot be," Aguilar must quite carefully construct her own public literary identity. As we saw in her devotional poetry, one strategy Aguilar uses is to suggest the "likeness" the Jewish poet has to Christian poets; writing of individual spiritual experiences and observations that exist outside of specific historical contexts in her devotional and nature lyrics, Aguilar was able to claim her poetic identity as "just like" that of Christian writers, and particularly the Romantic poets. But in other poems, Aguilar seeks to represent moments that are clearly marked by historical context, poems that explore the specific dimensions of Jewish religious vision in Aguilar's contemporary moment. It is in these poems that we discover another trajectory of Aguilar's poetic identity, one that expresses a poetics not only of Jewish "sameness" to hegemonic Christian identity and culture, but a poetics of Jewish difference.

"MY COUNTRY! OH MY COUNTRY!": EXPLORING THE LIMITS OF ANGLO-JEWISH PROPHECY

Aguilar's poem, "A Vision of Jerusalem," is subtitled, "While Listening To a Beautiful Organ in One of the Gentile Shrines."[27] Using a standard Romantic trope of situating the poem in a particular place, Aguilar immediately creates both a literal and symbolic structure for her Jewish vision: it occurs as she is literally within a Christian environment, a "gentile shrine" which also stands for the larger dominant Christian culture of Victorian England. The dramatic context of this poem thus literalizes Aguilar's larger theory of the limits of Jewish identity; the situation of the poem's speaker, surrounded by the sights and sounds of the "gentile shrine," ultimately dictates the kind of vision the speaker can generate. Thus, the poem is very different from those lyric poems explored in the earlier part of this chapter, where the speaker's devotion was cast in terms of her private and personal relationship with God at deeply individual moments: thoughts during the Sabbath, sitting alone with a sick relative, or musing on the natural world. Those lyrics seem to represent ahistorical moments in a Jewish woman's life. Here, in "A Vision of Jerusalem," however, the entire structure of the poem insists on locating the speaker's prophetic and redemptive vision of Jerusalem within an explicitly public Christian context at a particular historical moment. In this poetic context, Aguilar creates what we might term a conditional prophetic identity, one governed by the historical conditions of "captivity" which marks her experience as a Jew in the Diaspora.

The first lines, "I saw thee, oh my fatherland, my beautiful, my own! / As if thy God had raised thee from the dust where thou art strewn" initiate the ecstatic vision of Jerusalem which apparently comes upon the speaker in this midst of "listening" to the "Gentile" organ. Within the explicit Christian setting, and all of its sounds and sights, Aguilar's Jewish speaker demonstrates the power of her Jewish commitment by imaginatively transposing aspects of Christian worship into the powerful images of specifically Jewish redemption: the restoration of the Temple in Jerusalem. The second and third stanzas depict the speaker translating the complex sounds of the organ into sounds that reflect the celebratory instruments of Jewish Biblical history:

> Methought the cymbals' sacred sound came softly on my ear,
> The timbrel, and the psaltery, and the harp's full notes were near;
> And thousand voices chaunted, His glory to upraise,
> More heavenly and thrillingly than e'en in David's days. (lines 5–8)

Similarly, as she gazes on the Christian clergy in the "gentile shrine," she transposes them into "the sons of Levi," as well as seeing the priest himself as a vision of "th'anointed one."

> Methought the sons of Levi were in holy garments there,
> Th'anointed one upon his throne, in holiness so fair,
> That all who gazed upon him might feel promise be fulfill'd,
> And sin, and all her baleful train, now he had come, were still'd.
> (lines 9–12)

In the following (fourth) stanza the speaker goes on to envision "thousands of my people throng'd the pure and holy fane . . . Israel, forgiven, knelt within our own bright land." Thus even the Christian worshippers who surround her are transformed in her head into a "throng" of Jewish worshippers. The repeated use of "methought" in stanzas two and three contrasts with the more direct opening assertion "I saw thee, oh my father land" and the term "methought" emphasizes that this vision of Jewish worship in a Christian church is truly a production of this speaker's mind: no one else there, that is, is seeing what she sees.

What is especially significant about Aguilar's recontextualization of Christian worship service into images of specifically Jewish redemption is that the process reverses standard Christian typology, through which

New Testament authors invest Jewish texts and ritual with specifically Christian meaning. Aguilar's creation of Jewish meaning from a Christian service can be understood, then, in part, as a specifically Jewish response to centuries of Christian interpretations of Judaism that produced specifically Christian prophetic meaning. What makes the poem more complex is the apparent assertion that there is something universally uplifting about the organ service that speaks to the Jewish listener as well as its intended Christian congregation; in this way, "The Vision of Jerusalem" also suggests the compatibility of Jewish and Christian religious experience, an important part of Aguilar's larger theory of Judaism, as we saw earlier. Indeed, the organ music allows for a brief transcendence of the necessarily inhibiting circumstance of being the only Jewish person in the church.

If the first half of the poem depicts the "gentile shrine" as offering certain experiences that actually contribute to Jewish vision, the second half of the poem describes the immense difficulties involved in maintaining Jewish vision in a Christian culture. The fifth and sixth stanzas create an abrupt transition from the speaker's visionary state to recognition of her actual historical reality as a Jew in the Diaspora.

> My country! oh my country! was my soul enrapt in thee
> One passing moment, that mine eyes might all thy glory see?
> What magic power upheld me there? – alas, alas! it past,
> And darkness o'er my aspiring soul the heavy present cast.
>
> I stood ALONE 'mid thronging crowds who fill'd that stranger shrine,
> For there was none who kept the faith I hold so dearly mine:
> An exile felt I, in that house, from Israel's native sod, –
> An exile yearning for my *home*, – yet loved still by my God.
>
> (lines 17–24; emphasis in original)

The opening line of Stanza five is rich with double meaning; at the moment this speaker calls out to "my country," the disjunction of her visionary identity as a Jew in the restored Jerusalem, and her literal identity as an Anglo-Jew in England is made clear; her cry to "my country" reads on both levels. In addition, there is play on exactly what phenomenon has produced this religious vision; the line break that occurs on "was my soul enrapt in thee" raises the subtle question of what exactly the "thee" refers to: the more obvious reading would read the "thee" as referring to the vision of "my country" – namely Israel, and so suggest that the speaker's "enraptured" soul allowed her to transcend her literal national setting, namely, England. The line thus opens a space in which to read the

English Christian church service as that which provided "magic power [that] upheld"; acknowledging the "magic power" of the Christian service veers, I would argue, dangerously close to granting a mesmerizing power to Christianity which Aguilar so often fears can captivate Jewish women with the myth of Christianity's superior "spirituality."

Just as the power of the Christian shrine produces the vision, so too does her awareness that she is "alone" in this setting eventually destroy her vision of Jewish communal redemption. Aguilar clarifies that the obstacle to her vision occurs because of her specific historical context, "the heavy present." And if her vision had allowed her to imagine the future redemption of the entire community of Israel, it is this "heavy present" which now reveals her essential isolation in "that house." All that is left to her, upon making this recognition, is her awareness of being "loved still by my God." Aguilar calls on explicit passages of Biblical text to remind readers of the covenant between Israel and God; in Stanzas nine and ten, Aguilar quotes from Leviticus 26: 40–1, footnoting the reference as we have seen her do elsewhere.

> "If they their own iniquity in humbleness confess,
> And all their fathers' trespasses, – nor seek to make them less;
> If they my judgments say are right, and penitently own
> They reap the chastisement of sin, whose seeds long years have sown:
>
> "Then will I all my vows recall, and from them take my hand,
> My covenant remember, and have mercy on their land."
> So spake the Lord in boundless love to Israel his son;
> But can we, dare we say, these things we *do*, or we *have* done?
>
> (lines 33–40; emphasis in original)

God's Biblical words recall the terms of the covenant to restore Israel to Jerusalem; in quoting these words, Aguilar includes the words of God's own voice in her visionary poem, thus furthering the construction that this is a prophecy of sorts, albeit one that occurs specifically out of a strange Diasporic experience. The reference to "Israel his son" is a good example of Aguilar's constant awareness of a doubled audience of Christian and Jewish readers; with this reference, Aguilar uses language that "works" within Christian epistemology, while never relinquishing her commitment to Judaism – and this is a strategy she uses in countless poems; indeed, these verses have three different footnotes referencing Hebrew Biblical texts, as we saw in "Sabbath Thoughts" as well. Her emphasis on Israel as God's son, as opposed to the repeated images from Jewish texts of Israel as a daughter, suggest Aguilar's interest in claiming a masculine identity for Israel – perhaps in order to counter the Christian claim of Christ as the true son of God.

The last line of the above passage, "can we, dare we say, these things we *do*, or we *have* done," is perhaps the most important moment in this poem to question whether a Jewish voice can ever claim authority in a Christian culture. As Aguilar details in so many of her novels and historical studies, Jews in the Diaspora tended to face persecution whenever they displayed Jewish difference publicly.[28] Further, to speak of the sins of Israel is a daring act within the Jewish community itself; imagine how much more daring such Jewish speech might be in the space of the Gentile Church, which of course stands as a symbol for the larger English Anglican society as well. At this moment in the poem, then, Aguilar insists that although the Jewish need to "in humbleness confess" is a religious requirement for Jewish redemption, such a confession made "out loud" is a literal threat to Jewish communities living in a Christian culture. Thus, here again she reiterates how different historical settings necessarily mediate Jewish religious identity in fundamental ways, and she calls implicit attention to the danger her own public poetic utterance might bring.[29]

The poem concludes on a complex note of both hope and the ultimate recognition of the limited nature of the speaker's own prophetic power.

> Alas, my country! thou must yet deserted rest and lone,
> Thy glory, loveliness, and life, a Father's gifts, are flown!
> Oh that my prayers could raise thee radiant from the sod,
> And turn from Judah's exiled sons their God's avenging rod!
>
> And like an oak thou standest, of leaves and branches shorn;
> And we are like the wither'd leaves by autumn tempests torn
> From parent stems, and scatter'd wide o'er hill, and vale, and sea,
> And known as Judah's ingrate race wherever we may be.
>
> Oh! blessed was that vision'd light that flash'd before mine eye;
> But oh, the quick awakening check'd my soul's ecstatic sigh!
> Yet still, still wilt thou rise again my beautiful, my home,
> Our God will bring thy children back, ne'er, ne'er again to roam.
>
> (lines 41–52)

The speaker yearns that her "prayers" might "raise [Jerusalem] from the sod" and likewise restore Jewish people – the leaves and branches of the metaphorical oak of Israel; yet it is a yearning that her prayers cannot, in the end, complete. Likewise, the speaker acknowledges that she had a "blessed vision," yet it was tempered by the "quick awakening [that] check'd [her] soul's ecstatic cry." For Aguilar, it seems, Jewish ecstasy

and spirituality have been and continue to be "check'd" in the captivity
and oppression in the Diaspora.

What "A Vision of Jerusalem" demonstrates, then, is not only the
speaker's own powerful maintenance of Jewish self and prophecy while
surrounded by Christianity; what is striking about this poem is how it
asserts that Israel's God will "[m]y covenant remember" – even in this
very setting of Christianity. The poem represents an unconverted Jew
sitting among the Christian throng, a Jew who is not affected by the fact
that Christian culture generally casts Jews as "Judah's ingrate race." As
she points out the subjective limits of any religious – or poetic – "vision,"
Aguilar insists that only through God's agency can Jewish prophetic
vision truly be made manifest. The last line of the poem places God
as the agent of redemption, the one who will "bring . . . back" Jews to
Jerusalem, and implicitly, to Jewish observance. Setting the poem in
a "gentile shrine" reveals the delicate balance Aguilar strikes between
the idea of shared/universal spiritual traditions between Judaism and
Christianity, and the sharp differences that mark Jewish and Christian
vision in Victorian England.

Like the poems of the major Romantics who clearly influenced her,
Aguilar's poetry often relies on specific places to construct poetic inspiration, yet Aguilar's attention to the sheer limits of her own prophetic
agency is where she most clearly departs from the conventions of
Romantic poet/prophets. Aguilar knew that a Jewish woman would
never be claimed as a poet/prophet or "true woman" in Victorian
England; further, her goal of speaking to both Jewish and Christian
audiences substantively altered traditional models of English lyric poetic
communication, in which the poet could assume his or her audience's
investment in a certain set of shared Christian values. It is the tension
between her appropriation and transformation of English literary traditions that teaches us not only about the complexities of Anglo-Jewish
literary identity, but also of her own clear awareness of the literary privileges from which she was excluded in English literary history.

Aguilar's awareness of the contradictions of being a devout Jewish
woman poet in Victorian England necessitated a deeply pragmatic
approach to her religion and her writing. Neither her own Jewish practice
nor her writing were ever ends in themselves; on the contrary, her own
religious practice was constantly put in service of her larger community
as she sought to describe the most intimate moments of her own prayer
and devotion in her poetry, daring to reveal her private faith to the
"censorious world." If she had serious literary ambitions, and a need

to make money, she attempted to link these needs to her religious goals, resisting the temptations of the "high-sounding religion of flowing verse"; it was only after her death that so many of her non-religious writings were issued, suggesting Aguilar's own desire to resist publication for money only. Aguilar looked intently into Jewish history in the name of Jewish women; she refused to grant to Christianity the ownership of idealized womanhood, just as she refused to degrade her faith because she saw historical injustices to women as part of a larger historical problem of Jewish persecution in Diaspora history and cultures. Aguilar maintained that the Judaism of Biblical Israel was a powerful force for Jewish women's spiritual agency, and her poetry repeatedly asks contemporary Jewish women to claim their birthright, renew their spiritual practice, and thus support the redemption of all Jews who remain "captive." Read with and against the work of Christian women poets of her day, Aguilar emerges as a prophetic "voice in the wilderness" advocating Jewish renewal, and anticipating many aspects of the Jewish women's movements that would emerge full-blown over a century after her own death.

CHAPTER 6

Amy Levy and the accents of minor(ity) poetry

"Nothing," he said presently, "can alter the relations of things – their permanent, essential relations . . . 'They *shall* know, they *shall* understand, they *shall* feel what I am.' That is what I used to say to myself in the old days. I suppose, now, 'they' do know, more or less, and what of that?" (Amy Levy, "Cohen of Trinity")[1]

> Song nor sonnet for you I've penned,
> Nor passionate paced by your home's wide wall;
> I have brought you never a flow'r, my friend,
> Never a tear for your sake let fall.
>
> And yet – and yet – ah, who understands?
> We men and women are complex things!
> A hundred tunes Fate's inexorable hands
> May play on the sensitive soul-strings.
>
> Webs of strange patterns we weave (each owns)
> From colour and sound; and like unto these,
> Soul has its tones and its semitones,
> Mind has its major and minor keys.
> (Amy Levy, "In a Minor Key," lines 29–40)[2]

Amy Levy (1861–89) was, up until the early 1990s, almost a "lost" figure in British literary history. Today, she is gaining an increasing amount of critical attention, both for her fiction and her poetry. The reasons for Levy's critical resurrection are multiple; perhaps the most important event in her recent critical heritage was the 1993 publication of her selected writings, edited by Melvyn New, a volume which gave contemporary scholars access to Levy's writing from all genres, and Linda Hunt Beckman's 2000 publication of *Amy Levy: Her Life and Letters*. Levy's critical resurrection is also linked to the fact that so many of the issues she addresses in her writing speak to concerns of the contemporary critical moment: Jewish Diasporic identity, lesbian identity, women's emancipation, and more general theories of "otherness" within the English literary tradition. In addition, Levy was one of the first Jewish women to attend Newnham College, Cambridge and she was associated with a wide range of *fin-de-siècle* writers and intellectuals including Oscar Wilde, Olive Schreiner, Havelock Ellis, and Eleanor Marx; her poetry and fiction is often read in conjunction with the "New Woman" poets writing at the end of the century.

In this chapter, I want to focus on Levy as an author who explored the concept of "minority" writers long before such a category had any real cultural or critical meaning. Levy's poetry and literary theory makes a commitment to exploring minority as a concept rather than linking it to one specific personal identification; thus, her writing stands as an important transition to more modernist and post-modernist perspectives which do not assume the possibility of "universal" poetic utterance. Instead, her writing, and particularly her poetry, repeatedly highlights the intersection between various minority positions and the cultural discourses which construct and judge "others." Interrogating the ways dominant assumptions of Christianity and heterosexuality have structured the identity of the English poet and English literary conventions, Levy overtly constructs a number of "minority" voices and then sets them in relation to the conventions and discourses of English literary tradition. Whereas previous chapters have focused on the ways different women poets configured certain figures of religious or sexual identity in order to claim some more "universal" authority for their poetry, this chapter will focus on how Levy sought to rewrite the assumption that a "universal" poetic identity is in fact an ideal literary goal.

The two passages at the start of this chapter suggest some of the parameters of Levy's project and how she created a literary identity deeply linked to the concept of minority – while refusing to identify that identity with any single discourse of otherness. The first passage above is from Levy's later short story, "Cohen of Trinity." Giving her character the name "Cohen" (signifying the Jewish priestly class) and placing him at "Trinity" (a symbol of the elite Anglican university which symbolized the institutions of Christian culture) Levy immediately highlights the fact that her protagonist, Alfred Lazarus Cohen, represents the archetypal Jewish other in English high culture and educated society. The story details the rise and fall of Cohen, who, though kicked out of Trinity College, Cambridge, nevertheless publishes a smash success of literary work – "[h]alf poem, half essay, wholly unclassifiable, with a force, a fire a vision" (483). And yet, as he speaks to a non-Jewish acquaintance (who is also the narrator of the story) in the passage cited above, Cohen describes his ultimate disillusionment with his attempt at literary self-representation. Because, he suggests, "[n]othing ... can alter the relations of things – their permanent, essential relations" the literary desire to be known by a "they" (a public audience) is never truly realizable.

That idea of some "permanent, essential relation of things" is a complex and recurring concept in Levy's work, referring, I think, to the fossilized sense of tradition, the "common" and hegemonic assumptions of the normative that structure almost any kind of cultural discourse. In the context of "Cohen of Trinity," the assumptions "they" have about Jewishness are precisely those forces Cohen understands he can never change by writing. Thus, even as Cohen does transform the genres of his writing into something "wholly unclassifiable" in order to express his particular vision, it seems ultimately that even this kind of radical generic transformation could not provide a literary structure that could fully represent his Jewish self to mainstream Christian culture. The impossibilities of representing an "other" identity in literature are highlighted by Levy's choice to structure "Cohen of Trinity" not as a first-person narrative in the voice of Cohen, but rather with a non-Jewish narrator who consistently misunderstands Cohen throughout the story. With this generic strategy, which calls into question the very concept of the omniscient narrator from its very first lines, the story becomes as much about the subtle anti-Semitism that marks the narrator's misunderstanding of Cohen as it is about any "truth" of Cohen's life.

The title of Levy's second book of poetry, *A Minor Poet and Other Verse* (1884), is her most obvious declaration of her own self-proclaimed minority status, a volume in which the concept of the "minor" is explored in a variety of ways. What becomes clear is that for Levy, Jewish otherness was one of a variety of characteristics that could position a writer as "other"; along with Jewish identity, Levy's poetry also explores the complex dynamics of representing same-sex love in the conventions of English poetry. "In a Minor Key," cited above, connects the problem of articulating love for a woman to the very nature of the writing of poetry; it is one of many lyrics to women which have led most recent critics to identify Levy as a lesbian writer, a conclusion which I think is warranted and which this chapter assumes.[3] Earlier in the poem, the speaker has identified the loved object of the poem as a woman, as the speaker watches "for the least swift glimpse of your gown's dear fold" (line 14) and asks "Is it love today?" (line 25). In trying to figure out how to express her unnamed feeling, the speaker notes that she has used neither the conventions of "song nor sonnet" to represent her love, apparently finding those conventional forms of love poetry unsatisfactory.

"In a Minor Key" announces itself as neither a "song nor sonnet" in the conventional sense, but rather offers itself as a new generic response to the idea that "other" kinds of love may need another kind of poetry, a poetic that can indeed get at the "complex" and "strange," the "major" and "minor" tones. In this and many of her poems critiquing the conventions of heterosexual love poetry, Levy seems the most modern and precocious of poets, taking up what Adrienne Rich would later term "compulsory heterosexuality" as one her main themes in her poetry.[4] What I hope to illuminate in the readings that follow is how this interrogation of compulsory heterosexuality is deeply tied to Levy's understanding of the "compulsory Christianity" in English literary tradition. Repeatedly, Levy's poetry asserts that the poetic discourses of heterosexuality have deep historical and literary ties to religious discourses, specifically in the metaphors of heterosexuality that structured Hebrew devotional poetry as well as the Christian English lyric tradition. Demonstrating the contingency between discourses of literature, religion, and sexuality, Levy suggests that if poetry is to be able to represent the fine distinctions between the "tones" and "semitones" of the "Soul," and the "major and minor keys" of the "Mind," then poets will need a new set of conventions and assumptions about not only religious and sexual diversity, but also about literature itself. Resisting a poetic system which has often claimed the value of suffering which leads to religious redemption, which is often structured on a rubric of personal or religious conversion, and which uses heterosexual marriage as the sanctioned form of closure, Levy distinguishes her public literary identity from those of Aguilar, Barrett Browning, and Rossetti – and, of course, many other poets of her day.

All of us who work on Levy are in debt to those who have pursued important biographical research, and this chapter has benefited most significantly by Linda Hunt Beckman's research on Levy's biography – which goes far in correcting certain inaccuracies about Levy's life that were often included in previous studies.[5] Because the biographical evidence suggests Levy's lack of interest in religious practice, it is important to explain her appearance in a book about women's poetry and religious identity. Indeed, my emphasis on religious discourses in Levy's poetry may seem to contradict biographical studies which suggest, as Hunt Beckman effectively argues, that Levy herself was not a particularly religious or devout individual.[6] My argument for including Levy in this study is that regardless of her actual personal religious practices,

Levy was fully aware of the force religious discourses – and especially the hegemonic weight of Christian discourse – had in English poetry; part of her literary project was to expose the inherently Christian assumptions that structured so much poetic discourse in her day. Levy's explorations in the dynamics of religious discourses in her poetry, then, are not an indication of her personal religious beliefs *per se*, but rather reflect her deep insight that any poet would have to confront the religious assumptions of that overtly Christian literary tradition, particularly if one stood outside them as a Jew. In this sense, then, I suggest that Levy was fully cognizant of the powerful connections in the rhetorics of poetry and religion that I charted in chapter 2 – as my comparison between her literary theory and Matthew Arnold's in the next section of this chapter also suggests.

Occupying a number of marginal subject positions – female, Jewish, and lesbian – and maintaining awareness of a number of potential audiences – her Jewish community, the non-Jewish intelligentsia of her day, men and women, straight and gay/lesbian – Levy's role as a poet was always extraordinarily complex. Indeed, I speculate that the coincidence of Levy's suicide and the imminent publication of her last book of poems, *A London Plane Tree and Other Verse* (1889), sheds light on the central problem that lyric poetry – perhaps more than any other literary genre – posed for Levy. For, what made that last book of poetry stand out from almost all of Levy's other works is that it is a completely "lyric" volume – that is, it is a book of poems all written in the first-person voice, unlike her earlier *A Minor Poet and Other Verse*, which was primarily a volume of dramatic monologues with some lyrics scattered within. In this sense, *A London Plane Tree and Other Verse* threatened to give an audience the illusion that Levy was indeed exposing some true "self" to a kind of public perusal she so often mocks and distrusts in her own work. Leaving behind the model of the dramatic monologue that had dominated her earlier books of poetry, *A London Plane Tree and Other Verse* may have been a highly fraught volume for a poet who had repeatedly resisted a self-revelatory poetics. The lyric mode of this last book may have threatened to expose Levy to a kind of public examination of her own otherness, for despite the "distancing" effect Hunt Beckman describes in many of these poems, Levy had no assurance that her audience, steeped in the assumptions of post-Romantic lyric poetics, would read the volume as anything but an attempt at self-representation.[7]

The poems in *A London Plane Tree* explore, among other things, a particular affinity for the urban life of Jewish London, an unorthodox spirituality that refuses clear identification with either Christian or Jewish traditions, and her most direct intimations of lesbian sexuality. Made public, with Levy's name, they would have been subject to a Victorian ideology which, as Joseph Bristow observes, still upheld "strict binary divisions" between men and women; Bristow articulates the central problem this binary ideology might have posed to Levy: "how could Levy's lyric persona ever find a third 'sexless' position from which to speak? These poems actively raise rather than resolve such questions, making it hard to accord a specific gendered value to works that thematise their personas' outsider – and on occasion, uncanonical – status" ("All out of tune," 88). Adding to the impossibility of finding a "third sexless position" I would suggest that finding a spiritual/religious identity outside of a common binary understanding of Jewish/Christian identity was also one of the challenges of Levy's poetry. Often turning to both Jewish and Christian scriptural allusion in her work, Levy's use of religious discourse seeks to destablize obvious divisions between Jewish and Christian identity, while also resisting any clear location of self within those religious identities. In this chapter, I connect Levy's literary challenges to the assumptions of both heterosexual and Christian identity; indeed, it was Levy's work itself that taught me how religious and sexual discourses converge in the conventions of English poetry.

LEVY OF CAMBRIDGE AND THE CONTRAST WITH GRACE AGUILAR

> The sad rain falls from Heaven,
> A sad bird pipes and sings;
> I am sitting here at my window
> And watching the spires of "Kings."
>
> O fairest of all fair places,
> Sweetest of all sweet towns!
> With the birds, and the greyness and greenness,
> And the men in caps and gowns.
>
> . . .
>
> The sad rain falls from Heaven;
> My heart is great with woe –
> I have neither a friend nor honour
> Yet I am sorry to go.
> (Levy, "A Farewell (After Heine),"
> *A Minor Poet and Other Verse*)

Levy was born in 1861, in Clapham, the second daughter of Isabelle and
Lewis L. Levy.[8] When she was fifteen, her parents moved to Brighton,
where she was educated until she began her studies at Newnham College
in 1879. Thus, like Grace Aguilar, Levy spent much of her early life
outside a specifically urban Jewish community, though her family eventually settled in Bloomsbury, which then had a growing Jewish community;
Linda Hunt Beckman notes that while linked to Jewish life-cycles and
occasional synagogue attendance, the Levy family had "a casual attitude
toward religious observance" (*Amy Levy*, 13). Amy Levy's England and
Anglo-Jewish community was in many respects a very different world,
both literally and ideologically, from Grace Aguilar's. Born almost fifty
years after Aguilar, Levy was a child of emancipation, seeing in her lifetime the lifting of almost all bans on Jewish political and educational
restrictions.[9] Less restricted by institutional anti-Semitism, Levy was
nevertheless highly attuned to the ways anti-Semitism persisted in the
English social and cultural circles of her day. Thus, along with some
very different religious attitudes than Aguilar, Levy's later position in
history gave her a very different attitude toward Anglo-Jewry as a community. Whereas Aguilar constructed herself as a defender of Judaism,
and an apologist, Levy – like many second- and third-generation immi-
grants – chose to cast a critical eye on a community which was ostensibly
less vulnerable to political repressions than Aguilar's community.

Yet it was not only the relative security of the Jewish community that
may have shifted Levy's perspective from that of a previous generation of Anglo-Jewish women writers. Levy was also privy to a variety of
"New Woman" discourses endorsing the role of the emancipated intellectual, often single, woman, discourses that were not as readily available in
Aguilar's day – nor do we know if they had been whether Aguilar would
have embraced them as Levy did. By Levy's time, the separate spheres
ideology which relegated women's lives and identities to the moral, spiritual, private, and domestic realms and assigned to men the theological,
public, intellectual, and business realms, had begun to break down, offering some new possibilities for women in the worlds of work and education.
Further, the previous generations of successful women poets and writers
had also made the figure of the woman writer, if not equally respected
by the critical patriarchy, far less of a cultural anomaly than in the earlier
part of the century.

Levy's quite different historical position from Aguilar's made her far
less protective of Jewish tradition; unlike Aguilar's attempt to reclaim aspects of traditional Jewish spirituality as a vital source for Jewish women,

Levy has been much cited as a critic of traditional Judaism, mostly based on some essays she wrote in the 1880s and her novel, *Reuben Sachs*. Whereas Aguilar sought to rewrite Jewish woman's identity by claiming certain accepted doctrines of Christian womanhood as explicitly Jewish and then inserting Jewish womanhood into Romantic poetic conventions, Levy sought to rewrite Jewish womanhood through critical challenges to Christian poetic convention and its attendant assumptions of spirituality, gender, and poetry. However, if Levy was a critic of Anglo-Jewish social life in the latter part of the century, she did not fully dismiss the possibility of an idealized Jewish spiritual identity. More specifically, for Levy, the problem was how to find a connection to a distinctly Jewish spiritual sensibility in a moment when any religious identity was increasingly contested, when traditional Judaism limited women's access to Jewish education, and when religious discourse maintained powerful links to an assumed heterosexuality that Levy came to increasingly challenge in her work.

Perhaps the most important contrast with Aguilar's experience as an Anglo-Jewish woman was Levy's ability to attend Newnham College, Cambridge, which had only opened to women a few years before her entrance. As one of the first Anglo-Jewish women to gain a university education (though no women could yet take degrees at this time), Levy ultimately had a profoundly different attitude toward Christian Victorian society and its approach to women's education than Aguilar. For in Aguilar's day, it is safe to say, the Jewish community's general lack of commitment to providing a Jewish education for women was similar to the Christian community's lack of interest in providing education for women: neither group made educating women a priority. Aguilar saw the dangers of Christian women's education and literature for Jewish women, arguing that without a serious Jewish literature and attention to women's education, women might lose all connection to Judaism. Yet, by Levy's day, the institutions of Christian education had come farther in the "woman question," and while Jewish education for women was still a concept being developed through the German Haskalah (Enlightenment) movement, Christian/secular education in England was – at least in theory – available to women of both Christian and Jewish backgrounds. Christian culture provided for Levy that which her Jewish culture could not yet provide for a woman.

Levy's recognition of the privileges and challenges that accompanied her university training are evident in the ambivalent tone that marks so many of the poems about her Cambridge days. Thus, in her poem

"A Farewell," as her speaker sits and "watch[es] the spires of 'King's'" she is "sorry to go" even as she notes having "neither a friend nor honour." Of Levy's university years, Deborah Epstein Nord has written that "the experiences at Cambridge might well have heightened her feminist sensibilities while, at the same time, binding her to certain male traditions of learning and literature" ("'Neither Pairs Nor Odd,'" 747); we can add to that, of course, that any time at Cambridge, with its still mandatory chapel requirement, and institutional structures based on training Anglican clergy, would also have also "heightened" Levy's awareness of Jewish difference as she was thrust into a world in which the Christian identity of the university (both Cambridge and Oxford), was evident in simple college names like "Trinity," "Christ Church," and "Magdalen" Colleges.

Despite the difficulties of being Jewish in an overtly Christian environment, Levy's university experience seems to have offered her an even wider background and awareness of literature and languages (her specialization), work in German, and classics, that continued after her departure from university as well.[10] It is worth noting that even before her university experience, Levy was a precocious writer with obvious interests in literary subjects, offering up a review of *Aurora Leigh* at age thirteen, which apparently won her the "junior prize" at her school, and the next year another "junior prize essay" on the topic of David's character in the Bible – suggesting there was some emphasis on Jewish education in her early training.[11] Levy published her first verse at age thirteen in the feminist (suffragist) journal *The Pelican*. Her German studies at university had the added benefit of giving her access to a Jewish tradition of literature in translation, especially through the work of Heinrich Heine and Abraham Geiger's translations (from Hebrew to German) of Jehuda Halevi.

Finally, as research by Hunt Beckman and Emma Francis has suggested, Levy's university period may have also contributed to her own identification as a lesbian. This research has been useful in challenging one early interpretation of Levy's many love poems; writing in 1986, Deborah Epstein Nord suggested that these poems that address a female lover "seem rather like exercises, often spirited ones, in which she carries the convention to the point of taking a male poet's voice. Rather than revealing intimate feeling, they seem instead to be burying it almost completely" ("'Neither Pairs Nor Odd,'" 748). Biographical research now challenges the concept that Levy intended her love poems to be read in a male voice, suggesting instead that there is distinct evidence of Levy's own romantic attachments to women. Yet I would maintain with Virginia

Blain that even without such biographical "data," there still would be no reason to assume Levy was not writing love poems to women. Indeed, since this chapter argues that Levy has a clear investment in challenging conventions rather than "carrying" them as well as an investment in deconstructing the very idea that poetry can reveal "intimate feeling," it seems far more logical to assume that she did not represent heterosexuality as the normative default for her poetic personae.[12]

After university, Levy interacted primarily with figures we now consider part of a "mainstream" (though self-consciously radical at their time) of late Victorian writers: Olive Schreiner, Havelock Ellis, Vernon Lee, Clementina Black, Eleanor Marx and perhaps most significantly, Oscar Wilde; in addition, William Butler Yeats knew of her work, and thought her a promising poet.[13] Levy had an extensive publishing history in "mainstream" journals such as *Victoria Magazine, Temple Bar, Cambridge Review, London Society, Woman's World,* and *Gentleman's Magazine,* to name a few.[14] These contributions range from short stories, poems, and literary criticism to comments on contemporary life, and women's issues. She published three novels, *The Romance of a Shop, Reuben Sachs* (both in 1888), and *Miss Meredith* (1889), and three volumes of poetry: *Xantippe and Other Verse* (1881, while still at Cambridge) was reissued and expanded in 1884 under the title *A Minor Poet and Other Verse* and her last book of poems, published posthumously in 1889, was *A London Plane Tree and Other Verse.*

Along with her role in the *fin-de-siècle* literary and intellectual circles of her day, Levy also maintained her connections with the Anglo-Jewish literary community, most obviously through her work in the 1880s for *The Jewish Chronicle.* Along with her "Jewish" journalism and essays, Levy also wrote literature of Jewish content, including the novel *Reuben Sachs,* a few short stories, including "Cohen of Trinity," and translations of Heine and German versions of the poetry of Jehuda Halevi. And even while it seems that Levy's professional life was not centered in the Jewish community, it is worth noting that she remained very close to her family and especially her sisters, who were, it appears, more fully engaged in the daily cycles of Jewish religious and social life.[15] She continued to publish in journals and formats that emphasized both her feminism and her Jewish identification; at sixteen (see below) she wrote a scathing reply to an article in *The Jewish Chronicle* opposed to women's rights. Her involvement with the journal continued when in 1886 she served as a foreign "correspondent" on Jewish topics in Europe.

Compared with Aguilar, however, Levy represents a new generation of Anglo-Jewish women, and her approach to the idea of Anglo-Jewish female identity is vastly different than Aguilar's.[16] In an early letter written to *The Jewish Chronicle* on the subject of "Jewish Women and Women's Rights" Levy's position – at the age of sixteen – clearly rejects Aguilar's strategy of claiming the "domestic sphere" as a place of female spiritual agency; in part, the difference in approach comes from a difference in terminology; where Aguilar's use of "spiritual" often seems to embody a certain aspect of intellectual development, albeit one limited to women's private sphere, Levy sees the intellectual as a profoundly public realm, and one that may be more central to her concerns than "the spiritual." In the letter, Levy connects female intellectual oppression and sexual corruption, likewise challenging the notion that seclusion in the "domestic" maintains the sanctity of "homely happiness."[17] The article ends with a biting reference to the issue of suffrage; while stating she "has little to say, not having sufficiently considered it," Levy ends by asserting that "it might appear just to some minds that those who have to pay taxes should have some voice in deciding by whom those taxes should be imposed." She signs the letter, quite ironically, "Obediently yours, Amy Levy."

In this early piece in particular, Levy's position as an explicitly "Jewish" writer in an explicit "Jewish" forum is galvanized by her feminism, and so in this letter "patriarchal oppression" and "Jewish tradition" are implicitly merged in her argument – a central difference from Aguilar's approach. Emma Francis has argued that Levy's feminist critique and her critique of Anglo-Jewry are constructed on very different terms; Francis finds

Levy's explorations of femininity and the desires elaborated around it result in an increasing breakdown of the grounds of identification and differentiation. Her intervention into Jewish issues is governed by the opposite dynamic. Rather than breaking down identifications, her writing on Anglo-Jewry reinforces and overdetermines them; it translates identity into stereotype, which is repeated rather than repudiated. As we celebrate the sophisticated sexual politics of Levy's poetry it is vital to keep in mind that in other respects her work is profoundly politically unsanitary. ("Amy Levy,"201)

Other critics have also found Levy's attitudes toward Jewishness less appealing than her attitudes toward women's issues.[18] While it is clear that Levy does often call on a racial discourse of Jewish identity, a discourse many today find untenable, I do not conclude that Levy's use of this discourse necessarily demonstrates her deeply held racial bias or "self-hatred" for Jewishness and Judaism as a whole.[19] Indeed, though Levy does not ever idealize traditional domestic roles of women in Jewish

life, nor does she seem particularly interested in idealizing Biblical women
as ideals for Jewish women's identity, there are aspects of traditional
Jewish life and Jewish spirituality Levy does seem to revere at moments
in her writing. In a few works, Levy seems to creates a kind of nostalgia
for not only an ethnic or cultural ideal of Jewishness, but also for an
idealized sense of Jewish religious belief.

Levy's quite moving essay, "The Ghetto at Florence" (written for *The
Jewish Chronicle* in 1886) is one such essay.[20] Writing in a collective first-
person voice, "we," Levy describes the historical transformation of the
Ghetto and brings the history up to its present-day use for a carnival;
the speaker wonders if she can hear "human footsteps" of the past, or
see "the faces of ghosts, that peer wistfully through the grated lower
windows" (*Complete Novels and Selected Writings*, 519). She then offers the
following thought: "It is only sentimentalists, like ourselves, that trouble
themselves in this unnecessary fashion. There are a great many Jews here
to-night, evidently quite undisturbed by 'inherited memory' . . . We ourselves, it is to be feared, are not very good Jews; is it by way of 'judgment'
that the throng of tribal ghosts haunts us so persistently to night?" (520).
The "ghostly" presence of past Jews represents a form of "inherited
memory"; in a somewhat ironic twist, Levy calls this awareness of Jewish
history a kind of "judgment" or punishment for those who are not "good
Jews" – that is, I would interpret, observant Jews – and suggests Levy
identifies herself as one of these "bad Jews."[21]

Yet, this essay ends on a quite different note, as Levy goes on to suggest how difficult it can be to identify Jews in Florence, because they
seem too much like the non-Jewish Florentines; perhaps, she speculates,
"those old and mystic races, the Etrurians and Semites, were kinsfolk,
pasturing their flocks together in Asia Minor. But this is opening up
a very big question, over which wiser heads than our own have puzzled often and in vain" (520). Reaching back into a past even more
mythic than Biblical history, Levy suggests that Jewish and Italian "races"
were once linked, and so she challenges the common Victorian notion
of a particular Jewish racial identity. While perhaps not a notion of
racial identity that we might embrace today, it is crucial to see that
Levy's use of the racial discourse of her day is not without a certain
irony. Thus, after suggesting that supposedly distinct racial groups (as
understood by the inaccuracies of Victorian race theory) of "Semites"
and "Etrurians" might have found peaceful coexistence and even "kin"
among each other, Levy forecloses that topic with a typically ironic ges-
ture "to wiser heads than our own [who] have puzzled often and in vain"

202 Women's poetry and religion in Victorian Britain

about the "very big" question of racial identity; those "wiser" heads, it seems, have come, and she suggests, will come, to no truly convincing conclusions.

It is worth noting that Hunt Beckman's new research on Levy suggests that for a time in her early twenties, Levy did indeed disassociate from much of her Jewish heritage, though a shift in her attitude seems to have occurred by 1886, as is evidenced by her essays from that period and some of her later poetry (discussed below).[22] This tension between a more familiar "racial" discourse of Jewishness and a discourse of Jewish spirituality has been most remarked upon in Levy's most famous work, her novel, *Reuben Sachs. Reuben Sachs* is indeed a novel that not only seems to represent "bad Jews," but also was understood to be written by a "bad Jew" – that is, the way Amy Levy was seen by the Jewish community for writing a novel that reveals a less than complimentary vision of middle-class Anglo-Jewish community. However, later critics have noted the complexity in this text. As Meri-Jane Rochelson has written, "Levy's critique of Jewish materialism is in fact quite pointed, and not simply an expression of hostility toward Jews as a whole. It is also intimately joined to her feminist purpose" ("Jews, Gender, and Genre," 317); thus, Rochelson includes Levy's novel in the context of a "nineteenth century feminist literary tradition" (325). Likewise, Hunt Beckman suggests in an early article on Levy that the novel is "a jeremiad, a lamentation for a people that has sold its soul for money and power" ("Amy Levy and the 'Jewish Novel,' " 240). Extending these readings, I would suggest further that *Reuben Sachs* offers a specific mourning for the loss of "the people of the Book"–that is, the loss of Jewish religious and intellectual pursuits; within this lament for a lost spiritual center for Anglo-Jewry, Levy pays special attention to how women remain excluded from the linked worlds of male Jewish religious and intellectual activity.

As others have argued, the central character of the novel is in fact not Reuben Sachs, but rather his doomed love interest, Judith Quixano. As a live-in poor relation to a more socially and economically prominent Jewish family, Judith is at the mercy of the ruthless materialism that structures Jewish lives, and particularly Jewish women's lives in this novel. As Rochelson and Hunt Beckman suggest, Levy depicts Judith's plight as particularly desperate because of her exclusion from both education and a sense of Jewish identity that might bring some deeper spiritual meaning to her life. Contrasting the world of the political and social-climbing materialist Jewish community, however, are some brief glimpses at the "other" Jews in London, namely the world of Judith's family of birth that she has left behind in a search for social and financial improvement. In her only visit to her family of birth, we are introduced to Judith's father, a figure who represents one of the most morally and spiritually upright characters in Levy's Jewish world – albeit a total financial failure. His appearance in the novel itself is brief, yet offers an important commentary on Levy's ideas about Jews who maintain their religious scholarship even in the onslaught of modern pressures. Levy writes:

Long ago in Portugal there had been Quixanos doctors and scholars of distinction. When Joshua Quixano had been stranded high and dry by the tides of commercial competition, he had reverted to the ancestral pursuits, and for many years had devoted himself to collecting the materials for a monograph on the Jews of Spain and Portugal.

Absorbed in close and curious learning, in strange genealogical lore, full of a simple, abstract, unthinking piety, he let the world and life go by unheeded.

. . . Quixano's manners and customs were accepted facts, unalterable as natural laws, over which his children had never puzzled themselves. Some of them indeed had inherited to some extent the paternal temperament, but in most cases it had been overborne by the greater vitality of the Leunigers. But to-day the dusty scholar's room, the dusty scholar, struck Judith with a new force. She looked about her wistfully, from the book-laden shelves, the paper-strewn tables, to her father's face and eyes, whence shone forth clear and frank his spirit – one of the pure spirits of this world. (*Complete Novels and Selected Writings*, 225)

In this passage, Levy makes clear the deep alliance between Jewish male religious and scholarly identity; Joshua Quixano maintains the traditional link between "piety" and scholarship that defines the ideal Jewish man in earlier periods of Jewish history.[23] Thus, the figure of the "dusty scholar" who is "[a]bsorbed in close and curious learning" is also one of the only characters in the novel who is also "full of a simple, abstract, unthinking piety"; it is this piety which allows him to "let the world and life go by unheeded" – a sign that makes him a "failure" in the politically charged world of Reuben Sachs, but, I would argue, perhaps one of the few successes from the point of view of the novel, which does not at all endorse Reuben and Judith's morally corrupt political and social worlds as "ideal." Faced with her father as the representation of a lost Jewish spiritual identity, Judith is "struck . . . with a new force" and "look[s] about her wistfully"; Levy's narration and plot construction go on to suggest that this loss of a spiritual identity through the social and educational limits placed on Jewish women will be part of what determines Judith's unredeemed, ultimately miserable life. Thus at the moment a weeping Judith tells her father of her acceptance of a loveless marriage to a rich

Jewish convert, securing a life of material comfort for herself, the narrator speculates on her tears: "But she was Joshua Quixano's daughter – was it possible that she cared for none of these things?" (*Complete Novels and Selected Writings*, 281). Thus, Judith is marked through her father as a potentially spiritual and intellectual Jewish soul, yet as a woman, she has no opportunity to replicate his identity or achieve the satisfaction her father finds in being "one of the pure spirits of this world."

If it is this alliance between scholarship and piety that idealizes Jewish religious identity for Levy, it is also exactly the formulation that most nineteenth-century Jewish women were specifically unable to claim for their own lives. Thus, in the scene where Judith has a private and profound moment of spiritual crisis – a crisis in the sense that she realizes her loss of Reuben and her increasing entrapment in materialist society, Levy has Judith turn to poetry. Levy makes it clear that Judith is having a spiritual crisis at the start of chapter 15 through her use of an epigraph from Goethe for which Melvyn New offers the following translation: "Who ne'er his bread in sorrow ate,/Who ne'er the mournful midnight hours/Weeping on his bed has sate,/He knows you not, ye Heavenly Powers" (*Complete Novels and Selected Writings*, 546n). This line about knowing the divine through suffering thus opens the chapter in which Judith begins to experience those "mournful midnight hours" – thus suggesting she seeks to "know" heavenly powers. After rejecting a number of texts to soothe her, she settles on her cousin Leo's stash of poetry, Swinburne in particular. From poetry, Judith receives a moral lesson: "there was, after all, something to be said for feelings which had not their basis in material relationships" (269). Deprived of any access to that pious and scholarly life that protects her father's spirit, Judith must seek this, the simplest of moral and spiritual teaching that comes from English poetry.[24]

Here then, Levy's message seems most aligned with Aguilar's: without some form of moral education, Jewish women are deeply susceptible to the Christian cultural contexts in which they are imbedded. While Aguilar would take her Jewish women back to Jewish tradition and educate them within the Jewish community, however, Levy sees that the Jewish community – with a few exceptions – is actually no more morally healthy than the larger Christian culture; unlike George Eliot, who invested the Jewish characters in *Daniel Deronda* with exemplary spirituality and moral uprightness against a morally bankrupt Christian culture, Levy – while making many references to Eliot's text – refuses to idealize contemporary Jewish culture. In a sense, Levy suggests that there is no place for the spiritual or intellectual woman in Anglo-Jewish life, a critique that seems to make sense when we realize how deeply Levy depended on her own access to Christian institutions of learning.

Yet for those who condemn Levy for her attitudes toward Anglo-Jewry, it is important to note that Levy did not limit her critical eye to Anglo-Jewish society. Indeed, even more commonly, Levy explored the ways Christian culture repressed any possibility of authentic Jewish self-representation. In short, Levy often wrote from a position of dual critique aimed at both her own Anglo-Jewish roots and the limitations of the Christian literary culture to which she was also connected professionally and socially. Levy's own cultural literacy was rooted in primarily English texts and culture, in the discourses in which her intellectual life was maintained. Nevertheless, careful exploration also reveals her own Jewish cultural literacy, and her own desire to construct a poetic identity that can be covertly marked as Jewish even as it is embraced by Christian culture. To keep from becoming a Judith Quixano, to take control of the construction of a female Jewish intellectual identity, Levy calls on, critiques, and transforms a number of literary and religious discourses that wielded power in nineteenth-century English literary discourse. In particular, her poetic theory offers a running "conversation" with some of the theories and commentaries on Jewishness and poetry that were emerging, as I suggested in chapter 2, from the Christian literary establishment; Levy offers one such conversation with perhaps the central Victorian theorist of Christian and poetic culture, Matthew Arnold.

"SAYING SHIBBOLETH": LEVY'S THEORY OF MINOR POETRY

But for supreme poetical success more is required than the powerful application of ideas to life; it must be an application under the conditions fixed by the laws of poetic truth and poetic beauty. Those laws fix as an essential condition, in the poet's treatment of such matters as are here in question, high seriousness: – the high seriousness which comes from absolute sincerity. (Matthew Arnold, "The Study of Poetry," 184)

Heaven knows what would have become of them, people and poet alike, had it not been for this happy knack, or shall we say this tough persistence in joke-making under every conceivable circumstance ... (Levy, "Jewish Humour," *Complete Novels and Selected Writings*, 522)

If Grace Aguilar called on the work of the major Romantic poets, and especially Wordsworth, as a touchstone for her theory of Jewish women's spirituality, Levy finds her touchstone – or rather a point of departure – in Arnold and his dominant views on the nature of "great" poets and poetry. In particular, Levy's essays titled "Jewish Humour" (1886) and "James Thomson: A Minor Poet" (1883) can be read as direct responses to Arnold's poetic theory. As the juxtaposed passages above suggest, for Arnold, great poetry is governed by "the laws of poetic truth and poetic beauty," which, as I demonstrated in chapter 2, are fully aligned with a Christian theological perspective as well as a call for "high seriousness." Levy, on the other hand, celebrates a model of poetry rooted in "a nation whose shoulders are sore from the yolk of oppression," a poetic that must make "rueful humour" its law (*Complete Novels and Selected Writings*, 522). Looking over her work as a whole, it is possible to see that Arnold's idea of a set of fixed "laws of poetic truth and poetic beauty" corresponds to Levy's idea of a "permanent, essential relations . . . of things" which so delimit a poetic identity and voice. As her poetics emerges from these two essays, it is clear that Levy constructs a poetic system for the outsider, for the poet who does not or cannot necessarily embrace one universal set of laws and conditions to govern all poetic identities.

As I explored in chapter 2, Arnold's poetic theory falls in line with other Victorian thinkers by making literal and rhetorical connections between "great" poetic identity and some vision of a "universal" (and ultimately Christian) utterance. While evident throughout his literary criticism, this central importance of the idea of the universal is clearly articulated in his 1880 essay, "The Study of Poetry." Here, Arnold names two "fallacies" which often mistakenly guide the evaluation of great poetry: the "historical" and the "personal" estimate. Arnold explores the problem of having a "personal estimate" of poetry through an analysis of Robert Burns. He describes Burns' poetry as concerned primarily with "this world of Scotch drink, Scotch religion, and Scotch manners," and with this national/ethnic focus, Arnold suggests the "Scotchman" may have a particular "tenderness" for this sort of poetry (182). Yet, Arnold goes on to suggest that this personal connection to the poetry has nothing to with the poet's "greatness": "[b]ut this world of Scotch drink, Scotch religion, and Scotch manners is against a poet, not for him, when it is not a partial countryman who reads him; for in itself it is not a beautiful world, and no one can deny that it is of advantage to a poet to deal with a beautiful world" (182). Maintaining an evaluative hierarchy for the "beautiful" which refuses to identify with a particular identity other than "English" (and Christian), Arnold's poetic theory assumes that any expression of particular ethnic, religious or national identity is a detriment, is "not beautiful."

Levy counters this argument in an 1883 essay titled "James Thomson: A Minor Poet," published in two parts in *The Cambridge Review*. The title "James Thomson: A Minor Poet" immediately casts her essay within the context of the discourse on canonization which also implicitly structures Arnold's essay; Levy pursued this notion of major and minor writers in many places, most obviously in the title and title poem to her second book of poems, *A Minor Poet and Other Verse* (1884). In the essay on James Thomson, Levy has found a good foil for Arnold's derogatory ideas about "Scotch" poets, for like Burns, Thomson was a Scotsman and as Levy points outs, probably drank himself to death. Further, Thomson, Levy writes, "did not speak the Queen's English with the precision one would desire" ("James Thomson," 508); here again, she seems to comment on the requirements of the perfect English accent that Arnold associates with neither Scotsmen nor Anglo-Jews.[25]

Levy's audience for the James Thomson essay must have been remarkably like the audience for which Arnold wrote, a mainstream, predominately Christian literary audience. Throughout the essay, Levy makes use of the pronoun "our" to refer to herself and her English readers; she aligns herself with a "majority" readership. Yet while positioning herself to speak with authority to that hegemonic literary audience, Levy also works to redefine the very assumptions of English poetic value in which that audience is steeped – in particular, she challenges certain notions of poetic prophecy that inform Arnold's theories of poetic identity. The second paragraph of the essay poses a radical opposition to the idea that a poet should be valued for speaking universal prophetic truth for all. After noting that Thomson's recent death caused "but little stir," Levy writes:

There is nothing very remarkable in this; Homer, we know, had to beg his bread; contemporary cavaliers held Milton not too highly; and I cannot claim for James Thomson the genius of a Homer or a Milton. He is distinctly what in our loose phraseology we call a minor poet; no prophet, standing above and outside things, to whom all sides of a truth (more or less foreshortened, certainly) are visible; but a passionately subjective being, with intense eyes fixed on one side of the solid polygon of truth, and realising that one side with a fervour and intensity to which the philosopher with his birdseye view rarely attains. (501)

Levy calls on the same poetic reference points that have informed many discussions of poetic value: Homer and Milton. In making such references, Levy places Thomson within a certain tradition, even as she seems to distinguish Thomson from these illustrious forebears by saying he has not their "genius." But in her subsequent point, Levy seems to undercut the idea of the prophetic genius itself. Her description of the prophet, "standing above and outside things, to whom all sides of a truth (more or less foreshortened, certainly) are visible" initially appears quite conventional, yet Levy's "minor prophet" foregoes the objective vision and access to "all sides of a truth" in order to claim a "passionately subjective" identity "with intense eyes fixed on one side of the polygon of truth." Thus, this kind of poet chooses a subjective focus, and constructs a poem that challenges the poetry of "the philosopher" through a rejection of the "birdseye view" in favor of a vision that has "fervor and intensity." Levy questions, therefore, in the Thomson essay and elsewhere, the very crux of British literary tradition – that the true lyric poet has some sort of prophetic access to universal feeling and truth.

Though the Thomson essay is not explicitly concerned with the idea of the Jewish author, the theory of poetry Levy puts forth in this essay opens the door for a consideration of the Jewish author in English literary culture by recasting Arnold's insistence on the value of (Christian) universalized truth. Her 1886 article "Jewish Humour," published in *The Jewish Chronicle*, can be read as another major statement of Levy's poetic theory, and again, Levy uses "Jewish humour" to create a subtle retort to Arnold, in particular his critique of Heine in his 1863 essay "Heinrich Heine," already discussed in chapter 2.[26] Drawing briefly on that discussion, I will suggest that Levy responds directly to that work in her own re-evaluation of Jewish humor and Heine's identity as a specifically Jewish poet. "Jewish Humour" thus extends Levy's poetic theory from the Thomson essay, this time more explicitly addressing issues of Jewish identity and poetic evaluation.

As I argued in chapter 2, in his essay on Heine Arnold explores the specific qualities of Heine's "genius," but stops short of suggesting he is truly canonizable as a great poet; Arnold makes use of the New Testament text to assert that although Heine has the admirable quality of being able to translate the genius of Jewish humour to non-Jews, Heine is ultimately unable to live up to his potential as a "great" poet. Calling on specifically Christian reinterpretation of the idea of "Jewish chosen-ness" from Matthew, Arnold challenges the notion of Heine's poetic chosen-ness, that is, his relationship to poetic canonization, and his argument hinges on some specifically anti-Judaic and anti-Semitic impulses which I demonstrated earlier. In her essay, "Jewish Humour," Levy's treatment of Heine seems in direct response to Arnold's. Indeed, Levy values Heine for precisely the reasons Arnold ultimately condemns the poet, and Levy subtly condemns Heine for the very reasons Arnold praises him. Most importantly, she uses her discussion of Heine as an opportunity to challenge

Arnold's Christian typological emphasis, which necessarily reinterprets Heine from a Christian perspective. Levy reads Heine from within a Jewish perspective, and likewise chooses a very different Biblical context in which to situate her assessment of Heine. Most importantly, in "Jewish Humour," Levy exposes how certain Christian theological assumptions about universality and particularity are galvanized in the process of English "poetic canonization."

Where Arnold lauds Heine for being able to "translate" Jewish humour into a "universal" realm which – according to Arnold – non-Jews could easily apprehend, Levy reverses Arnold's evaluative formula, choosing instead to value the poet for his ability to speak in particular ways to Jews only. She writes:

> In general circles the mention of Jewish Humour is immediately followed by that of HEINE; nor is this a *non-sequitur*. For HEINE, in truth, has given perfect expression to the very spirit of Jewish Humour, has cracked the communal joke, as it were, in the language of culture, for all to enjoy and understand.
>
> The world laughs, and weeps and wonders; bows down and worships the brilliant exotic. We ourselves, perhaps, while admiring, as we cannot fail to admire, indulge in a little wistful, unreasonable regret, for the old cast clouts, the discarded garments of the dazzling creature; for the old allusions and gestures, the dear vulgar, mongrel words; the delicious confidential quips and cranks which nobody but ourselves can understand. (*Complete Novels and Selected Writings*, 521–2)

Here Levy explores exactly what Arnold had praised in Heine: his ability to present Jewish experience to non-Jews. Levy uses the terms "general circles" and "the world" to stand in opposition to "we" Jews in the piece. Yet ultimately, Levy suggests that Jews regret what is figured as Heine's betrayal of his Jewish community; Levy, in this case directly writing to a Jewish audience in *The Jewish Chronicle*, explores the value of having access to a language that only Jews can understand, and she longs for "delicious confidential quips" that are valuable precisely because they cannot be appropriated by non-Jews. Thus, for Levy, Heine demonstrates a particular humour that "nobody but ourselves can understand."

In contrast to Arnold's emphasis on Hebrew qualities – qualities that are in themselves abstract, universalized, and ahistorical character traits – Levy makes a direct connection between Heine's strength as a poet and his Jewish identity

> The Poet stretched on his couch of pain; the nation whose shoulders are sore with the yoke of oppression; both can look up with rueful humorous eyes and

crack their jests, as it were, in the face of Fortune. Heaven knows what would have become of them, people and poet alike, had it not been for this happy knack, or shall we say this tough persistence in joke-making under every conceivable circumstance ... (522)

Heine is a representative of particularly Jewish experience and suffering, rather than an exception to Jewish identity, as Arnold suggests when he writes of Heine: "But what Hebrew ever treated the things of the Hebrews like this?" ("Heinrich Heine," 128). For Levy, the ability to tell a Jewish joke, and by extension Heine's inclusion of Jewish humor in his poetry, is a mark of Jewish survival. And Levy claims this ethnic humor as having specific meaning for Jewish readers, thus countering the idea that poetic greatness can only be claimed when a poet transcends a specific national / ethnic identity. Further, Levy states that "only a Jew perceives to the full the humour of another ... a humour so fine, so peculiar, so distinct in flavour, that we believe it impossible to impart its perception to another" (*Complete Novels and Selected Writings*, 523), and here she seems to be pointing directly at Arnold's essay, refusing Arnold the right to claim he understands Heine, while also challenging the idea that the Christian reader can ever fully appreciate the "humour" of the Jew.[27]

As Levy's essay continues, she gets more explicit about the idea that only Jews can understand each other; in so doing, she moves the essay away from explicit attention to Heine and onto the specific issue of an Anglo-Jewish voice. The conclusion to "Jewish Humour" reads:

The old words, the old customs are disappearing, soon to be forgotten by all save the student of such matters. There is no shutting our eyes to this fact. The trappings and the suits of our humour must vanish with the rest; but that is no reason why what is essential of it should not remain to us a heritage of the ages too precious to be lightly lost; a defence and a weapon wrought for us long ago by hands that ceased not from their labour. If we leave off saying Shibboleth, let us, at least, employ its equivalent in the purest University English. Not for all Aristophanes can we yield up our national free-masonry of wit; our family joke, our Jewish Humour. (524)

Finding an "equivalent" for "saying Shibboleth" is for Levy a literal demand she makes of contemporary Jews, not a metaphorical abstraction of transcended Hebrew identity, and it links the expression of Jewish identity to the very forms of language with which an individual chooses to identify. The reference to "Shibboleth" also proves an interesting foil to Arnold's Christian references to Matthew, for Levy's reference to Judges 12 examines the idea of Jewish particularity from a positive standpoint.

In Judges 12: 4–6, "saying Shibboleth" is the test of pronunciation devised by the Gileadites to locate Ephraimites in their midst – that is, a sort of password test in order to identify "true" members of the Jewish community; if the term "shibboleth" was pronounced incorrectly, with the wrong accent, then the "other" could be identified. "Saying Shibboleth" is a figure that emphasizes the voice as a marker of identity, and so takes on an association with poetic identity as well. Further, Levy's choice of the "shibboleth" passage imbeds within itself a special reference to the stereotyped "accent" of the Anglo-Jew, who was often cited in English racist humor as speaking with a predominance of "sh" sounds. In short, Levy seems to suggest that Jews may have to "leave off" the markers of Jewishness that are stereotypically recognizable as Jewish and instead create equivalent markers that will allow Jews to recognize each other and their "humour" even as they speak the "purest University English" – thus not appearing to be recognizably Jewish to non-Jews.

In the end, Levy suggests that speaking with the same unmistakably "Jewish" accent of the past was no longer possible in the 1880s; nevertheless, she makes a claim for some kind of continued connection to Jewishness in the forms and accents of English culture. And in an even more pointed reference to Arnold's own comparative approach to Hebraism and Hellenism in his most famous work, *Culture and Anarchy*, Levy ends her passage by challenging his call for a renewed "Hellenism" in British culture, urging her readers that "not for all Aristophanes" can a specific commitment to Jewish identity be forfeited. Levy's "solution" to the problem of maintaining a minority identity within the form and accents of a dominant language is not without its complexities, however. Her theory of "saying Shibboleth . . . in the purest University English" seems, on closer examination, a quite difficult literary identity to achieve. For, as Levy herself sought this "equivalent" marker for Jewish identity while using accents (and thus poetic traditions) traditionally ascribed to English(men), she was also deeply aware of the ways university English – and the attendant Christian religious assumptions that structured this language – always already constructed Jewish voice and identity as other. As Levy suggests in a number of works, the perception of any accent, Jewish or otherwise, depends not only on how a speaker speaks, but what an audience is able to hear and understand; many of her poems, I will suggest, do indeed maintain specifically Jewish and lesbian markers, available to an audience who is able to identify them; for other audiences, the poems may read as if speaking in what Arnold termed in "The Study of Poetry" a "perfect poetic accent" or what

Levy terms the "purest University English." Yet as I suggest below, there are often markers of Jewish identity in many of Levy's poems, her own ways of "saying Shibboleth" to those who know how to identify that term.

It is not surprising, I think, given Levy's clear articulation of the problem of presenting a "minority" identity in the "accents" of University English, that her initial major poetic attempts and successes were not lyrics, but rather dramatic monologues. Writing dramatic monologues allowed Levy to avoid making reference to her own "minorities" as woman, lesbian, and Jew, while simultaneously allowing her to raise the problem of voicing difference in larger cultural contexts. Levy's innovations in the genre, as I have argued elsewhere, participate in what Isobel Armstrong has termed "the invention" of the dramatic monologue by Victorian women poets; Levy's dramatic monologues focus on representing speakers who stand in opposition to certain dominant cultural beliefs, and as a result find no authorizing audience to validate their poetic speech.[28] And along with making their more general point about the difficulty of any "minority" position, two of Levy's dramatic monologues in particular also manage to "say Shibboleth" – speak of a particularly Jewish identity and thus manage that "equivalent" marker and commitment to Jewish culture which she claims is central to the survival of Jewish cultural and literary identity.

The title poem to the volume *A Minor Poet* makes explicit many of the issues of authority described above; the title alone raises the problem of literary classification as a mode of cultural validation. Indeed, it is exactly the idea of cultural consensus which the speaker, "the minor poet," sets himself against. The poem begins *in medias res*, as the speaker lifts a "phial" of poison and locks the door to his room. He then discusses the two other times he has tried to commit suicide, the first time thwarted by his friend Tom Leigh, who delivered a lecture to the poet, described as

> ... all compact
> Of neatest newest phrases, freshly culled
> From works of newest culture: "common good";
> "The world's great harmonies"; "must be content
> With knowing God works all things for the best,
> And Nature never stumbles." Then again,
> "The common good," and still, "the common good";
> And what a small thing was our joy or grief
> When weigh'd with that of thousands ...
> ("A Minor Poet," lines 10–18)

Tom Leigh, who returns to speak at the end of the poem, articulates a position we have come to associate with Victorian England: the interest in placing man within larger, universalizing contexts such as Darwinism, or Christian fundamentalism, which assume there is the goal of the "common good" – whether natural selection or divinely based Christian morality – which governs all humanity. In these schemes, the individual's experience is minimized when seen in relation to that larger experience of all mankind; as the minor poet puts it, "our joy and grief" becomes of little importance when compared with the universal condition "of thousands." Read from a Jewish perspective, the "common good" poses a universalist and generally Christian approach to identity which suggests that all can participate in this "common good," an idea not easily reconciled with a theory of identity that maintains a commitment to group particularity like Judaism. Perhaps more importantly for Levy's context, accepting the very idea that "the common good" governs the world is particularly difficult when read from the perspective of Jewish historical oppression in the Diaspora.

The minor poet places this notion of a "common" philosophy against his own emphasis on the individual human experience.

> ... Gentle Tom,
> But you might wag your philosophic tongue
> From morn till eve, and still the thing's the same:
> I am myself, as each man is himself –
> Feels his own pain, joys his own joy, and loves
> With his own love, no other's. Friend, the world
> Is but one man; one man is but the world.
> And I am I, and you are Tom, that bleeds
> When needles prick your flesh (mark, yours, not mine).
>
> (lines 18–26)

The passage rejects the mediation of "philosophy," suggesting, rather, that no man escapes the "world" of his own feeling and experience, that no man can translate his own pain into universal necessity. In this sense, the poet seems to reject a lyric identity associated with Romantic and earlier Victorian poetry, a sensibility such as the one in Tennyson's *In Memoriam*, which asserts individual emotion in order to strike a universal poetic note. The minor poet upholds an absolute distinction between subject and object, using a figure of the body and a reference to Shakespeare – perhaps the most "universally" claimed author in English tradition – to make his point: "I am I, and you are Tom, that bleeds/When needles prick your flesh (mark, yours, not mine)."

This last allusion to *The Merchant of Venice* does more than emphasize
the individual quality of material existence; it makes reference to the
paradigmatic literary representation of Jewish isolation in Western culture. The passage ironically answers Shylock's rhetorical "If you prick
us, do we not bleed?" – a question which within the context of the play
is Shylock's claim to "sameness" rather than difference; thus the famous
lines seem to argue that even Jews share in a common human condition
of bleeding when pricked.[29] Levy's minor poet, however, recasts that
Shakespearean reference, pointing out the difference between "yours,
not mine" and so in fact highlighting the idea that one's own suffering
is felt most acutely by oneself. While it remains ambiguous whether this
"minor poet" is actually Jewish, the allusion suggests his identification
with Shylock as one persecuted by the common / Christian expectations
of society at large. Thus, the allusion to Shylock makes explicit that
Christianity has often served as the "philosophical" basis for much of
what passes as "common" belief in England, and reminds readers of an
archetypal moment of Jewish persecution – if, that is, a reader understands Shylock in those terms.

When the poet begins to address more specifically his own experience
in the world, he describes himself as an artist, an identity that super-
sedes the specific references to Jewish or religious identity. Nevertheless,
this poetic identity maintains some of the classic markers of the poet's
connection to "the divine." The minor poet describes himself as follows:

> A dweller on the earth,
> Yet not content to dig with other men
> Because of certain sights and sounds
> (Bars of broken music, furtive, fleeting glimpse
> Of angel faces 'thwart the grating seen)
> Perceived in Heaven. Yet when I approach
> To catch the sound's completeness, to absorb
> The faces' full perfection, Heaven's gate
> Which then had stood ajar, sudden falls to,
> And I, a-shiver in the dark and cold,
> Scarce hear afar the mocking tones of men . . .
> (lines 54–64)

This passage isolates more specifically the forms of alienation felt by the
speaker as a particular problem for the "minor" artist. It describes the
poet-speaker as a "perceiver" first of himself, then prophet-like in his
ability to grasp "certain sights and sounds . . . [p]erceived in Heaven,"
and finally of the "mocking tones of men." While seeming to embody

the ingredients for poetic identity, his artistic agency is thwarted by his inability to act on, or create a "completeness" and "full perfection." He differentiates himself from the real poets of the day, comparing himself to

> . . . one wild singer of to-day, whose song
> Is all aflame with passionate bard's blood
> Lash'd into foam by pain and the world's wrong.
> At least, he has a voice to cry his pain;
> For him, no silent writhing in the dark,
> No muttering of mute lips, no straining out
> Of a weak throat a-choke with pent-up sound,
> A-throb with pent-up passion. . .   (lines 92–9)

The "wild singer" is referred to at the end of the speaker's apostrophe to the authors of books on his shelf: Shakespeare, Goethe, Theocritus, Heine, and Shelley. The minor poet's inability to speak as a "bard" is at the heart of his dilemma; his supposed muteness seems clearly related to the search for an audience who might be able to "hear" and validate the poet's voice, and highlights the fact that this seeming dramatic poem emerges from a dramatic context in which no auditor serves to motivate the poet's speech. The closest he has to an audience in the opening section of the poem is an apostrophic relationship to "the sun" and to the absent "Tom." Thus the minor poet's impossible contradiction lies in his simultaneous desire for poetic authority, and his refusal to enter a system of "common" ideology and shared assumptions of poetic self-representation that would compromise his own experience and philosophy of particularity and alienation.

The poem's structure itself deftly demonstrates that the poet, even when he does speak, has not really been heard – much like the larger message "Cohen of Trinity" offers as well. Tom Leigh's role as second speaker in the poem highlights this connection, in his ultimate role as one who "misunderstands" the minor poet. As the minor poet's only intimate acquaintance, one referred to a number of times in the minor poet's own speech, Tom Leigh is a potential auditor turned speaker whose reportage of the scene of the suicide offers the reader a number of new clues about the minor poet's life; more importantly, however, Tom's report also indicates his own inability to accept the minor poet's ideas.

> I search'd and search'd;
> The room held little: just a row of books
> Much scrawl'd and noted; sketches on the wall,

> Done rough in charcoal; the old instrument
> (A violin, no Stradivarius)
> He played so ill on; in the table drawer
> Large schemes of undone work. Poems half-writ;
> Wild drafts of symphonies; big plans of fugues;
> Some scraps of writing in a woman's hand:
> No more – the scattered pages of a tale,
> A sorry tale that no man cared to read.
>
> (lines 178–88)

This "tale that no man cared to read" is perhaps the very tale the reader has just encountered from the "mouth" of the poet; Tom Leigh's details seem to confirm much of the minor poet's own explanation of his motives. But this secondary description illuminates our understanding (though not Tom Leigh's) even further; "wild drafts of symphonies" and "Large schemes of undone work" prove the poet's own unsatisfied expectations of himself as poet or musician, as well as confirming an evaluation of him as "minor" in that he never finishes, nor publishes his projects. The irony is not only that "no man cared to read" the tale of the poet's life, but also that he did not allow his work to be read; on some level, the minor poet has resisted the attempt to publish, and so when Tom notes "there was no written word to say farewell" (line 176), the very status of the monologue the reader has just read is called into question, suggesting that we had access to a voice of the poet never before recorded, except, perhaps to Tom himself in conversation with the poet.

As his monologue continues, however, Tom Leigh's comments also alert the reader to the fact that even he, the poet's only friend, has significantly misread the minor poet's predicament. What Tom Leigh cannot see is how alienated the poet was from the philosophical model of experience that is both Tom's and the "common" culture's. His final comment on the poet is as follows:

> Nay, I had deemed him more philosopher;
> For did he think by this one paltry deed
> To cut the knot of circumstance, and snap
> The chain which binds all being?
>
> (lines 196–9)

Tom's final assertion that there is a "chain which binds all being" is exactly the concept that the minor poet's philosophy at the start of the poem rejects. Thus, the final cryptic comment by Tom Leigh actually seems to prove the minor poet's premise that no man can really "understand" the experience of another. The poet's struggle, it seems, is in finding any human audience who might understand him and thus grant him a title, even a limited title like that of "minor poet."

Levy plays on the more conventional structures of a dramatic monologue which would often assume an auditor within the dramatic scenario of the poem; her replacement of this auditor role with lyric apostrophe and an address to an absent being whose own words negate the minor poet's are techniques that help Levy establish how crucial the role of audience acceptance is to the establishment of poetic identity. By exploring that very problem within her poem, Levy highlights the potential terror of an unacknowledged lyric voice, suggesting that to be an "other" or "minor" poet is to know the difficulty of finding an audience who can authorize the poet to claim a poetic and prophetic voice. Over and over again, I think, Levy's poetry and poetic theory suggests that even the most sincere poets risk their very identity as poets at the moment in which they speak from experiences which do not conform to hegemonic cultural expectations. Minor(ity), Levy seems to argue, is a status controlled by an audience rather than any intrinsic "beauty" or "truth" of a poet's speech.

With the challenge to the very premise that poetry can produce sympathetic identification between authors and readers, Levy thus challenges the most basic premise of post-Romantic poetic conventions, as well as the premises imbedded in Matthew Arnold's theories of universal poetry, and she continues this examination of lyric identity in many other poems which explore the "common" assumptions of sexual and religious identity that had marked English literary history. One of Levy's major poetic projects is to deconstruct a central metaphor that governs both Jewish and Christian traditions of religious poetry: the symbol of the divine/human relationship as heterosexual romance. The complex intersections between discourses of heterosexual romance and divine love recur in a variety of patterns in Biblical and English literary traditions. Levy takes on the power of these figures in one of her most radical poems, "Magdalen," a dramatic monologue that explores the tension between the sexualized and devotional discourses that have constructed the figure of Mary Magdalen. When linked with other lyrics that explore the relationships between divine and earthly love, we can see how Levy sought to challenge some of the basic Christian and heterosexual assumptions that have structured much English poetry.

"A WOMAN WITH A HEART OF STONE": CHALLENGING THE POETICS OF CHRISTIAN WOMANHOOD

They asked her, "Why are you weeping?" She answered, "They have taken my Lord away and I do not know where they have laid him." With these words she turned around and saw Jesus standing there, but she did not recognize him . . . Jesus said "Mary!" She turned and said to him, "Rabboni!" "Do not cling to me," said Jesus. (John 20: 13–17, Revised English Bible)

> . . . Was ever known
> A woman with a heart of stone?
> (Amy Levy, "Magdalen," *A Minor*
> *Poet and Other Verse*, lines 63–4)

"Magdalen" represents Levy's most pointed depiction of a woman who refuses the traditional terms of an explicitly Christian heterosexual identity. Instead, Levy's Magdalen represents herself as a Jewish woman who resists the dominant discourses of sentimentality, romance, Christianity, and indeed poetry that have served so often to construct the figure of the woman poet. The Biblical Magdalen is understood in some Gospel accounts to be the first Jewish figure to come face to face with the resurrected Jesus in his transformed, Christian identity, and it becomes Magdalen's role to report this transformation to the other apostles and initiate explicitly Christian history.[30] Susan Haskins has identified the discourse of some romantic bond between Mary Magdalen and Jesus as one of the many discourses surrounding Magdalen throughout the ages, though she notes that "the idea of a physical relationship between Christ and Mary Magdalen . . . was seized upon by several later nineteenth century artists and writers" (*Mary Magdalen*, 351). To Haskins' list of writers and works that attempted to describe a sexual relationship between Christ and Magdalen, I would add Levy and her poem, "Magdalen."

Levy plays on the very assumptions of Christian female identity with her choice of the culturally loaded figure Magdalen for the title of her poem. This title raises what I think is an intended ambiguity: the problem of figuring out exactly who is the speaking subject of the poem. Specifically, it is difficult to determine whether the speaking voice of the poem is (1) the historical figure Mary Magdalen – the first witness to Christ's Resurrection, especially foregrounded in the Gospel of John – or 2) the voice of a contemporary Victorian "Magdalen," the period's symbolic term for "fallen" woman. In the former interpretation, the poem would situate Mary Magdalen speaking after the Resurrection, ostensibly speaking to Jesus, and condemning him for having abandoned an earthly romance for his divine mission. Choosing to read the speaker as a contemporary figure, on the other hand, constructs the dramatic scenario of the poem as a Victorian woman speaking to a lover who has jilted her, given her a disease, and left her to die in a Victorian "Magdalen house" – a common Victorian Christian institution for the reform of "fallen" women.

Complicating this issue of reading a specific historical identity for this speaker are different sets of details in the poem, some of which support a Biblically linked reading, as I will argue, while others support a more contemporary reading, There are, for example, numerous scriptural allusions to symbols like the "thorn" and the "stone" (discussed below); likewise, the poem offers what seems to be the speaker's exploration and rejection of the very idea of religious faith, as well as references to God's foreknowledge of the story Magdalen tells. Yet there are also a number of details that work against an historically Biblical setting: the poem is set in a "bare, blank room" in a hospital/prison resonant of the Victorian Magdalen houses for the Christian reform of fallen women, complete with a "Pastor" who names her "sin"; likewise, certain colloquial, modern references to "handkerchiefs" and a "shawl" also contribute to the sense that the poem is set in Victorian England, suggesting that the speaker is not literally the Biblical Mary Magdalen, but rather only a symbolic "Magdalen" speaking from a more contemporary setting.

Given these textual complexities within the poem, it is not surprising that most recent critics of this poem have read it as a comment on contemporary Victorian life rather than a rewriting of a Biblical story. Indeed, I would contend that since the governing reading practices of the mainstream Victorian audience (and perhaps later critics) assume a Christian world view, this poem is "unreadable" if the speaker is imagined as the Biblical Magdalen; reading the poem in the voice of the Biblical Magdalen transforms that which can be understood as feminist outrage into quite shocking Christian blasphemy.[31] Thus, for most previous critics of the poem, reading the poem revolves around constructing the speaker as an "imprisoned prostitute" and seeing, for example, the poem as offering " a response to the social and hygienic problems created by prostitution" in Levy's own day (Francis, "Amy Levy," 188–9). While this quite literal reading of the poem is warranted, I want to suggest that the poem offers a simultaneous commentary – from both Jewish and feminist perspectives – on the politics of Christian Biblical interpretation; in my reading, Levy's speaker is identified with the historical Mary

Magdalen even as she also serves as a symbolic voice for more contemporary "Magdalens." Keeping both these identities intact is crucial, I think, to understanding how the poem imbeds a specific challenge to the hegemony of Christian symbol and interpretation in the more obvious narrative of a Victorian prostitute.[32]

Interpreting the last lines of the poem first helps to demonstrate the radical nature of Levy's project in "Magdalen." After describing her condition of alienation, and her misreading of a relationship she believed to be romantic, Levy's Magdalen ends her poem with the following statement:

> You, that I knew in days gone by,
> I fain would see your face once more,
> Con well its features o'er and o'er;
> And touch your hand and feel your kiss,
> Look in your eyes and tell you this:
> That all is done, that I am free;
> That you, through all eternity,
> Have neither part nor lot in me.
>
> (lines 79–86)

When Magdalen imagines how she "fain would see your face once more / Con well its features o'er and o'er / And touch your hand and feel your kiss, / Look in your eyes and tell you this . . ." Levy creates a specific rewriting of the Christian scriptural scene in the garden when Jesus, in his post-Resurrection state, comes to Magdalen and says "Noli mi tangere" (do not touch me) (John 17). The "noli mi tangere" moment is a crucial one in understanding that Jesus' crucifixion and Resurrection created an entirely new relationship with his apostles, and most obviously, Mary Magdalen, whom the Biblical text suggests had indeed gone forward to "touch" Jesus. According to the *New Bible Dictionary*, this phrase – ("noli mi tangere") indicates that "[c]learly Mary's relationship to her Lord, following his resurrection, is to be of a different kind and to continue in another dimension" (Douglas, ed., *New Bible Dictionary*, 793). If we allow Levy's Magdalen to be the Biblical Magdalen, then this scene becomes much more than a fallen woman's address to her lost man. Read as a specifically Jewish resistance to the Christian narrative, these lines offer a Jewish woman's fantasy of how she would revise Christian history.

If the Biblical Magdalen is on some level the first Christian convert, the first to acknowlege and witness the fact of Jesus' miraculous Resurrection and the new divine dimension of their relationship, Levy's Magdalen refuses to accept the terms of any "new dimension." Instead, the poem implies that in fact the "lost" you of the poem never really returns, having completely abandoned Magdalen while "seeing clearly in [his] mind / How this must be which now has been" ("Magdalen," lines 16–17). Reflecting back on the narrative of their relationship – "Now that the tale is told and done" (line 19), Magdalen is seemingly stupified by its "strange[ness]" (line 34) and is most upset that "you, who knew what thing would be / Have wrought this evil unto me" (lines 11–12), thus finding most fault in the idea of Jesus' foreknowledge of events. When she does fantasize a reunion, she chooses to "tell" Jesus of her rejection of his power over her "through all eternity," and thus she identifies herself as defiantly unconverted and unaccepting of any new relationship. Read in this historical Biblical context, Magdalen's refusal to accept his role in her "eternity" thus suggests she confirms her Jewish, rather than Christian identity in her last lines.

It is not only at this particular moment of fantasized reunion that Magdalen suggests she does not share Jesus' approach to their relationship; indeed, much of the rest of the poem charts exactly how Magdalen and her lover operated under quite different assumptions of the terms of their relationship; for Magdalen, theirs was a romantic relationship, an understanding clearly not shared by her Christ. This sense of their different understandings of their relationship is heightened by Levy's use of symbols that register on both romantic and devotional registers. For example, when Magdalen describes a romantic moment in the past, her language calls up a symbol instantly recognizable from a Christian and romantic discourse.

> And once my hand, on a summer's morn,
> I stretched to pluck a rose; a thorn
> Struck through the flesh and made it bleed
> (A little drop of blood indeed!)
> Pale grew your cheek; you stoopt and bound
> Your handkerchief about the wound;
> Your voice came with a broken sound;
> With the deep breath your breast was riven;
> I wonder, did God laugh in Heaven?
>
> (lines 25–33)

Magdalen believed she was participating in a romantic scenario with her lover: for her, the "rose" was a romantic symbol. Yet reading that passage with an awareness of Christian discourse, it seems that the image of blood from a thorn has a quite different meaning for Jesus. The moment the rose is connected with images of the "thorn" and "bleed[ing]" (both terms significantly enjambed) the entire weight of Christian narrative is galvanized, calling up – for a Christian reading audience – the crown of thorns and stigmata, and letting Magdalen see in retrospect that what had been a romantic moment for her was also symbolic of Christ's future suffering – and his own heightened awareness of that other narrative in which he alone was at the center. Thus, the reaction of the lover is what signals Magdalen's misunderstanding of the situation: though he appears to be concerned about Magdalen's wound, her comment that it was "[a] little drop of blood indeed" suggests that his reaction – growing "pale," offering "deep" sighs, and a "broken" voice – far outweighs the actual seriousness of her injury, and puts the spotlight on his suffering rather than hers. Seeing the moment in retrospect, now Magdalen "wonder[s]" about "God's laugh[ter]" at this moment, suggesting God knows full well how the moment plays out on the religious register. When Magdalen points to the ostensible foreknowledge of God, she understands herself as a pawn in the larger "divine" plan to which only Jesus and God have access.

There are other moments in the poem which suggest Levy's self-consciousness of Biblical symbol and her deconstruction of the hege-monic power of Christian interpretation. In her most cryptic use of Scripture, Levy has Magdalen make numerous references to the "heart of stone"; in so doing, Levy works to explore a conventional image of Jewish identity in a new context. Heading toward poetic closure, Levy has Magdalen note that her heart has "turn'd to stone" (line 52) adding that to her, the "future and the past are dead" (line 58). This statement triggers the following thought for Magdalen in which she repeats the figure "heart of stone" quite pointedly.

> If my heart were not made of stone,
> But flesh and blood, it needs must shrink
> Before such thoughts. Was ever known
> A woman with a heart of stone?
>
> (lines 61–4)

If we look to the Scriptures, both Jewish and Christian, to answer that final question, the individuals with hearts of stone are usually Jews: to name just a few examples, in Ezekiel 11: 19, the Jewish prophet named the Son of Man, addressing a lapsed Jewish community, promises to "take the stony heart out of their flesh and give them a heart of flesh";

in Corinthians 3: 2, the Jewish covenant is figured as "written in stone," compared with the "spirit of the living God" who writes with "fleshly tables of the heart." The difference in these two uses of the same symbol is not in their apparent meaning (heart of stone signifies unbelief), but rather in how the term gets revised in Christian history to suggest that all Jews are subject to such a heart, erasing the possibility contained in Ezekiel's prediction that the Jewish community will be granted a fleshy heart – salvation and belief – not through conversion, but rather by maintaining Jewish belief; it is later Christian interpreters of this symbol who recast the notion of the heart of stone as a symbol for all "misdirected" Jewish spirituality, that is, Jewish belief that rejects Jesus as Messiah.

Thus, when Magdalen asks "Was ever known a woman with a heart of stone," she ironically calls attention to her Jewish identity by using the very language which has condemned Jews in Christian culture for their refusal to convert. And so, as Magdalen repeatedly refuses to grant any "belief" in the "you" of the poem, she claims that identity of a "woman with a heart of stone"; her identification with this figure challenges the conventions of religious devotion and spiritual conversion which punctuate the discourse of the heart in Scripture, as well as positioning her, within a Christian epistemology, as a Jew. This idea of a "woman with a heart of stone" also registers on the literary level, challenging the notion that women were inherently sentimental, spiritual, and romantic, and so Levy has her Magdalen challenge the terms of what Angela Leighton has called the "poetics of the heart," a reliance on structures of sentimentality, feeling, and romance which Victorian women poets often galvanized in their poetry. Self-consciously naming herself as a woman with a heart of stone, Levy's Magdalen offers herself as a new figure for the woman poet.

Finally, because the recognition that Magdalen might be a Jewish woman is dependent on a reader's understanding of the original Jewishness of Jesus and his followers, it seems that Levy does indeed "say Shibboleth" to an audience who can recognize early Christian history as a narrative of Jewish conversion. Rather than letting herself be appropriated by a hegemonic religious narrative that would "convert" her experience into a symbol of Christian faith, Levy's Mary Magdalen resists both literal and metaphoric conversion, insisting instead that she speaks from a particular body that rejects any such symbolic or transcendent "truth." With her choice of Magdalen as the subject for the poem, Levy also reverses the familiar practice that Christian writers use to re-animate figures from Hebrew history for a Christian context.[33] In her representation of Magdalen, Levy engages in what might be best termed "anti-typology"; in her poem, a supposed Christian heroine refutes her ties to Christ and instead speaks an unrepentant narrative of a woman who resists all aspects of Christian conversion. In this sense, Levy separates her poetic strategies from women poets like Rossetti, Barrett Browning, and even Aguilar, who in radically different ways all sought to authorize the woman poet by making claim to some larger discourse of religious (Christian) transcendence or heterosexual "universality."

Those readings of the poem which ignore the scriptural allusions and thus de-literalize the title reference to Mary Magdalen uphold an assumed Christian perspective, insisting that Levy's reference to "Magdalen" can only be to that of a Victorian fallen woman. Yet I argue that Levy is aligning the voice of the Biblical Magdalen with a more contemporary fallen woman in order to highlight a process of enforced conversion and rewriting of Jewish identity that marks the work of the New Testament (from a Jewish perspective); likewise, the dual imagery works in the other direction, suggesting that the Victorian fallen woman, subjected to the institutions and rhetoric of Christian conversion, might be understood as like a Jewish woman. Thus, Levy chooses a central moment from the Christian Scriptures and destabilizes conventional Christian interpretations of that moment by suggesting an alternative perspective and approach, one that potentially takes into account the historical fact that Jesus' first followers were Jews. Symbolizing a Biblical (Jewish) woman as a simultaneous figure of a contemporary prostitute, Levy links the identities of the unconverted Jewish woman and the fallen Victorian prostitute, suggesting there are deep connections between the woman who refuses the discourses of the Christian faith and the woman who refuses the model of the chaste and sentimental female heart.

"Magdalen" is not the only poem in which Levy makes connections between the traditions of devotional verse and the conventions of heterosexual love poetry.[34] Her most humorous of these, "The Ballad of Religion and Marriage," clearly links both Jewish and Christian discourses when it refers to both the "Father, Son and Holy Ghost" and "Jehovah," aligning both Judaism and Christianity in their joint commitment to rituals of heterosexual courtship, a commitment Levy's speaker names "dreary" as she daringly notes: "Daily the secret murmurs grow; / We are no more content to plod / Along the beaten paths – and so / Marriage must go the way of God" (*Complete Novels and Selected Writings*, 404–5, lines 13–16).

In other poems, Levy makes explicit links between these overlapping religious traditions and the poetry they have produced, a poetic tradition which repeatedly – and often intentionally – blurs the boundaries between devotional and love poetry. One of her early lyrics published in *Xantippe and Other Verse* (1881) seems clearly linked to Levy's interest in Christian symbol as demonstrated by "Magdalen"; along with recasting certain implications of Christian symbol, I will suggest that "A Prayer" also draws on a lesbian subtext as well. The very title of "A Prayer" immediately puts it in a religious context, and the structure of a prayer is maintained with direct addresses to "My God" and "Great God." The poem also makes reference to the conventions of Christian poetics, capitalizing not only references to God as "Thee" but also as "Love." Yet rather than pray for a specifically religious connection, this poem requests of God the right to imagine a new kind of love, one that can replace the speaker's own alienation from conventional love on earth. Noting that "not mine is the bliss / Of claspt hands and lips that kiss" ("A Prayer," lines 4–5), and "never shall entwine / Loving arms around mine" (lines 10–11), the speaker makes it clear that the conventional images of love do not apply to her.

We might expect that this "prayer" to God might be for a religious love to replace the lack of earthly love; as the poem continues, however, it becomes clear that the speaker seeks a love that might replace both hegemonic heterosexual and Christian ideals of love. Thus, unlike some devotional poems in which the loved object is merged with the figure of the divine, here Levy's speaker prays not for any specific union with God, but rather prays for the power of imagination that will give her at least a fictive love, if not "real" love on earth. By the last lines, the poem has become a prayer for a specifically poetic inspiration:

> Yet grant me this, to find
> The sweetness in my mind
>   Which I must still forego;
> Great God which art above,
> Grant me to image Love,–
>   The bliss without the woe.
>   (lines 25–30)

Levy situates her own desire to "image Love" in a new way within an explicitly religious discourse; only God it seems, has the power to grant her a new kind of poetic image and a new kind of love to imagine, if not attain. Seeking an imagery of "Love" that offers "bliss without the woe," the speaker longs neither for the familiar figure of the suffering Christ as embodying love, nor for an earthly love that might entail a degree of "woe" – a woe she seems to experience in her own extreme isolation.

The oblique references to Christian symbol in "A Prayer" echo the symbolism in "Magdalen," likewise seeking a way to deconstruct the assumptions of Christian and heterosexual romance that structured so much poetic utterance. In "A Prayer," the speaker figures herself as Christ before Resurrection. She writes:

> Lonely as in a tomb,
>   This cross was on me laid;
> My God, I know not why;
> Here in the dark I lie,
>   Lonely, yet not afraid.
>
>   (lines 14–18)

As a speaker who seeks something that she finds unattainable on earth, this speaker aligns herself with a Christ-like figure, suggesting that like Christ in that intermediary stage between his human life and Resurrection, she too lies in wait for some new kind of resurrection which will heal her current suffering. This simultaneous identification with Christian imagery and the desire for a new kind of "Love" which does not seem to be Christian love suggests that the speaker is both using and revising Christian symbol in this poem in order to construct a new vision of "Love."

The revision of the conventions of Christian love seem most pointed at the moments when the speaker differentiates her own desire from that of "men." The clues that suggest that the speaker desires to image a lesbian sexuality occur in the lines in which the speaker compares herself to those "men" on earth who do attain love on earth. Still calling on the image of herself locked in a tomb, the speaker says to God:

> It has seemed good to Thee
>   Still to withold the key
>   Which opes the way to men;
> I am shut in alone,
> I make not any moan,
>   Thy ways are past my ken.
>
>   (lines 19–24)

In withholding a "key" that men seem to have, a figure which "opes the way" to their desire, God has relegated the speaker to a very specific kind of aloneness that is dependent on her lack of a "key" – a potentially phallic image. The double play on the idea of the moan as both a lament and a sound of sexual pleasure furthers the possibility that this speaker is referring to a love for women which "men" are granted, but not the speaker. Thus, "A Prayer" begins to create links between a discourse of religious devotion, and a discourse of an "other" kind of love, and thus seeks to create a new language of "imaging" – that is, a new poetry, that will likewise construct a new sexual and religious identity for the speaker.

While some might argue that Levy's repeated uses of Christian symbol are a sign of her disassociation from Jewish identity, I would suggest that her interests in exploring Christian symbol are no different than when Christian women poets explore Jewish symbols and identity to help construct their own Christian selves. In both cases, the turn to the "other's" religious discourse is not a sign of identification with that discourse, but a recognition of the deep historical, theological, and discursive links between Jewish and Christian identity, and a desire to place oneself in what these poets seem to suggest is a larger continuum of religious identity. Often positioning certain symbols or moments in Christian discourse as central to a given poem, Levy rarely lets those symbols sit easily; likewise, the common knowledge of her Jewish identity, as marked by the Jewish name that Levy never replaced with a pseudonym, would bring to these poems an awareness of her Jewish identity.[35] This awareness of Levy's Jewish authorship insists that a reader question the use of Christian images and see how Levy uses them often as a specific refusal of alliance with Christian literary identity.

"SHALL I WANDER IN VAIN FOR MY COUNTRY?" LEVY AND JEWISH LITERARY TRADITION

Along with having an interest in connecting and simultaneously deconstructing discourses of Christianity, Levy also makes direct connections to Jewish traditions of poetry. We know, for example, that Levy worked on a series of translations of the twelfth-century Spanish/Hebrew devotional poet Jehuda Halevi which appear in Lady Katie Magnus' essay "Jehuda Halevi," first published in and later reprinted in the volume of Magnus' collected essays, called *Jewish Portraits* (1888).[36] Along with these translations, Levy also demonstrates her literary heritage as a Jew in other poems as well. While many of her poems call on religious imagery in order to create a tension between the discourses of religious and sexual identity, some of Levy's poems take on the specific issue of religious faith in its own right; two poems from *A London Plane Tree and Other Verse* serve as examples of Levy's work regarding Jewish religious (as opposed to cultural or racial) identity. "Lohengrin," a sonnet, uses imagery from

Wagner's opera by the same name as an extended metaphor for the loss of one kind of faith and its replacement with something from the past. Where "Lohengrin" calls on a specific discourse of the English sonnet tradition to articulate the longing for a return to her Jewish roots, another poem, "Captivity," is rooted more clearly in the tradition of Jewish poetic lament concerning the exile from a mythic Jewish homeland, yet it too transforms the conventional Jewish longing for "freedom" from exile into a very different kind of meditation about the internal spiritual losses wrought by Jewish assimilation in the Diaspora.

I would speculate that Levy's interests in Wagner's opera, *Lohengrin*, are rooted in the strange ending which resists conventions of heterosexual and Christian closure and offers a somewhat mysterious alternative.[37] Wagner's character Lohengrin is often interpreted to represent the bearer of Christianity, a shining knight of the Grail who arrives to protect and marry the heroine, Elsa, who has been falsely accused of murdering her missing brother, Gottfried. The condition of their love and marriage, Lohengrin tells her, is that she can never ask about his name or his origins. This proves to be an impossible condition for Elsa, and so at the end of the opera, Lohengrin leaves the heartbroken Elsa because she could not offer him total trust and faith. Yet, at the moment of his leaving, Elsa is reunited with her lost brother (who in fact had been the mystical swan that drew Lohengin's vessel); thus, as she loses her true romantic love and symbol of Christian faith, Elsa regains her lost brother who is likewise restored to power and honor, reclaiming the ancient family throne.

Levy's octet recounts the Wagner source quite faithfully.

> Back to the mystic shore beyond the main
>   The mystic craft has sped, and left no trace.
>   Ah, nevermore may she behold his face,
> Nor touch his hand, nor hear his voice again!
> With hidden front she crouches; all in vain
>   The proffered balm. A vessel nears the place;
> They bring her young, lost brother; see her strain
>   The new-found nursling in a close embrace.
>
> (lines 1–8)

Levy's recounting, stripped of specific referents that tie it to the opera, becomes a generalized narrative of loss and redemption. What the "she" gets is a reunion with her origins, her brother, as a sort of replacement for the loss of her romantic love. The emphasis on "mystic" gives the opening a sort of ambiguous spirituality which is coupled with the romantic failure that she is never to see his face or "hear his voice" again; Levy's version creates a deep sense of grieving with the figure of her "hidden," "crouch[ed]" "front" and the vain offering of "balm" to soothe her. Perhaps most striking is the enjambment on "strain" in the seventh line; this odd verb suggests that while she does indeed have a "close embrace" with "her young, lost brother," it is a complex moment of both loss and reunion, requiring a certain intensity of effort even in the desire for closeness.

Levy's concluding sestet draws this narrative into a different, and seemingly less mythic, more contemporary context; significantly, the sestet opens with a direct address to God.

> God, we have lost Thee with much questioning.
> In vain we seek Thy trace by sea and land,
> And in Thine empty fanes where no men sing.
>> What shall we do through all the weary days?
>> Thus wail we and lament. Our eyes we raise,
> And, lo, our Brother with an outstretched hand!
>
> (lines 9–14)

In what is one of Levy's most direct commentaries on religious belief, the sestet states clearly that "questioning" has brought a loss of connection to God, and replaced it with a "vain" "seek[ing]." Likewise, it seems to be a collective rather than personal loss, as she notes that "no men sing" in the "fanes" – which can mean temple or church; without this possibility of faith, Levy's speaker – now signficantly collective – is at a loss for what to "do through all the weary days."

In Levy's reading of Wagner's narrative, then, the "shining knight" who seeks to redeem Elsa with a new identity, is relinquished, and a new relationship with family, the "Brother," is enabled through this loss of the assumed ideal knight. If we read this sonnet with an awareness of Levy's own complex attitudes toward her Jewishness and her repeated interest in linking Jewish and Christian history and symbol, we can speculate that the "Lohengrin" narrative was for Levy a narrative of return rather than conversion. Further, it gestures toward the complex relations between Jewish and Christian history, in which Lohengrin, the "new" manifestation of Christianity who emerges out of a "old" Jewish order, is unable to complete his mission, and so Elsa must reunite with that old order, the "Brother," as the only possible form of redemption. Levy's capitalization of "Brother" suggests this figure has divine implications, one who can soothe the "wail[ing]" and "lament[ing" of the previous line. Significantly, the line "And lo, our Brother with an outstretched hand" does not quite specify its outcome, only implying – especially through the use of "lo" – that there is a sort of redemption implied here, one that comes from connection within a family. "Lohengrin" seems one of Levy's most complex religious poems, one which voices a desire for reconnection and a sense that true spiritual solace can only come from within a "family" context, even if that return to original roots entails a loss of idealized romance with the other.

In another poem from her last volume, Levy makes even stronger allusion to a Jewish literary tradition, and likewise to the complex questions of home and identity raised in the context of Jewish assimilation. "Captivity" stands out as quite a unique poem in Levy's body of work, a poem whose title alone connects to a tradition of Jewish poetry on the pain of Jewish exile and Diasporic identity. The poem begins by describing the dual fates of the "lion in chains" and the "captive" bird, each of whom remember the land of their freedom, the "forest" and the "woodland" respectively, and who "strain" and "bea[t]" against the fetters and cages of their present captivity. Levy's speaker goes on to imagine what might happen to these figures if "loosed" from their cages.

> If the lion were loosed from the fetter,
> To wander again;
> He would seek the wide silence and shadow
> Of his jungle in vain
>
> He would rage in his fury, destroying;
> Let him rage, let him roam!
> Shall he traverse the pitiless mountain,
> Or swim through the foam?
>
> If they opened the cage and the casement,
> And the bird flew away;
> He would come back at evening, heartbroken,
> A captive for aye.
>
> Would come if his kindred had spared him,
> Free birds from afar –
> There was wrought what is stronger than iron
> In fetter and bar.   (9–24)

Rather than being able to relish the possibility of freedom, the lion and bird are both unable to live in their original homes. In the lion's case, the "jungle" can no longer be found, either destroyed or too distant, and he is left to "rage," apparently in vain. The case of the bird seems more complex; the bird, "a captive for aye," inevitably returns to the cage rather than being able to relish freedom; even more complex is the idea that he could only return to the cage "if his kindred had spared him." Those "free birds from afar" is seems, must also relinquish a desire to "hold" the bird who has a connection "stronger than iron" to the boundaries of his captivity; the image of the bird is one who has very little free will of his own, either in alone in captivity or with "kindred."

The raging lion and the eternally captive bird set up a certain contrast in the problem of identity in exile. One example deals with the problem of actually locating a lost metaphorical homeland, while the other deals with the problem of an internal assimilation. The concluding four stanzas of the poem move into a first-person voice, linking the speaker to the same problems described allegorically by the lion and bird.

> I cannot remember my country,
>   The land whence I came;
> Whence they brought me and chained me and made me
>   Nor wild thing nor tame.
>
> This only I know of my country
>   This only repeat: –
> It was free as the forest, and sweeter
>   Than woodland retreat.   (lines 25–32)

The speaker identifies with both bird and lion, now having no memory of that land from "whence I came," but only the present knowledge of now being neither "wild thing nor tame." Rather than any actual memories of "my country," Levy's speaker can "only repeat" (line 30) words about that country, that it was "free as the forest, and sweeter / Than woodland retreat" (lines 31–2). The speaker can only describe her lost country through reference to myths and literary language, suggesting she has no tangible relationship or memory of it for herself.

The poem ends in a series of unanswered questions which offer a somewhat different kind of resolution than that of more traditional Hebrew poets who contrast the captivity of Diaspora with the freedom of spiritual union in Jerusalem. Levy writes:

> When the chain shall at last be broken,
>   The window set wide;
> And I step in the largeness and freedom
>   Of sunlight outside;

> Shall I wander in vain for my country?
> Shall I seek and not find?
> Shall I cry for the bars that encage me,
> The fetters that bind?
> (lines 33–40)

The speaker seems to assume that eventually the "chain shall at last be broken" – that is, there seems to be an assumption that ultimate freedom is inevitable, perhaps in the form of death. However, even when turning to a familiar spiritual concept of finding light – "stepp[ing] in the largeness and freedom / Of sunlight outside" – the speaker does not yet rejoice, but can only if she will ever be able to fully escape her "captivity," or even have the clear desire to do so. Certainly on some level, this poem relates to the experience of being an Anglo-Jew, and links that condition to the centuries of Diasporic existence in "exile" which marks the Jewish literary tradition. The idea of a "lost homeland" resonates from Jewish history; that the speaker cannot remember the "land whence (she) came" implies she never was in that country, or that its existence in her life is only imaginary. But the poem is really concerned with the process that accompanies Diasporic displacement. The final lines are the most important in their description of the psychological effects of oppression, of creating a condition in which nothing except the "captivity" can be imagined or desired.

This idea of being at home nowhere is a theme Levy refers to repeatedly in her work, using it to describe her religious identity, her cultural identity, and her sexual identity at various different moments. "Captivity" seems to offer Levy's most Jewish version of being caught between two worlds, a version whose title and references to a "lost land" position her more directly in line with a tradition of Jewish Diasporic poetry longing the loss of the land of Israel – a "place" that is always symbolic of a spiritual state in Jewish literature, rather than a mere geographical location. On some level, "Captivity" seems to speak to some of the same issues Grace Aguilar explored in "A Vision of Jerusalem," which also voiced a longing for union with the Jerusalem of the past. But where Aguilar is able to end her poem with the idea that "still wilt thou rise again my beautiful, my home / God will bring his children back, ne'er again to roam," Levy's poem characteristically only ends with unanswered questions that pose the impossibility of finding a "home"; fearing that she would eventually "cry for the bars that encage [her]," Levy's depiction of the pains and alienation of Diaspora life (without the deep spiritual conviction that marks Aguilar's poetic) is bleak, moving, and offers a new dimension of Jewish literary longing, this time marked by the profound ambivalence of the assimilated Jew.

"SOME OTHER WHERE": CONCLUSIONS AND FURTHER QUESTIONS

> Somewhere, I think, some other where, not here,
> In other ages, on another sphere,
> I danced with you, and you with me, my dear.
> (Levy, "A Wall Flower," *A London Plane
> Tree and Other Verse*, lines 4–6)

Whereas each of the women examined so far in this book has chosen to claim a universal authority through discourses of Christianity or heterosexuality, Levy stands out as from her antecedents as a poet who eschews alliance with the hegemonic poetic and religious identities with which so many women poets of the period aligned themselves. Levy's version of the woman poet challenges the figure of the "spiritual" woman writer that Aguilar, Barrett Browning, and Rossetti found invaluable for their own poetic authority; further, many of Levy's lyrics challenged a poetic woman's assumed commitment to heterosexuality which was at the heart of many Victorian women's claims to poetic authority. Finally, Levy's poetry resists certain patterns of redemptive closure – spiritual and sexual union/transformation, a discourse of emotional and spiritual "conversion" that often marks the English Christian lyric tradition and which many of the women writers of her day used to create their own poetic identities and authorities.

In this sense, Levy stands as an important transition from women poets who sought some kind of literary authority through their alliance with and reconfiguration of certain dominant discourses of religion and sexuality; in Levy's case, she steps back one step, and rather than seeking to reconfigure the relationships between religion, poetry, and sexuality to create her own literary authority, she calls those very relationships into question. And yet, she also seemed to have an awareness that such poetic strategies would probably not be embraced in her own day. As she suggests in her late poem, "A Wall Flower," Levy created a poetic system that she imagined might be more suited to "[s]omewhere . . . some other where, not here, " some future cultural moment where her representations of Jewish, lesbian, and unconventionally spiritual identity might be more readily understood. The recent renewal of interest in Levy suggests that ours is the moment she may have sought.

Yet of course, Levy also exists in a tradition of Anglo-Jewish women poets, and I have tried to suggest that in much of her work, she situates herself within certain Jewish literary traditions as well as English. When we read the writing of Aguilar and Levy together, it becomes clear that the Anglo-Jewish woman poets carried with them an awareness of both the conventions of English literary history and Jewish literary history. In many ways, Aguilar and Levy align themselves with different sides of both these traditions; Aguilar found her connections to Romantic poets, and thus she created a personal lyric poetic that sought to depict a private Jewish spirituality that could nevertheless speak in "Christian" terms. Her ties to a Jewish literary tradition are to a poetry that offers a direct address to God, a tradition rooted in the Psalms and the poetry of personal relationship to the Divine. Further, Aguilar seeks to portray Jewish spirituality as a voice for universality, often arguing in her poetry that Judaism contains within it all the roots of Christian spirituality and womanhood that Christian writers claimed as uniquely their own.

Levy, on the other hand, challenges the assumptions of the Romantic lyric, and the very idea that any one person can speak universally; this assumption necessarily affects her approaches to both spirituality and poetry. Rather than endorse an obvious link to any specific Jewish doctrine or theology, Levy prefers to keep her references to Judaism and Jewishness somewhat veiled. Rather than claim Judaism as encompassing the terms of Christian womanhood, Levy poses distinct challenges to those assumptions of spiritualized femininity, often calling on a Jewish perspective to destabilize the hegemonic power of both Christian and heterosexual rhetoric. Her goals are not as a "apologist" for Judaism, but rather as a defender of all forms of "minority," and so unlike Aguilar, Levy is willing to turn her critical eye on Jewishness – most specifically in her prose writing. Her poetry, I have suggested, never makes the same kinds of spiritual commitments as Aguilar's did, but nevertheless does offer a "marker" of a Jewish sensibility, suggesting that Levy did indeed attempt to "say Shibboleth" in her poetry to those who could recognize the Jewish accents imbedded at certain moments. If, as I argued in chapter 2, Victorian poetic discourses were deeply tied to the discourses of Jewish and Christian relations, then I would argue that Levy was fully aware of the weight of that religious discourse on English poetics and the special implications it had for women's poetic identity.

In closing this book, my hope is that I will not be closing a chapter of feminist literary criticism which takes seriously the work of women who sought to address issues of religious identity in their poetry. Focusing on only four women, two of them already quite famous, I have sought to ask some new questions about the ways we read some of the now canonized texts of Christian Victorian women poets, as well as draw attention to some lesser-known Jewish women poets and their engagement, albeit from a very different perspective, with issues of religion and poetry. I have also sought to highlight a dialogue within Victorian women's poetry about Jewish/Christian relations. If this book offers nothing else, I hope it suggests that Jewish identity was a deeply significant issue within the world of Victorian poetics. In posing this issue, I hope too that the explicit Christian bias of so much English literary history can be more openly revealed, and revive questions about the politics of aesthetic evaluation which have marginalized so many Jewish writers in the English tradition.

Because feminist theory has taken up the problem of gender bias in aesthetic evaluation, it can be a useful starting place for deconstructing religious biases in literary evaluation as well. Rita Felski begins to probe the problem of "feminist aesthetics" in *Beyond Feminist Aesthetics: Feminist Literature and Social Change* (1989). Felski summarizes the problem with most theories of feminist aesthetics, and their respective methods, as follows:

> feminist criticism is necessarily a contradictory enterprise; it produces tensions and problems which cannot be resolved by thinking either dualistically (whereby literature and ideology are separate spheres) or monistically (whereby literature is indistinguishable from political ideology) . . . The notion of feminist aesthetics presupposes that these two dimensions of textual reception can be unproblematically harmonized, assuming either that an aesthetically self-conscious literature which subverts conventions of representation forms a sufficient basis for a feminist politics of culture (a position that can be regarded as both elitist and politically naive), or that texts which have been politically important to the women's movement are automatically of aesthetic significance . . . A dialectical interaction between politics and aesthetics is compressed into an identity which attempts to construct a normative aesthetic on the basis of feminist interests. (180–1)

Like Felski, I believe that the project of articulating a feminist aesthetics is fraught with contradiction; further, I believe that *all* aesthetic evaluations of literary works have been based on political distinctions – or religious assumptions – and that categories of "good and bad" literature are produced by those particular sets of political, cultural, and religious beliefs. Thus, to follow Felski's thinking about feminist aesthetics in relation to this project, I would note that the critical desire to separate ideological values from aesthetic ones is not only a question for feminist analyses, but is equally important when examining poetry which was culturally defined through its relation to Christian theology.

How might we begin to productively rethink this relationship between "great poetry" and the assumed normativity of Christian values? As I think Amy Levy suggests, rethinking generic definitions might be a starting place. If we accept that aesthetic evaluation in the English literary tradition has indeed been predicated on a set of deeply held Christian assumptions about literature, then we can begin to see how literary form itself can be linked to religious values. Thus, Christian perspectives may find intrinsic value in poetic lyric which privileges narratives of individual redemption, constructions of unitary subjects, patterns of conversion or personal transformation as modes for closure. These are only some of the figures and genres which have come to be claimed as representative of the English poetic tradition, without always naming them as Christian *per se*. The alternatives to these generic patterns might position communal identity as more valuable than individual redemption, might posit multiplicity of perspectives and a community of voices, as in a tradition of Talmud and midrash, over unitary or monologic identity, might emphasize narratives of persistence rather than conversion or transformation, and might replace narratives of redemptive closure with narratives of perpetual hope. This list of alternative modes of literary values is not meant to be conclusive, but rather only suggestive of a method that could challenge the often naturalized, universalized, and essentialized categories of "great literature" through which certain theological assumptions are recast as "aesthetic" values.[38]

Beyond these larger theoretical questions about literary value, however, there are still so many practical questions to be asked about the study of women, religion, and poetry in this period, and so many women poets who explored religion and women's identity whose work still remains under-studied. There is so much more work to be done to move beyond even the simple binaries of Jewish/Christian with which this book is concerned, and to explore women's poetry of different Christianities (Catholic and numerous Protestant denominations) as well as Buddhist, Hindu, and spiritualist movements in the nineteenth century. There also remain any number of other Jewish women poets from the nineteenth century who remain virtually unknown to Victorian studies.[39]

How will this work get done? It seems that first, we must help our students – the future critics – understand the central role religion played in Victorian literature; their decreasing knowledge about specific religious traditions, the language of the Bible, and general religious history all work against those budding scholars who may have an interest in this work. In an era of multicultural curriculum reform, it seems particularly important to teach our students that just as racial difference structures many of our current historical discourses on diversity, in Victorian England religious difference too was a major source of diversity and conflict. I hope too that we continue to make space in feminist critical discourse to acknowledge the important and complex roles religion played in Victorian women's lives, moving past the assumptions I charted in chapter 1 that assume organized religious traditions have only stifled women's literary creativity. In my close readings of these four poets' literary strategies, I have sought to highlight not only the relations between Jewish and Christian women in this era, but also to recognize the sheer creativity and complexity of their poetry and theology. I hope this book suggests that religious texts, ideas, and belief systems offered women a wellspring of both intellectual and artistic creative acts, and that in both rewriting versions of patriarchally defined religious traditions or finding a unique kind of identification within those traditions, Victorian women poets have left us a rich legacy from which to explore the very meaning of women's religious identity. By assuming too that these women achieved an artistry with religious discourse equal to that of their male counterparts, I hope to create here a critical space where these women poets will not only be recognized, but in which their complex negotiations with religious discourse might "dance" with my own perspectives as a feminist scholar and a religious woman.

Notes

1 For more on the related project of revealing the anti-Semitic impulses in Victorian prose, fiction, and non-fiction, see Cheyette, *Constructions of "the Jew,"* and Ragussis, *Figures of Conversion.* I use all three terms – Judaic, Jewishness, and Hebraic – in this book; "Judaic" refers to specific aspects of Judaism (the religion); "Jewishness" is used more generally to refer to aspects of Jewish culture and identity, and "Hebraic" is used to refer to the textual traditions of the Hebrew language and Hebrew Bible.

2 See Jill Robbins' Introduction, "Figurations of the Judaic," in *Prodigal Son/Elder Brother,* for an excellent discussion of the ways Judaism and Jewishness are always inscribed in the discourse of Christianity. See also Langmuir, *History, Religion, and Antisemitism,* Part 3, "The Religious Roots of Antisemitism."

3 It has also asked me to reconsider some of the theories of those ground-breaking feminist critics whose work in feminist literary criticism has been directly responsible for my success in the academy. I do my critique of past work with full awareness of my own debt to the critics who came before me, confident that they will see my critique as part of the logical and healthy progression of feminist thought. With such an acknowledgment I hope to separate my analysis from the work of some who critique feminist critics without recognition of our mutual intellectual debts to each other.

4 Feminist literary scholarship of the last thirty years, as powerful as it has been in rewriting literary history and theory, necessarily reflects the values of the first generation of women to attain political success within the academy. This group of feminist literary scholars has, for the most part, been deeply troubled by the patriarchal claims of institutionalized religious traditions, and their critique has been both crucially important for feminist thought, and not always fully theorized. See note 5 below on Moody's theory regarding womanist scholars; see also Rubin-Dorsky and Fishkin, eds., *People of the Book*; many women scholars identify quite overtly their antipathy to religion as a reason they became academics. See also Susan Gubar's essay on her own feminism in relation to her Jewish identity in "Eating the Bread of Affliction."

5 Here, I am in debt to Joycelyn Moody's theory of the ways the "black church woman" remains a potential embarrassment to womanist literary critics, a theory she described in a 1997 talk at the Harvard Divinity School and has since published in her *Sentimental Confessions*, 152–77. There are other issues of sentimentalism that also make contemporary readers of Victorian women's poetry uncomfortable; see Jerome McGann's introduction to *The Poetry of Sensibility*.

6 For more on the history of Rossetti's canonization, see Lootens, *Lost Saints*, chapter 5.

7 *Ibid.*, 162–88.

8 Indeed, Angela Leighton writes: "Rossetti's reputation as a minor lyricist and unfashionably religious poet has only been challenged in the last decade or so" (Leighton and Reynolds, eds., *Victorian Women Poets*, 356), However, Lootens points out in her chapter on Rossetti that though we in the twenty-first century may not like the terms with which Rossetti was canonized in her day, she clearly was an important model for women's poetry, not merely understood as a "minor lyricist."

9 Jerome McGann's article "The Religious Poetry of Christina Rossetti," the volume of essays titled *The Achievement of Christina Rossetti* (ed. Kent), and G. B. Tennyson's *Victorian Devotional Poetry* are good exceptions here.

10 It is important to consider the political fates of other non-Anglican groups in England in this context; for example, Jewish emancipation was inherently linked to Catholic and Dissenting emancipation. However, The Catholic Relief Act of 1829 brought Anglo-Catholics political citizenship in England almost thirty years sooner than Anglo-Jewish emancipation. Despite the vexed relationship between Catholicism and Anglicanism in English history, then, it was clearly easier to enfranchise Christian "others" rather than non-Christian others in Victorian England.

11 See especially Krueger, *The Reader's Repentance*, for an analysis of the relationships between women's preaching and the novel.

12 Dr. Linda Moody explores related issues in her current project on nineteenth-century women's hymn writing. See Moody, "Religio-Political Insights of 19th Century Women Hymnists and Lyric Poets."

13 Sexual orientation and class are other important manifestations of power which affect systems of oppression; while I acknowledge the crucial importance of those categories of analysis, in this book I am focusing my analysis on intersections between discourses of religious and sexual difference. See chapter 6 for Amy Levy's poetry, which creates a linked critique of religious tradition and heterosexist discourse.

14 See G. B. Tennyson, *Victorian Devotional Poetry*, for statistics; he notes that between 1827 and 1873, 379,000 copies were published – one copy for every sixty inhabitants in England – and that if we calculate publishing after the copyright ran out, it is likely over half a million copies of *The Christian Year* were sold by the end of the century (227).

15 See my "Canonizing the Jew: Amy Levy's Challenge to Victorian Poetic Identity" for more on the theological structures that informed Victorian poetics.

16 Aguilar's novels have received more attention than her poetry; see Ragussis, *Figures of Conversion*, and Galchinsky, *The Origin of the Modern Jewish Woman Writer.*

2 "SWEET SINGERS OF ISRAEL": GENDERED AND JEWISH
OTHERNESS IN VICTORIAN POETICS

1 See Landow, *Victorian Types*; see also Cheyette, *Constructions of "the Jew,"* who calls on certain patterns of typology, though his analysis and method focus on a "Semitic" discourse and are thus significantly uninterested in theological questions *per se.*

2 In 1848, two separate anthologies of women's poetry came out, George Bethune's *The British Female Poets*, and Frederic Rowton's *The Female Poets of Great Britain.* Their simultaneous emergence in 1848 can be used to suggest how the very idea of the woman poet had gained critical credence by the mid-nineteenth century.

3 For more on the statistics about women poets and the literary market in nineteenth century England, see Mermin, *Godiva's Ride*, chapters 3 and 4, Armstrong, *Victorian Poetry*, chapter 12, and McGann, *The Poetics of Sensibility.* See also Paula Feldman's anthology, *British Women Poets of the Romantic Era.*

4 See especially the works listed in the Bibliography by Lipman, Salbstein, Jacob Katz, and David Feldman for studies of the political emancipation of the Jews. See David Katz, *The Jews in the History of England*, and Endelman, *The Jews of Georgian England; Radical Assimilation* for studies of historical context prior to emancipation. See Ragussis, *Figures of Conversion;* "Representation, Conversion," and Cheyette, *Constructions of "the Jew,"* for more specific relationships between the history of Anglo-Jewish and Victorian literary history.

5 The original debate on a "Jew Bill" on issues of Jewish naturalization was in 1753, which failed; though the issue of naturalization was dealt with in 1826, a series of bills from 1830 to 1858 sought to find ways to allow Jews to serve in Parliament without having to take the oath "on the true faith of a Christian." See David Katz, *The Jews in the History of England*, 381–9, for a summary of these bills and debates. See note 4 above for more detailed studies.

6 See Ruether, *Faith and Fratricide*, and Langmuir, *History, Religion, and Anti-semitism*, for detailed discussions of anti-Judaism in relation to or contradistinction with anti-Semitism. The connection I trace between poetics and Judaic discourse is related to, but not identical with, the emphases on Jewish racial difference so emphasized in other recent scholarship.

7 This issue of whether to emphasize theology in feminist Jewish studies was a central debate in the early work by Jewish feminist theologians like Cynthia

Ozick and Judith Plaskow. See Ozick, "Notes Toward Finding the Right Question," and Plaskow's "The Right Question is Theological," in Heschel, ed., *On Being a Jewish Feminist*; see also Plaskow, *Standing Again at Sinai*, and Rachel Adler, *Engendering Judaism*. The refusal to consider specifically theological questions and the attendant emphasis on "cultural" and "racial" studies has led to what I think is an over-simplification of Jewish identity in many recent works which focus on anti-Semitism and Jewishness; see Langmuir, *History, Religion, and Antisemitism*, for a cogent analysis of why anti-Semitism limits certain important issues surrounding historical Jewish oppression.

8 Clearly, my use of the term "Romantic" is not meant to be exhaustive or comprehensive, as I am not considering the specific contours of the theological/poetic systems of, say, Coleridge or Blake. For more specific work on particular Romantic poets and religion, see Prickett, *Romanticism and Religion*, and Jasper, *The Study of Literature and Religion*.

9 For more on the contrast between Carlyle's formula for prophetic/poetic identity and earlier formulations of this figure, see my "Victorian Poetry and Religious Diversity," in Bristow, ed., *The Cambridge Companion to Victorian Poetry*.

10 For more extensive reading on Romanticism and gender, see Mellor, *Romanticism and Feminism*, and Ross, *The Contours of Masculine Desire*.

11 See chapter 1, note 14.

12 G. B. Tennyson, *Victorian Devotional Poetry*, 69–70.

13 Stopford Brooke was the author of numerous books of literary criticism. Besides the text mentioned in this chapter, he also authored *The Development of Theology as Illustrated in English Poetry From 1780 to 1830* and many other works of literary criticism, most of which had numerous editions in England and America.

14 I am in debt to one of this typescript's readers for pointing out that Tennyson's *In Memoriam* (1850) offers a similar theory of "personal theology" in action, and was probably a very influential text in the development of the concept of theology as "felt truths."

15 Byron's *Hebrew Melodies* (1815) are an important example of this idealization.

16 Mary Schneider calls the essay "baffling" and notes that its "statements cannot be put together into a coherent theory" (*Poetry in the Age of Democracy*, 128). Ruth apRoberts, *The Biblical Web*, 114 calls the essay "a rather uncomfortable piece of work" and while noting Arnold's interest in "Heine's Jewishness," apRoberts stops short of offering any reading of the essay's closure. Perhaps the most astute reading of this essay comes from Joseph Carroll, who suggests that Arnold's "evaluation of Heine fails of justness for the . . . reason that Arnold is ultimately unwilling to attribute to Heine the significance warranted by Heine's influence on Arnold himself" (*The Cultural Theory of Matthew Arnold*, 232).

17 Obviously, the question of Heine's Jewish identity is made more complex by his own conversion to Protestantism when he was twenty-eight (1825); for more on the complexities of Jewish conversion to Christianity and its

effects on Jewish identification, see Gilman, *Jewish Self-Hatred*, 167–87; Ritchie Robertson, *Heine*, 76–101.

18 Nevertheless, racial difference, in the Heine essay, does not seem to be the more vexed problem it will become in *Culture and Anarchy*, and this is, I think, because Arnold is not compelled to find any *Englishness* in Heine *per se*. For more on Arnold and a racialized Jewish identity see Ragussis, *Figures of Conversion*, 211–33, and Cheyette, *Constructions of "the Jew,"* 13–23.

19 The phrase "many are called, few chosen" refers to the parable in Matthew of the king's wedding feast for his son. The guests whom the king originally invites do not come, and in their place, the king invites whomever can be found on "highways"; when one of these shows up without a wedding garment, however, the king has him bound and cast out. From within a specifically Christian reading of Jewish identity, this parable might describe the Jewish refusal to enter into a "new" Christian covenant with God in honor of his "son." Thus, the reference to "chosen" refers specifically to those who accept the king's invitation for the wedding of his son and honor it accordingly, in contrast to those who are "called" and do not respond.

20 There has been considerable critical interest in Arnold's relationship to Jews and Judaism. Most often cited is the fact that he had many Jewish friends, and was an ardent admirer of the Jewish actress Rachel. See DeLaura, *Hebrew and Hellene*, and Brownstein, "Representing the Self."

21 For an alternative reading of this passage, see Ragussis, *Figures of Conversion*, 223–4.

3 ELIZABETH BARRETT BROWNING AND THE "HEBRAIC MONSTER"

1 Excerpted from two of Barrett Browning's letters to Mitford in *Letters*, 13 March 1844 (II: 395), and 22 March 1844, (II: 400).

2 Though at this point in her life Barrett Browning was not yet a Browning, I have opted to use her full name, Barrett Browning, throughout the chapter, for clarity. In truth, she was known and published as Elizabeth Barrett until her marriage in 1846; after she was known as Mrs. Browning to many; I have opted to preserve both her identities.

3 See Mermin, *Elizabeth Barrett Browning*, 81–2, for more on Barrett Browning's relationship with Horne.

4 Although she saw very clearly the ambiguous implications of Horne's essay about herself, she refused to tell him of her dismay for fear of hurting his feelings, and likewise repeatedly begged Mitford to not convey her disappointment to Horne. See Browning, *Letters*, II: 394–400, for two letters in which she complains about Horne's descriptions of her, including this passage.

5 Of course, the entire notion of a saving a "relic" – a body part of a saint – is quite alien to Jewish practice. Horne's imagery thus displays his lack of Jewish knowledge and his Christian assumptions.

6 Mary Russell Mitford was one of Barrett Browning's closest friends, and an important literary figure of the day, known especially for her tales of rural life, *Our Village*, 1824–32, and her gift book, *Findens' Tableaux* (1838–41), to which Barrett Browning contributed as a favor to her friend. Mitford also gave Barrett Browning her favorite gift, the spaniel Flush.

7 The term "the Hebraic" in this chapter refers to references, allusions, and knowledge of the Hebrew Bible and Hebrew language, and is thus slightly different than references to Jewishness. See chapter 1, note 1.

8 See also Tricia Lootens, *Lost Saints*, for more on the complexities of Barrett Browning's canonical history. In particular, Lootens notes that "metaphoric monuments to Barrett Browning's glory tended to teeter between evocations of a Comtean honorary 'Great Manhood' and of the 'eternal,' generic category of femininity" (121).

9 This and all subsequent page references to Barrett Browning's Prefaces and poems (with the exception of *Aurora Leigh*), refer to the page numbers in the 1916 Oxford University Press edition, *The Poetical Works of Elizabeth Barrett Browning with Two Prose Essays*, ed. Humphrey Milford, which reproduces all of her prefaces as well as poems.

10 See Landow, *Victorian Types, Victorian Shadows*, chapter 1. For a more extended study on the history of European approaches to Hebrew linguistics, see Olender, *The Languages of Paradise*.

11 In the Torah, for example, vowels, (or "dots") are left out of the written text, rendering meaning somewhat obscure for one not well versed in the language; this elimination of vowel indicators occurs in many other important Hebrew texts as well.

12 According to Mermin, *Elizabeth Barrett Browning*, 19, 47 and Forster, *Elizabeth Barrett Browning*, 67, Barrett Browning began studying Hebrew in the early 1830s.

13 Mermin (*Elizabeth Barrett Browning*) and Smith (*Poetics*) discuss the difficulty for women poets in being considered "representative"; but one way Barrett Browning got around this problem – as did other women poets of the period – was by claiming the position of "the Christian" from which to speak.

14 This poem does not appear as part of "A Supplication for Love" in the Milford edition of Barrett Browning's poems, but rather as its own poem (295). Milford does not recreate the order of each book of Barrett Browning's, so it is possible this poem was separated from others. It does appear as part of the larger poem in other editions; see the 1900 Houghton Mifflin edition (*Complete Poetical Works*) for the original ordering of poems.

15 See Lewis, *Elizabeth Barrett Browning's Spiritual Progress*, 50–2, for a summary of other critics' work on this passage.

16 Lootens, *Lost Saints*, 122.

17 It is not fully clear that Barrett Browning chose the correct tense in her Hebrew in this example; her term is for "blessing" in the future tense rather than the noun form that would make more sense.

18 Further on in the poem, the poet is described as being alone "as Jacob at the Bethel stone," another connection between the poet's visionary experience and the Hebrew Scriptures (Genesis 28:10–20). In the Biblical version, Jacob dreams that angels travel up and down a ladder between earth and God's throne. In "A Vision of Poets," then, Barrett Browning has rewritten Jacob's dream to suggest that the angelic intermediaries between earth and heaven are actually poets.

19 The source for this interpretation is in Rashi's commentary on Deuteronomy 34:5. See Plaut, *The Torah*, 1582, note 5.

20 Barrett Browning inserts her own footnote here which reads: "The coincidence consists merely of the choice of subject; the mode of treating it being wholly different."

21 Sandra Donaldson's exhaustive *Elizabeth Barrett Browning: An Annotated Bibliography* gives two references to the poem, both of which refer to a book published in 1868 by A. A., titled *The True Mary: Being Mrs. Browning's Poem: "The Virgin Mary to the Child Jesus"* (New York, Thomas Whittaker). Donaldson, *Annotated*, 115–16. Helen Cooper devotes two paragraphs to the poem in her 1988 text, suggesting that it explores the "practical implications" of the life of "the blessedest of women" (Cooper, *Elizabeth Barrett Browning*, 43–4). Marjorie Stone categorizes the poem with those that seek to "transform silent or marginalized women into speaking subjects" and links the poem to later feminist theory in its representations of "women short circuiting a male economy in which they function as objects of exchange" (Stone, *Elizabeth Barrett Browning*, 13); Mermin mentions the poem only to suggest *The Seraphim* is a "woman's book" (*Elizabeth Barrett Browning*, 68). Linda Lewis makes no mention of the poem in her important work on Barrett Browning's religious poetry, *Elizabeth Barrett Browning's Spiritual Progress*.

22 The "daringness" of this poem is cast into sharp relief when we consider it against a much more passive image of Mary provided by Barrett Browning in "The Seraphim":

> A woman kneels
> The mid cross under,
> With white lips asunder,
> And motion on each.
> They throb, as she feels,
> With a spasm, not a speech . . .
> (lines 477–82)

23 I include Jewish narrative here, since the reference to "Crown me a King" could also refer to the Jewish Messiah, whom prophecy said would be a king as well. Once again, then, Barrett Browning might be alluding to Mary's Jewish knowledge.

24 The setting of the poem echoes Coleridge's "Frost at Midnight", and is an interesting contrast to Grace Aguilar's "Angels," which I think also alludes to the Coleridge poem. See chapter 5.

25 All citations from *Aurora Leigh* are taken from the Margaret Reynolds edition (Norton Critical) which reproduces the 1859 revised "fourth" edition (313).

26 See Mermin (*Elizabeth Barrett Browning*), and the works listed in the Bibliography by Cooper, Falk, Friedman, Hickock, Rosenblum, Gelpi, and Stone for more explicit attention to Barrett Browning's women.

27 This issue of whether the feminist politics of *Aurora Leigh* are "radical" or "conservative" is at the heart of the critical debate surrounding this text, though a few critics include an extended discussion of religion in their feminist approach (with the exception of Linda Lewis, Dorothy Mermin, and Helen Cooper). See the works listed in the Bibliography by Blake, Case, Cooper, David, Friedman, Gelpi, Kaplan, Mermin, Stone, and Zonana.

28 For more on Christian typology from both Jewish and Christian perspectives see the works listed in the Bibliography by Erich Auerbach, Charity, A. Cohen, Frei, Landow, Josipovici, Miner, ed., and Ruether.

29 See Lewis, *Elizabeth Barrett Browning's Spiritual Progress*, Mermin, *Elizabeth Barrett Browning*, and Hickock, *Representations of Women*, for more limited attention to the role of Miriam in this poem. Holmes ends her article on Barrett Browning's use of Miriam by stating: "Barrett Browning reached back to the earliest part of the most sacred story of her society to find a model for Aurora Leigh to imitate" ("Elizabeth Barrett Browning," 604–5); it is this reading of Miriam's role in the poem that is most prevalent among recent critics, and with which my argument takes particular issue.

30 See Pellegrini, "Whiteface Performances," 125–30 for a more detailed analysis of some nineteenth-century Jewish women actresses.

31 See *ibid.*, 119, for more on the Jewish woman versus "the angel in the house."

32 See chapter 6 in this volume, and Rochelson, "Jews, Gender, and Genre," and Hunt Beckman, "Amy Levy and the 'Jewish Novel,'" for readings of women's plight in *Reuben Sachs*.

33 This poem occurs in Hemans' series of sonnets titled: "Female Characters of Scripture" in *The Poetical Works of Mrs. Hemans*, 641–5.

34 The emphasis on "whiteness" here is a familiar repression of what historically we could construct as Miriam's Semitic skin.

35 It is often surmised that it is Miriam, referred to only as "Moses' sister" in Exodus 2:4–8, who really enables his adoption by Pharaoh's daughter. See Plaut, *The Torah*, 388.

36 There is some midrashic reading that suggests Miriam married; however, she stands out from other Biblical female prophets in not being immediately identified as "wife of" in the first mention of her name.

37 Most English translations of Miriam's song are an exact replica of Moses' earlier words, and Hebrew scholarship offers two interpretations of the relationship between Miriam's and Moses' songs. In his commentary on the Torah, Plaut offers two interpretations of Miriam's song which suggest some earlier authorial source, making her a "performer" (many interpretations also stress her role as a "dancer") rather than an original poet (Plaut, *The Torah*, 487). It is unclear whether Barrett Browning had access to such

information, but her inclusion of Miriam "sing [ing] the song she chooses" asserts choice, agency, and creativity into the Miriam narrative.

38 Barrett Browning has provided another element which ruptures Romney's complete typological identification with either Moses or Christ, namely, his blindness. The Biblical Moses ends his life in a moment of "vision" on Pisgah, and Barrett Browning explicitly points this out in Book V when Sir Blaise also compares Romney to Moses at the end of his life "getting to the top of Pisgah hill"; Blaise goes on to make the typological link to Romney with a qualifier: "Leigh . . . is scarce advanced to see as far as this" (*Aurora Leigh*, V: 730–8).

39 The reference to the "Selah-pause" displays Barrett Browning's sophisticated knowledge of Hebrew terms, the "Selah-pause" being alternatively interpreted as the moment in the service when the voice is raised up in response to the instruments, or a moment when there is a pause in the voice that directs the instruments. But even more interestingly, the 1870 *Treasury of Bible Knowledge* suggests that the pause would occur "where very warm emotions would have been expressed," just as they have been in the text of the poem (Ayre, *The Treasury of Bible Knowledge*, 809).

40 It is crucial to distinguish my reading here from those Christian feminist readings of religious history which suggest that Christianity brought "freedom" to women from the oppressive practices of Judaism. There has been much debate about this idea in the discourse of feminist theology (see *Journal of Feminist Studies in Religion* entry in the Bibliography). Suffice to say here that while I do not claim Christianity offers women any "freer" roles than Judaism, I do imagine Barrett Browning to understand Christianity as a "freer" state than Judaism in her own Christian epistemology.

41 For example, in her important article on the poem, Joyce Zonana argues that the last lines in which Aurora speaks the text of Revelation can be read as a moment in which Aurora emerges as her own "muse" and "takes her place as a triumphant goddess, embodying through her words the promise of her name, conclusively demonstrating that the woman artist can both see and sing, by her own eyes inspired" ("The Embodied Muse," 241). While this reading offers crucial analysis of the discourse of the "muse" in the poem, seeing Aurora as "goddess" at the end of this poem is exactly the reverse of Barrett Browning's larger argument about an ideal female Christian poetic identity.

4 CHRISTINA ROSSETTI AND THE HEBRAIC GOBLINS OF THE JEWISH SCRIPTURES

1 See Lootens, *Lost Saints*, chapter 5, on ways critical communities then and now have constructed Rossetti's image.

2 The SPCK is an Anglican organization founded in 1698 with the Queen of England as a patron. Self-described as an missionary agency, it was concerned with Christian conversion on many levels, including Jewish

conversion. It emphasized then and now the publication for study of Christian texts.

3 See especially Kent, *The Achievement of Christina Rossetti*, Leighton, *Victorian Women Poets: Writing Against the Heart*, Gilbert and Gubar, *Madwoman* and the works listed in the Bibliography by Armstrong, Harrison, and Whitla.

4 William Michael Rossetti helped create this distinction by separating certain poems in volumes he edited under the rubric "Devotional Pieces."

5 Without over-speculating, I think it safe to say that the critics who have been interested in Rossetti as a "great artist" have thus been less interested in exploring the anti-Judaism of the poems I explore in the first part of this chapter because they are less interested in the particularities of her theological vision.

6 Here, my analysis and evaluation of Rossetti's use of anti-Judaism in "creative" and "imaginative" ways draws on Anthony Julius' formulations about T. S. Eliot's anti-Semitism; Julius argues, rather provocatively, that "Eliot ... put[s] anti-Semitism to imaginative use" and claims that Eliot's poetry is "is one of anti-Semitism's few literary triumphs" (*T. S. Eliot*, 33). This idea that anti-Semitism can be a tool for generating complex artistic texts is a useful way to move past the idea that so-called "great art" cannot contain deeply problematic ideological content.

7 Linda Peterson likewise uses an approach that combines gendered and religious analysis in her "Restoring the Book."

8 Critics who have explored religious texts in relation to Rossetti's understanding of female poetic identity include Harrison, Peterson, and Cantalupo; however, none of these critics have taken up Rossetti's concern with Jewishness *per se*.

9 Stanwood's emphasis on "originality" is at the heart of the problem literary critics have with overtly religious texts. Peterson addresses this problem, noting it is "easy to see why this devotional work has been held against Christina Rossetti as an artist," and explores the various ways Rossetti's devotional prose and poetry have been categorized as "conventional" ("Restoring the Book," 214–16); Peterson argues that Rossetti "uses typology to disrupt Victorian gender ideology, and to suggest that a female heroine – and, by implication, a female artist – might be an active and original reader, interpreter and creator of biblical types" (Peterson, "Restoring the Book," 216). What Peterson misses are the ways Rossetti's investments in a "woman's" typology galvanize a powerful anti-Judaism.

10 Stanwood describes the Benedicite as an apocryphal canticle, often used as an alternative to the morning prayer in *The Book of Common Prayer* ("Christina Rossetti's Devotional Prose," 234).

11 G. B. Tennyson links Rossetti to the Tractarian movement in his *Victorian Devotional Poetry*, 197–211.

12 See Peterson, "Restoring the Book"; Peterson likewise sees Rossetti as offering "alternative readings" of women's roles, and suggests the radical nature of this project when she writes: "throughout the nineteenth century, then,

whether in Anglican circles or even in more radical Dissenting sects, the common view was women might read the biblical text for their own private or domestic use, but they were not to interpret actively, originally, or publicly" (212–13).

13 This heterosexualizing of the relationship between the human and divine also occurs in Judaism, of course. See below, my discussion of Rossetti's use of the Hebrew prophetical texts of Jeremiah and Isaiah.

14 Clearly acts of transgenderedness today might be seen as analogous to a kind of conversion of bodies rather than spirit; however this concept is more contemporary than is useful for this particular analysis.

15 Mermin also points out this passage, writing "[Rossetti's] didactic and devotional works assert women's inferiority with a relentless stringency and with an undertone of rebellion and pain she finds hard to subdue; but part of the comfort she finds in religion is the promise that in the soul's relation to Christ, gender, finally, does not matter" ("Heroic Sisterhood," 116).

16 At another moment in *Seek and Find*, Rossetti suggests that the repeated images of sibling relationships in the Bible, and particularly in the New Testament descriptions of the relationship between Judaism and Christianity, offers another way to understand difference from a Christian perspective, a point that sheds light on many of her poems that deal with sister relationships.

17 This choice of Hebraic material contrasts sharply with Barrett Browning's interest in the Miriam/Moses narrative, or Aguilar's interest in female figures of Hebrew Scriptures. These intertextual links to Lamentations could be to other similar moments and images in Jeremiah's prophetic texts as well as some of the Psalms, with all of which Rossetti would have been very familiar. I do argue, however, that there are certain indications that Lamentations held a special importance for Rossetti, in this poem and in *Goblin Market* (see below).

18 See Robert Browning's dramatic monologues "Cleon," and "An Epistle Containing the Strange Medical Experience of Karshish, the Arab Physician." In both cases, Browning offers the perspective of a non-Christian who glimpses the power of Christian revelation in the course of the poetic utterance.

19 For readings of *Goblin Market* see Casey, "The Potential of Sisterhood," Gilbert and Gubar, *Madwoman*, Hickock, *Representations of Women*, Kathleen Jones, *Learning Not to Be First*, Leighton, *Victorian Women Poets*: *Writing Against the Heart*, Mayberry, *Christina Rossetti*, Mermin, "Heroic Sisterhood."

20 I am in debt to one of my Mills College undergraduates, Erin Merk, and her research on the Biblical references in this poem, for this specific link to Isaiah's text.

21 In a 1991 talk at Rutgers University, Cora Kaplan, using Victorian figures of ethnography, pointed out that the goblins also represent ethnic and racial "others," thus emphasizing the figures of colonization and racial difference.

22 While certain Hebrew prophetic texts do make mention of a virgin birth, it is not an idea that carries the same kind of textual and theological weight that it does in the Christian appropriation of this idea in the Gospels.

23 There are of course female figures in the Bible who are not bound by hetero-sexual relationships, most specifically Devora and Miriam (though Devora is claimed as a wife and mother where Miriam is not). Here, I am specifically referring to the narratives of the matriarchs Sarah, Rebecca, Rachel, and Leah, who have great spiritual significance through their relationship to hus-bands and children. Rossetti seems remarkably uninterested in these figures of female identity in her poetry because, in part, I think, she remains uncom-fortable attributing women's religious agency and power to heterosexually defined roles.

24 See Whitla, "Questioning the Covention," 114n, for more on the letter to Webster in the context of "Monna Innominata."

25 Some would also point to biographical parallels in Rossetti's own life; there is critical speculation about the two potential suitors in her life and conflicts between her and their religious commitments. This em-phasis on biographical data does not characterize my approach to her poetry, however. See Battiscombe, *Christina Rossetti*, and Packer, *Christina Rossetti*.

26 The strange, unexplained shift of terminology from "donna innominata" in the Preface to the title "Monna Innominata" indicates a shift of empha-sis away from a simple exploration of "woman's voice" to the exploration of a "religious woman's voice"; the Italian "monna" is both an archaic term for "woman" as well as carrying echoes of the word for "nun," namely "monaca."

27 Whitla makes this case quite convincingly ("Questioning the Convention," 93–6).

28 For a detailed reading of the epigraphs in the sequence, see Harrison, *Christina Rossetti in Context*, 142–85, 199–200, and Whitla, "Questioning the Convention," 97–109.

29 Rossetti's version bears some resemblance to the Apocrypha version of the Book of Esther, a later Greek translation which adds 107 verses to the original Hebrew text. See also Whitla, "Questioning the Convention," 125.

30 Rossetti's figuration of Esther clearly echoes the tradition of the male poet/speaker figuring his lady as an oppressive captor; this strategy works to figuratively reverse the gender hierarchy of male power that governs the objectification of the woman in the sonnet tradition; see Harrison, *Christina Rossetti in Context*, 181; Whitla, "Questioning the Convention," 125. Of course, the image of the sexualized Jewish woman is also a common stereotype of anti-Semitism. See Pellegrini, "Whiteface Performances."

31 There are many other examples in the Hebrew Bible of women who seem to act outside the laws of sexual honor only to have these actions revealed in a larger narrative of Jewish history which renders them justifiable. See especially stories of Tamar (who pretends to be a prostitute to seduce her father-in-law), or Ruth, the Jewish convert who seduces a kinsman; both women's actions are later revealed to produce children who are essential players in Jewish history.

5 "JUDAISM RIGHTLY REVERENCED": GRACE AGUILAR'S THEOLOGICAL POETICS

1 Review of Grace Aguilar's *The Spirit of Judaism*, *The Voice of Jacob*, 1 April 1842, 111–12.

2 The most detailed work to date is in Michael Galchinsky's 1996 *The Origin of the Modern Jewish Woman Writer* (which focuses primarily on her fictional prose and theology to a lesser degree), Philip Weinberger's 1971 dissertation on Aguilar, "The Social and Religious Thought of Grace Aguilar," Michael Ragussis' exploration of her novel in *Figures of Conversion*; all Aguilar scholarship remains in debt to Beth-Zion Lask Abrahams' 1952 article on Aguilar's life and works, "Grace Aguilar," originally given as the Lady Magnus Memorial Lecture before the Jewish Historical Society in 1947; the text was subsequently published in the Transactions of that society in 1952. For recent work on Aguilar's poetry, see Daniel Harris, "Hagar in Christian Britain: Grace Aguilar's 'The Wanderers.'" I am indebted to many of Harris' ideas in this article for the development of my own thoughts about Aguilar's poetry.

3 After her death, Aguilar's mother did publish some of her more explicit works of theology, most notably in the volume *Essays and Miscellanies: Choice Cullings from the Manuscripts of Grace Aguilar*, which includes commentaries on the prophets Daniel and Isaiah, liturgical prayers, and a series of "Sabbath Thoughts" which refute certain Christian claims about Judaism and Jews. It seems significant here that Aguilar did not choose to publish these overtly theological texts in her own lifetime.

4 See, for example, her list of these "spiritual" women writers in the conclusion to *The Women of Israel*, 566.

5 Indeed, I would suggest speculatively that her fiction, as others before have analyzed, tends to be more concerned with historical and cultural aspects of Jewish identity, rather than the explicitly theological.

6 This biographical material is based on the work of both Abrahams and Galchinsky, whose pioneering scholarship on Aguilar should be noted as crucial to all future evaluations.

7 See Abrahams, "Grace Aguilar," 138, for more on Aguilar's relationship to Christian worship services.

8 Abrahams makes similar conclusions about the relationship between Aguilar's life and her comments in *The Jewish Faith*; see "Grace Aguilar," 139.

9 There are a number of different theories regarding what illness Aguilar actually had. See Abrahams, "Grace Aguilar," Galchinsky, *The Origin of the Modern Jewish Woman Writer*, and Valman, *Gender and Judaism*.

10 See Leeser's comments in "Reviews and Literary Notices" in *The Voice of Jacob* 3.73 (10 May 1844): 142, and Aguilar's response to those comments, written to Leeser's own journal *The Occident* 2.7 (October 1844): 340–2. Abrahams also mentions this letter, referring, perhaps tellingly, to "poor Leeser" ("Grace Aguilar," 144).

11 See *The Jewish Chronicle* 3.28, (October 1, 1847), for these comments.

12 It is quite difficult to ascertain the actual extent of Aguilar's Jewish education. She clearly knew Hebrew, though how much is hard to tell; she clearly had access to some Talmudic learning, though much of it may have been gleaned from the three volumes of *The Hebrew Review and Magazine of Rabbinical Literature* from which she often cites. This journal was published by Morris Raphall from 1834 to 1836, and it is a quite remarkable weekly series of translations from the Mishnah, important later Rabbinical sources, summaries of Talmudic precepts, and historical information. Aguilar also published at least one poem in the journal; her "Lament for Judea" appears in 3.73 (Friday, 17 June 1836). For more on *The Hebrew Review*, see Finestein, *Jewish Society in Victorian England*, 245 and Galchinsky, *The Origin of the Modern Jewish Woman Writer*, 210. Later in her life, Aguilar seems to have found someone to study with, a "Mr. Theodores of Manchester," whom she acknowledges after a specific Talmudic citation from Rabbi Arni (Yebamoth), writing in *The Women of Israel* that she is "indebted to the kind suggestions and valuable information" of this man (511).

13 See especially her commentaries on the prophetic books of Daniel and Isaiah in *Essays and Miscellanies*.

14 Leeser explores the problem of the "professional" male commentator in his Preface to the volume, in which he highlights the special value this text by a woman offers to readers (*The Spirit of Judaism*, 6).

15 See also Weinberger's dissertation, "The Social and Religious Thought of Grace Aguilar," which links Aguilar to Maimonides' thought.

16 The notion of individual spiritual devotion is of course a central tenet of Hasidism, which emerged in the eighteenth century as a powerful new mode of orthodox Jewish communal life and practice. It is unlikely that Aguilar would have had access to the primary texts of Hasidism, though she may have been aware of its historical emergence.

17 See especially Amy Levy's volume *A London Plane Tree and Other Verse*, and Emily Marion Harris' *Verses*.

18 There is currently no version of Aguilar's poetry in print; only one poem has been anthologized in the recent interest in Victorian women's poetry; see Armstrong and Bristow, "A Vision of Jerusalem," *Nineteenth-Century Women Poets*, 348–9. Poems discussed in this chapter appeared in Isaac Leeser's periodical *The Occident and American Jewish Advocate*. Leeser collected all the poems he published in *The Occident* and printed them as an "Appendix" to his 1864 stereotyped edition of *The Spirit of Judaism*; there is some evidence of his editing that edition of the poems, making some stylistic and punctuation changes from the *Occident* versions. It is this collection (from *The Spirit of Judaism*) which I have used when quoting from Aguilar's poetry. I also offer the *Occident* citations for reference; page numbers refer to the volume pages, rather than to individual issue pagination. "Night," 2.1 (1844): 22–6; "Ocean," 2.2 (1844): 81–2; "Hymn to Summer," 2.5 (1844): 241–2; "Autumn Leaves," 2.8 (1844): 384–5; "Autumn Winds," 3.10 (1845): 503–5; "The Evergreen," 78–9.

19 See *The Occident and American Jewish Advocate*, 1.2 (1844): 599–600.
20 Here, Aguilar apparently calls on the deep linguistic relationships between Arabic and Hebrew word roots, referring to them by using Hebrew transliteration of Arabic. It is not clear to what extent Aguilar actually understood Arabic or its relationship to Hebrew, though her point here does refer to a clear link between the two languages.
21 See *The Occident and American Jewish Advocate*, 1.5 (1843): 236. In the headnote to this poem, Leeser announces that he expects more poetry from Aguilar in subsequent issues. The numbering of the *Sabbath Thoughts* sequence (I–IV) occurs in the later edition.
22 Of course, traditional Judaism also puts an emphasis on men's acts of prayer along with their study of Torah and public worship, so Aguilar's emphasis on prayer does not exclude men *per se*.
23 Though this poem appeared in an explicitly Jewish venue, Aguilar's footnoting strategy suggests she wrote it with a heterogenous audience in mind, and supports Abrahams' suggestion that Aguilar would send her work just as easily to Christian as well as Jewish periodicals as well as Aguilar's own interests in making Judaism "rightly reverenced" by Christians.
24 See *The Occident and American Jewish Advocate*, 5.3 (1847): 139–41.
25 See Scheinberg, "'Measure yourself to a prophet's place'" for more on the comparison between Aguilar's and Christian women's approaches to Biblical women.
26 Likewise, in her poem "The Rocks of Elim," which replays the Red Sea narrative, Aguilar pays little attention to Miriam's role.
27 See *The Occident and American Jewish Advocate* 1.2 (1844): 541–2.
28 See Galchinsky, *The Origin of the Modern Jewish Woman Writer*, for more on how Aguilar understood the perils of revealing Judaism publicly.
29 This is a point Aguilar echoes in her passionate and angry response to a review Isaac Leeser wrote of one her novels, *The Records of Israel*, and his assertion that she had represented the community as "anti-Jewish" since they did not execute capital punishment on a murderer. Aguilar argues that though the community may not have followed "Mosaic" law, they were certainly fully "Jewish"; she sees their observance of Mosaic law as hindered by their lack of power in a Christian culture. Thus, she suggests that historical circumstance must be taken into account in evaluating Jewish observance.

6 AMY LEVY AND THE ACCENTS OF MINOR(ITY) POETRY

1 See *The Complete Novels and Selected Writings* of Amy Levy, ed. New, 485.
2 From *A Minor Poet and Other Verse*, 83–4.
3 Emma Francis, Linda Hunt Beckman, Joe Bristow, and Virginia Blain all have offered biographical evidence or literary readings which support the supposition that Levy articulated desire for women in her life and works.
4 Rich, "Compulsory Heterosexuality."
5 See Hunt Beckman's Prologue, *Amy Levy*, 2–7.

6 See *ibid.*, chapters 2 and 6 especially, for more on Levy's upbringing and attitudes toward religion.

7 Hunt Beckman examines a number of lyrics from this last volume, calling for more critical attention to them, *ibid.*, 189–97.

8 Because most of the biographical information on Levy has been more than amply represented elsewhere, I will not offer a full biography here; I would refer readers to Hunt Beckman's recent critical biography, *Amy Levy*, noted above.

9 For more on the exact condition of Jewish life before and during Levy's lifetime and the changes that occurred in Anglo-Jewish rights from the 1840s, see Baron, *A Social and Religious History of the Jews*, Endelman, *Radical Assimilation*, Galchinsky, *The Origin of the Modern Jewish Woman Writer*, David Katz, *The Jews in the History of England*, Lipman, *Three Centuries of Anglo-Jewish History, Social History of the Jews in England, A Social History of the Jews*.

10 Hunt Beckman, *Amy Levy*, 75.

11 I am grateful to Linda Hunt Beckman for alerting me to and providing copies of these early writings.

12 As Blain has deftly argued in her "Sexual Politics of the (Victorian) Closet; or No Sex Please, – We're Poets," "the gendering of the persona (the lyric 'I'; or even, on occasion, the dramatic 'I') in Victorian women's poetry is a locus of complexity that deserves closer attention"(136); Blain goes on to suggest that "the modern trope of the closet might usefully enlarge our perception of one kind of alternative standpoint from which a Victorian women poet could offer a critique of heterosexuality" (135). As this chapter suggests, I think Levy was deeply invested in offering that critique.

13 Yeats, *Letters to the New Island*, 87. See also Hunt Beckman, *Amy Levy*, 213.

14 See Abrahams, "Amy Levy," and Hunt Beckman, *Amy Levy*, for complete details on Levy's publishing history.

15 Hunt Beckman, *Amy Levy*, 13.

16 Wagenknecht states "If there is any one cause with which Amy Levy identified herself, it is female emancipation" (*Daughters of the Covenant*, 74–5) and Nord has included Levy in a study of urban nineteenth-century women who "found it difficult to reconcile the goals of their work with the dictates of femininity . . . had a highly ambivalent relationship to female culture and . . . vacillated between female and male identification" ("'Neither Pairs Nor Odd,'" 753). See also Levy's letter to *The Jewish Chronicle* when she was sixteen on the topic of women's education ("Jewish Women and Women's Rights").

17 Hunt, "Amy Levy and the 'Jewish Novel'" and Rochelson, "Jews, Gender, and Genre," discuss Levy's idea about women in *Reuben Sachs* in more detail.

18 See Rochelson, "Jews, Gender, and Genre," 314–17 for a summary of the reviews of *Reuben Sachs*, and Hunt Beckman, *Amy Levy*, 179–81. Hunt and Rochelson's own criticism on *Reuben Sachs* refutes the idea that Levy's novel was only derogatory toward the Jewish community of her day.

19 For more on this issue of "self-hatred" see especially Rochelson, "Jews, Gender, and Genre," and Hunt Beckman, "Leaving the Tribal Duckpond."

20 Hunt Beckman, *Amy Levy*, 118–19, together with Melvyn New, *Complete Novels and Selected Writings*, suggests this essay was a sort of turning point for Levy's sense of Jewishness, recasting some phases of potential internalized Jewish self-hatred that Hunt Beckman charts in earlier years.

21 See Rochelson, *The Children of the Ghetto*, Introduction, for more on how Israel Zangwill, writing only slightly after Levy, also creates a certain nostalgia for traditional Judaism.

22 Hunt Beckman, *Amy Levy*, 110–15.

23 See Boyarin, *Unheroic Conduct*, 33–80, for more on how traditional Jewish culture imagined the ideal Jewish man – in contradistinction to the Western Christian ideal of the male hero.

24 See also Rochelson, "Jews, Gender, and Genre," 321, for more on the importance of this poetic moment.

25 Jewish and Scottish accents were made much fun of in Victorian culture, and the two identities were connected in English culture through their "suspicious" potential "other" national affiliations. See Ragussis, "Jews and other 'Outlandish Englishmen'," on the drama and the often linked representation of Scotch and Jewish caricatures.

26 Levy may also have been responding to George Eliot's essay on Heinrich Heine, though her echoes, as I suggest, are more suggestive of Arnold's essay.

27 Levy's emphasis on "humour" may also respond to Arnold's use of the term in *Culture and Anarchy*, where Arnold uses the italicized term to distinguish certain kinds of racial and cultural characteristics, as in the phrase "Eminently Indo-European by its *humour*" (Arnold's emphasis, 142).

28 For more on the specifics of Levy's use of internal auditors, see Scheinberg, "Recasting Sympathy and Judgment"; for Armstrong on women and dramatic monologue, see *Victorian Poetry*, 325–6.

29 See Shakespeare, *The Merchant of Venice*, Act III, Scene 1.

30 Only recently have feminist theologians reclaimed Magdalen as one of the apostles; for a rereading of Magdalen's role as an apostle, see Farley, "A Feminist Consciousness."

31 See New, *Complete Novels and Selected Writings*, 14, Armstrong, *Victorian Poetry*, 374–5, Francis, "Amy Levy," 188–190 and Leighton, "'Because men made the Laws'" for an example of the conventional critical reading of "Magdalen" as the voice of contemporary Victorian fallen woman.

32 Susan Haskins traces the various ways Mary Magdalen was interpreted in different historical periods. Important for this reading are her comments on nineteenth-century depictions of Magdalen; Haskins suggest that in the *fin-de-siècle* period, the focus was on "the nature of the relationship between her and Christ . . . explored with a freedom characteristic of the age" (*Mary Magdalen*, 347). Haskins also notes that the Pre-Raphaelite images of Magdalen "created a strong, confident and sexually powerful woman."

These then would have been the cultural contexts for Levy's own exploration of the figure.

33 See Kohut, *A Hebrew Anthology*, for an amazing number of such "Hebraic" poems from the English tradition; the editor of this volume notes that the volume "admits the work exclusively of *Christian* authors" (viii, author's emphasis).

34 "A Ballad of Religion and Marriage," was, significantly, never publicly printed in Levy's lifetime, perhaps for its quite explicit rejection of heterosexual courtship rituals (Hunt Beckman, *Amy Levy*).

35 Hunt Beckman also notes that Levy never chose to change her name, citing the conjunction of feminist principles as articulated in a poem titled "Rondel" in which Levy notes: "married or Single, I do not require / To change my name"; Hunt Beckman suggests the poem carries a second level of meaning, referring to Levy's refusal to anglicize her own name (*Amy Levy*, 138).

36 Levy seems to have been working on these translations in conjunction with Lady Katie Magnus, who cites Levy's work in her own essay "Jehuda Halevi." Hunt Beckman notes that Magnus may have "help[ed] Levy feel more positive about her Jewish background, for Lady Katie moved in the larger gentile world of letters and yet remained strongly affiliated with the Jewish community" (*Amy Levy*, 77). Hunt Beckman also notes that Levy's datebook demonstrates Levy's meetings with Magnus in Europe, and that they may have met as early as 1882.

37 Though Wagner has been much studied for his anti-Semitism and its evidence in later operas, *Lohengrin* (the opera) is not much discussed in current studies of Wagner's anti-Jewish sentiments.

38 An excellent example of such critical work can be found in Ragussis' *Figures of Conversion*; in chapter 2, Ragussis argues that the genre of the English novel can be read as presuming a "conversion" narrative that is rooted in English theories of Jewish conversion. Another recent study of literary form and anti-Semitism is Julius' *T. S. Eliot, Anti-Semitism, and Literary Form*.

39 Emily Marion Harris, Lady Katie Magnus, Alice Julia Montefiore Lucas, and Celia and Marion Moss are only some of the Jewish women poets of the ninenteenth- and early twentieth-century England who deserve further attention.

Bibliography

A. A. *The True Mary: Being Mrs. Browning's Poem: "The Virgin Mary to the Child Jesus".* New York: Thomas Whittaker, 1868.

Abrahams, Beth-Zion Lask. "Amy Levy." *Jewish Historical Society of England Transactions* 11 (1926): 168–89.

"Grace Aguilar: A Centenary Tribute." *Jewish Historical Society of England Transactions* 16 (1952): 137–58.

"Amy Levy: Poet and Writer." *Jewish Affairs* 16.4 (1961): 8–11.

Adler, Rachel. *Endgendering Judaism: An Inclusive Theology and Ethics.* Philadelphia: Jewish Publication Society, 1998.

Aguilar, Grace. "Lament for Judea." *The Hebrew Review and Magazine of Rabbinical Literature* 3.73 (17 June 1836).

The Spirit of Judaism. Ed. Isaac Leeser. Philadelphia: No. 1 Monroe Place, 1842. (Includes collected poems at end of volume.)

"Editorial Correspondence." *The Occident* 2.7 (1844): 340–2.

The Women of Israel. New York: D. Appleton and Co., 1901 (1845).

"History of the Jews in England." *Chamber's Miscellany of Useful and Entertaining Facts.* Edinburgh: W& R Chambers, 1847.

Essays and Miscellanies. Philadelphia: A. Hart, 1853.

"The Authoress." *Home Scenes and Heart Studies.* 1853. 13th edn., London: Groombridge and Sons, 1876, 227–44.

The Jewish Faith: Its Spiritual Consolation, Moral Guidance, and Immortal Hope. Ed. Isaac Leeser. Philadelphia: 1227 Walnut Street: 1864 (1846).

Alderman, Geoffrey. *The Jewish Community in British Politics.* Oxford: Clarendon Press, 1983.

apRoberts, Ruth. *The Biblical Web.* Ann Arbor: University of Michigan Press, 1994.

Armstrong, Isobel. *Victorian Poetry: Poetry, Poetics and Politics.* London: Routledge, 1993.

Armstrong, Isobel and Virginia Blain, eds. *Women's Poetry, Late Romantic to Late Victorian: Gender and Genre, 1830–1900.* Houndsmill, Basingstoke: Macmillan, 1999.

Armstrong, Isobel and Joseph Bristow, eds. *Nineteenth-Century Women Poets.* Oxford: Oxford University Press, 1996.

Arnold, Matthew. "Heinrich Heine." In *Lectures and Essays in Criticism. (The Complete Prose Works of Matthew Arnold, Vol. III)*. Ed. R. H. Super. Ann Arbor: University of Michigan Press, 1962, 107–32.

"The Study of Poetry." *Matthew Arnold: English Literature and Irish Politics. (The Complete Prose Works of Matthew Arnold, Vol. IX)*. Ed. R. H. Super. Ann Arbor: University of Michigan Press, 1973, 161–88.

Culture and Anarchy. Ed. J. Dover Wilson. Cambridge: Cambridge University Press, 1988.

Atkinson, Clarissa W., Constance Buchanan, and Margaret Miles, eds. *Immaculate & Powerful: The Female in Sacred Image and Social Reality*. Boston: Beacon, 1985.

Auerbach, Erich. "Figura." Trans. R. Manheim. *Scenes from the Drama of European Literature*. Minneapolis: University of Minnesota Press, 1959 (reissued in 1973 and 1984). 11–76.

Auerbach, Nina. *Communities of Women*. Cambridge: Harvard University Press, 1948.

Ausubel, Nathan and Maryann, eds. *A Treasury of Jewish Poetry*. New York: Crown, 1957.

Ayre, Rev. John. *The Treasury of Bible Knowledge*. London: Longmans, Green, 1870.

Baron, Salo W. *A Social and Religious History of the Jews*. 3 vols. New York: Columbia University Press, 1937.

Battiscombe, Georgina. *Christina Rossetti: A Divided Life*. New York: Holt, Rinehart and Winston, 1981.

Bell, Mackenzie. *Christina Rossetti: A Biographical and Critical Study*. London: Hurst and Blackett, 1898.

Bethune, Geo. W. *The British Female Poets: With Biographical and Critical Notices*. New York: Allen Brothers, 1869 (1848).

Biale, Rachel. *Women and Jewish Law: The Essential Texts, Their History & Their Relevance for Today*. New York: Schocken, 1984.

Black, Eugene C. *The Social Politics of Anglo-Jewry 1880–1920*. Oxford: Basil Blackwell, 1988.

Blain, Virginia. "Sexual Politics of the (Victorian) Closet; or No Sex Please, – We're Poets." In *Women's Poetry, Late Romantic to Late Victorian: Gender and Genre, 1830–1900*. Eds. Isobel Armstrong and Virginia Blain. Houndsmill, Basingstoke: Macmillan, 1999. 135–63.

Blain, Virginia, Patricia Clements, and Isobel Grundy, eds. *The Feminist Companion to English Literature*. New Haven: Yale University Press, 1990.

Blake, Kathleen. "Elizabeth Barrett Browning and Wordsworth: The Romantic Poet as Woman." *Victorian Poetry* 24 (1986): 387–98.

Love and the Woman Question in Victorian Literature. Brighton: Harvester Press, 1983.

Bloch, Ariel and Chana Bloch, trans. *Song of Songs: A New Translation with an Introduction and Commentary*. Afterword Robert Alter. New York: Random House, 1995.

Boyarin, Daniel. *Unheroic Conduct: The Rise of Heterosexuality and the Invention of the Jewish Man.* Berkeley: University of California Press, 1997.

Breen, Jennifer, ed. *Victorian Women Poets, 1830–1900: An Anthology.* London: Everyman, 1994.

Bristow, Joseph, ed. *Victorian Women Poets.* New Casebooks. London: Macmillan, 1995.

"'All out of tune in this world's instrument': The 'Minor Poetry' of Amy Levy." *Journal of Victorian Culture* 5 (1999): 76–103.

Brontë, Charlotte. *Villette.* Harmondsworth: Penguin, 1985 (1853).

Brooke, Stopford A. *Theology in the English Poets: Cowper–Coleridge–Wordsworth and Burns.* 4th edn, London: C. Kegan Paul, and Co., 1880.

The Development of Theology as Illustrated in English Poetry from 1780 to 1830. London: Philip Green, 1893.

Brooten, Bernadette. "Early Christian Women and Their Cultural Context: Issues of Method in Historical Reconstruction." In *Feminist Perspectives on Biblical Scholarship.* Ed. Adela Yarbro Collins. Chico, CA: Scholars Press, 1985. 65–91.

Browning, Elizabeth Barrett. *The Religious Opinions of Elizabeth Barrett Browning.* London: Hodder and Stoughton, 1906

The Poetical Works of Elizabeth Barrett Browning with Two Prose Essays. London: Humphrey Milford/Oxford University Press, 1916.

Letters of Elizabeth Barrett Browning to Mary Russell Mitford 1836–1854. 3 vols. Eds. Meredith B. Raymond and Mary Rose Sullivan. Winfield, KS: Armstrong Browning Library of Baylor University, The Browning Institute, Wedgestone Press, and Wellesley College, 1983.

Complete Poetical Works of Mrs. Browning. Cambridge Edition. Cambridge, MA: Houghton Mifflin, 1900.

Aurora Leigh. Ed. Margaret Reynolds. Norton Critical Edition. New York: W. W. Norton, 1996 (1856/9).

Browning, Robert. *The Poems.* Vol I. Ed. John Pettigrew. New Haven, CT: Yale University Press, 1981.

Brownstein, Rachel M. "Representing the Self: Arnold and Brontë on Rachel." *Browning Institute Studies* 13. Ed. Adrienne Munich Auslander. New York: CUNY Browning Institute Studies Inc., 1985. 1–14.

Buchanan, Constance H. *Choosing to Lead: Women and the Crisis of American Values.* Boston: Beacon, 1996.

Byrd, Deborah. "Combating an Alien Tyranny: Elizabeth Barrett Browning's Evolution as a Feminist Poet." *Browning Institute Studies* 15 (1987): 23–42.

Calisch, Edward. *The Jew in English Literature, as Author and Subject.* 1909. Port Washington, NY: Kennikat, 1969.

Cantalupo, Catherine Musello. "Christina Rossetti: The Devotional Poet and the Rejection of Romantic Nature." In *The Achievement of Christina Rossetti.* Ed. David A. Kent. Ithaca, NY: Cornell University Press, 1987. 274–300.

Carlyle, Thomas. "The Hero as Poet." (Lecture III). (1840). *On Heroes, Hero-Worship and the Heroic in History*. Ed. Michael K. Goldberg. Berkeley: University of California Press, 1993.

Carroll, Joseph. *The Cultural Theory of Matthew Arnold*. Berkeley: University of California Press, 1982.

Case, Alison. "Gender and Narration in *Aurora Leigh*." *Victorian Poetry* 29 (1991): 17–32.

Casey, Janet Galligani. "The Potential of Sisterhood: Christina Rossetti's 'Goblin Market.'" *Victorian Poetry* 29.1 (1991): 63–78.

Chadwick, Rev. John W. *et al. Women of the Bible by Eminent Divines*. New York and London: Harper and Brothers, 1900.

Charity, A. C. *Events and Their Afterlife: The Dialectic of Typology in the Bible and Dante*. Cambridge: Cambridge University Press, 1966.

Cheyette, Bryan. *Constructions of "the Jew" in English Literature and Society: Racial Representations, 1875–1945*. Cambridge: Cambridge University Press, 1993.

Christ, Carol P. and Judith Plaskow. *Womanspirit Rising: A Feminist Reader in Religion*. San Francisco: Harper and Row, 1979.

Cohen, Arthur A. *The Myth of the Judeo-Christian Tradition*. New York: Harper and Row, 1957.

Cohen, Rev. Dr. A. *An Anglo-Jewish Scrapbook 1600–1840: The Jew Through English Eyes*. London: M. L. Cailingold, 1943.

Cohen, Rachel. "Grace Aguilar's Diary." *B'Nai Brith Magazine* 44.3 (1929): 109–10.

Coleridge, Samuel Taylor. *Biographia Literaria or Biographical Sketches of My Literary Life and Opinions*. Ed. George Watson. London: J. M. Dent & Sons Ltd., 1906.

    The Portable Coleridge. Ed. I. A. Richards. New York: Penguin Books, 1987.

Cooper, Helen. *Elizabeth Barrett Browning, Woman and Artist*. Chapel Hill: University of North Carolina Press, 1988.

Cruden, Alexander. *Cruden's Compact Concordance*. Ed. John Eadie. London: Oliphants, 1968.

Dallas, E. S. *Poetics: An Essay on Poetry*. London: Smith, Elder, and Co., 1852.

David, Deirdre. *Intellectual Women and Victorian Patriarchy*. Ithaca, NY: Cornell University Press, 1987.

    "'Art's a Service': Social Wound, Sexual Politics, and *Aurora Leigh*." In *Critical Essays on Elizabeth Barrett Browning*. Ed. Sandra Donaldson. New York: G. K. Hall, 1999. 164–83

Davidoff, Lenore and Catherine Hall. *Family Fortunes: Men and Women of the English Middle Class, 1780–1850*. Chicago: University of Chicago Press, 1987.

DeLaura, David. *Hebrew and Hellene in Victorian England: Newman, Arnold, and Pater*. Austin: University of Texas Press, 1969.

Donaldson, Sandra, ed. *Elizabeth Barrett Browning: An Annotated Bibliography of the Commentary and Criticism, 1826–1990*. New York: G. K. Hall-Macmillan, 1993.

    Critical Essays on Elizabeth Barrett Browning. New York: G. K. Hall, 1999.

Douglas, J. D., ed. *The New Bible Dictionary*. Grand Rapids, MI: William Eerdmans, 1967.

Drabble, Margaret and Jenny Stringer, eds. *The Concise Oxford Companion to English Literature*. Oxford: Oxford University Press, 1987.

Edgecombe, Rodney S. *Two Poets of the Oxford Movement: John Keble and John Henry Newman*. London: Associated University Presses, 1996.

Eliot, George. *Middlemarch*. New York: Signet (New American Library), 1964.

Daniel Deronda. New York: Penguin Books, 1983.

Ellis, Sarah Stickney. *The Women of England: Social Duties, and Domestic Habits*. New York: J. and H. G. Langley, 1845.

Encyclopedia Judaica. Jerusalem: Ketev Publishing, 1971.

Endelman, Todd M. *The Jews of Georgian England 1714–1830*. Philadelphia: Jewish Publication Society of America, 1979.

Radical Assimilation in English Jewish History 1656–1945. Bloomington: Indiana University Press, 1990.

Europa Biographical Dictionary of British Women. London: Europa Publications Ltd., 1983.

Evslin, Bernard, ed. *The Spirit of Jewish Thought*. New York: Routledge (Grosset and Dunlap), 1969.

Ezell, Margaret, J. M. *Writing Women's Literary History*. Baltimore, MD: Johns Hopkins University Press, 1993.

Faber, Geoffrey. *Oxford Apostles: A Character Study of the Oxford Movement*. London: Faber and Faber, 1974.

Fairchild, Hoxie Neale. *Religious Trends in English Poetry*. Vol. IV. New York: Columbia University Press, 1957.

Falk, Alice. "Elizabeth Barrett Browning and Her Prometheuses: Self-will and the Woman Poet." *Tulsa Studies in Women's Literature* 7.1 (1988): 69–85.

"Lady's Greek Without the Accents: Aurora Leigh and Authority." *Studies in Browning and His Circle* 19 (1991): 84–92.

Farley, Margaret A. "Feminist Consciousness and the Interpretation of Scripture." In *Feminist Interpretation of the Bible*. Ed. Letty M. Russell. Oxford: Blackwell, 1985. 41–51.

Feldman, David. *Englishmen and Jews: Social Relations and Political Culture 1840–1914*. New Haven, CT: Yale University Press, 1994.

Feldman, Paula. *British Women Poets of the Romantic Era*. Baltimore, MD: Johns Hopkins University Press, 1997.

Felski, Rita. *Beyond Feminist Aesthetics: Feminist Literature and Social Change*. Cambridge, MA: Harvard University Press, 1989.

Finestein, Israel. *Jewish Society in Victorian England*. London: Vallentine Mitchell, 1993.

Forster, Margaret. *Elizabeth Barrett Browning: The Life and Loves of a Poet*. New York: St. Martin's, 1988.

Fowler, Rowena. "Browning's Jews." *Victorian Poetry* 35.3 (1997): no pagination. Online, Internet, 23 July 1999. Available: http://vp.engl.wvu.edu.

Francis, Emma. "Amy Levy: Contradictions? – Feminism and Semitic Discourse." In *Women's Poetry, Late Romantic to Late Victorian: Gender and Genre, 1830–1900*. Eds. Isobel Armstrong and Virginia Blain. Houndsmill, Basingstoke: Macmillan, 1999. 183–206.

Frankel, William. *Friday Nights: A Jewish Chronicle Anthology*. London: Jewish Chronicle Publications, 1973.

Fraser, Hilary. *Beauty and Belief: Aesthetics and Religion in Victorian Literature*. Cambridge: Cambridge University Press, 1986.

Frei, Hans W. *The Eclipse of Biblical Narrative*. New Haven, CT: Yale University Press, 1974.

Friedman, Susan Stanford. "Gender and Genre Anxiety: Elizabeth Barrett Browning and H. D. as Epic Poets." *Tulsa Studies in Women's Literature* 5 (1986): 203–28.

Frontain, Raymond-Jean, and Jan Wojcik, eds. *Old Testament Women in Western Literature*. Conway, AR: UCA Press, 1991.

Frow, Ruth and Edmund Frow. *Political Women 1800–1850*. London: Pluto Press, 1989.

Galchinsky, Michael. *The Origin of the Modern Jewish Woman Writer: Romance and Reform in Victorian England*. Detroit: Wayne State University Press, 1996.

Gelpi, Barbara Charlesworth. "*Aurora Leigh*: The Vocation of the Woman Poet." *Victorian Poetry* 19.1 (1981): 35–48.

Gilam, Abraham. *The Emancipation of the Jews in England 1830–1860*. New York: Garland, 1982.

Gilbert, Sandra M. and Susan Gubar. *The Madwoman in the Attic: The Woman Writer and the Nineteenth-Century Literary Imagination*. New Haven, CT: Yale University Press, 1984.

Gilfillan, George. "Female Authors No. 1: Mrs. Hemans." *Tait's Edinburgh Magazine* 14.2 (1847): 359–63.

Gilman, Sander. *Jewish Self-Hatred: Anti-Semitism and the Hidden Language of the Jews*. Baltimore, MD: Johns Hopkins University Press, 1986.

Gordis, Robert. *The Dynamics of Judaism*. Bloomington: Indiana University Press, 1990.

Greer, Germaine. *Slip-shod Sibyls: Recognition, Rejection and the Woman Poet*. London: Viking, 1995.

Grimmett, Jennifer and Malcolm Thomis. *Women in Protest 1800–1850*. New York: St. Martin's, 1982.

Gubar, Susan. "Eating the Bread of Affliction: Judaism and Feminist Criticsm." *Tulsa Studies in Women's Literature* 13 (1994): 293–316.

Hall, Mrs. S. C. "Grace Aguilar. *Pilgrimages to English Shrines*." London: Arthur Hall, Virtue and Co., 1853.

Harris, Daniel. "Hagar in Christian Britain: Grace Aguilar's 'The Wanderers.'" *Victorian Literature and Culture* 27.1 (1999): 143–70.

Harris, Emily Marion. *Verses*. London: George Bell and Sons, 1881.

Harrison, Antony H. *Christina Rossetti in Context*. Chapel Hill, NC: University of North Carolina Press, 1988.

Victorian Poets and Romantic Poems: Intertextuality and Ideology, Charlottesville: University of Virginia Press, 1990.

Harshberger, Luther H. and John A. Mourant. *Judaism and Christianity: Perspectives and Traditions*. Boston: Allyn and Bacon, 1968.

Haskins, Susan. *Mary Magdalen: Myth and Metaphor*. New York: Riverhead Books, 1993.

The Hebrew Review and Magazine of Rabbinical Literature. Ed. Morris Raphall. London: Simpkin and Marshall: 1834–6.

Helsinger, Elizabeth K., Robin Lauterbach Sheets, and William Veeder, eds. *The Woman Question: Society and Literature in Britain and America 1837–1883*. 3 vols. Chicago: University of Chicago Press, 1983.

Hemans, Felicia. "The Song of Miriam." *The Poetical Works of Mrs. Hemans*. New York: Worthington Co., 1887, 642.

Herder, Johann Gottfried. *The Spirit of Hebrew Poetry*. 2 vols. Trans. James Marsh. Burlington, VT: Edward Smith, 1833.

Heschel, Susannah. "Anti-Judaism in Christian Feminist Theology." *Tikkun* 5.3 (1990): 25–8, 95–7.

Heschel, Susannah, ed. *On Being a Jewish Feminist: A Reader*. New York: Schocken, 1983.

Hickock, Kathleen. *Representations of Women*. Westport, CT: Greenwood, 1984.

Hoffman, Lawrence A. *The Canonization of the Synagogue Service*. London: University of Notre Dame Press, 1979.

Holmes, Alicia E. "Elizabeth Barrett Browning: Construction of Authority in *Aurora Leigh* by Rewriting Mother, Muse, and Miriam." *Centennial Review* 36.3 (1992): 593–606.

Homans, Margaret. *Women Writers and Poetic Identity*. Princeton, NJ: Princeton University Press, 1980.

Horne, Richard Hengist. *A New Spirit of the Age*. London: Henry Frowde/Oxford University Press, 1907 (1844).

Hunt (*now* Hunt Beckman), Linda. "Amy Levy and the 'Jewish Novel': Representing Jewish Life in the Victorian Period." *Studies in the Novel* 26.3 (1994): 235–53.

Hunt Beckman, Linda. "Leaving the Tribal Duckpond: Amy Levy, Jewish Self-Hatred, and Jewish Identity." *Victorian Literature and Culture* 27.1 (1999): 185–202.

Amy Levy: Her Life and Letters. Athens: Ohio University Press, 2000.

Hyneman, Rebecca. *The Leper and Other Poems*. Philadelphia: A. Hart, 1853.

Isaacs, Abraham. *The Young Champion; One Year in Grace Aguilar's Girlhood*. Philadelphia: The Jewish Publication Society of America, 1913.

Jasper, David. *Coleridge as Poet and Religious Thinker*. Allison Park, PA: Pickwick, 1985.

The Study of Literature and Religion: An Introduction. Minneapolis, MN: Fortress, 1989.

Jay, Elisabeth, ed. *The Evangelical and Oxford Movements*. Cambridge: Cambridge University Press, 1983.

Jenkins, Ruth. *Reclaiming Myths of Power: Women Writers and the Victorian Spiritual Crisis*. Lewisburg, PA: Bucknell University Press, 1995.

Jones, Edmund, ed. *English Critical Essays (Nineteenth Century)*. London: Oxford University Press, 1921.

Jones, Kathleen. *Learning Not to Be First: The Life of Christina Rossetti*. Moreton-in-Marsh: The Windrush Press, 1991.

Josipovici, Gabriel. *The Book of God*. New Haven, CT: Yale University Press, 1988.

Journal of Feminist Studies in Religion 7.2 (1991). "Special Section on Feminist Anti-Judaism." 95–133.

Julius, Anthony. *T. S. Eliot, Anti-Semitism, and Literary Form*. Cambridge: Cambridge University Press, 1995.

Kaplan, Cora. Introduction. *Aurora Leigh with Other Poems*. London: The Women's Press, 1978.

Lecture. Rutgers University, NJ, 1991.

Katz, David. *The Jews in the History of England, 1485–1850*. Oxford: Oxford University Press, 1994.

Katz, Jacob. *Emancipation and Assimilation: Studies in Modern Jewish History*. Farnborough, Hants.: Westmead, 1972.

Jewish Emancipation and Self Emancipation. Philadelphia: The Jewish Publication Society, 1986.

Keble, John. *The Christian Year*. London: Parker and Co., 1827.

"Tract No. 89." *Tracts for the Times by members of the University of Oxford* (J. H. Newman, J. Keble, W. Palmer, R. H. Froude, E. B. Pusey, I. Williams, and others), vol. v. London: J. G. F. and J. Rivington; Oxford: J. H. Parker, 1839–66.

Keble's Lectures on Poetry 1832–1841. 2 vols. Trans. Edward Kershaw Francis. Oxford: Clarendon Press, 1912. (Translation of *Praelectiones Academicae*).

Kent, David A., ed. *The Achievement of Christina Rossetti*. Ithaca, NY: Cornell University Press, 1987.

Knoepflmacher, U. C. "Projection and the Female Other: Romanticism, Browning, and the Victorian Dramatic Monologue." *Victorian Poetry* 22 (1984): 139–59.

Kohut, Alexander. *A Hebrew Anthology*. Cincinatti, OH: S. Bacharach, 1913.

Krueger, Christine L. *The Reader's Repentance: Women Preachers, Women Writers, and Nineteenth Century Social Discourse*. Chicago: University of Chicago Press, 1992.

Landow, George P. *Victorian Types, Victorian Shadows*. London: Routledge and Kegan Paul, 1980.

Langbaum, Robert. *The Poetry of Experience*. Chicago: University of Chicago Press, 1957.

Langmuir, Gavin I. *History, Religion, and Antisemitism*. Berkeley: University of California Press, 1990.

Larson, Janet. "Lady Wrestling for the Victorian Soul: Discourse, Gender and Spirituality in Women's Texts." *Religion and Literature* 23.3 (1991): 43–64.

"The Late Miss Grace Aguilar." *The Jewish Chronicle* 4.1 (8 October 1947): 263.

Leeser, Isaac. "Review of *Records of Israel.*" *Voice of Jacob* 3.73 (10 May 1844): 142.

"Obituary" (Grace Aguilar). *The Occident and American Jewish Advocate.* 5.8 (1847): 419–20.

Leftwich, Joseph, ed. *Yisroel: The First Jewish Omnibus.* London: John Heritage, 1933.

Lehmann, Ruth P. *Anglo-Jewish Bibliography.* London: The Jewish Historical Society of England, 1973.

Leighton, Angela. *Elizabeth Barrett Browning.* Key Women Writers. Ed. Sue Roe. Brighton: The Harvester Press/John Spears, 1986.

——. "'Because men made the Laws': The Fallen Woman and the Woman Poet." *Victorian Poetry* 27.2 (1989): 109–27.

——. *Victorian Women Poets: Writing Against the Heart.* Charlottesville, VA: University Press of Virgina, 1992.

Leighton, Angela, ed. *Victorian Women Poets: A Critical Reader.* Cambridge, MA: Blackwell, 1996.

Leighton, Angela and Margaret Reynolds, eds., *Victorian Women Poets: An Anthology.* Oxford: Blackwell, 1995.

Levine, Philippa. *Victorian Feminism 1850–1900.* Tallahassee: Florida State University Press, 1987.

Levinger, Elma Ehrlich. "Grace Aguilar, a Defender of Her Race." *Great Jewish Women.* New York: Behrman's Jewish Book House, 1940. 121–5.

Levy, Amy. "Jewish Women and Women's Rights." *The Jewish Chronicle* (5 February 1879): 5. (Response to letter of 31 January 1879: 5.)

——. *Xantippe and Other Verse.* Cambridge: E. Johnson, 1881.

——. "James Thomson: A Minor Poet." *Cambridge Review* (21 February 1883): 240–1; (28 February 1883): 257–8.

——. "The New School of American Fiction." *Temple Bar* 70 (1884): 383–9.

——. *A Minor Poet and Other Verse.* London: T. F. Unwin, 1884, 1891.

——. "Report from a Foreign Correspondent." *The Jewish Chronicle.* (26 March, 30 April, 28 May, 1886.)

——. "Jewish Humour." *The Jewish Chronicle.* (28 August 1886; reprinted in New, ed., *The Complete Novels and Selected Writings of Amy Levy*).

——. "The Jew in Fiction." *The Jewish Chronicle* (4 June 1886): 13.

——. "Jewish Children." *The Jewish Chronicle.* (5 November 1886; reprinted in New, ed., *The Complete Novels and Selected Writings of Amy Levy*).

——. *Reuben Sachs: A Sketch.* London: Macmillan, 1888 (reprinted in New, ed., *The Complete Novels and Selected Writings of Amy Levy*).

——. "The Poetry of Christina Rossetti." *Woman's World* 1 (1888): 178.

——. "Woman and Clublife." *Woman's World* 1 (1888): 364.

——. "Cohen of Trinity." *The Gentleman's Magazine* 1889. Rpt. in *Yisroel: The First Jewish Omnibus.* Ed. Joseph Leftwich. London: John Heritage, 1933 and in New, ed., *The Complete Novels and Selected Writings of Amy Levy.*

——. *A London Plane Tree and Other Verse.* London: T. F. Unwin, 1889. New York: F. A. Stokes, 1890, 1891.

The Complete Novels and Selected Writings of Amy Levy. Ed. Melvyn New. Orlando: University Press of Florida, 1993.

Lewis, Linda. *Elizabeth Barrett Browning's Spiritual Progress: Face to Face with God*. Columbia: University of Missouri Press, 1998.

Lewis, Sarah. *Woman's Mission* (1st American edn). New York: Wiley and Putnam, 1839.

Lindsay, L. *Letters on Egypt, Edom, and the Holy Land*. London: Henry G. Rohn, 1858.

Lipman, V. D. *Social History of the Jews in England, 1850–1950*. London: Watts, 1954.

Three Centuries of Anglo-Jewish History. Cambridge: N. Heffer & Sons, 1961.

A History of the Jews Since 1858. London: Leicester University Press, 1990.

Loewenstein, Andrea Freud. *Loathsome Jews and Engulfing Women*. New York: New York University Press, 1993.

Lootens, Tricia. *Lost Saints: Silence, Gender, and Victorian Literary Canonization*. Charlottesville: University Press of Virginia, 1996.

Lowth, Rev. Robert (Bishop). *Lectures on the Sacred Poetry of the Hebrews*. Trans. G. Gregory. London: Thomas Tegg & Son, 1787.

Magnus, Lady Katie. "Jehuda Halevi." *Jewish Portraits*. New York: Bloch Publishing Company, Inc. 1925.

Manning, Henry Edward, ed. *Essays on Religion and Literature: By Various Writers*. London: Henry S. King, 1874.

Manuel, Frank E. *The Broken Staff: Judaism Through Christian Eyes*. Cambridge, MA: Harvard University Press, 1992.

Martin, Loy D. *Browning's Dramatic Monologues and the Post-Romantic Subject*. Baltimore, MD: Johns Hopkins University Press, 1985.

Mayberry, Katherine J. *Christina Rossetti and the Poetry of Discovery*. Baton Rouge: Louisana State University Press, 1989.

Mayer, Hans. *Outsiders: A Study in Life and Letters*. Trans. Denis M. Sweet. Cambridge, MA: MIT Press, 1982.

McGann, Jerome. "The Religious Poetry of Christina Rossetti." *Critical Inquiry* 10 (1983): 127–44.

The Poetics of Sensibility: A Revolution in Literary Style. Oxford: Clarendon Press, 1996.

Mellor, Anne K., ed. *Romanticism and Feminism*. Bloomington: Indiana University Press, 1988.

Mermin, Dorothy. "The Damsel, the Knight, and the Victorian Woman Poet." *Critical Inquiry* 13 (1986): 64–80.

Elizabeth Barrett Browning: Origins of a New Poetry. Chicago: University of Chicago Press, 1989.

Godiva's Ride: Women of Letters in England, 1830–1880. Bloomington: Indiana University Press, 1993.

"Heroic Sisterhood in *Goblin Market*." *Victorian Poetry* 21.2 (1983): 107–18.

Meyers, Carol. *Discovering Eve: Ancient Israelite Women in Context*. Oxford: Oxford University Press, 1988.

Michie, Helena. *The Flesh Made Word: Female Figures and Women's Bodies.* New York: Oxford University Press, 1987.

Miller, J. Hillis. *The Disappearance of God.* Cambridge, MA: Belknap, 1963.

Milman, Henry Hart. *The History of the Jews.* 2 vols. London, 1829. New York: Thomas Y. Crowell, 1881.

Milton, John. *Paradise Lost.* Ed. Scott Elledge. Norton Critical Edition. New York: W. W. Norton, 1975.

Miner, Earl, ed. *The Literary Uses of Typology.* Princeton, NJ: Princeton University Press, 1977.

Mitchell, Sally. *The Fallen Angel: Chastity, Class and Women's Reading, 1835–1880.* Bowling Green, OH: Bowling Green University Press, 1981.

Mitford, Mary Russell. *Our Village.* 5 vols. London: G. and B. Whittaker, 1824–32.

Modder, Montagu Frank. *The Jew in the Literature of England.* Philadelphia: The Jewish Publication Society, 1939.

Moltman-Wendell, Elizabeth and Jurgen Moltman. *God His and Hers.* New York: Crossroads Press, 1991.

Moody, Joycelyn. *Sentimental Confessions: Spiritual Narratives by 19th Century African American Women.* Athens: University of Georgia Press, 2000.

Moody, Linda A. "Religio-Political Insights of 19th Century Women Hymnists and Lyric Poets." *Janus Head* 2.1 (1999): 73–99.

Morais, Henry Samuel. "Grace Aguilar." *Eminent Israelites of the Nineteenth Century.* Philadelphia: Edward Stern, 1880.

Myers, Jody and Jane Rachel Litman. "The Secret of Jewish Femininity: Hiddenness, Power, and Physicality in the Theology of Orthodox Women in the Contemporary World." In *Gender and Judaism: The Transformation of Tradition.* Ed. T. M. Rudavsky. New York: New York University Press, 1994.

Naman, Anne Aresty. *The Jew in the Victorian Novel.* New York: AMS, 1980.

New, Melvyn, ed. *The Complete Novels and Selected Writings of Amy Levy.* Orlando: University Press of Florida, 1993.

Newman, Amy. "Feminist Social Criticism and Marx's Theory of Religion." *Hypatia* 9.4 (1994): 15–37.

Newman, John Henry. "Poetry, with Reference to Aristotle's Poetics." *Essays Critical and Historical.* Volume I. London: Longmans Green and Co., 1910. 1–29. (First published in *London Review*, 1829).

Nord, Deborah Epstein. "'Neither Pairs Nor Odd': Female Community in Late Nineteenth Century London." *Signs: Journal of Women in Culture and Society.* 15.41 (1990): 733–54.

Norton, David. *A History of the Bible as Literature.* 2 vols. Cambridge: Cambridge University Press, 1993.

"Obituary" (Grace Aguilar). *Art Union* 113 (1847): 378.

"Obituary" (Grace Aguilar). *The Jewish Chronicle.* (1 October 1847).

Olender, Maurice. *The Languages of Paradise: Race, Religion, and Philology in the Nineteenth Century.* Trans. Arthur Goldhammer. Cambridge, MA: Harvard University Press, 1992.

Ostriker, Alicia. "A Word Made Flesh: The Bible and Revisionist Women's Poetry." *Religion and Literature* 23.3 (1991): 9–26.

Ozick, Cynthia. "Notes Toward Finding the Right Question." In *On Being a Jewish Feminist*. Ed. Susannah Heschel. New York: Schocken, 1983. 120–51.

Packer, Lona Mosk. *Christina Rossetti*. Berkeley: University of California Press, 1963.

Panitz, Esther L. *The Alien in Their Midst: Images of Jews in English Literature*. London: Associated University Presses, 1981.

Parry, Ann. "Sexual Exploitation and Freedom: Religion, Race, and Gender in Elizabeth Barrett Browning's 'The Runaway Slave at Pilgrim's Point.'" *Studies in Browning and His Circle* 16 (1988): 114–26.

Pellegrini, Ann. "Whiteface Performances: 'Race,' Gender and Jewish Bodies." In *Jews and Other Differences: The New Jewish Cultural Studies*. Eds. Jonathan and Daniel Boyarin. Minneapolis: University of Minnesota Press, 1997. 108–49.

Peterson, Linda. "Biblical Typology and the Self-Portrait of the Poet in Robert Browning." In *Approaches to Victorian Autobiography*. Ed. George P. Landow. Athens: Ohio University Press, 1979.

"Restoring the Book: The Typological Hermeneutics of Christina Rossetti and the PRB." *Victorian Poetry* 3–4 (1994): 209–32.

Phillips, Ann. *A Newnham Anthology*. Cambridge: Cambridge University Press, 1979.

Philipson, David. *The Jew in English Fiction*. Norwood, PA: Norwood Editions, 1977. Reprint of the 1889 edn. published by R. Clarke, Cincinatti, OH.

Plaskow, Judith. "The Right Question is Theological." In *On Being a Jewish Feminist*. Ed. Susannah Heschel. New York: Schocken, 1983. 223–33.

Standing Again at Sinai: Judaism From A Feminist Perspective. New York: HarperCollins, 1990.

Plaskow, Judith and Carol Christ, eds. *Weaving the Visions: New Patterns in Feminist Spirituality*. New York: HarperCollins, 1989.

Plaut, W. Gunther, ed. *The Torah: A Modern Commentary*. New York: Union of American Hebrew Congregations, 1981.

Pratt, Mary Louise. "Arts of the Contact Zone." In *Ways of Reading*. 5th edn. Ed. Donald Bartholomae and Anthony Petrosky. Boston: Bedford St. Martins, 1999. 582–95. (Reprint of Address to Modern Language Association, 1990).

Price, Warwick James. "Three Forgotten Poetesses." *The Forum* 47 (1912): 361–75.

Prickett, Stephen. *Romanticism and Religion: The Tradition of Coleridge and Wordsworth in the Victorian Church*. Cambridge: Cambridge University Press, 1976.

The Prophets: A New Translation of the Holy Scriptures According to the Masocretic Text. Philadelphia: The Jewish Publication Society of America, 1962.

Quilter, Harry. "Amy Levy: a Reminiscence and a Criticism." *Preferences in Art, Life and Literature*. London: Swan and Sonnenschein, 1892.

Ragussis, Michael. "Representation, Conversion, and Literary Form: *Harrington* and the Novel of Jewish Identity." *Critical Inquiry* 16 (1989): 113–43.

Figures of Conversion: "The Jewish Question" & English National Identity. Durham, NC: Duke University Press, 1995.

"Jews and Other 'Outlandish Englishmen': Ethnic Performance and the Invention of British Identity under the Georges." *Critical Inquiry* 26.4 (2000): 773–97.

Review of Grace Aguilar's *The Spirit of Judaism. The Voice of Jacob* (1 April 1842): 111–12.

Rich, Adrienne. "Compulsory Heterosexuality and Lesbian Existence." In *Powers of Desire: Politics of Sexuality.* Eds. A. Snitow, C. Stansell and S. Thompson. New York: Monthly Review Press, 1983. 177–205.

Richardson, Alan. "Romanticism and the Colonization of the Feminine." In *Romanticism and Gender.* Ed. Anne. K. Mellor. Bloomington: Indiana University Press, 1988. 13–25.

Riede, David G. "Elizabeth Barrett: The Poet as Angel." *Victorian Poetry* 32.2 (1994): 121–37.

Robbins, Jill. *Prodigal Son/ Elder Brother: Interpretation and Alterity in Augustine, Petrarch, Kafka, Levinas.* Chicago: University of Chicago Press, 1991.

Robertson, Linda, K. "Writers, Social Conscience, and the *Other* Victorian England." *Studies in Browning and His Circle* 20 (1993): 133–6.

Robertson, Ritchie. *Heine.* London: Weidenfeld & Nicolson, 1988.

Rochelson, Meri-Jane. "Jews, Gender, and Genre in Late-Victorian England: Amy Levy's *Reuben Sachs.*" *Women's Studies* 25 (1996): 311–28.

Rochelson, Meri-Jane, ed. *Children of the Ghetto.* Detroit: Wayne State University Press, 1998.

Rosenberg, Edgar. *From Shylock to Svengali: Jewish Stereotypes in English Fiction.* Stanford, CA: Stanford University Press, 1960.

Rosenblum, Dolores. "Face to Face: Elizabeth Barrett Browning's *Aurora Leigh* and Nineteenth Century Poetry." *Victorian Studies* 26.3 (1983): 321–38.

"Casa Guidi Windows and *Aurora Leigh*: The Genesis of Elizabeth Barrett Browning's Visionary Aesthetic." *Tulsa Studies in Women's Literature* 4.1 (1985): 61–8.

Ross, Marlon B. *The Contours of Masculine Desire: Romanticism and the Rise of Women's Poetry.* New York: Oxford University Press, 1989.

Rossetti, Christina. *Seek and Find.* London: Society for the Promotion of Christian Knowledge, 1879.

The Family Letters of Christina Georgina Rossetti. Ed. William Michael Rossetti. New York: Haskell House Publishers, 1968 (1908).

The Complete Poems of Christina Rossetti. 3 vols. Ed. Rebecca Crump. Baton Rouge: Louisana State University Press, 1979–90.

Poems and Prose. Ed. Jan Marsh. London: Everyman, 1994.

Roth, Cecil. *Anglo-Jewish Letters 1158–1917.* London: Soncino Press, 1938.

A History of the Jews in England. Oxford: Clarendon Press, 1941.

Rowton, Frederic, *The Female Poets of Great Britain*. (Philadelphia: Henry C. Baird, 1853 [1848]). Facsimile edn, ed. Marilyn L. Williamson: Detroit: Wayne State University Press: 1981.

Rubin-Dorsky, Jeffrey and Shelley Fisher Fishkin. *People of the Book: Thirty Scholars Reflect on Their Jewish Identity*. Madison, University of Wisconsin Press, 1996.

Ruether, Rosemary Radford. *Faith and Fratricide: The Theological Roots of Anti-Semitism*. New York: Seabury, 1974.

Ruskin, John. *Sesame and Lilies and Unto This Last*. Introduction by Alice Meynell. London: The Gresham Publishing Company, 1865/1871.

Saintsbury, George. *A History of Nineteenth Century Literature (1780–1895)*. New York: Macmillan, 1896.

Salbstein, M. C. N. *The Emancipation Of the Jews in Britain: The Question of Admission of the Jews to Parliament, 1828–1860*. Rutherford, NJ: Associated University Presses, 1982.

Scheinberg, Cynthia. "Elizabeth Barrett Browning's Hebraic Conversions: Feminism and Christian Typology in *Aurora Leigh*." *Victorian Literature and Culture* 22 (1995): 55–72.

"Canonizing the Jew: Amy Levy's Challenge to Victorian Poetic Identity." *Victorian Studies* (1996): 173–99.

"Recasting Sympathy and Judgment: Amy Levy, Women Writers, and the Victorian Dramatic Monologue." *Victorian Poetry* 35.2 (1997): 57–75.

Interview. "Feature: An Interview with Cynthia Scheinberg." *Wick*: Harvard Divinity School Student Journal of Literature and Religion (Summer 1997). 2.

"'Measure yourself to a prophet's place': Biblical Heroines, Jewish Difference and Women's Poetry." In *Women's Poetry, Late Romantic to Late Victorian: Gender and Genre, 1830–1900*. Eds. Isobel Armstrong and Virginia Blain. Houndsmill, Basingstoke: Macmillan, 1999. 263–91.

"Victorian Poetry and Religious Diversity." In *The Cambridge Companion to Victorian Poetry*. Ed. Joseph Bristow. Cambridge: Cambridge University Press, 2000. 159–79.

Schneider, Mary. *Poetry in the Age of Democracy*. Lawrence: University of Kansas Press, 1989.

Schreiner, Olive. *Letters of Olive Schreiner 1876–1920*. Ed. S. C. Cronwright-Schreiner. Westport, CT: Hyperion, 1976. (Reprint of London: T. Fisher Unwin, 1924.)

Schussler Fiorenza, Elizabeth. *In Memory of Her: A Feminist Theological Reconstruction of Christian Origins*. 10th anniversary edn, New York: Crossroad Publishing, 1994.

Selkirk, J. B. *Ethics and Aesthetics of Modern Poetry*. London: Smith, Elder, and Co., 1878.

Shairp, J. C. *Culture and Religion in Some of their Relations*. Boston: Houghton Mifflin, 1883 (1870).

Shakespeare, William. *The Merchant of Venice*. Ed. W. Moelwyn Merchant. New York: Penguin Books, 1967.

Shaw, David. *The Lucid Veil: Poetic Truth in the Victorian Age*. London: Athlone Press, 1987.

Showalter, Elaine. *A Literature of Their Own: British Women Novelists From Brontë to Lessing*. Princeton, NJ: Princeton University Press, 1977.

Silberstein, Laurence J. and Robert Cohn, eds. *The Other in Jewish Thought and History: Constructions of Jewish Culture and Identity*. New York: New York University Press, 1994.

Smith, Sidonie. *A Poetics of Women's Autobiography*. Bloomington: Indiana University Press, 1987.

Sollars, Werner. *Beyond Ethnicity*. New York: Oxford University Press, 1986.

Spielman, Mrs. Meyer A. "Jewish Woman Writers." Presidential Address to the Union of Jewish Literary Societies. 10 November 1913.

Spivak, Gayatri. "The Politics of Translation." In *Destablizing Theory: Contemporary Feminist Debates*. Eds. Michele Barrett and Anne Phillips. Stanford, CA: Stanford University Press, 1992. 177–200.

Stanwood, P. G. "Christina Rossetti's Devotional Prose." In *The Achievement of Christina Rossetti*. Ed. David A. Kent. Ithaca, NY: Cornell University Press, 1987. 231–49.

Starzyk, Lawrence J. *The Imprisoned Splendor: A Study of Victorian Critical Theory*. London: Kennikat, 1977.

Stedman, Edmund Clarence. *Victorian Poets*. Boston: Houghton Mifflin, 1891.

Stedman, Clarence E. *A Victorian Anthology 1837–1895*. New York: Houghton Mifflin, 1894, 1895.

Stephen, Leslie and Sir Sidney Lee, eds. *Dictionary of National Biography*. London: Oxford University Press, 1973.

Stone, Marjorie. "Gender Subversion and Gender Inversion: *The Princess* and *Aurora Leigh*." *Victorian Poetry* 25 (1987): 101–27.

  Elizabeth Barrett Browning. Women Writers. New York: St. Martin's, 1995.

Suggs, Jack M., Katherine Sakenfeld, and James Mueller, eds. *The Oxford Study Bible*. New York: Oxford University Press, 1992.

Taylor, Barbara. *Eve and the New Jerusalem: Socialism and Feminism in the Nineteenth Century*. New York: Pantheon, 1983

Tennyson, Alfred Lord. *In Memoriam*. Ed. Robert Ross. New York: W. W. Norton, 1973.

Tennyson, G. B. *Victorian Devotional Poetry: The Tractarian Mode*. Cambridge, MA: Harvard University Press, 1981.

Todd, Janet, ed. *British Women Writers*. New York: Frederick Unger, 1989.

Trevelyan, G. M. *English Social History*. New York: David McKay, 1942.

Trible, Phyllis. *God and The Rhetoric of Sexuality*. Philadelphia: Fortress, 1978.

Tuchman, Gaye and Nina Fortin. *Edging Women Out: Victorian Novelists, Publishers, and Social Change*. New Haven: Yale University Press, 1989.

Umansky, Ellen. "Creating a Jewish Feminist Theology." In *Weaving the Visions: New Patterns in Feminist Spirituality*. Eds. Judith Plaskow and Carol Christ. New York: Harper Collins, 1989. 187–98.

Umansky, Ellen and Dianne Ashton, eds. *Four Centuries of Jewish Women's Spirituality: A Sourcebook*. Boston: Beacon, 1992.

Valman, Nadia. *Gender and Judaism in Victorian England*. Unpublished manuscript (in progress).

Vrete, Mayir. "The Restoration of the Jews in English Protestant Thought 1790–1840." *Middle Eastern Studies* 8 (1972): 3–50.

Wagenknecht, Edward. *Daughters of the Covenant: Portraits of Six Jewish Women*. Amherst: University of Massachusetts Press, 1983.

Weinberger, Philip. "The Social and Religious Thought of Grace Aguilar." Dissertation, New York University, 1971. Ann Arbor: University of Michigan Press, 1971.

Wheeler, Michael. *Heaven, Hell, and the Victorians*. Cambridge: Cambridge University Press, 1994.

Whitla, William. "Questioning the Convention: Christina Rossetti's Sonnet Sequence 'Monna Innominata.'" In *The Achievement of Christina Rossetti*. Ed. David A. Kent. Ithaca, NY: Cornell University Press, 1987. 82–131.

Wilde, Oscar. "Amy Levy." *Woman's World* 3 (1890): 51–2.

Williamson, Audrey. *Wagner Opera*. London: John Calder, 1962.

Wolffe, John. "Anglicanism." In *Nineteenth Century English Religious Traditions: Retrospect and Prospect*. Ed. D. G. Paz. Westport, CT: Greenwood, 1995.

Woolford, John. "Elizabeth Barrett and William Wordsworth." *Studies in Browning and His Circle* 20 (1993): 48–61.

Wordsworth, William. "Preface to Lyrical Ballads" (1802). In *Lyrical Ballads: Wordsworth and Coleridge*. Eds. R. T. Brett and A. R. Jones. London: Routledge: 1988 (1963). 240–72.

The Writings (Kethubim): A New Translation of the Holy Scriptures According to the Masocretic text: third section. Philadelphia: The Jewish Publication Society of America, 1982.

Yeats, William Butler. *Letters to the New Island*. Ed. Horace Reynolds. Cambridge, MA: Harvard University Press, 1934. 87.

Yeazell, Ruth Bernard, ed. *Sex, Politics and Science in the Nineteenth Century Novel*. Baltimore, MD: Johns Hopkins University Press, 1986.

Zatlin, Linda Gertner. *The Nineteenth Century Anglo-Jewish Novel*. Boston: Twayne, 1981.

Zonana, Joyce. "The Embodied Muse: Elizabeth Barrett Browning's *Aurora Leigh* and Feminist Poetics." *Tulsa Studies in Women's Literature*. 8.2 (1989): 241–62.

Index

Abrahams, Beth-Zion Lask, 150, 151, 153–4, 250 n.2, 8, 252 n.23

Aguilar, Grace, 5, 6, 20, 22, 23–4, 61, 146–89, 224; accused of Jewish Protestantism, 153–5; Biblical references: Leviticus, 26:40–1, 186, I Kings, 19:12, 172, Proverbs, 168; compared to Elizabeth Barrett Browning, 176–7; compared to Samuel Taylor Coleridge, 165–6; compared to Amy Levy, 196–97, 199–200, 204, 205, 224, 232–3, 234; construction of religious authority, 150; construction of literary authority 20, 147, 183; Jewish education, 251 n.12; and Isaac Leeser, 152, 157, 158, 176, 252 n.29; and Biblical women: Deborah, 174, 178, 180–3, Hannah, 174, 178–80, Miriam, 174, 176–8, 180; manuscript copy books, 153; and public/private spheres, 155–60, 162, see also separate spheres; and Romantic poetics, 160–4, 166–7, 169; use of Christian typology, 184–5; and the *Voice of Jacob*, 147, 151, 180; and William Wordsworth, 161–2; *Works*: "Angels: Written While Watching At Past Midnight, Alone By the Bedside of a Beloved Friend," 165–7, "The Authoress," 149–50, 161, 181, *Communings with Nature*, 163, "The Evergreen," 163–5, 166, 167, *The Days of Bruce: A Story of Scottish History*, 152, *Essays and Miscellanies*, 152, *Home Influence*, 151, 152, *Home Scenes and Hearth Studies*, 152, *Israel Defended*, 152, *The Jewish Faith: Its Spiritual Consolation, Moral Guidance, and Immortal Hope*, 146, 148–9, 151, *The Magic Wreath*, 152, *A Mother's Recompense*, 152, *The Records of Israel*, 152, 252 n.29, "The Rocks of Elim," 252 n.26, *Sabbath Thoughts*, 167–70, 173, 186, "Sabbath Thoughts I" 168–70, "Sabbath Thoughts VI," 170–2, *The Spirit of Judaism*, 147, 148, 152, 156, 157, 161, 169, 175, *The Vale of Cedars; or The Martyr*, 152, "A Vision of Jerusalem: While Listening to a Beautiful

Organ in One of the Gentile Shrines," 22, 183–8, *The Women of Israel*, 161–2, 173–82

anti-Judaism, 31, 36, 44, 58; distinguished from anti-Semitism, 37; see also Elizabeth Barrett Browning, Christina Rossetti

anti-Semitism, 37, 57, 131, 247 n.6

apRoberts, Ruth, 241 n.16

Armstrong, Isobel, 8, 212

Arnold, Matthew, 27, 38, 45, 52, 53, 55–60, 184; Hebraism, 57–9, 211; analysis of Robert Burns, 206; compared with Amy Levy, 206–12; *Works: Culture and Anarchy*, 55, 57–60, 210, "Heinrich Heine," 55–7, 208–10, "The Study of Poetry," 206, 211

Ayre, John, Reverend, 85

Barrett Browning, Elizabeth, 5, 6, 20, 22, 28, 61, 62–105, 224; Biblical references: Deuteronomy, 75, 79, Exodus, 91, 92, 95–6, 98, 102, Genesis, 72, Isaiah, 70, Luke, 1:31, 78, Psalm LXXX, 70, Revelation, 21:1–20, 102; compared to Christina Rossetti, 103–4, 111, 144; compared to Grace Aguilar, 176–7; construction of female poetic identity, 28, 65, 89, 95–8, 101–3, 104–5; figuration of Mary, 79–84; figuration of Miriam, 22, 69, 76, 84–7, 89–105; figuration of Moses, 79–90, 92, 95–100, 102; and Hebrew language, 67, 70, 71, 76; and Jewish Biblical women, 68, 69, 79, 89–105; and Jewishness, 63–7, 73–6, 79–80, 89–105; and John Milton, 72, 77; and Mary Russell Mitford, 62, 63, 64, 243, n.6; relationship to Hebrew language, 28, 63, 67, 70, 73–4, 79; religious affiliation, 67; and Richard Hengist Horne, 62–5, 242 n.4; and Robert Browning, 104–5; and Robert Burns, 66; use of Christian typology, 20, 22, 87–94, 98, 104; *Works: Aurora Leigh*, 21–3, 28, 67, 68, 76, 84–104, 144, "Drama of Exile," 28, *Poems* (1844), 71, "The Seraphim," 28, 244 n.22, *The Seraphim*

272

CAMBRIDGE STUDIES IN NINETEENTH-CENTURY LITERATURE AND CULTURE

General editor
Gillian Beer, *University of Cambridge*

Titles published